S0-AZE-538

Dear Reader:

The book you are about to read is the latest bestseller from the St. Martin's True Crime Library, the imprint *The New York Times* calls "the leader in true crime!" Each month, we offer you a fascinating account of the latest, most sensational crime that has captured the national attention. St. Martin's is the publisher of John Glatt's riveting and horrifying SE-CRETS IN THE CELLAR, which shines a light on the man who shocked the world when it was revealed that he had kept his daughter locked in his hidden basement for 24 years. In the Edgar-nominated WRITTEN IN BLOOD, Diane Fanning looks at Michael Petersen, a Marine-turned-novelist found guilty of beating his wife to death and pushing her down the stairs of their home—only to reveal another similar death from his past. In the book you now hold, HER DEADLY WEB, Diane Fanning investigates a former nurse and the violent deaths of her two husbands.

St. Martin's True Crime Library gives you the stories behind the headlines. Our authors take you right to the scene of the crime and into the minds of the most notorious murderers to show you what really makes them tick. St. Martin's True Crime Library paperbacks are better than the most terrifying thriller, because it's all true! The next time you want a crackling good read, make sure it's got the St. Martin's True Crime Library logo on the spine—you'll be up all night!

Charles E. Spicer, Jr.
Executive Editor, St. Martin's True Crime Library

Other True Crime Accounts by
DIANE FANNING

Mommy's Little Girl

A Poisoned Passion

The Pastor's Wife

Out There

Under the Knife

Baby Be Mine

Gone Forever

Through the Window

Into the Water

Written in Blood

**From the True Crime Library of
St. Martin's Paperbacks**

HER DEADLY WEB

Diane Fanning

St. Martin's Paperbacks

HER DEADLY WEB

Copyright © 2012 by Diane Fanning.

Cover photos: Spider web on barbed wire © Nilsson, Huett, Ulf/Getty Images. Raynella Dossett © AP photo/Wade Payne.

All rights reserved.

For information address St. Martin's Press, 175 Fifth Avenue, New York, NY 10010.

EAN: 978-0-312-53459-2

Printed in the United States of America

St. Martin's Paperbacks edition / January 2012

St. Martin's Paperbacks are published by St. Martin's Press, 175 Fifth Avenue, New York, NY 10010.

10 9 8 7 6 5 4 3 2

To Ed Dossett, Dave Leath,

and all who loved them

HER
DEADLY
WEB

CHAPTER 1

The humidity was rising and not a single speck of blue could be seen in the cloud-covered sky as Raynella Dossett Leath turned into the driveway of her farm near Knoxville, Tennessee, on March 13, 2003. She drove past the family vegetable patch, where newly planted onion sets thrust fresh green sprouts up through the dark soil.

She continued on past an outbuilding to the house she'd called home for nearly twenty years. In the time she lived beneath its roof, she'd lost a husband and a son; raised one daughter to adulthood and marriage; and now prepared for the high school graduation of her third child.

Stepping on the porch, unlocking the closed door and crossing the threshold, she entered a lifeless dwelling. David Leath, a barber who had been her husband of ten years, lay dead in the marital bed.

She picked up the receiver of the telephone on the table beside his body and punched in 911.

The emergency dispatcher answered the incoming call at 11:23 that morning.

"County 911."

"Help me! Help me!" Raynella shrieked, choking on her words.

"Ma'am, where are you?"

"Please help me!" she yelled as she struggled to breathe.

"Ma'am, what's going on?"

"My—my husband shot himself—three—uh—three-oh-three-one Solway. Hurry!"

"Okay, where is your husband?"

"He's still in the bed. Please hurry!"

"Ma'am"

"I'm going to vomit."

"Ma'am?"

Raynella uttered wordless shrieks and moans.

"Ma'am?"

Raynella gagged and made inarticulate sounds.

"Ma'am, I need you to calm down so I can get some help to you. Okay?"

The dispatcher sent units to the address to investigate a reported suicide attempt. Dispatch informed the emergency personnel: "She's called in, says her husband shot himself. The phone's off the hook, the line is open, and the caller can still be heard screaming."

The first responder to the scene, Deputy Sergeant David Amburn of the Knox County Sheriff's Office, arrived at 11:32. He found Raynella lying facedown in the grass in the front yard. He thought that she, too, had been shot or injured. He bolted out of his vehicle shouting, "Ma'am, ma'am," as he ran to her.

He knelt down and nudged her. She burst into unintelligible cries and wails then shouted, "Help him. Help him. He's been shot." She was, he said, a woman "overcome with grief." He helped her onto the porch and went into the house with Deputy Chief Keith Lyons.

They found David Leath, age fifty-seven, dead in his bed. He had a black hole in his forehead over his left eye surrounded by copious gunpowder stippling, consistent with a shot fired from close range. He lay on his right side with his right arm extended straight out and his left arm bent at the elbow, with his wrist turned under and resting on the mattress.

Beside that hand was an old blue steel Colt .38 double-action revolver with a black grip.

Investigator Perry Moyers arrived at the solid brick house at 11:51. Raynella was on the front porch now with a rag in her hand. At five feet eight inches and 170 pounds, with stark blue eyes and steel-colored hair, Raynella cut an imposing figure. She was wearing blue jeans, white Skechers tennis shoes, and a gray and white long-sleeved shirt layered with a gray sleeveless shirt. He looked her over but saw no signs of any blood transfer stains. He thought that was odd. Raynella was a nurse: surely she had attempted CPR on her husband.

Moyers went inside where Sergeant Robert Lee directed him to the left and down the hallway to the bedroom. He heard the sound of a clothes dryer running and made a mental note to follow up on that observation.

The deceased David Leath appeared to Moyers's trained eye as if he'd been tucked into bed for comfort. A pillow in a green pillowcase was in between his head and shoulder, another between his legs. He lay on a blue sheet, and a white quilt with pink and green accents neatly covered the lower half of his body.

His position simply did not look right: Moyers thought it seemed unlikely for someone who had committed suicide. He wondered if the scene was staged.

A plate of food—oatmeal, toast, and jelly—sat on a table beside the bed. It had not been touched. It bore no blood evidence on its surface. There were neither lip marks on the drinking glass standing beside the plate nor any other indication that anyone had drunk a drop of the milk inside it.

Moyers saw early signs of lividity discoloring David's skin. That in all probability meant his death could not have occurred in the last half hour. He pressed a finger down on the skin's surface. Where he applied pressure, he observed blanching, suggesting that death could not have occurred much more than five hours earlier. The exposed parts of his body were cool to the touch, but under the covers the toes were still warm. Moyers estimated the time of death as between 6:00 and 9:00 that morning.

Three officers in training were on the scene, learning from their more experienced colleagues. Before lifting the weapon from the bed to demonstrate the proper handling of a gun at a death scene, Moyers noted that the holes in the blue bedsheet indicated there had been a fold in the fabric when the gun was discharged.

"When you rotate the cylinder out, you need to be careful not to turn it," he said holding the revolver up so that all the new officers could see. "Then you need to draw the cylinder as you see it on a piece of paper." Moyers made his drawing, but at the time he did not notice the most significant piece of evidence the gun contained.

Raynella came into the house with her married daughter, Maggie Dossett Connaster, and asked, "What's going on here, boys? What's going on?"

Moyers talked with Maggie while Detective Steve Webb spoke to Raynella. She informed Webb that it had been a typical morning. Katie was running a little late but she left home for school at 8:15. Raynella said she'd prepared and served her husband breakfast in bed. "He always tells me I bring it too hot to melt the butter." The detective thought that was an odd statement but didn't question her about it. Before leaving the house, she tuned the television to the Joyce Meyer show, a religious and inspirational program that aired at 8:30.

She also told him that the house was locked when she returned home. When Webb asked her why her husband would commit suicide, Raynella said, "He just found out yesterday that his mother has cancer."

After a moment of silence she added: "Well, he's finally at rest. He can finally rest."

She volunteered her journal, handing it to the investigator, saying that it chronicled their family life and contained documentation of Dave's health and state of mind. In response to the detective's question, she said that she started the washer and the dryer just before leaving home at 9:00 that morning. Lead investigator Moyers silently wondered why the dryer was still running three hours later.

Moyers looked for signs of the grief and sorrow noted in Raynella by the first responder but saw none. Instead he a observed a woman in control, taking charge of the situation. That made him very uncomfortable.

He also wasn't pleased to see the gathering of the who's who of Knoxville's legal and political world in front of the Leath home: public defenders, local Republican Party leaders, lawyers, and at least one judge. They were clearly there in support of Raynella, their attention not wavering even when a burst of misty drizzle blew through the gloomy afternoon. Investigator Moyers knew the pressure the powerful could apply. Their involvement always made an investigation difficult and delicate.

But what troubled Moyers the most was the evidence uncovered in the bedroom. Techs dug a bullet out of the wall. It had passed through the headboard with a piece of the victim's hair attached. They dug another bullet out of the floor under the bed. And a third bullet was lodged in David Leath's head—the one that had pierced his skull above his left eye, transected his brain stem, and killed him instantly.

The evidence wasn't in harmony with the widow's story. Was it really a suicide?

CHAPTER 2

Cindy Wilkerson, David Leath's daughter from a previous marriage, arrived at the scene of her father's death. Investigator Moyers noted that the thin blond woman had a faraway look in her eyes as she struggled against the ugly truth that her father was gone.

Crime scene technicians continued their grim but necessary work. Brad Parks set up the stringing of the scene. He ran a line from the point of impact out along the angle of entry to find the trajectory of each bullet. This information would give investigators an indication of the location of the gun when the trigger was pulled.

After the body was on its way to the morgue for an autopsy, techs moved the mattress, revealing spatters and puddles of bright red. Crimson drops fell from the bed to the floor, splashing up on the molding running along the base of the wall. The blood stood in stark contrast to the white lid on the clear plastic storage box tucked beneath the bed frame.

Techs collected the oak headboard with its intricate carved medallions and posts, and the pillow where David rested his head. They cut out a piece of the wall and collected the gun. They confiscated a pair of rubber gloves from the bathroom.

Gordon Armstrong was unaware of the drama playing out

at the home of his best friend, David Leath, until his wife, Gail, telephoned him at work. "David committed suicide. He shot himself."

"I don't believe he'd shoot himself."

"There was a handgun beside him."

"That makes even less sense: Dave hated guns."

When Gordon returned home, he received a phone call from Raynella, who was now at her daughter Maggie's home because her own house was sealed by law enforcement. "Gordon, can you go up to the house and pick up the will?"

Gordon, half out of his soiled work clothes, said, "Just as soon as I can get ready."

Before he could get out the door, Raynella called again. "Never mind, Gordon. Maggie's got to go down there to get something else and she'll pick up the will."

Later that evening, Gordon wanted to see if Raynella needed anything else. Maggie picked up the phone and said, "She's not going to talk to anybody tonight."

In the background, Gordon heard Raynella ask, "Who is it?"

"Gordon," Maggie said.

"Come on. I will talk to him," Raynella said, taking the phone.

Gordon expressed his sympathy, shared his sorrow, and reminded Raynella that if she needed anything at all, she need only let him know.

The next morning, at 8:15, Detective Moyers and three other detectives observed as Dr. Darinka Mileusnic, the assistant chief medical examiner for Knox County, performed an autopsy on the body of David Leath.

She made a thorough external examination of the man stretched before her on the stainless steel table. She noted scars and his wedding band, and described the body as "that of a well-developed, well-nourished, and well-built white male appearing the stated age of fifty-seven years. The body measures 68 inches in length and weighs 201 pounds. The scalp hair is brown with gray and short with a residual layer of dried-out hair spray."

She noted that he was tanned and wore a short mustache and beard. She observed one shrunken eye below the gunshot entry wound and the remaining eye with its green-blue iris and cloudy cornea.

She noted a number of developing health problems internally: a fatty liver, an enlarged heart and spleen, and mild atherosclerosis with small areas of severe blockage. Dr. Mileusnic removed the copper-plated bullet that took his life when it traveled from his forehead through his brain, ricocheting off the interior backside of his skull before burrowing into the right occipital lobe.

When the autopsy was complete, the doctor released the body to Cremation Options as the widow had instructed. David's body was cremated that same day. Raynella had prepaid for the service, although David had a plot in the cemetery next to his parents and had expressed his desire to be buried there.

Cindy was shocked and dismayed when she learned of the cremation: she knew Raynella had gone against her father's oft-expressed wishes. Gordon was likewise surprised: his thoughts went to the dark places he'd been trying to avoid. He was certain his friend had not committed suicide; that left only murder. There were only three people living in that home. David was dead; that left Raynella and her daughter Katie. Who had pulled the trigger?

CHAPTER 3

Three days after David's death, the Reverend Henry Lenoir officiated over a memorial service at Solway United Methodist Church in Solway, Tennessee. The family was there to greet friends and neighbors and the ceremony began at 3:30 that Sunday.

In the middle of her words about the passing of her husband, Raynella spoke a phrase that puzzled many of the attendees: "I was nothing but Dave's hood ornament." In lieu of flowers, Raynella requested donations to David Leath's Grandchildren's Memorial Fund.

The sheriff's office released the Leath home on Monday. Investigator Moyers met Raynella at the house to turn it over. He informed her that they believed David's death to be a homicide.

"Am I a suspect?" she asked.

"The only person who is not a suspect is me," the detective said.

The following day, Raynella invited people to her home for a meeting. Among attendees were David's fellow barber and shop co-owner Hoyt Vanosdale. He was a man of average height and weight, his face framed by gray-brown hair and adorned with glasses and a beard. Also present was David's daughter, Cindy Wilkerson. When they arrived, a lawyer from

James A.H. Bell's office, the firm representing Raynella's interests, was already at the home. He had a tape recorder and asked everyone why they thought David had committed suicide.

Hoyt spoke up, saying he did not believe that David had shot himself.

The attorney said, "I guess our conversation is over."

Rising to his feet, Hoyt said, "You got that right," and left the meeting.

A few days later Hoyt returned to Raynella's home to see if she needed anything, volunteering to be available for his former partner's widow through the difficult aftermath of David's death. Before he left, Raynella handed over a small, heavy cardboard box and asked that he deliver the package to Cindy. She did not tell him the contents of the container. And he didn't peek inside.

Hoyt turned the box over to Cindy, who opened it to see what was inside. She found in it her father's cremains. To Cindy, this discovery was like learning about her father's death all over again.

The first of April brought an abundance of activity in the case. Because Raynella's first husband had been the Sixth Judicial District attorney general, the local prosecutor's office did not feel they should be involved in the investigation. "To avoid even the appearance of any conflict of interest, I have asked that a special pro tem prosecutor from outside Knox County be appointed to assist law enforcement in this case," sitting attorney general Randy Nichols announced.

Raynella's attorney, James Bell, told the media, "I have specifically asked the sheriff's department if she is a suspect, a target, or a subject of an investigation. They just say they can't tell me. I have asked if there are any suspects in the case, and they say they can't tell me that, either." He continued with a defense of his client: "Raynella Dossett Leath did not kill David Leath. She loved him, and anyone who says she killed him had better be prepared to come into court and deal with me over it."

David's daughter, Cindy, was simply befuddled. She told the *Knoxville News Sentinel*, "I don't know anything. I don't know if they're calling it a suicide or a homicide. I would like to know something, but no one has told me anything." She added that she doubted her father would have killed himself, and if he had, he would not have done it with a firearm "because he was terrified of guns. Anybody who knew him knows that."

The day after Nichols's conflict-of-interest announcement, Bill Reedy and Chuck Pope, both of the Tenth Judicial District attorney general's office, were assigned as special prosecutors to work with Knox County Sheriff's Office on the case. They met with meet with lead investigator Perry Moyers and other Knox County Sheriff's Office officers the next day.

After the meeting, Bill Reedy spoke to reporters, telling them that the investigation into the death of retired West Knoxville barber David Leath would rely on circumstantial evidence. He warned that the state budget cutbacks that resulted in the closing of two crime labs might mean it would take longer to accumulate evidence results.

"It is also very clear that to develop a suspect in this case will require the use of investigative subpoenas, a new procedure available to us. We are going to have to develop a good deal more evidence by way of such things as telephone records and other things to confirm or deny things that have been said to police by some parties close to the victim."

He went on to describe the case as "a death investigation that we are treating as a homicide and will continue to do so, unless something comes back from the complete autopsy results and forensic tests that tell us something different. But everybody who has looked at the crime scene and the evidence that was collected have concluded that is most probably not a suicide."

When the results came back from the forensics labs, it was clear that the gun recovered at the scene was the weapon that fired all three of the bullets. It was more shots than typically found in a suicide, but it still did not prove homicide beyond a shadow of a doubt.

However, the final autopsy report bolstered the other forensic evidence. It concluded: "Examination of the skin surrounding the gunshot wound of entrance reveals gunpowder stippling which covers an area of 3.8 inches in diameter. Scene investigation and wound features, particularly the extent of gunpowder stippling, are inconsistent with self-inflicted gunshot wound. The manner of death is homicide."

Law enforcement now knew with certainty that Raynella's pronouncement of suicide was wrong: David Leath had not taken his own life.

CHAPTER 4

Dewey Large, born on May 11, 1922, in Mill Creek, Tennessee, and Annie Irene Owens, born on June 17, 1925 in Dillon County, South Carolina, both attended Berry College near Rome, Georgia, at the time that the United States stepped into World War II. The conflict interrupted Dewey's education. Dewey and Annie married when he enlisted in the U.S. Army Air Corps. He earned a Purple Heart, among other medals, while Annie studied and graduated from college.

After the war, Dewey continued his education at the University of Tennessee, earning a bachelor of science in education. He later became the principal at Pi Beta Phi Elementary School in Gatlinburg, Tennessee. They settled in nearby Pigeon Forge, in a big white house on a hill above the church. Their first child, Floanna, was born on January 26, 1945.

Their second daughter, Raynella Bernardene, arrived on October 25, 1948. Dewey earned a master's degree in chemistry and physics, in 1952, from the University of Tennessee. Their only son, Marcus, was born that same year. The family settled in Oak Ridge, twenty-five miles outside of Knoxville, where their final child and third daughter, Robyn, rounded out the family in 1956. According to family friends, Dewey and Annie carefully planned the separation between the birth of each child to ensure that each one of them would have a singular high school experience.

Annie was a schoolteacher in both their first home in Sevier County as well as in Oak Ridge. She loved organic gardening, arts and crafts, reading, and music. She was a master quilter and quilt designer. She served as crew chief for the annual Berry Alumni Work Week quilters' group for years.

Dewey, meanwhile, had gone on to work at the Oak Ridge Institute of Nuclear Studies as the coordinator of the science fair program. He was one of the founders and a longtime curator of the American Museum of Atomic Energy and eventually retired from the environmental management division of the U.S. Department of Energy in 1986. After his retirement, he focused on one of his chief concerns: the safe containment and storage of nuclear waste.

Oak Ridge was a very unusual town. According to legend, its future was foretold by John Hendrix, an east Tennessee mystic. In the early 1900s he revealed a vision. "In the woods, as I lay on the ground and looked up into the sky, there came to me a voice as loud and sharp as thunder. The voice told me to sleep with my head on the ground for forty nights and I would be shown visions of what the future holds for this land," he said.

"And I tell you, Bear Creek Valley someday will be filled with great buildings and factories, and they will help toward winning the greatest war that will ever be. There will be a city on Black Oak Ridge . . . Big engines will dig big ditches, and thousands of people will be running to and fro. They will be building things, and there will be great noise and confusion and the earth will shake. I've seen it. It's coming."

His seemingly mad vision proved true, twenty years after his death.

The area of Oak Ridge was selected by the U.S. Army Corps of Engineers in September 1942. Major General Leslie Groves liked the isolation of the poor Appalachian farmland, the low population, the plentiful energy from the nearby Tennessee Valley Authority, and its location in a long valley surrounded by ridges that protected it from natural disasters—and offered the rest of the world a measure of protection from Oak Ridge in case of an accident. The government quickly acquired a total of sixty thousand acres that sat atop the county line between Anderson and Roane counties.

It might have been a poverty-stricken rural area, but it was a region of lush beauty in the shadows of the Great Smoky Mountain National Park. The region was originally home to Cherokee Indians drawn to the area by the many rivers and lakes that dotted the countryside. Every spring was heralded with the blooming of white dogwoods and the whites, pinks, and reds of rhododendron. In the fall, the hills looked like they were on fire with a blaze of oranges, reds, and yellows as the leaves of deciduous trees turned before falling to the ground to await the coming snow and ice.

When fall arrived in 1942, the residents were thinking less about the glorious foliage than the tragic sense of déjà vu they were experiencing. In the early thirties, 2,900 families had been relocated out of the area by the Tennessee Valley Authority. The building of Norris Dam, part of the rural electrification project, necessitated their departure. Some of the refugees left behind farms and homes that had been in their families since early settlers arrived in the area. With the completion of the dam, all those beloved acres were submerged in water, as if they had never been.

Now, a decade later, the federal government was shoving more families out of their homes; it was the second forced relocation for some. Thousands came home from work and school to find eviction notices slapped on their front doors. Most of them were given six weeks to move out, but others had as little as two weeks. Some were forced to move before receiving payment for their property. By January 1, 1943, they were all gone.

Construction began a month later. By April, fences and checkpoints at the seven gates were up and the guards in position in the towers beside them. An architectural firm designed both the four secret industrial buildings and the town. One of the facilities, K-25, was massive. Covering forty-four acres, it was the largest building in the world at the time.

The first residents to arrive on the site lived in tents until more permanent dwellings were erected. Prefabricated modular homes, apartments, and dormitories—most constructed of "Cemesto" panels made of bonded cement and asbestos—rose through the town in a rush. Boardwalks were built because no one had time or patience for allowing the cement to dry.

In May, the emissaries swept through campuses across the country, hiring chemistry majors. Seventy-five thousand educated people with a median age of twenty-seven descended on the new city almost overnight. They were greeted by ominous billboards. One had the hear-no-evil, see-no-evil, speak-no-evil monkeys in the background, topped with Uncle Sam sporting rolled-up shirtsleeves. The message read: "What you see here, What you do hear here, When you leave here, Let it stay here." One had an eyeball with a swastika and read: "The enemy is looking for information, guard your talk."

Except for a handful of scientists, the new arrivals were told in training: "We cannot tell you what you are going to do, but we can tell you how to do it and we can only tell you that if our enemies achieve what we are attempting before we do, God help us!"

It was a secret city. Not on any maps. It didn't even have a formal name until 1949. Prior to that time, it was quietly referred to as the Clinton Engineering Works. The only person who could carry a camera in town was the official Army photographer. The manufacturing plants and the city itself were a twenty-four-hour-a-day operation. More than eight hundred buses ferried people to and from work on three shifts.

Every week, thousands of laden railcars barreled into the

city. They left without any cargo. The end product of this relentless effort left town once or twice a week in briefcases carried by lieutenants who caught a train to Chicago and then another to New Mexico. Within the borders of the city behind the gates, everyone, including children, had to wear identity badges or dog tags.

Security for the city was as tight as for a military base in a country at war. If you didn't have a badge, you needed a pass to enter its borders.

This was home base for the Manhattan Project. Sixty cents for every dollar spent on this massive federal undertaking were expended within the boundaries of Oak Ridge.

The project's mission: to enrich the uranium needed to obtain the radioactive material that would be dropped on Japanese cities and bring World War II to an end. When the first bomb fell on August 6, 1945, the citizens of Oak Ridge finally knew what they'd been doing for the past two years.

Even after the war, though, the secrecy continued. Turner Construction Company erected the city and administered it until 1947 when it fell under the authority of the U.S. Atomic Energy Commission, which planned the transition to independent control. That came in 1959 when the town was finally incorporated and badges were no longer required.

Dewey Large brought his family to an idyllic, charmed setting when he accepted his job in Oak Ridge. The town had a lot of uncommon amenities, including a free bus system to get around town and virtually no crime. No one ever locked their houses. A kid could ride his bike up the movie theater, leave it parked outside, watch a show, and never worry: his bike would be right where he left it.

The city swimming pool was a three-acre lake cemented in by the Army Corps of Engineers. In it, every child was given swimming lessons each summer. There wasn't a real downtown area, but residents called a centrally located strip mall "downtown." It was an enriched environment where children thought nothing of encountering a woman in a sari and showed no surprise when their next-door neighbors were replaced by the family of a foreign scientist for a year in the international exchange program.

Raynella's family attended Robertsville Baptist Church, located next to the junior high school. That was where five-year-old Raynella met Beverly Heth, who remained a close friend all the way through college. The two girls were in the choir together at church and the chorus at school. Raynella had a beautiful singing voice and often performed solos.

Since everyone in the newborn community was a transplant, no one had extended family in town; neighbors filled that role for one another. The sense of community was very strong. Raynella and Beverly were in and out of each other's homes throughout their childhoods. But neither of them knew what their dads did for a living other than that they worked, as everyone's father did, at the plant.

People of color were segregated initially in a section called Scarboro. Those homes were built with outdoor bathrooms. But as scientists from all over the world began descending on Oak Ridge, that had to change. The wives of the scientists were appalled by the conditions in Scarboro and launched a fund-raising campaign to install indoor plumbing in every home. The process of integrating the schools began in the upper grades and over the years trickled down to the primary grades. Oak Ridge High became the first integrated school in the South in 1955. Although there were some racist incidents, including fistfights, graffiti, and other indignities, the change happened with far less discord than the desegregation in subsequent years in other cities.

When Raynella Large attended elementary school, her classes were still segregated. They wouldn't be by the time she reached Robertsville Junior High.

Like all other residents of Oak Ridge, Raynella wore an identification tag, but because she was a child, her surname was not visible. In fact, her teachers never referred to her or to any of the students by their last names, because of security. Officials nursed a strong fear that someone might attempt to abduct children of the top scientists at the facilities.

Everyone here, even the children, was acutely aware of the perils of the cold war. Across the country at this time, schoolchildren practiced duck-and-cover exercises under their desks and in windowless hallways. Here in Oak Ridge, it was far more extreme. They all knew that they were living in one of the top five targets selected by the USSR in the event of a war.

Beginning in third grade, Raynella, like all the children in this community, practiced walking home from school all alone to make sure she could accomplish that task without any help. On Wednesdays at noon, loud air raid sirens pierced the air for a solid minute, reminding everyone of perilous times and their vulnerable position. Children rushed from their classrooms to crawl into the basement and pack tightly into the deepest corners, often places with earthen floors and walls.

Sometimes the children were taken out in the woods for training exercises. They were taught to cover themselves with leaves and bushes to hide from the fighter pilots sent to kill them after the war with Russia began. Their city was a permanent no-fly zone. When an occasional military plane went through the airspace, most children looked up and wondered if it was an enemy aircraft.

Twice a year, the residents practiced a complete evacuation of the town—an exercise that had to be completed in ninety minutes. All stores closed. The three plants shut down. Housewives grabbed any children they had at home. Everyone jumped into their cars. Parents were not allowed to go to the schools to get the children there.

Teachers walked students to the assigned major pickup points, some as much as a mile away. Older students and teachers carried the little guys who could not walk far enough or fast enough.

All seven roads leading out of town went in one direction.

The residents traveled out of the city on roads predetermined by each individual's location at the time the drill began. They stopped at the pickup points. As each car pulled up, kids were crammed into cars with no regard to family connections. They then drove to their assigned shelters as far as seventy-five miles away and awaited the all-clear signal to return to homes, jobs and schools.

And yet, throughout all of this, the average child felt safe and secure. Beverly said that although she and Raynella lived with a sharp concept of the dangers of the cold war, they did not feel the stress of it. They always had a sense that no matter what, they would survive. Maybe because they felt prepared. Maybe because their parents conspired to remain silent about the biggest threat in their lives: the plants themselves and the lethal quality of the substances they contained.

Raynella and her siblings were educated in an exceptional system. Children started Spanish or French in second grade. By the time Raynella attended Robertsville Junior High, she also had the option of Latin. At Oak Ridge High School, German and Russian were also available for study. Of course, in a city full of scientists, the school science curriculum was extraordinary.

Raynella was at the top of the heap, even in this enriched environment. She took accelerated classes, was an officer in the German club and participated in the chemistry and physics clubs. She served on the committee that planned the junior-senior prom and she played clarinet in the marching band. There were three social clubs for young women at the school: the Penguins, the Swankettes, and the group Raynella joined, the Sub Debs. She spent a lot of time at her residence on Wadell Circle studying; education was very important in her home and in her city.

When she did socialize, it was typical early-sixties fare. A lot of mingling happened at the Wildcat Youth Center. Friday nights she went to football games, followed by the dance at the Wildcat Den. The school usually won the state championships in football, basketball, and track; with a student body of more than three thousand students, they could be very picky about who made the teams.

Saturday nights meant movies and driving around and around Shoney's, which Raynella often did in a 1931 maroon Ford with black fenders and a rumble seat owned by friend and sometimes date Jim Campbell. Drinking alcohol, a big problem at the time for high school students across the country, wasn't much of a concern in Oak Ridge. Even adults rarely had alcohol in their homes: the city, the county—the whole area—was dry.

Raynella often spoke to Jim in German. He replied in French. Somehow they seemed to understand each other but baffled all those around them—and that was the point. They hung out together a lot in the junior and senior years. They dated occasionally, threw paper wads at each other across the school hallways often, and hung together at lunchtime.

Raynella was never in trouble and was known for being upright and honest. One friend described her as "an all-American girl. What you'd want your daughter to be in the fifties or early sixties. I expected her to grow up and be just like June Cleaver, the mother in the television show, *Leave it to Beaver*." Raynella graduated from high school in 1966.

Many people praised Oak Ridge as the best place to raise a family—"a virtual Camelot," according to her high school friend Jim Campbell. There was a dark side, though—one that would not be apparent for years. The long-term effects of beryllium exposure would sicken and destroy some families in Oak Ridge. Jim lost his father to cancer, his mother to pulmonary fibrosis, and a sister—all as a result of exposure to beryllium. His remaining sister developed an autoimmune disease and Jim had a recent diagnosis of a lung disease—all, he believed, caused by the beryllium that came home on his father's clothing.

One of Raynella's other classmates said, "We watched and have continued to watch the deaths of so many of our friends and family since I was a small child—even class-mates who died at a very early age. Of the seven houses around mine, at least one or two members of the household have had breast or lung cancer."

That fall, Raynella left Oak Ridge, going off to East Tennessee State University in Johnson City, Tennessee, north of Knoxville, to earn her nursing degree. Beverly, her close friend since kindergarten, moved into the same dormitory just across the hall from Raynella.

During Raynella's sophomore year, she headed home for Thanksgiving break. Beverly sat in the front passenger seat of a car just ahead of her, driven by a friend. Beverly unlocked her seat belt to turn around and speak to people in the backseat. As she did, a car turned in front of their vehicle.

In the collision, Beverly flew partially through the windshield. Raynella pulled over and administered first aid while soothing Beverly with a constant stream of encouraging words. She stayed with her friend in the emergency room.

Nurses wiped at Beverly's face. She told them to stop because there was glass in her eyes, but they wouldn't listen. Raynella spoke to them emphatically, finally getting them to pause long enough to verify the presence of glass. Beverly credited Raynella with saving her vision. Raynella did not leave Beverly's side until her friend's parents arrived. Beverly said, "It was Raynella being Raynella . . . She was kind. She was cheerful. She never was a bully. She was always good."

At the university, Raynella participated in competitive rifle shooting, becoming a very good markswoman. She also met the man she would marry, William Edward Dossett.

CHAPTER 5

Magdalena Snodderly, born April 8, 1906, was the third child in a family of five girls and two boys. She married Henry Dossett in Campbell County, Tennessee, where she worked as a schoolteacher. Henry came from a huge family. His father was married to Mary Telitha Hunter and had had seven children, four boys and three girls. When Mary passed away, the widower married Minnie Allen. That couple had ten children divided equally between the sexes. Their oldest son was Henry.

When World War II commenced, Henry moved up to Ohio to help the war effort by working in a tire manufacturing plant. His wife, Magdalena, lived with her parents, Charles and Belle Snodderly, during that time, on a farm just seven and a half miles east of Oak Ridge. Belle passed away in 1943.

When Henry returned to Tennessee after the war, he helped his father-in-law on the farm. Magdalena taught at the Solway School for a while and then became a fourth-grade teacher at Ball Camp School. She was a heavyset woman— so much so that few were aware she was pregnant until she gave birth to William Edward "Eddie" Dossett on January 4, 1948.

The day Magdalena went into labor was frigidly cold.

Her sister Paralee "Pat" Graves bundled up her son, Ray, and rushed to the farmhouse. Dr. Cobb was on hand to deliver the baby. He handed the newborn to Pat, who cleaned him, swaddled the infant, and placed him in a cradle. In that little bed, Cousin Ray met the new family member who would become his close friend while he lay under a blanket, just minutes after his birth.

Ray remembered his aunt Magdalena as a very loving and compassionate woman who passed along those traits to her son. Eddie would come over to his house to watch television, since Pat and Cleon Graves were the first family in the valley to own a set. Typically the boys watched Westerns, but Eddie could not stand the violent parts. When Indians were on a rampage or cowboys were shooting it out for each other, Eddie would get up and leave the room. When he came back, if the confrontation was still in progress, he'd leave the room again.

When Eddie was five and a half years old, his father, Henry, moved thirty-five miles north to care for his ailing mother, Minnie, in Jacksboro. Every weekend, Magdalena and Eddie made the trip to visit Henry. Just as Minnie had recovered enough to allow Henry to return home to his wife and son, the tables turned. Henry was diagnosed with throat cancer. Magdalena had to work and care for her young son; taking care of a seriously ill husband around the clock wasn't possible. Henry stayed in Jacksboro to be nursed through the illness—and even more debilitating chemotherapy—by his mother.

In 1955, Eddie's grandfather Charles Snodderly died. His aunt Pat led the effort to get the other siblings to sign the farm over to Magdalena, enabling her to remain there, raising her son and teaching at the school. The next year young Eddie would face a more crushing loss.

One weekend in March 1956, Aunt Pat and Cousin Ray accompanied Eddie and his mother on their visit to Henry in

Jacksboro. Henry was in high spirits. His chemotherapy was over and finally his beard had begun sprouting again. He couldn't wait for it to grow back. No one knew it at the time, but it was already too late for Henry: the cancer had metastasized and was silently growing in his brain.

On Saturday, March 31, Eddie and Magdalena went into town to shop for Easter. Everyone who saw her that day thought she looked healthy and happy.

Eight-year-old Eddie awoke on Easter morning, April 1, 1956, to find his mother lying on the floor beside his bed. When he couldn't rouse her, he ran to the nearest neighbor. An ambulance was called, but when they arrived, it was obvious that Magdalena was gone, killed by a massive heart attack.

Because of her size, the family had to special order a casket for her. It took a few days, but finally she was brought home the following Thursday, and family gathered round to sit up all night with her, bidding her farewell. She was buried in the Solway Methodist Church cemetery.

After his mother's death, Eddie went back and forth between the homes of two of his mother's sisters. He'd stay with his aunt Lana for a week and then move over to his aunt Pat's house.

Two months after Magdalena died, Eddie lost his father to cancer. Now he was an orphan. He owned a farm, but at his age, there was no possibility that he could care for it. His aunt Pat was executrix of Magdalena's estate, and another sister, Aunt Lana, became Eddie's guardian. Lana had two children, a daughter older than Eddie and a son, Bob, who was younger.

Eddie settled into the home of his aunt and uncle, Lana and Reuben Bailey. By all accounts, Lana was a good cook, housekeeper, and mother—a kind woman who treated her nephew well. Reuben, however, had a temper and was pretty hard on the young, grieving boy. Eddie used to complain to Aunt Pat that he had to do all the chores while Bob took it easy, and he said he was blamed for everything, while Bob got away with murder.

The Baileys rented out the two houses on Eddie's farm property, collecting the income until Eddie turned eighteen. Eddie also brought a Social Security death benefit check into the household. Aunt Pat often questioned her sister Lana about those two sources of money, wondering if any of it was being saved for Eddie's education. Because of disagreements over those funds and Eddie's treatment, Lana and Pat had a falling-out that lasted for a few years.

In grade school, Hazel Masters, one of Eddie's teachers, remembered, Eddie was exceptionally kind and friendly. Eddie went to Karns Junior High and then on to Karns High School. The school had an interesting population: half of the students came from farming families, the other half had parents working at the Oak Ridge nuclear facilities.

Eddie was a popular young man among his class of 180 students. All four years of his high school career, he was in the Pep Club, the Latin Club, and the 4-H Club. As a junior and senior, he added even more activities. Both years he was on the football team, the high school newspaper staff, the Lettermen's Club, the Quill and Scroll (a reading and writing club), and the High-Y Club (affiliated with the Young Men's Christian Association). He also and played intramural sports.

In his junior year he was in the junior play and was the national winner of the current events quiz competition. As a senior, he was a chemistry aide and became vice president of the Lettermen's Club, president of the 4-H Club, and sports editor of the school newspaper.

In a final tribute to his popularity, his classmates awarded him an award for best school spirit. For the yearbook photograph, he wore his letterman jacket and stood next to his co-winner, cheerleader Donna Price.

When Eddie bought his first car, he selected one of the hottest cars of its time, a yellow and white 1957 Chevy. He had a serious relationship with Maxine Hensley. They dated for a couple of years in high school and continued dating when Eddie went off to college. Friends thought they would marry when he graduated from college.

Eddie's choice of an institution for higher education was a foregone conclusion. His uncle Burgin, one of his father's half brothers, had been president of East Tennessee State University since 1949. Before that, Burgin Dossett had worked on every level in the education field, from teaching in a one-room schoolhouse to being chairman of the Tennessee Board of Education. When Democratic governor Harry Hill McCalister decided not to run for reelection in 1936, Uncle Burgin tossed his hat in the ring. He came in second in a field of three in the primary election.

Eddie graduated from Karns High School in 1965 and went more than one hundred miles away to East Tennessee University in Johnson City on a football scholarship. His aunt Lana drove him up to the school. His cousin Ray Graves, who had a narrower face than he but sported the same dark blond hair and and had the same blue eyes, made the trip north along with Eddie's girlfriend Maxine Hensley. As they pulled away, Eddie had tears in his eyes. Maxine cried all the way home. Lana tried to comfort her, promising, "He'll be home for weekends."

Eddie and Maxine continued to date while he was a freshman. One weekend when he was back at home, he called Ray because his car broke down on Oak Ridge Highway. As smart as Eddie was, Ray and his brother Pat knew he was not in the least mechanically inclined, so they went to his rescue expecting almost anything.

When they arrived, Ray asked, "What happened?"

"I don't know," Eddie said. "It started knocking and then it just quit."

Ray looked under the hood. The first thing he did was check the oil. When he pulled out the stick, it was bone dry. "Eddie, you don't have any oil in this car. Didn't you check it?"

"The guy at the gas station said he checked it and it was okay."

"Eddie, you can't trust a stranger with something that important. You need to check it for yourself."

The motor was fried. Eddie bought a new one and his cousins hauled out the old one. Maxine wound up picking up Eddie so they could go out that Saturday night.

On Sunday, Eddie headed back to the university. Maxine didn't know it yet, but her days with Eddie were numbered.

In Eddie's sophomore year, a new student arrived on campus. She would change his life. Her name was Raynella Large, and she was the woman he would marry.

CHAPTER 6

Eddie's uncle Burgin retired from his position as university president in 1968. The following year, Eddie graduated from East Tennessee State with a degree in business and became a first lieutenant in the Army Reserve. Raynella was only nine months younger than Eddie, but she started school one year later. Because of that, she still did not have her degree when they decided to marry in the summer of 1969.

Raynella was a lovely bride. Her lacy white dress, tall stature, and straight posture gave her a regal appearance. Her long dark hair, parted in the middle, framed a sweet face full of promise. Eddie's dirty-blond hair swept across his forehead. His face was still round with the chubbiness of youth, but he was built with the sturdiness of a linebacker. Even at this young age, they were a formidable-looking couple.

Raynella's mother was not pleased. She did not approve of the marriage and bore a grudge toward her son-in-law. She refused to speak to Eddie for the first thirteen years of his marriage to her daughter.

The newlyweds moved to the Knoxville area in Eastern Tennessee, embraced by the Cumberland Plateau of the Appalachian mountain chain on one side and Great Smoky Mountains National Park on the other. The city began its life as a fort named after George Washington's secretary of war, Henry Knox. When Tennessee became a state in 1796, Knoxville was its first capital.

Knoxville is home of many notable natives, including Pulitzer Prize–winning novelist and playwright James Agee; actress Patricia Neal; actors David Keith and Brad Renfro; director Quentin Tarantino; Dave Thomas, founder of Wendy's; Dr. William Bass of Body Farm fame; and musicians Flatt and Scruggs, Chet Atkins, and the Everly Brothers. The soft drink Mountain Dew was born here in the 1940s. In 1974, Walter Cronkite named it the "Streaking Capital of America" after five thousand people met on Cumberland Avenue, stripped, and raced down the road.

Ed started at the University of Tennessee Law School in 1969, while Raynella finished her nursing degree and got a job at Parkwest Medical Center. Later, she'd return to the University of Tennessee to teach nursing classes.

Ed graduated from law school in 1972. He and Sharon Bell, a friend from law school, set up a law office downtown on one of the lower floors of the old Bank of Knoxville building at the corner of Church and Market streets. Norman Jackson had an office in the same building on a slightly higher floor. Ed, Sharon, and Norman came into frequent contact coming and going from their offices. They decided to consolidate to share overhead expenses and moved in together on the eleventh floor.

When Ron Lewis graduated from law school, he joined the group. When BankFirst purchased the building and wanted to office their in-house lawyers in the space now occupied by Ed, Norman, Sharon, and Ron, the four attorneys moved into an office in West Knoxville.

Their staff consisted of two secretaries, Kaye Holden Clift and Donna Price Corbitt. In addition to working with Ed, the two women became close friends with his wife, Raynella. Kaye was the receptionist and Norman's secretary.

Donna did the secretarial work for other attorneys. Soon Ed and Kaye began an affair that would last, on and off, for years.

Norman remembers Ed as an affable person, an easy person to share the informal working relationship. Ed's favorite saying was "Adversity makes you stronger." It seemed that was how he viewed any setback as well as the difficulties of his childhood. He referred to Reuben Bailey as "that man who raised me." He never said anything more about the man, either positive or negative. To most of the friends he met as an adult, Ed's childhood remained cloaked in mystery.

Although Ed would get excited about things from time to time, he never exhibited any signs of a bad temper. Norman and Ed became fast friends, helping each other out whenever they could. "When Ed told you something, you could take it to the bank," Norman said.

In addition to their career, Norman and Ed had another thing in common: both owned family farms. They spent more time talking about farming than the law. Ed was proud of being a farmer and a country lawyer. "He had some rough corners, but he had a big heart," Norman recalled.

Ed demonstrated the latter in his criminal law practice, always willing to "go the extra mile" for those less fortunate. "He'd work harder for the ordinary man than for someone in a privileged position," according to Norman.

When Ed's good friend, county law director Charlie Maner, was temporarily unable to perform his job in 1978, Ed filled in during his absence. On December 22 of that year, Raynella and Ed had their first child, Raynella Magdalena "Maggie" Dossett, named after her mother and the paternal grandmother she would never know.

The couple had been living in a mobile home on Melton Hill Lake, but with the birth of Maggie they moved to Ed's family farm. Coming home from Knoxville, Ed drove west, turning northwest at Dead Horse Lake. An hour farther west was the oddly named Frozen Head State Park, the place where Martin Luther King Jr.'s assassin James Earl Ray was captured after his escape.

The family lived in a single-wide trailer while Ed worked on their new home. Ed was determined to build the house using lumber from his own land. He spent months cutting down trees and hauling the logs down to the lumber mill. Once they were cut into boards, he dried them on the farm, turning them frequently to make the boards straight and true. Architect Bob Carroll designed his new home and oversaw the progress of the work.

Ed bulldozed the old farmhouse and laid a new, larger foundation on the same spot. He did most of the work constructing this home, getting advice and assistance from contractor friend Murt Compton. His home-cured lumber was so hard, it often bent twenty-penny nails. He often joked that so many of those nails had fallen into the basement, they didn't need to use any rebar in the cement.

He constructed his new home as sturdy as a fortress, wanting it to last well beyond his own lifetime. He enlisted some help for the finish work, including cousin Pat Graves, who was the electrician who did the wiring for the house.

Ed had been hankering for a mule for quite some time. He wanted to use it to plow tobacco fields and his vegetable garden. A couple of his cousins had one for sale. Ed brought the mule home and his cousin Ray joined him at the farm to check out the animal. Ray now worked for the University of Tennessee's agricultural experimental station in Oak Ridge and was Ed's go-to guy for all farming questions.

They hooked up a log to the animal's harness to see how well he'd pull a plow. The second they let go, the mule took off running. Ed and Ray ran after it, finally getting it to stop. Ed said, "I think my cousins slipped one past me. They said this mule would do anything. They said he'd even let you ride him."

Ray decided to put that last claim to the test. He bounded

up on the mule's back. The mule reared up on his hind legs, slashing the air with his front hooves. Ray dismounted as quickly as he could.

Ed recognized an opportunity to advance his legal career in 1982 when Ron Webster, the Sixth Judicial District attorney general since 1968, announced his retirement. When Ed decided to run for the position, no one thought he had a chance. "He didn't care. He just went for it," Norman Jackson said.

The moment Ed entered the race, Annie Large changed her attitude about son-in-law. She attended many election events, wearing a smile and getting close to Ed whenever a camera was in the vicinity.

Raynella dedicated herself to the election, running errands, mailing and delivering campaign materials, and doing every bit of general grunt work a bid at public office required. At the same time, one of Ed's colleagues in the law office, Sharon Bell, was also campaigning, seeking the position of general sessions judge.

Ed's election-night party was planned for the Howard Johnson's on Clinton Highway. He must have been pretty confident of his chances. He invited his cousin Elizabeth Perril to travel down from Illinois to be there as the results rolled in from the polling places. Elizabeth couldn't make it but could only imagine the celebration: Ed defeated his opponent Randy Nichols. Sharon Bell won that night too.

The next day, Norman Jackson went into the city-county building and was greeted with warm welcomes from everyone he saw. He laughed at their congratulations. Sure, two of the attorneys in his law office had won their elections, but for Norman that meant he'd lost two people who contributed to the overhead costs. It was a bittersweet victory.

Sheriff Tim Hutchison gave Ed Dossett a five-shot blue steel pistol when he was elected, saying he'd need a gun for protection, now that he was locking up the bad guys. Ed never did much of anything with the gun. No one paid any attention to it for nearly thirteen years.

As soon as Ed assumed his new position, he needed to hire an administrative assistant. He picked his private practice secretary and sometime lover, Kaye Clift, to work for him in the attorney general's office.

The following year, Ed and Raynella's family grew by one more with the birth of William "Eddie" Dossett Jr. Ed became Big Eddie, and the baby was Little Eddie.

In the early 1980s Ed's secretary, Kaye, met Steve Walker. He was the manager of Marshall Transmission, where Kaye brought her car in for repairs. In 1983 they married. Kaye introduced Steve to Ed and Raynella, and the couples socialized together on occasion. Kaye stopped working for Ed in 1984 for the birth of her first child, Kevin.* The couples kept in touch through visits to the hospital when children were born and on half a dozen occasions at the Dossett farm. Raynella never visited the Walkers at their home; she wasn't very social, rarely attending the functions held by Ed's office.

Ed, however, was at the Walker house frequently—far more than Steve knew at the time. Ed also visited Steve at the transmission shop to talk about farming. "We didn't have any other common interest, except my wife, and I didn't know about that at the time," Steve said.

---

* The names of Steve and Kaye Walker's sons have been changed to protect their privacy.

CHAPTER 7

Ed often said, "I'm a farmer first and a lawyer second."

Jim McMillan, the son of one of the neighboring farmers, witnessed the reality of that statement firsthand. He was just a teenager when he started going with his dad and Ed Dossett to livestock sales. It was hard to look at Ed in his overalls and imagine him as a district attorney general. He was nothing more than a farmer among a herd of farmers. He didn't throw his weight around or display any pretensions. He treated everyone as his equal.

When Ed was involved with anything related to his agricultural work, he drove around in an old, ratty green pickup truck. Teenage McMillan spotted the vehicle in the parking lot at a cattle sale one day. He pulled out a piece of paper and jotted down the license plate number.

Then Jim went looking for Ed. "We've got a problem out our way," he said.

"What's that?" Ed asked.

"Somebody keeps racing up and down the road that runs by our place, tossing out beer cans in our yard."

Even though they lived in a dry county, Ed couldn't get too upset about someone drinking beer. Ed liked an occasional cool one on a hot summer day. He never bought it himself, though, because it wouldn't look good if he was recognized coming out of the store with a six-pack. He'd send a farmhand to the nearest place to legally buy beer to bring it back.

Nonetheless, he found driving while drinking and littering one of his fellow farmers' properties in the process not at all acceptable. "You need to get his plate number and call the sheriff. Or call me," Ed said.

"I've got his license plate number right here," Jim said, struggling to conceal a smirk. He pulled the piece of paper out of his pocket and handed it to Ed.

The district attorney general looked down at the number and recognized it right away. A prosecutorial scowl hardened his face. "Now, boy, don't you do that!" Then Ed grinned, slapped Jim on the back, and burst into laughter.

At the livestock sales, Jim noticed the prosecutor-farmer's preference in beef cattle. Ed liked to buy polled Herefords. The breed had white faces, a white stripe down their backs, and no horns. They were as gentle as dairy cows. Even when Ed picked out a bull, he'd look for the most passive one he could find. He built up a herd that was so tame that when he went out to feed them, it was like mingling with a bunch of overgrown puppies.

Although Jim was comfortable around Ed and enjoyed passing time with him, Raynella was another story. When she came around, Jim made himself scarce. He didn't care for Ed's wife, thinking she was a low-class woman who had married Ed with the expectation that she'd now be treated like a princess by everyone. Jim also thought she bossed her husband around too much. In his opinion, Ed was a different man when he wasn't around Raynella. He seemed to relax outside of her presence.

Ed put a lot of time and energy into upgrading his farm to handle his herd. He'd built a pole barn with an enclosed area on both sides and a covered open area in the middle of the two. He asked his cousin Ray to come over and advise him about his plans for the barn. "I want to put a gate up at each end here," he said pointing to the empty space. "That way I'll have a confined area for the cattle when I need to load them up for market."

"Well, Eddie, that space is twenty feet wide. If you use just one gate on each end, you're not going to like it. Put in two ten-foot gates on each end. It'll give you a smaller entrance so you have better control of the cattle. Then, if you need to get a vehicle or a piece of equipment in here, you can open up both gates."

Ed was eager to learn from the wisdom of others. He followed Ray's advice and it met his needs perfectly.

Ray came around on another day when Ed needed advice. Ed was out on his tractor pulling a drill, planting a field of sudex, a hybrid of sorghum and Sudan grass. At the time it was considered to be a great crop for grazing cattle. He was having a devil of a time getting the tractor to keep working. It was jamming up, and he had to stop often to get it to work right.

Ray was driving by when he spotted his cousin out in the field. "You having a problem?" he asked.

"Yeah, I don't think I have enough seed."

"Well, Eddie, if you're planting a five-acre field and you know you need one bag of seed for each acre, you ought to buy six bags. You can take it back it if you don't use it. You want me to run up to the co-op and get you some more?"

"If you don't mind," Ed said.

Ray drove down the road to the feed and seed store. While he was gone, Ed continued working, but the problem worsened. Every few feet that he proceeded, the supply of seed in the drill dropped. The descending level aggravated its tendency to seize up and stop. Ed barely made it ten feet before he'd have to stop and free up the drill again. The last time he stepped off the tractor to mess with the drill, he fixed the problem; but before he could regain his seat, the tractor started moving forward.

He grabbed at it, trying to hoist his body up to the controls, but it was going too fast. It knocked him down and ran over him. He wasn't seriously injured, but the tractor tore his overalls and ripped off his shirt.

When Ray arrived back with the seed, he found an ashen, disheveled Ed standing beside his tractor. The vehicle had stopped only when it ran into a barn.

"Ray, you gotta promise me: Don't say anything to Raynella about this," Ed pleaded.

"Why not, Eddie?"

"She'll want me to sell this place. She'll worry I'll get killed if I keep farming."

On June 10, 1985, the Dossett's third and last child, Nancy Kathalena, whom they called Katie, was born, rounding out the family of five. Shortly after that, Ed took a job-related trip to Chicago. He took a side jaunt to visit his cousin Elizabeth Perril while he was in the area.

Elizabeth was a committed dog lover and, of course, allowed her pets in her home. Ed usually teased her about that, saying that wasn't the way she was raised. Like Ed, she grew up on a farm where dogs stayed outside.

That day, he told her a story about his dog. "I took the dog to the vet."

"Really, why?" Elizabeth asked.

"I don't know. I can't remember. But they wanted to know the name of my dog. I said, 'Name? He's a dog. I call him Dog.'"

Elizabeth chuckled. "Then what happened?"

"Well, they said he had to have a name: they needed for their records. I said, 'Okay, just call him George.' And they said, 'George? Why do you want to call him George?' And I said, 'Because George is the father of our country and this dog's the father of most of the puppies born in the county.'"

The story was vintage Ed. Decades later, it still made Elizabeth laugh.

CHAPTER 8

Kaye Walker resumed her job at the district attorney general's office. One day she returned home from work in state of fury over an incident that day in Ed's private office. His quarters had a private bathroom with a shower.

Kaye watched as a woman entered Ed's office for an interview. She was behind closed doors much longer than usual. When the woman came out with wet hair, Kaye knew she had taken a shower. She reached the logical conclusion that Ed had had sex with that woman, and she was angry.

Her husband, Steve, listened to her vent about the impropriety. He understood why she'd be mad about her boss using his office for extramarital sex, but he did think she was over-reacting a bit. Of course, Steve had no idea about why it affected her so personally.

Ed plowed into his work, making news in a few locally significant cases. One case involved University of Tennessee quarterback Tony Robinson, a onetime Heisman Trophy contender whose collegiate career ended on October 19, 1985, when his right knee was injured in a game against Alabama. Before that injury, he set three records for the Volunteers: most completions, with 29 in a game against Florida; most yards passing, 387 against UCLA; and most offensive yards in that same UCLA game.

Robinson lived in an off-campus apartment with Kenneth "B.B." Cooper, a Volunteer fullback from 1981 to 1984. According to the arresting officers, the two young men began the sale and distribution of cocaine less than a month after Robinson's injury, on November 8. From that date until their arrest on January 8, 1986, there were five incidents of distribution to undercover police officers, totaling forty-six grams of cocaine. Robinson was involved on three occasions and Cooper in all of them. Ed also obtained a conspiracy indictment against them both.

At the time of his arrest, a detective asked Robinson, "Did you know there was cocaine in the bag you handed me?"

"I don't know what it was," Robinson said. "I don't mess with it. It was closed and I don't touch the stuff."

Nonetheless, both men faced a total of twenty-five counts, making them eligible for life in prison. Robinson's attorney, Bob Ritchie, wanted diversion for his client so that he would not have to admit guilt and could do community service work instead of going to prison. In order for that to be possible, Ritchie asked Dossett to drop the counts against Robinson to one possession charge, saying that the charges were arbitrarily broken into multiple counts.

Ed fired back in a letter to Ritchie: "Mr. Robinson's active involvement in the sale and delivery of cocaine was not an impulsive or casual flirtation with this substance, but an extensive activity involving connections to other members of the community involved in drug traffic and distribution of this substance to fellow University of Tennessee students. During this time, Mr. Robinson furnished money for the purchase of cocaine, delivered cocaine to undercover agents and delivered cocaine to other members of the University of Tennessee football team."

Attorney Bob Ritchie said the Ed's allegations were "unfounded, untrue and baseless." The prosecutor was "trying to turn the public's mind against Tony Robinson." Sportswriters across the country came out in support of Robinson and his lawyer's allegations.

Despite Ed's strong stance, he negotiated a plea bargain for the men that would punish them but not ruin their lives. Both men entered no-contest pleas. Robinson pled on three counts of cocaine delivery, which netted him a six-year sentence—150 days at the county penal farm and the rest on probation. Cooper was convicted on four counts, resulting in an eight-year sentence but reduced to the same short sentence working at the county farm. Robinson went on to play for the Washington Redskins, leading his team to a 13–7 win over the Dallas Cowboys during the strike of 1987.

After taking the required courses and obtaining a second degree, Raynella was certified as a clinical social worker and received a license from the state on January 13, 1986.

Delana, one of Ed's cousins, passed away that year. Elizabeth Perril and her husband drove down from Illinois for the funeral. They planned to stay at a hotel, but Ed insisted they stay in his home, and they accepted. Elizabeth said that after that weekend, she swore that she'd never stay at Ed's house again. She couldn't bear spending that much time around Raynella.

Elizabeth said that Ed's wife had a nasty temper and "she was full of herself," always going on about how great she was. Every minute Elizabeth was at the farm, she felt the sting of Raynella's forced, artificial hospitality.

CHAPTER 9

One of the rising stars on Ed's staff of assistant district attorneys was Ted Barnett, a thirty-one-year-old native of Knoxville and the first African American prosecutor in Knox County. He'd worked in the Nashville public defender's office before returning home to join Ed's team. "He was an outstanding young man and very proactive attorney and prosecutor," Eighth Judicial District attorney general Paul Phillips said.

Ted took two weeks of vacation in December 1987. He was expected back in the office on December 28, the Monday after Christmas. When didn't show up for work that day, Ed was concerned by his absence. He asked his staff to keep calling Ted's home until they reached him.

With still no word from Ted on Tuesday, Ed sent Rex McGhee and another staff member over to the young attorney's two-story Brandau Street home in the old, established neighborhood of College Hills surrounding the campus of Knoxville College. They knocked but got no answer. They left a note on the door asking him to call the office. Rex told Ed that Ted's car was not at his home.

By Wednesday, Ed Dossett was alarmed. He took Rex McGhee and another member of his staff with him and went to the house. Again they knocked. Again no one responded.

Ed borrowed a ladder from a next-door neighbor and propped it against the house beneath an open window on the second floor. Inside, he unlocked the front door and let the others into Ted's home.

Walking through scattered empty bottles of wine and liquor, they thought they glanced in every room. Their greatest fear was that they'd find Ted dead from an accident, an illness, or an act of violence. They spotted an apparent semen stain on the sheet of the unmade bed but no sign of their colleague. They were relieved that they did not find a body during their cursory exploration.

On the day of New Year's Eve, Ed Dossett sent one of his investigators over to Ted's home with instructions to do a more thorough search. Opening a door that the previous searchers thought led to a closet, the investigator discovered a partially completed, unheated bathroom addition jutting off the side of the house. Their worst fears were realized in that cold, forbidding room.

The water ran in the sink, the toilet, and the shower, making the room more chilly and damp. Light streamed in through the unfinished siding and up through the cantilevered floor.

Electrical cords—one with the iron still attached—bound the hands and feet of the young lawyer. He was fully clothed and obviously deceased. His head lay on the rough lumber sub-flooring beside the toilet and slightly beneath the sink. His legs stretched into the shower. His throat was slit. Defensive slices covered his hands and arms. Stab wounds riddled his body, with the greatest number in his back and on his buttocks. Mold grew on his wounds and cuts. The middle finger of one hand was raised in an obscene salute. It could have been Ted's last message to his attacker or a sick joke staged by the perpetrator.

Horrified, the investigator called the attorney general's office. Ed Dossett and many of his staff rushed over to Ted's home.

Veteran Knoxville Police Department investigator Art Bohanon received a message from the dispatcher: "Call the DA's office ASAP. They asked specifically for you."

Bohanon grabbed the phone. He was connected to Assistant District Attorney Bob Jolley who described the scene at Ted's house and asked him to go there immediately. "Don't tell anybody," Bob said. "The chief is the only other person at the KPD who knows about this."

Art raced to the College Hills neighborhood. Kneeling on the floor beside the body, he saw dozens of stab wounds. Worst of all, some of them had begun to pull together, an obvious sign of healing. He feared that meant Ted's death had not been quick. Ted had endured days of torturous suffering before he died.

Medical examiner Dr. Randall Pedigo arrived at the scene. He confirmed Bohanon's conclusions and estimated that the victim had died weeks earlier. When the body was taken to the morgue, Art called in the forensic team and the lead investigator in this new case, Knoxville police detective Gary Moyers, brother of Knox County Sheriff's Department investigator Perry Moyers.

When Gary Moyers arrived on the scene, the crime lab people were already at work, gathering fingerprints and other evidence. The house was crawling with patrol officers and Ted's coworkers, including District Attorney General Ed Dossett.

Somehow, the previous day, the attorney general's staff overlooked vital indicators of foul play. To Moyers's eye, the signs of a violent crime were obvious. He walked through the living room and into a formal sitting room. Blood spatter dotted the walls; streaks of cast-off blood ran across the doors and ceiling. Blood stained the blue couch and displayed the signs of an attack on an area of the carpet. A new chandelier lay broken in an open box. Slivers of glass littered the floor. The light fixture appeared to have been used to bludgeon the victim. The cardboard box was smeared with dried blood and bloody fingerprints. A bloody mop bore evidence of a cleanup.

He entered the bathroom to view the body. The water still ran. The room was cold and damp; it had preserved the body well.

How the attorney general and his staff missed this important evidence boggled Moyers's mind. He could only reach one conclusion: they were looking for something else. Perhaps they sought case files that could indicate impropriety on Ted's part. Or perhaps they wanted to keep the lid on Ted's homosexuality.

The prosecutors and their staff huddled together at the crime scene looking nervous, upset, and concerned. Ted was well liked in the office, and the grief at his loss was apparent. But the overwhelming emotion they exhibited was regret for their actions during the last couple of days. Gary Moyers said, "They realized they'd stepped in a bucket of poop and didn't know how to get it off their boots."

A chagrined Ed Dossett admitted he should have called in trained investigators immediately instead of relying on a pack of lawyers to do the work of forensic specialists.

Gary Moyers sent out a Knoxville Police Department BOLO ("be on the look out") for Ted's missing 1982 blue Oldsmobile. They searched records and found the car had been involved in a recent hit-and-run. They listed the vehicle as stolen on the National Crime Information Center (NCIC) database. They made television announcements and put up billboards asking for information from the public.

Gary received a call from John Williams, one of Ted Barnett's friends, who'd seen the Knoxville Police Department alerts about Ted's Olds. "I know where your car is," he said.

"Where?" Moyers asked.

"It's in Columbus, Georgia, and the guy driving it is in jail."

"You're kidding me," Moyers said.

"No. I know the guy. He's Jeffrey Middlebrook. He's been up here in Knoxville."

The arrest was made on Monday, December 28, the same day Ted was supposed to return to work. John—who by coincidence was visiting in Georgia over the holidays—spotted a car that looked like the one Ted drove. When he looked closer and spotted a Knox County sticker on its bumper, he was certain it was his friend's car. It didn't seem right, so he called the Columbus Crimestoppers line and reported the suspicious vehicle.

The Columbus Police issued a notice about the car and a patrolman spotted the Oldsmobile and pulled it over. Middlebrook produced the registration at the officer's request, explaining that his friend Ted Barnett lent him the car to make the trip down to Columbus. However, Jeffrey did not have a driver's license, so the officer arrested him for operating a motor vehicle without one. Since Ted's Oldsmobile had not yet been entered in NCIC at that time, an alert didn't come up in the department's search of the national database.

On December 31, investigator Gary Moyers called down to Columbus and verified the information provided by John Williams. Detectives Moyers and Tom Stiles drove down to Georgia that night. They questioned their suspect first thing in the morning on New Year's Day. Middlebrook confessed to stabbing Ted repeatedly over several days to make sure that he was dead. If that was true, it meant that Ted's throat was not slit in the initial attack.

Middlebrook admitted that his motive was to steal Ted's possessions. He told the detectives that he'd sold or given away much of his take. That part of his story was verified when, a few days later, a man came into the police department for an interview wearing one of Ted's shirts.

Although Moyers and Stiles doubted some of the details, they had enough to press charges against Middlebrook. Before they could take him back to Tennessee, they had to follow proper extradition proceedings and obtain the necessary paperwork. Since it was a legal holiday, no courts were in session. They worried they'd be stuck in Georgia for days.

The Columbus police came to the rescue, calling a judge at his home. Local police officers, detectives Moyers and Stiles, and Jeffrey Middlebrook all drove over to the judge's house. The judge conducted the extradition hearing in his dining room. Middlebrook waived his right to fight the order, consenting to return to the scene of the crime, and the three men were on their way back to Knoxville, Tennessee.

Details of Middlebrook's story changed with each telling. On the drive home he offered up another motive: self-defense. According to the suspect, he was the victim of an intense sexual advance by Ted Barnett. Middlebrook claimed he was repulsed by Ted's proposal but Ted would not back off. In the subsequent struggle, Ted got the upper hand and, Jeffrey said, he was forced to stab Ted to protect himself from sexual assault.

This story did not ring true. The forensic techs searching Ted's home found a letter written by Middlebrook while he was incarcerated at Brushy Mountain State Penitentiary. It began: "Dear Teddy Bear." That missive gave credence to Middlebrook's claim that Ted was gay, but it also made a lie of his statement that he found Ted's seduction attempt disgusting.

The detectives doubted the sexual assault story. Too many times they'd heard perpetrators trying to put the blame for their crime on the victim. Later, when they questioned Ted's friends, investigators found some who had suspected Ted was homosexual. Those who knew him best said that he habitually trolled the basketball courts looking for sexual conquests. Some of his willing liaisons were with Jeffrey Middlebrook. Ted kept quiet about his sexual preferences at work. In 1987, an openly gay lifestyle would not have been a good career move for a prosecutor in Tennessee—or in many other places, for that matter.

Moyers decided that Ted's homosexuality was irrelevant. To him, it was obviously a homicide connected to the theft of the victim's property.

During the ride to Knoxville, Middlebrook also claimed that he was not in the house alone. Another man and two women who were twins partied with him there. At one point he said that the man helped him murder Ted. Then he contradicted that statement by alleging that none of the others were aware that the body was in the home.

Moyers followed up with the people who Middlebrook claimed were in the house. The twins answered the detective's questions in a straightforward manner. They admitted to hanging out at the house for a couple of days but said they never opened the door that led to that bathroom. They said they didn't even know that a bath was behind the door. Since there were two other baths in Ted's home—one upstairs and one downstairs—Moyers believed it was a plausible scenario. The two women expressed horror that a dead body was in the house while they were having a good time.

Then Moyers ran down James "Big Head" Payne, the man Middlebrook placed in Ted's house. "You got a warrant for me?" Big Head asked.

"No," Moyers admitted.

"Then I ain't got nothing to say to you."

That attitude raised Moyers's suspicions, but the forensic techs never found anything to link Big Head to the murder. They had one unidentified fingerprint on the doorsill of the bathroom. It didn't match Big Head, either of the twins, Ted or anyone in the attorney general's office, or anything in the fingerprint database.

Upon returning to Tennessee, Middlebrook gave a final statement, a new version of events that matched the forensic evidence better than anything he had told detectives in the first two interviews. He admitted to multiple sexual encounters with Ted and previous visits to the prosecutor's home.

He had appeared in court in December on charges that he committed a burglary at an old library. The judge let him go with time served on the condition that he leave the city.

Middlebrook said that he assessed his situation to determine what to do next. To get out of town, he needed a car and some cash. He knew Ted had both. He went over to Ted's home after his last day of work before vacation. Middlebrook intended to take what he wanted using whatever means were necessary.

When he arrived, he and Ted went into the sitting room and sat on the blue sofa. Ted put his arms around Middlebrook and the two started kissing. Middlebrook realized that in order to get the money and car, he would have to kill Ted. He excused himself and slipped into the kitchen. Out of sight, he grabbed a knife and slid it up his sleeve.

Returning to the sitting room, Middlebrook sat down next to the prosecutor. Ted kissed him again. Middlebrook pulled out the knife and raised it up in the air. Ted sensed the movement, saw the descending blade, and fought for his life. Ted had the clear physical advantage: he was athletic, six feet two inches, and about 190 pounds. Middlebrook was not in great condition and was a smaller man at five feet six inches and about 170 pounds.

They tumbled off the couch and onto the floor. Ted soon gained the upper hand and was on the verge of overpowering his assailant. Ted's hand was on the knife. As he wrested it from Middlebrook's grasp, the attacker reached into an open box, pulled a lighting fixture out of it, and bashed it repeatedly over Ted's head.

Middlebrook said he regained control of the knife and slashed Ted's throat. He then stabbed him multiple times in the back and the buttocks. He tied the dying man's feet and hands with cords and dragged him into the adjoining bathroom. Once he shut the door, he claimed, he never went in that room again.

At some point, he said, he drove out to Lonsdale to pick up the twins and invited Big Head over to make it a foursome. Middlebrook had sex with one of the twins in Ted's bed without a thought for Ted's body discarded on the bathroom floor.

That scenario had its flaws. It didn't account for the signs of healing on some of Ted's wounds. However, since Middlebrook admitted to spending a week in the house, he could have done everything he said over a period of days rather than minutes. The slit to Ted's throat had to have come at the end at the attack, just before he dragged his victim's body into the bathroom.

Because of the obvious conflict of interest in Ed Dossett's office, the Tennessee Association of Attorneys General assigned the prosecution to Eighth Judicial District attorney general Paul Phillips in Huntsville. Ted's current and past case files were thoroughly reviewed. Investigators sought any signs that favoritism had been shown by Ted to anyone who engaged in sexual relations with him—particularly Jeffrey Middlebrook. They found nothing to indicate any wrongdoing on the part of the deceased prosecutor.

With a confession in hand, the law enforcement investigators thought it would be an easy prosecution. Moyers thought Middlebrook was headed to death row. The state might have gotten the death penalty if not for two pieces of bad news that made the risks of a trial too great.

One bit of unwanted information came from the morgue. At the scene, Dr. Pedigo estimated the time of death within a period when law enforcement could prove that Jeffrey Middlebrook was still in Knoxville. Pedigo, however, did not perform the autopsy. That procedure was done by Dr. John Evans, who was a doctor but not a forensic pathologist. Evans estimated a window for the homicide occurring between Christmas and December 28. Defense attorney Gordon

Bell knew he had evidence of Middlebrook's presence in Georgia during that time, and he intended to use it.

The other unfortunate development for the state happened in the courtroom. The judge delivered a blow to the case when he ruled that the final statement—the one that most definitively linked Middlebrook to a capital crime—was inadmissible because of Middlebrook's vague suggestion that he might want a lawyer.

Prosecutor Phillips reviewed all the evidence. Everything he saw was consistent with Pedigo's original estimate but didn't fit with Evans's time frame. He called in the renowned forensic anthropologist Dr. William Bass, creator of the University of Tennessee's Body Farm, a three-acre laboratory where bodies are exposed to the elements for the scientific study of decomposition.

Bill Bass examined the forty-six photos from the scene of the crime as well as pictures taken during autopsy. He scoured the autopsy report, gathered meteorological data, and analyzed it all. The telling piece of evidence was the mold he discovered on Ted's body combined with the chilly weather during the period in question. That data convinced Bass that Evans was wrong. His conclusions were consistent with Pedigo's original estimation. Bass believed Ted Barnett died well before Christmas, on or around December 18.

Testimony from Bass would add a lot of weight to the already hefty evidence in the hands of the prosecutors. Attorney Gordon Bell started bargaining for a sentence short of the death penalty that Middlebrook now faced. The prosecutors were willing to deal because they knew the defense had ammunition to use at trial. They reached an agreement on July 16, 1989, on the eve of the defendant's scheduled court date.

Middlebrook pled guilty to second degree murder and armed robbery. He received thirty-five years and twenty-five years, respectively, for these two crimes—a total of sixty years. Middlebrook will be eligible for parole on July 10, 2040.

Ed Dossett was relieved. He worried that a good defense might shred him and his office for their foolhardy invasion of Ted's home. Now that wouldn't happen. There would be no trial, and the bad guy was behind bars for a long time.

CHAPTER 10

On February 1, 1988, Ed Dossett tackled another sports star: Tennessee basketball player Elvin Brown. He was arrested for shoplifting $18 worth of blank video cassette tapes. Although it was only a misdemeanor charge, Elvin was kicked off the team and missed the remaining ten conference games of the season. At the time, he already had the most total steals and the most steals per game of any player in a three-year season.

Ed and Brown's attorney, Tom Dillard, reached an agreement that would enable Elvin to be eligible to play in the next season. He had to perform fifty hours of public service, enroll in Project First Offender, a counseling program, and pay $100 in court costs.

Kaye Walker gave birth to her second child, Kyle, in 1988. Steve Walker naturally thought Kyle was his biological son. Kaye wasn't so sure, but she didn't share her doubts about the boy's parentage with her husband.

Fledgling reporter Betty Bean was assigned a breaking news story one evening. Her editor told her to call the district attorney general at home for his comment. It was sometime between 8:00 and 9:00 p.m. when she dialed the number.

Since Ed was a publicly elected official, it was considered appropriate to call him about an important story before they went to press.

Apparently Raynella didn't agree with that assessment, and she was the one who answered the phone. According to Betty, Raynella chewed out the young journalist, showing her no mercy, and told her to never call at such an indecent hour again.

Betty was shocked. It was her first encounter with the prosecutor's wife. She'd already met Ed at the big blowout Christmas party that attorney Zane Daniels hosted in his home every Christmas. Ed struck her as a big party boy. She remembered spotting him dancing, twirling his jacket in the air over his head.

Ed's officemate Norman Jackson said, "Ed was not a big hell-raiser. He was a 100 percent guy. Anything he went at, he went 100 percent. He didn't do anything halfway. Some people saw him as a hard-nosed politician, but that was just his 100 percent character. He was ambitious without being ruthless. He gave his all to farming, to law, and when he relaxed, he really relaxed. If he wanted to raise hell, he could do a good job of that too."

Ed closed down four adult businesses in 1989. He argued that pornographic peep shows are a health hazard because of sex acts in unclean booths. In January 1990, Judge Frederick McDonald ruled that the shows were illegal in Knox County but that the shops could remain open and resume selling adult books.

Raynella retired from her position as charge nurse at Parkwest Medical Center and devoted herself to the farm, her children, and her husband in 1990, at the age of forty-two. In the warm weather she frequently took her children over to Dave Leath's place to swim in his pool. Leath was a childhood friend of Ed's who lived nearby. He was the divorced father of one and a popular and well-liked barber in

West Knoxville. It appeared as if all was well in Ed's life. He lived on the 165-acre family farm with his wife and three children and had no concerns about reelection. But his cousin Ray remembered two things that seemed to be harbingers of what followed.

Ed often teased Raynella, telling her she was crazy because between her nursing degree and her social work degree she spent too much time with crazy people.

In 1990, Ed was at a board meeting for the farming co-op. He didn't look well and he complained about his stomach hurting. Ed said, "I think she's trying to kill me. I'm married to the meanest woman in the world."

Ed didn't crack a smile; nonetheless, everyone, including Ray, took the statements lightly. The future would make Ray doubt his judgment.

CHAPTER 11

In 1991, Ed was cultivating support within the powerful Tennessee Farm Bureau as part of his plan to run for the office of governor, and unlike his uncle Burgin in his failed bid in 1936, Ed would be a candidate for the Republican Party. But when Ed went into the hospital for an appendectomy in October 1991, his whole world fell apart.

He expected a simple procedure with a short recovery time. Instead, the situation became very complicated. During the procedure, his surgeon discovered adenocarcinoma of the appendix that involved the small intestines and metastasized to other organs.

Raynella planned a meeting of Ed's closest friends and associates at the Andrew Johnson Hotel. She said she wanted to talk to them all about Ed's situation.

Just before Norman Jackson left to go to the hotel, he received a call from Sharon Bell. "I don't want you to walk in that meeting not knowing what's going on," she said, and told him about Ed's illness and the gloomy prognosis.

Raynella shared the sad news with a select few that day, but she withheld the news from the media. She simply said, "He is recovering at home from exploratory abdominal surgery."

When asked if he had cancer, she snapped, "My husband's health is not public information. My husband is ill and that's all that needs to be printed." She said she would answer the questions of family and friends individually. Then she added, "He is recovering beautifully. He is coming back. He's working, he's signing indictments."

As soon as Ed was ambulatory, he went out to Sevier County and bought some young apple trees. His cousin Ray came to the farm to help him plant them. He knew Ed had cancer but he had a hard time believing anything could kill Ed; after all Ed had been through in his life, Ray believed he could survive anything.

In the middle of setting the trees, Ray said, "Ed, you know what Confucius say about a man who plants trees: he has faith in the future." Nearly two decades later, that little quip remained a reason for regret.

On November 19, Assistant Attorney General Rex McGhee told the *Knoxville News Sentinel*, "He's performing all of his duties through his assistants or by himself." He added that Ed had worked in the office three days the previous week and was in touch with them every day.

Reporters asked about the many rumors floating around the community: that Ed was dead, that he had had his liver removed, and that meetings were under way to choose his replacement. In response to those queries, McGhee joked, "We also heard he had twins."

In the spring of 1992, Elizabeth Perril made the 600-mile trip down from Illinois to visit her ailing cousin Ed. Raynella refused to allow her into the house. Elizabeth returned home, completing the 1,200-mile round trip without a glimpse of him. Raynella sent her a letter explaining that Ed was too ill to have visitors. Elizabeth knew no matter how sick he was,

Ed would have wanted to see her after she traveled so far to be by his side.

Contrary to the opinion expressed in Raynella's letter, many were still optimistic about Ed's recovery that spring. A rumor raced through the attorney general's office that the tumors were gone. It was a false hope that disappeared forever that summer.

Ed Dossett was still running his office in early June 1992. He tackled the high number of DUI cases clogging his office as well as the Knox County grand jury. It had gotten so bad that offenders were repeating their offenses again and again before they were even indicted. It took an average of eighteen months to dole out justice. Ed secured local and federal money to form a special DUI unit in his office and hired his former law office comrade and now veteran Knox County prosecutor Ronald Lewis to spearhead the effort.

A month later Ed's condition had deteriorated. Ed was sitting back in his recliner when Norman Jackson came by for a visit on July 10. After they visited for a while, Norman left the home wondering if he'd ever see Ed again.

Ed's aunt Pat made a habit of stopping by for a visit every other night. On Tuesday, July 11, her son Ray went with her. Ed was weak but he insisted on getting out of bed and into his rocking chair. Pat and Ray watched him struggle with aching hearts.

When he was finally settled, they had a long chat. They didn't discuss his death explicitly, but Ed expressed one regret: "I wish I started having my children when I was younger than I did."

On July 8, 1992, Jim McMillan stopped by in the morning to talk with Ed. He noticed the same weakness, adding that it was a challenge for Ed to sit up, slide his feet into his slippers, and move to his chair.

Donna Corbitt and Kaye Walker went out to the farm to visit Ed that afternoon. Kaye returned home that evening very distressed. "He's dying," she told her husband Steve.

"He's bedridden. He can't get out of bed. He can't even sit up. He can't talk. I'm not sure he knew I was there."

That same day, Robert Leath drove over to the Dossett farm. The Dossett and Leath clans had been close for decades. Robert wanted to check on Ed's condition and visit with him for a while. To his surprise, when he arrived, Raynella refused to allow him to come into the house. It bothered him as he drove back home, but he wouldn't have given it another thought if it weren't for the events that occurred the following day.

Tennessee was in the national news on July 9, as presidential candidate Bill Clinton named his choice for vice president: Carthage, Tennessee, native Al Gore. It was a celebratory day for the state but a sorrowful one in Knox County.

Raynella claimed that Ed asked to go out to the pasture to see and feed his herd of cattle. At that point Raynella's stories diverged. In one version she said that she helped him outside and then went back into the house. When she returned, he was lying in the gateway of the fence.

The story she told Knox County sheriff's detective Darrell Johnson was a bit different. According to him, Ed was standing at a corral gate, watching Raynella give food pellets to the cattle, when something spooked the livestock. "She heard a commotion, and when she turned around, Mr. Dossett was already on the ground and the cattle were exiting the corral. We don't know what spooked them and she does not have any idea."

She also said that she was so angry at the cattle, she went to the house and got a gun. She shot the one she thought stepped on Ed. She added that she didn't kill the animal, just wounded him.

At a press conference that evening, Sixth Judicial District assistant attorney general Dave Jennings, gave yet another version. "He and Raynella were feeding cattle when the cattle surged and Ed was knocked down and trampled."

At any rate, Raynella said she attempted CPR before racing back to the house and to call 911 at 3:30 that afternoon. She said she told the dispatcher that Ed had no pulse.

Raynella told Ray that she tried to call 911 on her cell phone but couldn't get an operator. She claimed she couldn't remember the phone number for Parkwest Medical Center— a place she worked for many years. She said she called the only number she could remember at the time: Sims Market & Deli on Hardin Valley Road.

The proprietor called for an ambulance and headed up to the farm. He and his son Jason were the first to arrive on the scene. A Rural/Metro ambulance soon followed, and Raynella was by her husband's side when it arrived. Ed was taken to Fort Sanders Parkwest Medical Center where the forty-four-year-old man was declared dead on arrival.

Ray was down in his tobacco patch when his daughter-in-law called to deliver the news that Ed was deceased. Ray picked up his mother and the two of them drove up to the Dossett Farm. They wondered if Ed had done it to himself. Ray, Pat, and Ferrel Moore were talking to Raynella and Donna Corbitt when a deputy and medical examiner Randall Pedigo approached her and said that she'd have to come into the sheriff's office to give a statement.

Donna asked, "Do you want me to go up there with you?"

Raynella shook her head. "This is something I need to do for myself."

Ray thought it was odd that Raynella didn't want a friend along for comfort. But at that time he thought nothing more of it.

Steve Walker was a bit puzzled by his wife's extreme reaction to Ed's death. Kaye was bawling and teary-eyed for days. He thought it was an odd way to behave at the death of her employer, since she was aware that he had cancer and knew it was terminal. He assumed the event rocked his wife that badly because it was the first time someone close to her had died.

Steve also couldn't understand Ed's death. He said, "Kaye, you told me he was unable to talk, can't sit up in bed, and now he's out feeding cows?"

Kaye had no answer for him, but Deputy Jeff Sellars told him: "They're telling us to lie out there. There's not a mark on him. Cows won't step on a man unless they're in a confined space."

Later, Investigator Mike Lett told Steve, "I would never let it go if I thought it was murder. I thought he died and she took him up there to get more insurance money."

Jim McMillan, who knew Ed's cattle almost as well as his own, found the whole incident too incredible to believe. "You couldn't blow up a stick of dynamite under that herd and get 'em to stampede." He didn't believe Raynella's story, and his heart was full of grief. "We lost one hell of a good man in Ed Dossett; we need more like him."

Ray Graves thought the whole story sounded peculiar, as if something was being left unsaid. "A cow won't even run over a dead or injured animal. If it's still and not moving, they are not going to run over it unless they are forced to back up to where they can't see it." After hearing Raynella's version of events, he could not visualize how it would take place. To him, "it sounded like something out of a cowboy and Indian show."

Ray's mom asked him, "Do you think she had anything to do with his death?"

"I don't think so, Mom," Ray said. He didn't want her to worry about that possibility.

His aunt Mary asked the same question. "I don't know," he said.

Any worries Ray had at the time, though, were buried in the sorrow of losing his cousin. "He's a better man than me.

He was good with us on the co-op board. He acted on his own behalf as a legal adviser to us and helped us make some right decisions at a critical time."

Ed's high school friend Chris Cawood, who spent all his life working with beef and dairy cattle, also thought the story sounded fishy. "Most of the members of Karns High's class of 1965 thought he was dying or dead when he was taken out to the paddock," he said. "They thought it was done to collect double indemnity on the life insurance policy and wouldn't have been surprised if it had been Ed's idea."

Bob Bailey, the cousin in the home where Ed was raised, was scared to death of Raynella. After Ed's death, he wouldn't stay by himself at his house on the Dossett property.

These suspicions didn't make it to reporters from the *Knoxville News Sentinel*. Instead of looking into the possibility of a crime, they were busy calling people who knew Ed Dossett. The morning paper was full of their comments. Criminal defense attorney Bob Ritchie said: "I had tremendous respect for him as a prosecutor and as a man. He epitomized the prosecutor who struck hard blows, but never foul blows."

In the criminal court, Judge Randy Nichols said, "Eddie and I campaigned against each other in '82. We never said an ill word about each other. I always thought he was a nice guy. I'm real sad for his family."

Judge Ray Lee Jenkins added: "This is a loss to the community and the criminal justice system. All of us will miss him."

"I am just very saddened," court clerk Martha Phillips said. "I had remained optimistic that he would beat the cancer. He was a good friend of mine, and he will be greatly missed."

George Bonds, executive secretary of the Tennessee District Attorney General Conference said, "I am shocked to hear it."

The Knoxville Police Department released an official

statement to all media: "His death is a great loss to law enforcement and he will be sorely missed."

In honor of the man they lost, the attorney general's office and the criminal courts were closed the Friday after his death as well as the following Monday.

CHAPTER 12

When Ed was declared dead, his body was delivered to the medical examiner, Dr. Randall Pedigo. Initially, Raynella opposed an autopsy, as did the prosecutors in Ed's office. Pedigo said he had a "policy" of erring on the side of the family in cases where a judgment call was required. In most situations like this one, he simply would not have done an autopsy.

In this case, he persuaded Raynella to allow him to perform the procedure because the insurance company would need it to confirm his death by agricultural accident, making Raynella eligible for benefits from the accidental death policy. She did ask that they not disturb Ed's head, and Pedigo agreed. The head was X-rayed to check for fractures, but not a cut was made. Later, many questioned whether it really was policy or if Raynella received special treatment because of her standing in the community. Ed's family would wonder if there was something more sinister behind her reasons.

Ed's breastbone and some of his ribs were broken, his lungs had hemorrhaged, and there was a hoof print on the bib of his overalls. The autopsy report mentioned the presence of an ostomy bag and a Foley catheter but did not once cite the presence of his implanted morphine pump. His body was covered with abrasions, and he had several petechial hemorrhages on his chest and back.

Internally, multiple tumors invaded his colon, small intestine, stomach, liver, spleen, appendix, and the tail portion of his pancreas, leaving him in a greatly weakened state. But according to the autopsy report, "the extent of the patient's tumor was severe and the patient was felt to be terminal; however, the cause of death cannot be attributed to the malignancy." The report concluded that "the cause of death was by trampling by cattle and therefore accidental."

Pedigo later said there were suspicions about Ed's death, but people wondered about insurance fraud, not murder. "There was a lot of talk and speculation that it was made to look like an accidental death to collect double indemnity. Some people even speculated that it might have been Ed Dossett's idea."

Many in Knox County had suspicions about the ethics of the medical examiner. Randall Pedigo had been Knox County medical examiner since 1983. He was also an associate professor of surgery at the University of Tennessee. Three years before performing the incomplete autopsy of Ed Dossett's body, Pedigo came under the scrutiny of the pharmacy department at the University of Tennessee Medical Center. Susan Watkins, a UT pharmacy supervisor, noticed the large number of narcotic prescriptions Pedigo had written for family members. She spoke to Steven R. Ross, the pharmacy director, about her concerns.

Ross spoke to Dr. Pedigo, telling him that it gave the appearance of wrongdoing. Pedigo said he understood the problem and it wouldn't be repeated. Pedigo no longer filled prescriptions for family members at that pharmacy. Instead he wrote narcotic scripts for three different patients—an FBI agent, a deputy at the Knox County Sheriff's Office, and a fellow professor—and filled them at other drugstores around town.

Ross became alarmed in 1991 when he learned that a local

pharmacist had refused to honor the prescriptions for a narcotic painkiller that Pedigo had written for his father. Ross went to the head of surgery, Dr. Kimball Maull, and laid the problem in his lap.

Maull talked to Pedigo about his prescribing patterns. Soon thereafter, Pedigo took a four-month leave of absence and checked into a Memphis clinic for treatment of chemical dependency. He returned to his job as medical examiner in Knoxville, but the board of medical examiners restricted his license for overprescribing addictive painkillers. They also ordered him to participate in the Impaired Physicians Program after he admitted to being an alcoholic since he was a teenager and also having a narcotic addiction.

Just a few months after Ed's death, the office of District Attorney General Randy Nichols wanted to prosecute the doctor. However, a Knox County grand jury declined to indict Pedigo on charges that he abused his position as medical examiner to get prescription narcotics.

CHAPTER 13

On July 10, a deputy went out to the Dossett farm. He looked for any signs of injury to the cattle but couldn't find a single one with a bullet wound. His story was backed by a bush hog operator who checked out the grazing herd a few days later. But why, they wondered, would Raynella make up a story like that?

On Saturday, July 11, the family received friends from 4:00 to 8:00 p.m. at Weaver's Cumberland Memorial Chapel. Police officers in formal dress uniforms flanked Ed's casket. The funeral at 2:00 p.m., on Sunday, was moved from Solway United Methodist, where Ed was a member, to Solway Church of God Family Life Center because the Methodist Church was not large enough to handle the anticipated crowd.

The day was hot enough to raise blisters on a camel. Nonetheless, hundreds of people were in attendance including judges, lawyers, county officials, law enforcement officers, farmers, Republican and Democratic political figures, and friends and neighbors. One of the eight pallbearers was Ed's childhood friend David Leath.

The service was not conducted by Ed's minister but by one of Ed's law school classmates, the Reverend Howard

Hinds, pastor of West View United Methodist Church. Raynella requested that memorial donations be made to the Dossett Children's Education Trust Fund.

Reverend Hinds read scripture and offered some personal remembrances of Ed, describing him as "a man of grace, a man of honor and a man of justice." He then opened the floor with an invitation for others to speak about Ed.

Helen R. Gault, longtime Republican activist who had campaigned hard for Ed during his first election, said: "He was so very honest. He was simply one of the best men in politics I ever worked with."

Hazel Masters, one of Ed's grade-school teachers, said, "He was one of the greatest treasures I ever had in my thirty-two years of teaching."

Then Ed's nine-year-old son broke everyone's heart as he spoke simply and from his heart about his father. "He was a hard worker. He was kind."

Ed's widow, Raynella, was the last person to speak. She acknowledged that her husband had known and loved many of the people there that day. "I know Ed would have wanted me to personally thank you for everything you did for him in his lifetime."

She reminded the mourners: "All of our lives will be sad without him. He always made you laugh." She concluded with a word of encouragement: "What we need today is for you to be celebrating life."

After her words, a soloist sang "Amazing Grace" while Raynella hugged all three of her children. After the service, a long line of cars followed the Dossett family to the farm with a motorcycle escort provided by the Knoxville Police Department. Ed was buried on the farm. Although burial on private property was not allowed in many states, it was perfectly legal in the state of Tennessee. A municipality could outlaw the practice within their borders, but out in an unincorporated rural area that was not a problem. The landowner was required to report the existence of the graveyard whenever the land was sold. The buyer of the property was then required to provide access to the cemetery in perpetuity.

The relatives of Ed Dossett said they were upset about the arrangement. They told investigators that Ed wanted to be buried next to his mother in the Solway Methodist Church cemetery. They said that they were certain that Raynella knew that too. Yet, there she was, violating her dead husband's wishes.

The police honor guard, wearing white gloves, was on hand to bid Ed a final farewell with "The Star-Spangled Banner," a salute of firearms, and "Taps."

Later, at the house, Ed's family was not pleased with the widow's post-funeral behavior. "Raynella was laughing and carrying on as if nothing had happened," Elizabeth Perril said.

At the courthouse on July 13, the day before the attorney general's office reopened after Ed's death, a crowd of lawyers, clerks, and judges squeezed into a courtroom. The criminal-court judges made their decision to appoint Rex McGhee as acting attorney general until Governor Ned McWherter could decide on a permanent replacement for Republican Ed Dossett.

Senior Deputy Assistant Attorney General Rex McGhee stood before criminal-court judge Ray Lee Jenkins, with his wife on one side and Raynella Dossett on the other. He was sworn into the position at noon.

Fear of the unknown raised its head in Ed's old office. Four Republican state legislators met with Democratic Governor Ned McWherter. "The tragedy of General Dossett's death has caused some concern among employees," Senate Minority Leader Ben Atchley said. "We would hope that there wouldn't be any wholesale firings of employees."

McWherter brought up the number of state officials fired when Republican governor Lamar Alexander took office but added, "I don't follow that policy." He said he believe the district attorney general's office "is above any kind of political partisanship."

The staff still trembled when, in August, the governor appointed Democrat Randy Nichols to fill the position. He was the man Ed had defeated in 1982 and was now a Knox county criminal-court judge. Although Ed's second eight-year term would not have concluded until 1998, Nichols would serve just two years of Ed's term until a special election in 1994. He brought in a few of his own people but didn't rock the office boat overmuch.

The month that Nichols took office, Dr. Pedigo presented the toxicology report to the prosecutors. For a reason that's unclear, the morphine intoxication mentioned in the report did not trigger further investigation.

Ray ran into Raynella down at the courthouse soon after the funeral. "You know I hate that about Ed. Me and him was going to farm together when he retired," he said.

Raynella shrugged. "If he lived, he would have had a lot of operations."

Ray wasn't sure what she meant but he continued, "Ed made me promise once not to tell you about something that happened. But he's gone now, so I guess I can."

"What is it? What is it? Tell me. Tell me," Raynella pressed.

"Well, we was up there drilling sudex and he run out of seed. Well, he was trying to get that drill to work. And I went to get the seed. And when I got back, he was down at the barn and as white as a sheet."

"Yeah, what happened?" Raynella asked.

"Well, the tractor ran over him"

"Oh," Raynella said, and turned around and walked away.

Ray stared at her departing back, stunned at her subdued reaction.

Less than six months after Ed's death, his widow was giving new meaning to the phrase "unseemly haste." She married her husband's good friend, Dave Leath, on January 9.

CHAPTER 14

Robert and Mayme Leath of Knox County, Tennessee, had a daughter, Charlene, in 1942, but Robert really wanted a son. He'd grown up with four sisters but he was the only boy in his family. He felt an old-fashioned responsibility for continuing the Leath family line. He got his wish on October 22, 1945, when his son David was born.

When Dave was little, instead of sucking on his thumb like other kids, he shoved his two middle fingers into his mouth and didn't break that habit until he went off to first grade. Dave didn't like school at all. Early in his educational experience, if he felt he'd had all he could take for that day, he'd leave the classroom and make the short walk home.

"He was a mean little devil—mischievous, like all little boys," his cousin Frieda said. They two saw a lot of each other while growing up. Frieda's mother got sick and died when she was only three months old. She was raised by her and Dave's grandparents, who didn't have a car or telephone. Dave's family stopped by the house nearly every day to check up on them and see if they needed anything.

Dave's father worked as a machinist, eventually winding up at the nuclear power plant in Oak Ridge. His mother was employed as a cook in the cafeteria of Fairview Elementary School. One of her coworkers was Lana Bailey, who raised her nephew, Ed Dossett, from the time he was eight years old. Both women lived within walking distance of the school and each other. As a result, Dave and Ed—just four months apart in age—came early to school with their mothers and played together until class started. They went back and forth between each other's houses throughout their childhoods.

Their relationship began because of the most important women in their lives: their mothers. They had no way of knowing then that in the last chapter of both of their lives, the most pivotal person would be their wives—as it happened, the same woman.

Dave dated Peggy Vanosdale in high school. After his junior year, he dropped out and went off to Tri-City Barber School to learn his trade. When Peggy graduated, the two wanted to get married. At that time, you could not get married at the age of seventeen in Tennessee unless you had written permission from your parents. Dave and Peggy decided it would be easier to drive across the state line. On August 7, 1962, with Peggy's sister, Charlene, and her boyfriend serving as witnesses, the couple wed in Ringgold, Georgia—a frequent choice for elopers, made famous seven years later by the marriage of Tammy Wynette and George Jones.

The newlyweds returned to Knox County and moved in with Dave's parents. Peggy got a job at Whiteway, one of the five-and-dime stores always built next door to the White Store, the leading grocery chain in the Knoxville area in the sixties.

Dave, of course, wanted a job cutting hair. He caught the eye of brothers Bill and Mel Cooper, who made it a habit of checking out the new talent at the barber school for their shop. They perceived potential in Dave and hired him to work at the Cooper Barber Shop on Western Avenue in Knoxville.

When the Cooper brothers saw the boom in development occurring in West Knoxville, they eyed the area for expansion. They decided to open a second shop in the new Suburban

Plaza shopping center at Kingston Pike and Winston Road. They sent Dave Leath and Paul Wilson over as co-managers.

Dave was nineteen years old when he took over the middle of three barber chairs there in the West Hills community of Knoxville. Paul established his permanent position in the front chair. Years later, when the Cooper brothers passed away, Dave and Paul become the owners of the shop.

Peggy became pregnant right after the wedding. Their daughter Cindy was born one month early on April 6, 1963, with a herniated belly button that required surgery when she turned a year old. The delivery was difficult for Peggy: she had complications from excessive bleeding that caused her to spend a full five days in the hospital.

She also learned that her Rh factor was negative and Dave's was positive. This genetic combination can produce an Rh-positive child. If it does and the fetus's blood enters the Rh-negative mother's cardiovascular system, she will create antibodies. Those antibodies would perceive the developing baby as an intruder and attack its blood cells, breaking them down, causing anemia and, in severe cases, brain damage or even death.

Today, there are successful treatment options for this condition, but they were not available in 1963. Peggy's doctor urged her not to have any additional children, because the risk was too great.

In 1964, Cindy had her hernia operation, and the couple began building a new home on a piece of property given to them by Peggy's parents. Construction was completed in 1965, and the young family of three finally moved out of Dave's parents' home.

Life developed into a pleasant pattern of work, home, and family outings. Dave owned a '57 Chevy hardtop when the couple married. He loved working on it and keeping it looking good. Peggy and the baby piled into it on Saturday nights for a drive down to the stock car races at Smoky Mountain Speedway in Maryville, Tennessee. From an early age Cindy loved those trips. The races at Maryville were a family affair, with kids running around everywhere. At first it was the other children that Cindy enjoyed, but soon she came to love the competition on its own merits. Every summer Dave, Peggy, and Cindy took a family vacation by the ocean—often to Daytona Beach, where there was car racing too.

In 1968, Dave hired Peggy's brother, Hoyt Vanosdale, as the third barber at the shop—the beginning of decades with Dave, Paul, and Hoyt working side by side. Despite outward appearances, Dave had not completely settled into a quiet life. Since he was twelve years old, he was always cutting up with his friend Gordon Armstrong. In their twenties, both men were married and still pulling Halloween pranks. They went out one year looking for trouble.

Using kerosene, they set the railroad crossing guardrail on fire. Dave didn't realize that his father-in-law Charlie Rowe came home across those tracks every night.

When Gordon's wife Gail learned about it, she said, "What are you two trying to do, kill Dave's father-in-law?"

They also played pranks on each other. One of Dave's favorite tricks happened when Gordon sat in the chair for a haircut. On numerous occasions Dave distracted Gordon while Paul gathered up hair clippings from the floor and stuffed them into the pipe Gordon carried in his back pocket. After Dave finished cutting his hair, Gordon pulled out his pipe, lit it, and gagged. Gordon couldn't remember how many times he fell for that one. In return, Gordon plaited clipper cords together so that when Dave reached for a pair, two more were entwined with it, making it impossible for Dave to work until he unraveled the mess.

Beneath the fooling around, there was a strong bond of friendship that made each man go the extra mile for the other. Gordon named his oldest son Gordon Jr., but everyone called him Butch. When Butch was one year old, Gordon took him up to the barbershop to have Dave give him his first haircut. Dave didn't like to cut kids' hair, and normally he would pass a child off on another barber; but this was his good friend Gordon's son, so he made an exception.

Gordon sat in the chair with Butch on his lap, but the moment Dave turned on his clippers, Butch got hysterical. Dave turned them off right away and said, "I'll come over tonight and I'll cut his hair at your house."

That night they waited until Butch was sound asleep. Gordon held his son, laying the boy's head on his shoulder. Dave cut one side of his hair. Then Gordon shifted Butch over to the other side and Dave finished the cut. Even with that special service Dave wouldn't accept money: he never did let him pay for his or his son's haircuts. If Gordon tried to force money on him, Dave would yell at him, "Get out of here!"

Gordon said that they could always count on each other in times of tragedy too. When Gordon had a death in the family and required a hair cut to go to a funeral, Dave told him to stay where he was. Dave came over to Gordon's mother-in-law's house to give his friend an emergency haircut.

The most telling sign that Dave had not yet adopted the mantle of family man became obvious to Peggy in 1970. Right after the family returned from a vacation in Daytona Beach, she learned that Dave was romantically involved with another woman. Peggy filed for divorce.

Cindy was seven years old when her parents called it quits. Initially, Dave was caught up in the excitement of his new relationship, and he was a lackadaisical father for a couple of years: irregular in visits, not good at remembering important dates, and drinking heavily. Cindy and her mother maintained a close relationship with Dave's parents, Robert and Mayme. After a short while, they coaxed Dave back into a more active role as a dad. He remembered birthdays and holidays, and the two grew very close.

He and Cindy resumed their road trips to NASCAR and dirt track races, often accompanied by Dave's aunt Mac. They traveled to Caswell County Raceway, Bristol, Bulls Gap, and other venues. On occasion, Dave's cousin Frieda went with them. Driving back from one race, they stopped at a restaurant for a bite to eat.

Dave told their waiter that he and Frieda were getting married the next day at a church on Kingston Pike. He didn't bother mentioning that they were cousins but invited the young man to the wedding.

Back in the car, Frieda laughed and said, "I can't believe you told him that. You are the biggest liar. I'll never believe anything you say ever again."

The relationship that signaled Dave's pulling away from his marriage to Peggy came to an end with a traumatic event in late 1970. Dave was chopping wood when a piece of tree bark flew up and into his eye. It hurt a lot, but Dave just thought it was one of those minor accidents that cause pain because of the sensitivity of the injured area. He went to bed thinking he'd feel better in the morning. But when he awoke, his eye was very swollen. He went to the doctor and learned his retina detached. He would never see out of his left eye again, and his eye would atrophy and pucker.

Dave grew very self-conscious of that fact. He almost always wore sunglasses, even in the house and at night. If he talked to someone without his sunglasses, he wouldn't look at them because he didn't want the other person have a direct view of his eye.

He also grew far more aware of his physical appearance overall. Dave was serious about keeping his trim shape, going to the YMCA to work out regularly. He liked wearing his jeans so tight that he couldn't carry a wallet. He crammed his driver's license in his right front pocket and a wad of cash in the left. When he spent the money, he'd replace it with cash he'd stashed in the barn and under rocks, according to Gordon, who said his friend didn't like banks much.

As the years took their toll on his looks, Dave invested in cosmetic procedures. He had hair implants, a tummy tuck, and a face-lift. Some people said Dave was vain, but according to Cindy it went back to the accident, when he grew painfully aware of every flaw in his appearance.

It was the late seventies before Dave got serious about a woman again. He met Debbie Shelton at the doctor's office. They dated a couple of years and married in the summer of 1979. Dave built a new home on the property behind his mother's house. He put in a swimming pool, did extensive landscaping, and created a showcase for Debbie. When the relationship all came to an end, he was bewildered and confused. He said, "Every morning, she packed my lunch, walked me to the door, and said, 'Have a nice day.' One day, that seemed the same as all the others, I came home and Debbie and all the furniture was gone."

Dave told Gordon that Debbie had plans to marry her employer-doctor. She thought the doctor would leave his wife and kids after she left Dave but he didn't. That breakup sent Dave into a tailspin; for a short time, he drank heavily.

One of the steadying forces in his life was his friendship with Gordon. Through good times and bad, their lives intertwined. It seemed based on getting laughs at the other's expense, but beneath the digs a strong current of attachment flowed. Gordon remembered numerous occasions when he went into the barbershop and said, "What I'd like you to do . . ."

Dave cut him off every time. "I'm the barber; I'll cut your hair how I think it needs to be cut. Just sit there and be quiet."

Gordon got his pay back when he was at Dave's place doing grading on his property. Dave said: "I want—"

Gordon cut him off: "Who's in the grading business?"

Dave said, "You are."

Gordon nodded and said: "Get over there and watch and let me do my work."

The two men had a standing, friendly wager on NASCAR

races, the payoff being an RC Cola and a moon pie. No matter who was racing, Dave always bet on Dale Earnhardt. "I'll take Dale, and you can have the rest of 'em."

"I'd gig 'em a bit if Earnhardt didn't win," Gordon said. When Earnhardt won, Gordon would go to the barbershop, get a moon pie and RC out of the vending machine, and set it down beside Dave and deliver the same line: "There you go, Crook."

Another bedrock for Dave was his daughter, Cindy. She cemented their bond when she told him she wanted to follow in his footsteps. Dave was surprised and delighted. When she graduated from high school, he drove her to Tri-City Barber School and introduced her to the staff and faculty. His pride was apparent in the glowing way he spoke of his daughter and by the perpetual presence of his smile. To Cindy's delight, her father's instructor, Walt McGuinness, was hers too.

Dave's little girl was now all grown-up. On July 3, 1982, Dave performed the bittersweet role of father of the bride. He and Peggy walked Cindy down the aisle together. She married David Wilkerson.

In mid-March 1982, Dave's sister, Charlene Hendrix, succumbed to the systemic scleroderma that had sickened her for many years. She left behind her son, Bryan, who was still in high school.

The localized form of the disease hardens and tightens the skin. The type Charlene had moved also to the connective tissues and internal organs, ravaging the heart, the lungs, the kidneys, and the digestive tract. Her death was not a surprise, but it was still a shock to Dave: his big sister had not yet reached her fortieth birthday.

Two decades later, Cindy would consider the significance of her aunt Charlene's death in mid-March.

CHAPTER 15

Through ups and downs, Dave and Gordon continued to be the go-to friends for each other. When Gordon's younger son, Brian, had an accident in the Army in 1989, Brian was in the Veterans Affairs hospital for months. When he finally came home, Gordon opened the door and Dave stood there with big tears in his eyes. Dave normally kept his emotions in check. But on this day he was overcome with his grief for Brian's injuries. He cried with so much anguish, he couldn't speak. He put an arm around Gordon's shoulder and gave him a couple of empathetic squeezes. No words or actions from anyone else meant as much to Gordon as that moment with Dave.

Dave often turned to Gordon when he encountered one of those situations out in the country, when a firearm was needed. Dave just didn't like handling guns. When coyotes were bothering his dogs, he called on Gordon. His friend came over with his sons and spotlighted and shot the coyotes.

Snakes were another problem; Dave was scared of them. One day he called Gordon: "You better come over quick, there's a snake by the pool."

"Kill it," Gordon said.

"I can't," Dave said. "You come over and do it."

Gordon came over with his granddaughter. He gave the

girl a stick and told her to chase the snake out of the bushes. Dave freaked out and ran into the house.

Gordon and Dave often worked side by side helping out Dave's dad with chores on his property. Whenever they did, Robert cooked up his signature meal: fried chicken, mashed potatoes, and southern-cooked green beans with bacon. Mayme fixed iced tea. "Everybody loved her sweet tea," Gordon remembered. "It was the best."

One of their projects at the elder Leath's house involved taking down a large tree situated between the house, the garage, and the woodworking shop. It was a risky job: they had to remove the tree without damaging any of the surrounding buildings.

Gordon borrowed pole climbers from a friend who worked for the utility company. He propped his stepladder by the tree to make getting down a bit easier, then he and his son Butch eased their way up the trunk, trimming branches. When they were near the top, the running chain saw slipped out of Butch's hand. It fell down with its blade landing upright on the top rung of the ladder, cutting through every step all before it hit the ground. Fortunately, no one was hurt.

Dave wasn't responsible for the broken ladder, but they were doing a favor for his dad. Before Gordon and Butch realized that Dave was gone, he'd driven to the store and returned with a new ladder.

Nineteen ninety was a year of pure joy for Dave. His daughter Cindy gave birth to her first child on September 11, and it was a boy. She named him Tyler. "What do you want him to call you?" Cindy asked.

"Big Daddy," Dave said.

"Big Daddy?"

"Yea, I'm too young to be called Paw Paw."

And Big Daddy it was from that moment forward.

Tyler quickly became a major focus in Dave's life—more important to him than anyone. Cindy worked the evening shift, and as soon as Tyler was old enough, Dave made a habit of picking him up to go out for milk shakes while his mother was at work and sometimes bringing her lunch and visiting with her during her meal break.

When Tyler started school, Dave took care of his grandson during spring break and on holidays. He never wanted to bring the boy back home, telling Cindy, "Don't worry about him. He's in good hands. I'll bring him back when I'm ready."

The close ties of youth that bound Dave to Ed Dossett stretched a bit thin during Dave's years at Karns High and Ed's time away at college and law school. They renewed their bond years later, aided in large part by their mutual membership in the Solway United Methodist Church.

Dave was a frequent visitor to the farm, where he helped Ed out with his chores. He was there so often that some people thought he was Ed's farmhand. Throughout the fall of 1991 and into the summer of 1992, Dave prayed with the rest of the church congregation for Ed's recovery.

Dave was at work on July 9, 1992, when a phone call brought the tragic news of Ed's death. Dave, Paul, and Hoyt closed down the barbershop and drove out to Dossett farm to offer assistance and condolences to Ed's widow.

Dave performed a final duty in respect of his childhood friendship, serving as a pallbearer at Ed's funeral. After that, his relationship with the widow Dossett grew closer.

It was a Thursday in late August or September 1992 when Dave and Raynella had their first date. That night he brought Raynella a single rose. From that day on, Dave repeated that gesture every Thursday.

He told his cousin Frieda that Raynella had asked him out on a date.

She said, "Dave! He's not even cold in the ground yet."

Dave flung his arms around in frustration. "I knew you'd say that."

"That's what everybody's gonna say, Dave."

A few months later, when Dave told his fellow barbers about his plans to marry Raynella, they were aghast. "You movin' kind of quick, ain't ya?" Hoyt asked. "People are gonna think you were there before the other one left."

His daughter Cindy wasn't any more encouraging than his coworkers. "You're not just marrying Raynella. There's three kids living at home. You're getting a package deal."

Dave brushed all the warnings aside and even agreed to sign a prenuptial agreement to protect Raynella's assets in case of a divorce. Nothing shook Dave's commitment to exchange wedding vows for the third time.

CHAPTER 16

Raynella and Dave married on January 9, 1993—a short six months after Ed Dossett's death. The service was held at Solway United Methodist Church. His cousin Frieda refused to attend. Dave told her he might never forgive her for that.

Dave sold the home he'd built, retaining a tract of adjoining land, and moved into the house built by Ed Dossett. It seemed an odd pairing: Raynella, who placed a premium on higher education, exchanging vows with Dave, the high school dropout. But to all appearances the couple deeply cared about each other. Dave built a greenhouse for Raynella. She bought him a custom truck with a matching horse trailer. Dave got vanity plates for her car bearing the nickname he had given her: NELL NELL.

The couple was often seen holding hands and acting like two people in love. Raynella, who had never been a NASCAR fan, even went to the races in Daytona with her new husband for the first couple of years of their marriage.

Raynella packed Dave's lunch every workday and started his vehicle to warm it up for him on cold mornings. She waited on him hand and foot; Dave was delighted by her solicitousness. However, at times it made Cindy a little uneasy. Raynella treated Dave like a king, but sometimes it seemed like she was overdoing it.

Her niggling thoughts felt justified when Cindy found Dave sitting outside in his truck crying. Dave would not tell her what was wrong; he just said, "It will work out."

Cindy suspected that either the reality of a home filled with kids might be eroding his romantic vision of marriage or there was a more serious problem in the relationship. She said, "Daddy, if there's something wrong, you don't have to stay. You can get out of it."

But Dave repeated, "It'll work out."

After marrying Raynella, Dave started going to bed around 8:00 p.m. because he shifted his YMCA workout time to 4:00 or 4:30 in the morning. Cindy wondered if the early hour he went to bed had something to do with a desire to escape the drama of living in a home with two teenage girls. Raynella liked Dave going to the Y because she wanted him to stay healthy.

Gordon said that when he and his wife went out to dinner with Raynella and Dave, he noticed that Raynella always ordered Dave's meal to make sure he ate right. In addition to packing his lunch every day, she frequently dropped by the barbershop mid-morning with an energy drink or a fruit juice.

However, all those healthy meals made Dave crave junk food. First thing, whenever Gordon picked up Dave, they'd stop at a convenience store. Dave would load up on Cheetos, M&M's, and cookies. If Dave didn't finish his goodies, he'd try to get Gordon to take them, because Dave knew he'd get grief from Nell-Nell if he took the snacks into the house.

On Thanksgiving Day, 1993, Dave went out to hunt quail with his dad; his only nephew, Bryan Hendrix; and neighbor Jeff Massey. Dave did not care for hunting, but his dad loved going out for quail, dove, and rabbits. In order to spend time with his dad, Dave often grabbed a shotgun and went along with him. As a rule, Dave never fired a shot.

After trekking across the fields for hours, the men headed home. They were crossing the final field that led to the yard when Robert jerked to a stop and sat down hard on the ground. Dave knelt down by his father and realized it was serious. Leaving the guns and bird dogs with Bryan, Dave and Jeff carried Robert to the car and raced to the hospital.

Bryan explained what happened to Mayme. She turned off the oven, leaving the turkey inside of it. Then she called Frieda and said, "Come and get me. I need to go to the hospital."

"Aunt Mayme, maybe you ought to wait at home. You can't do anything at the hospital."

"I have to be there. I'll walk there if I have to."

Frieda took her into town to be by her husband's side. But it was too late: Robert died of a massive coronary before he reached the hospital. Dave took his dad's death hard. He began to drink heavily again for a short while. A cousin often had to guide him into his own home and into bed.

Dave wanted to be rid of anything that reminded him of his daddy. He had his mother sell his dad's truck and then he bulldozed down the stand-alone garage where Robert always parked it.

After Robert's death, Dave's revulsion toward guns grew even stronger—an abhorrence that, a dozen years later, would fill everyone he knew with disbelief.

CHAPTER 17

Beginning in November of 1993 and into the spring of 1994, medical examiner Randall Pedigo ordered excessive quantities of Versed from a South Carolina distributor. This drug was often used before surgery or medical procedures like colonoscopies in order to cause drowsiness, relieve anxiety, and prevent any memory of the events. It is also sometimes given as part of the anesthesia during surgery to produce a loss of consciousness.

In late January of that year, twenty-two-year-old Derek* visited Pedigo's Cherokee Bluff condominium. Pedigo gave Derek an injection. The young man fell asleep wearing boxer shorts and woke up nude.

Pedigo had friends in Shelby County, in the Memphis area, with whom he often stayed when he made an overnight trip to the western part of the state. Their son, Jeremy, was a nineteen-year-old student. He frequently visited Pedigo in his home in Knoxville, watching videos, sharing meals, and sleeping in the guest room. Sometimes the doctor treated Jeremy for an old shoulder injury with the injection of what Pedigo called a muscle relaxant. Jeremy said on occasion, at

---

* The names of all of Dr. Pedigo's victims have been changed to protect their privacy.

night, the doctor stuck a needle into his buttocks, claiming that he was inoculating him against hepatitis B.

Jeremy introduced Dr. Pedigo to Austin, a nineteen-year-old student and a friend from home. Austin spent a few nights at Pedigo's condo. In February 1994, Austin came down with a fever and stomach virus. The doctor took him home and into the guest bedroom. He gave the young man a couple of injections in his arm. Austin was admiring the view out the window when the drowsiness hit. Pedigo said, "Just lay down on the bed."

Austin awoke the next morning with no memory of anything that happened after that comment.

Nat, a seventeen-year-old family friend, visited Pedigo's condo in mid-March. The doctor gave him an injection in his hip. Nat immediately fell asleep and remembered nothing more.

In May, Pedigo brought Leo, a sixteen-year-old who aspired to be a physician and Kenny, his thirteen-year-old brother, to the condo to take photographs for a medical presentation. He put a red X on a spot he identified as the incision point and took pictures that showed their pubic areas but not their genitals.

On May 27, Nat invited Pedigo to go to his high school graduation. There the doctor met Shane, a fifteen-year-old boy from East Tennessee. With Shane's parents' permission, he supposedly gave the boy a hepatitis B inoculation. He spent a lot of time with Shane over the next few weeks, flying him, along with two other young people, to an air show in Chattanooga the first weekend in June.

Trenton, a twenty-two-year-old student at the medical center, expressed an interest in observing surgeries. Pedigo volunteered to allow Trenton to watch him in the operating room. The two lunched together that day and made plans to go on rounds together the next day. "I thought it was cool that a doctor was so open and receptive to me," Trenton later said.

After following the doctor around on June 1, Trenton went

to Pedigo's condo, where the doctor insisted that he needed a hepatitis B vaccination. Trenton thought the doctor had drawn far too much serum into the syringe but said nothing, assuming Pedigo knew what he was doing. The doctor was still massaging the injection spot on his buttocks when he lost all memory of the evening. "I was dead to the world all night," he said.

Less than two weeks later, Pedigo invited eighteen-year-old Sean to spend the night, in order to watch him perform his job the next day. The two had met in May at a substance abuse support group meeting for health care workers. He, too, received an injection that the doctor called a hepatitis B inoculation.

The following day, June 14, Pedigo, an avid hunter, picked up Trenton to go shooting. They had dinner at Applebee's and returned to the condo. Trenton said that he received no injection that night.

Dr. Pedigo picked up Shane for a weekend of shooting. They went out to dinner and returned to Pedigo's place. Shane recalled no shot that night. The next day the doctor and the boy flew to Jackson, Tennessee, and then on to Murfreesboro, where they met Trenton and his father.

On Father's Day, June 19, Shane and Pedigo flew back to Knoxville. The next day the doctor asked Trenton if he'd like to go on rounds with him, but Trenton said he couldn't because he had to study.

Pedigo called Leo's mother and asked if her son would like to follow him around the University of Tennessee Medical Center that day. Leo shadowed him on his trauma rounds. They spent the evening together and eventually drove over to the Cherokee Bluff condo in a county-issued Ford Bronco so that Leo could go with him on his next trauma call. Pedigo referred to himself as "Daddy" and called the boy "Kiddo." While there, Pedigo reminded Leo that he needed a vaccination for hepatitis B, a disease that is an exposure risk for all medical personnel.

Pedigo told Leo to lower the bottom half of the hospital scrubs and lie across the bed in the guest bedroom. "I added a sedative to the shot to take out the sting," Pedigo said.

It's not certain if Pedigo actually inoculated the boy against hepatitis B, but he certainly shot Leo full of Versed. Leo turned around to look at the doctor after he removed the needle and that's all he remembered until sometime in the middle of the night. Leo awoke briefly and noticed a large, hairy man, nude from the waist down, lying beside him in the bed. He fell back into a deep sleep before he could react.

The next morning Leo awoke with Pedigo stroking his hair and telling him to get up. Leo was confused. He had gone to sleep wearing hospital scrubs but now he was wearing underwear. Then he remembered the moment he woke up earlier. He asked, "What were you doing in my bed last night?"

Pedigo said, "You must have been dreaming. I slept in my own bedroom."

Leo went on rounds with the doctor again that day, but his memory of that moment in the wee hours of the morning of June 21 was too vivid to ignore. When he got home, he told his mother. She took him to East Tennessee Children's Hospital.

CHAPTER 18

District Attorney General Randy Nichols's sleep was disturbed at 1:30 in the morning by a phone call delivering the disturbing news about the incident at his medical examiner's home. At 10:00 that same morning, he was on the phone with Gary Gerbitz, his counterpart in Hamilton County, asking him to serve as special prosecutor, since the Sixth Judicial District attorney general's office had close ties to Randall Pedigo. "We've got a situation up here we've got to get out of. In fact, we're out of it now, and we're looking for somebody to handle it. Will you?"

Gerbitz, a native of Cleveland, with a law degree from the University of Tennessee, had served in the prosecutor's office for twenty-one years. He agreed to take on the case. He was accustomed to handling sticky situations.

Knoxville police investigator Tom Pressley met with Leo and his mother that morning. Immediately after those interviews, he began work preparing a search warrant with assistance from the Hamilton County attorney general's office. "The phone line on the search warrant was open two hours at a time just talking back and forth," Gerbitz told the *Knoxville News Sentinel*.

Pressley did not lead the team into Pedigo's home, though.

In addition to his job as medical examiner for the county, Pedigo was a longtime firearms instructor for local law enforcement agencies. To avoid any possible allegations of special treatment, agents from the Tennessee Bureau of Investigation were put in charge.

Dr. Pedigo spent the morning of June 22 observing a surgical procedure at the University of Tennessee Medical Center. At 1:00 that afternoon he arrived home still wearing blue hospital scrubs. Eight officers from the Tennessee Bureau of Investigation and the Knoxville Police Department, under the command of Special Agent Steve Richardson, converged on the Cherokee Bluff complex, confronting Pedigo in the parking lot.

Richardson approached Pedigo and said, "We need you to come down to the police station for questioning."

Pedigo said he would comply but insisted he needed to change out of his scrubs and into street clothes first. Richardson agreed as long as the officers could accompany him into his condo. Up to this point, Pedigo had displayed a calm demeanor. Once they went inside, he became agitated.

Pedigo changed his clothing and then wandered around. At one point he sat down on a couch on top of a holstered gun. Police officers immediately took charge of the weapon. Without warning, the doctor rushed out of the room and down the stairs. Richardson raced after him, yelling, "What are you doing? Where are you going?"

"I just want to make sure the door down here is locked." Richardson anticipated that the suspect would slip out the door and escape.

Back upstairs, Pedigo dawdled around his coffee machine, appearing to be stalling in every way he could.

Richardson, growing impatient with his behavior, said, "It's time to go."

Seven law enforcement officers went through the door ahead of Pedigo. Richardson was right beside the medical examiner. He was half inside and half outside the condo when

Pedigo jumped back inside, shoved Richardson through the door, slammed it shut, and threw the dead bolt.

While a few officers battered on the front door, others ran around to the rear entrance. Once the front door was open, Richardson led the men inside. He found Pedigo in the downstairs den. Pedigo reached into a recliner and pulled out a .45-caliber pistol, assumed a shooter's stance, and cocked the gun.

Richardson dropped to a kneeling position with his 9mm weapon in hand. Pedigo aimed his gun at the special agent. Richardson fired.

Pedigo spun to his right and stumbled backward but remained on his feet. Richardson shouted, "Stop. Drop your weapon."

Pedigo pointed his pistol at Richardson again. Richardson fired again. He fired four more times not, stopping until the doctor dropped his gun and fell to the floor.

Five of the shots hit Pedigo, including one into his right eye, but he was still alive. Bleeding and in pain, Pedigo begged, "Go ahead and finish me off."

An officer said, "You know we can't do that."

"Damn, I can't even kill myself right," Pedigo said.

Pedigo was rushed to the hospital, where he underwent four hours of surgery to repair the damage done by gunshot wounds to his face, arms, and chest.

Up in Hamilton County, Attorney General Gerbitz was walking down the hall when someone yelled to him, "The thing may be over. They just shot Pedigo six times."

Gerbitz thought, *Oh, he's dead.*

But Pedigo had survived, and while he was under the knife, law enforcement put his home under intense scrutiny. They found sixty Polaroid pictures of young nude males. Most of the subjects were asleep in bed with the bedding pulled away from their bodies. Some lay on their backs, others on their sides. Among them were close-up shots and views in which the boys' faces could be clearly seen.

They discovered an additional 150 photographs taken with a 35mm camera of other males. The subjects of those shots were either patients or volunteers who had taken part in mock disaster drills at the medical center. Many of them were aware that Pedigo had taken snapshots: he said they were for instructional purposes.

They found syringes and vials including several bottles marked *Hepatitis B*. Later testing, however, revealed no trace of the vaccine but clear evidence of the presence of Versed.

Lock experts drilled into the gun safe and confiscated the doctor's weapons. In total, they uncovered ninety-seven weapons: rifles, shotguns, pistols, and one .30-caliber machine gun. They confiscated the doctor's Rolodex and monthly phone bills, and obtained a list of Pedigo's frequent visitors from the guards at Cherokee Bluff.

The next day, while Pedigo recovered from surgery at the hospital, his family, on his behalf, retained the services of attorney Bob Ritchie. The University of Tennessee Medical Center issued a quick statement that, at their hospital, Pedigo did not have access to the drugs found in the search of his condo.

On June 29, a Knox County grand jury issued an indictment charging Randall Pedigo with attempted murder for aiming his pistol at a Tennessee Bureau of Investigation agent. No evidence about the possible sexual abuse charges were presented in this session.

The fiscal year for the medical center ended on June 30. In light of Pedigo's current circumstances, they declined to renew his contract with its salary of $48,480 per year. For now, Knox County allowed him to retain the title of medical examiner; however, they relieved him of his duties for the duration of the investigation. Dr. Sandra Elkins, an assistant medical examiner in Memphis, was hired on an interim basis to perform the functions of a medical examiner. The county issued the final paycheck on Pedigo's salary on July 2.

All expenses of the medical examiner's office came from the budget of the sheriff's office, although the sheriff had no power to hire or fire the medical examiner. But the sitting sheriff, Tim Hutchison, was also Pedigo's patient. Since he was running for reelection at the time of Pedigo's arrest, he faced endless criticism for his professional and personal connections to the doctor.

Investigators got busy trying to identify the subjects of all the photographs they recovered from Pedigo's home. Among them were pictures of several Knoxville police officers wearing bulletproof vests but no shirts. None of the men were aware that the snapshots had been taken.

More alarming were the full nude photographs of another officer taken during surgery. The procedure was usually done with local anesthetic, but this man had received a general anesthetic and was not aware of anything that had occurred in the operating room.

Detectives showed the photographs to many young men in an attempt to identify the subjects. Jeremy pointed to some of the Polaroid shots and said, "These are me. I look pretty dead asleep there."

Jeremy's friend, Austin, was shaken by pictures. "I never consented to anything like that. I never consented to anything with any man ever. I mean, I have a girlfriend."

Sean could not identify any of the photographs as depicting him, but he was still distressed. He didn't want to look but he did, and wondered how many people were victimized by that man. In every interview, investigators found traumatized young men and devastated families. In all, they identified eight men in the nude photographs.

Defense lawyers were on top of the case as well, questioning Pedigo's ability to testify against their clients in other cases. Within weeks, attorney Doug Trant filed fifty motions seeking evidence from the prosecutors for two of his clients charged with murder: Thomas Dillon and Dorcie Jenkins.

Dr. Pedigo performed hernia repair surgery on Dillon in 1993 while he was an inmate in the Knox County Jail. "There is no way that Dillon can be satisfied whether or not any of the photographs are of him without viewing the said photographs. If the photographs are of him, he is certainly entitled to know because he may be the victim of a sexual assault as well as using the photographs to impeach Dr. Pedigo at trial."

Even in light of Pedigo's obvious disregard to professional ethics and the law at this time—or perhaps because they were too distracted by his other professional and sexual misconduct—no authority raised any concerns about the autopsy Pedigo had performed on the body of Ed Dossett.

CHAPTER 19

The Knox County sheriff was not the only one facing election that year. Forty-five-year-old Randy Nichols, the former judge who the governor appointed to replace Raynella's first husband, Ed Dossett, as district attorney general, was up for his first election in 1994. In March, Ron Webster, the fifty-five-year-old private practice lawyer who held the office for the fourteen years before Dossett, announced he'd run against Nichols.

On July 30, the day after the *Knoxville News Sentinel* printed their second editorial endorsing the Democrat's candidacy, Raynella Dossett Leath came out in support of Nichols. She sent a letter to more than one thousand of her fellow Republicans urging them to turn their backs on their party's candidate because he was an "inaccessible man" who would "prosecute unequally" and carry out a "vendetta" against political rivals. "Please do not return Knox County to the stranglehold of an individual who displays years of obsessive behavior, laced with various attempts to hurt my late husband, Ed," she wrote. She added that Nichols had been doing a good job since replacing her deceased husband. Nonetheless, her support seemed more anti-Webster than pro-Nichols.

A lot of Raynella's fellow Republicans were appalled at

her behavior. Talking trash about their party's candidate was not something the party faithful ever did in public. Endorsing the other party's candidate was equally disturbing to many of her political friends.

Despite their disapproval, Raynella backed a winner. On August 4, Nichols won the election with 58 percent of the vote. Some said that Webster lost the election because of his negative campaigning. Others said that Raynella's support made a pivotal difference.

That summer, Ray Graves worried that his nephew, Little Eddie, was being neglected. One day, the eleven-year-old boy hopped on a tractor and drove it off. He went across a field then started down a hill. He lost control of the big piece of machinery, running it into the road toward an oncoming vehicle. That car backed up as quickly as it could to get away from the runaway tractor.

Eddie was heading straight for the creek when he ran into a ditch and the tractor overturned. The boy's injuries were minor, but still Ray worried. Even out in the country, there were a lot of ways for a kid to get into trouble.

On August 9, with attorneys Bob Ritchie and Ken Irvine by his side, Dr. Randall Pedigo entered the Blount County courtroom of Judge D. Kelly Thomas Jr. for arraignment on the attempted murder charges. He'd lost his right eye, his face was scarred, and he wore a brace on his left arm because of injuries to his arm and wrist.

District Attorney General Gerbitz told the judge: "I think it is obvious to everyone, surely it is to the defense as it is to the prosecution, that there are going to be other charges that are the basis of this shooting. We anticipate in the very near future creating other indictments."

When the judge asked Pedigo for his plea, the doctor said, "Your Honor, I am not guilty."

The judge then moved to the dozen motions filed by the

defense. One of them requested a review of the evidence seized from Pedigo's condominium, including the photographs, syringes, drug bottles, and bedclothes taken in connection with the original molestation allegation.

Gerbitz objected: "It's huge in quantity and has not even been gone through other than to be logged."

However, Judge Thomas felt that the defense should be able to review everything and ordered the prosecution to make it all available on or before August 23.

The defense also moved that the weapons removed from the condo should be released to his client. The prosecution did not object and the judge ruled in favor of the defense.

The other motions were not addressed that day but included one arguing that the search of the condominium was illegal and the evidence obtained should be suppressed.

Sealed indictments against Pedigo were handed down by the grand jury on the doctor's forty-fourth birthday, October 18, 1994. They were unsealed when Pedigo turned himself in at the Knox County Jail. He was charged on sixteen counts: one count of rape, one count of aggravated rape, three counts of sexual battery, five counts of aggravated sexual battery, and six counts of unlawfully dispensing controlled substances. The counts listed as aggravated meant that Pedigo caused bodily injury to the victims at the time that the sexual acts were committed.

Defense attorney Bob Ritchie objected to the indictments, since all of the victims were called "John Doe" and no ages were given for any of them and because all of the offenses were listed as happening on or before July 1, 1994. "The charges against Dr. Pedigo are unprecedented in their vagueness," he wrote. "They do not indicate who was supposed to have been assaulted, [or] when or where the alleged assaults took place. It is impossible to tell from the presentments anything about the charges against him.

"It is unfair to file such serious charges in this totally unprecedented manner. It will be impossible to investigate, much less defend, these charges unless the court requires the prosecutor to set forth what they claim Dr. Pedigo has done. If the prosecution has reliable charges against Dr. Pedigo, one would think four months of intensive investigation could have produced something more than the charges filed today."

Pedigo was released on the same $100,000 bond set when he was charged with attempted murder in the summer. At the November 16 arraignment, Pedigo said, "Your Honor, I am not guilty of each and every one of these charges."

At that hearing, Ritchie and Gerbitz agreed to consolidate the current charges with the attempted-murder count filed in August.

They were all back in court on December 8 for a hearing about the legality of the search of Pedigo's condo. The judge ruled that the search was legal and the evidence admissible.

A Hamilton County assistant district attorney told the *Knoxville News Sentinel*: "I watched him during the suppression hearing, and I was quite surprised at his reaction. I mean, he was there up front walking through the cameras and I thought, *He's not going to take a plea. That swinger's going to trial.*"

Both sides prepared for the day in April.

CHAPTER 20

At 8:00 a.m. on December 14, fifteen-year-old Maggie Dossett slid behind the wheel of a GMC pickup. Her brother, eleven-year-old Eddie Dossett, sat on the passenger side of the vehicle. Eddie was in fifth grade at Karns Intermediate School. He was on the Warriors basketball team and the Marlins baseball team and had a blue belt in taekwondo. He was a team leader of his youth group at Solway United Methodist Church.

Maggie drove out of the farm and down Solway Road a tenth of a mile before turning right on George Light Road. Three-tenths of a mile later, she reached the intersection with Pellissippi Parkway.

Failing to yield to oncoming traffic, she drove into the path of a 1974 Volkswagen driven by thirty-two-year-old Michael W. Carpenter of Oak Ridge. The VW broadsided the truck and Eddie flew out of the passenger's-side window.

Since Maggie had only a learner's permit, a licensed driver needed to accompany her. According to official reports, her mother, forty-six-year-old Raynella Dossett Leath, was seated next to her in the front seat of the family truck. However, a responder to the scene said that Raynella was not in the car. He said that she'd heard the accident up at the farm and raced to the scene.

One of Raynella's neighbors was first to arrive at the site of the accident. He said when he arrived, Raynella was not there. Another woman who saw the collision and recognized the Dossett truck drove up to the house and brought Raynella down to the intersection.

When Ed's cousin Ray asked the neighbor why he didn't speak to the authorities about Maggie driving without an adult in the car, he said it was because of fear: he was afraid of Raynella. "Ray, she could set out in her driveway and shoot me in my home." He thought it would be a waste of time, anyway. He didn't think law enforcement would believe a poor black farmer over the wealthier, white prosecutor's widow.

Emergency responders transported all four people assumed to be involved in the collision to the University of Tennessee Medical Center. Eddie was in critical condition. Michael Carpenter was in serious condition. Maggie was treated and released. Raynella had no signs of injury.

Gordon Armstrong and his third wife, Gail, rushed to the hospital to be by Dave's side and visit Eddie. As Gordon expected, his friend Dave was clearly dismayed. Maggie's seemingly apathetic reaction to her seriously injured little brother surprised Gordon. Katie, who was Maggie and Eddie's sister, was clearly distraught but in Gordon's opinion Maggie showed no signs of concern.

On December 16 at 10:20 a.m. Eddie died of injuries from the car wreck. Two afternoons later, Raynella and her daughters received friends at Solway United Methodist Church. They returned to the church the following day at 4:00 p.m. for the funeral service, officiated by Reverend Lucretia Hurley-Browning and the Reverend Jim Browning. In lieu of flowers, Raynella requested that memorials be made to the church.

The public was welcome and the line stretched long outside of the church. It was a damp day of bone-aching cold. When Dave's cousin Frieda arrived, she noticed that many of people standing in line were elderly; some of them were shivering.

Frieda ducked into the basement of the church, went upstairs, and found Cindy. They redirected the line through the lower entrance so that everyone could take shelter inside. Little Eddie's coaches and team members at Karns Intermediate School served as honorary pallbearers.

The funeral was just days before winter solstice and daylight was in short supply. By the time the procession left the church, it was dark outside. A slow, steady line of cars belonging to those invited to a private interment on the farm wended their way down the country road.

Cars circled around the spot where Eddie would be laid to rest. Their headlights provided the only illumination as his coffin was lowered into the ground next to his father's grave. Many could not understand why his burial couldn't wait until morning. It seemed an undignified way to bid farewell to a young man who'd lost his life way too soon.

Ed Dossett lost both parents at a young age; now decades later, the boy thought to be his only son was gone. Many felt it was better that the man hadn't lived to see that day.

The following January, District Attorney General Randy Nichols recommended to law enforcement that charges be brought against Michael Carpenter for driving without a license because of his previous DUI. He also encouraged them to not press any charges against Maggie Dossett.

The Tennessee Highway Patrol didn't see it his way. On February 3, 1995, they cited Maggie with failure to yield. The prosecutor's office took the case to juvenile court and moved for dismissal. His request was honored. But the question remained: Would Nichols have done the same for anyone in this position? Or did he give the Raynella and her family preferential treatment?

It was in the month of Eddie Dossett's death that the truth about Ed's other child was revealed to Steve Walker. Back in April, Steve and Kaye Walker had gone out to dinner. Over their meal, Kaye informed her husband that she wanted a divorce. She was in love with another man, Talmadge Morrell, she said. However, she did not confess her affair with Ed Dossett. Both Steve and Kaye wanted custody of Kevin and Kyle, and a bitter battle began.

In a custody hearing, Kaye's attorney dropped a bombshell, claiming that Steve should not be given custody because he was a third party. She claimed that a blood test revealed that Kyle was the biological son of Ed Dossett.

Steve's attorney, John O'Conner, argued that that fact was irrelevant. In the state of Tennessee, he said, when a child is born into a marriage, the child becomes the property of the marriage. It was the first time Steve was made aware of the affair. He never even suspected. But, he came to believe, Raynella knew about it all along.

Steve and Kaye agreed to keep the information secret for the sake of the children. Steve, who'd raised the boy as his own, said he loved him and still considered him his son. He agreed to pay child support without any argument.

After all, Steve had a good example of how a man should behave under these circumstances. His own legal father was not his biological father but never treated Steve like anything but his son. He'd been working for his biological father, Marshall Hargis, for years without knowing of their genetic connection. He'd been made manager and then partner at Marshall's Transmission. Kaye broke the news to him that everyone else seemed to know: Marshall was really Steve's father.

CHAPTER 21

In the nine months since Randall Pedigo's arrest, six victims filed civil actions against the doctor totaling millions of dollars in damages. Some of the suits named the University of Tennessee Medical Center and the Knox County Sheriff's Office as codefendants.

In criminal court, once Judge Thomas upheld the legality of the search of Pedigo's home, negotiations for a plea bargain began in earnest. On Friday, March 31, the doctor pled guilty to four Class D felony counts of unlawfully dispensing an illegal substance and four Class E of sexual battery. (The classes of felonies in Tennessee ranged from A, the worst offenses, down to E; below that level, the charge became a misdemeanor.) Eight of the other original counts as well as the attempted murder charge were dropped altogether.

In the state of Tennessee, each defendant is classified by range from mitigated to career offender. Based upon the criminal record of the convicted person, a judge classified an offender and sentenced him according to that range. A mitigated ranking meant that the individual had no prior offenses on their record. A standard offender, Range I, has zero to one prior offense. A multiple offender, Range II, has two to four priors. A persistent offender, Range III, has five or more priors. A career offender has multiple prior felonies of varying classes. Judge Thomas placed Pedigo in the Range I category.

A typical offender in his group would, on average, receive a two- to four-year sentence on each Class D count and one to two years for each Class E count. Pedigo, then, faced the possibility of twelve to twenty years in prison.

The plea bargain reached was far more lenient. Judge Thomas sentenced him to eight years in prison but required him to spend only one year at the Knox County Penal Farm. For the remaining seven years Pedigo faced supervised probation.

In the courtroom, Pedigo said, "Certainly I've made some mistakes in my life and some very serious mistakes. I never intended that anyone be harmed, and for this I am truly sorry."

Unfortunately, Pedigo didn't stop talking then. In typical predator fashion he proceeded to whine about his fate. "I've been blinded. I've been crippled. I'm in daily pain, and I'm going to spend a year in jail. That is a lot of punishment."

The judge ordered the doctor to report to the Knox County Detention Center on April 28 to begin serving his sentence.

Outside of the courtroom, Pedigo focused on himself. He said he would serve his time and become a productive, meaningful member of society. When reporters reminded him about his victims, he said, "They need to be put back together too. At this time, all I can really do is pray for them."

Many were ready to criticize the prosecutor for the leniency of Pedigo's sentence. Gerbitz told reporters at the *Knoxville News Sentinel*, "If I could have gotten a life sentence for this despicable character, I'd have done it. But it isn't even within the realm of reason."

The nature of the crime did support the agreement, but it was an embarrassing incident for the victims, many of whom did not want to testify. One had moved out of state; another had contemplated suicide. Additionally, because of the use of Versed, the young men had little or no memory of what actually occurred, making it highly dubious that the state could have obtained a guilty verdict at trial on the assault and rape charges.

Sean, however, spoke out against the agreement. He felt betrayed. He wanted to confront his abuser on the witness stand in open court. He told the newspaper, "We were going to convict this man for something he had done. In the end, it didn't seem like the punishment fit the crime."

Gerbitz acknowledged that not all the victims or the public were happy with the end result, but he told reporter John North, "Here's a guy who's done a dastardly deed, and I can understand them not liking it. But that has nothing to do with the plea agreement. If the public isn't satisfied with the law the way it is, make sure your legislators change the law."

Pedigo officially resigned from his position as Knox County medical examiner on April 14. Sandra Elkins, serving in his absence, was hired to replace him despite her month of in-patient treatment in the Impaired Physician Program for the abuse of prescription drugs in 1989.

The University of Tennessee Medical Center immediately made it clear that Pedigo would not be allowed to admit patients to the university facility. The Department of Health began the process of filing charges to revoke Pedigo's medical license. The doctor surrendered to authorities at 11:30 a.m. on April 28, 1995.

That month brought good news to David Leath. His daughter Cindy provided a salve for his sorrow over the loss of his stepson Eddie. On April 21 she gave birth to his only granddaughter, Lindsey.

CHAPTER 22

If Randall Pedigo had done a complete autopsy or if he had pressed authorities about the results of the toxicology tests, charges may have been filed against Raynella Dossett Leath for the death of her first husband, Ed Dossett. But Pedigo did nothing and, as a direct result, the nightmare for Steve Walker began in April 1995.

That month, Steve got a phone call from Donna Corbitt. "Raynella wants to talk to you. Would you come out to the farm?"

When Steve arrived, he walked through the side door straight into the kitchen. Maggie was there and they talked for a minute before she left to pick up her sister Katie at a ball game. Dave walked through and the two men spoke briefly.

Then Raynella got down to business. "I hear your children aren't your children. That they could've been Ed's kids."

They talked for a couple of hours, commiserating over their spouses' infidelity and Steve's divorce. Raynella called Kaye "a devil in a red dress." They looked at pictures of their children and talked about how much they loved them. Steve left not really sure why Raynella had wanted to see him.

Despite Raynella's negative words about Kaye, the two women were still friends. In fact, they had lunch together on May 18.

Six days later Raynella, with her hair up under a ball cap, dropped by Steve's place of employment, Marshall's Transmission, at 11:00 a.m. They went out to Raynella's car to talk. She told Steve, "I found some stuff today at the farm that proves your children are Ed's children. Ed hid some papers in the barn about the affair and about the boy. I thought you might want to come out and see them."

They drove out to the farm, talking about Ed's death and the infidelity. "I knew he had not been faithful but I loved him anyway," Raynella said.

She pulled into the driveway and stopped when she saw her mother in the vegetable garden. They talked for a while, and then Raynella said. "I'm taking Steve up to the barn to show him something."

They drove past the house. Just as they passed Ed's grave, Raynella stopped the car again. "Well, I'm sure you're mad at Ed," she said. "Right there is his grave. If you want to piss on it, I'll turn my back and you can. I sure wouldn't blame you."

Steve thought that was an odd offer. He said, "Yes, I'm mad but I don't need to do that."

The pole barn was an outbuilding that had an open passageway with gates at either end. It was where they gathered cattle to load them up into chutes that led into trucks.

Raynella pulled up to the gate and parked. She pointed inside and said, "The papers are in a bucket in the corner."

Steve climbed over the fence and went over to the spot she indicated and realized the bucket was full of paint. At first, he assumed he was looking in the wrong place. He turned around to get clarification.

Raynella had a towel wrapped around her hand. In the towel she clutched a revolver. She fired two .38-caliber shots in his direction and shouted, "I'll kill you, you bastard, and your ex-wife, and then I'll raise your son!"

Fortunately, Steve was not hit. He ran out the other end of the barn with Raynella at his heels. He came around the side of the barn and heard another shot. He ran down into a patch of woods. He tripped over fallen branches and got scratched up by brambles, though he hardly noticed. His mind was focused on one thought: *I have to get out of here.*

Eventually, he made it through the woods and into a pasture. He had no idea where he was. He walked up a hilly field, feeling a bit safer. Then he heard her car and saw it barreling across the field. He took off running again.

She caught up with him quicker than he thought possible and fired at him. He ducked into another patch of woods and climbed over a fence, falling on the other side, spraining his ankle. He lay on the ground helpless as Raynella approached. "Why do you want to kill me?" he asked.

She fired again and missed.

"If you kill me, I can't raise my kids and you can't raise your kids," Steve pleaded.

Now she was standing over him on the other side of the fence. "Steve, I used to be a better shot than that, but I can't miss you from here," she said aiming down at his head.

Steve knew he was about to die. Raynella pulled the trigger again. The gun clicked: the barrel was empty. She smiled. "Steve, things have gone on. Let me get something, wrap your foot up. C'mon into the house and let's talk about this," she said.

Steve wasn't fooled by her change of mood but he wanted to disarm her before he did anything else. "Okay. But I don't trust you now. Leave that gun here."

"Okay, look," she said, "I'll make an act of good faith." She dumped the empty cartridges from the gun and laid the weapon on the fence post.

She headed back to the car, expecting Steve to follow her. The short break in the pursuit had given Steve the opportunity to catch his breath after the fall. He jumped up, ignoring his injured ankle, and grabbed the gun. He took off running. He stopped at a big house and knocked on the door but got no answer.

Fearful that Raynella was following him, he hid deep in a large culvert. He heard a car come up the driveway. He didn't see it but he was sure it was Raynella. He was certain she'd find him and shoot him dead. Then he heard the car pull away, but still he waited.

Raynella went into town. She stopped at Gordon's Drugs and talked to Mike Gordon. She stopped in at the paint store. And apparently she visited or called Kaye Walker.

While Steve was still in hiding, Kaye called Kid's Place, where the children went for day care after attending Rocky Hill School, and said, "Don't let Steve pick the kids up: he's gone crazy."

When the call was reported to the owner, Pam Hughson, she didn't buy it. She knew Kaye was a control freak and that Steve was the parent who almost always picked up the boys. The kids were always eager and happy to see him, the youngest running straight to him for a hug. She said, "It's horse malarkey. He can have the kids unless someone has court papers."

Out somewhere in the country, Steve slid cautiously out of the culvert and headed again to a stretch of woods. He kept moving, following a fence line, until he reached a mobile home. Again he knocked on a door. This time he got an answer.

He told the older couple living there that he'd had car trouble. They allowed him to use the phone and he called Marshall Hargis. "I've had some trouble and I need you to come get me."

"Where are you?" Marshall asked.

Steve asked the couple and then told Marshall, "Sam Lee Road."

Steve went down to the street to wait for his ride. Still fearful that Raynella might be looking for him, he attempted to hide behind a tree. Steve was a large man, though, and when Marshall spotted him, he laughed. "Steve, what do you think you're doing? A cow could hide behind that small tree as well as you do."

Steve called his mother and asked her to pick up the boys. Marshall called the Knox County Sheriff's office and they sent deputies out to investigate. Before they arrived, Raynella called 911 to report that Steve had stolen her revolver.

Dewey Large was there with his daughter when law enforcement arrived. Raynella's mother, Annie, was in the house but Raynella told the deputies that they could not talk to her mother because her health was poor. Steve believed that she didn't want them talking to Annie because she'd seen him drive up to the pole barn with Raynella and she was bound to have heard the shots. If she answered truthfully, Raynella's version of events would have been undermined.

Raynella said, "I heard the cattle bellowing so I grabbed my gun and went out to the barn to investigate." When she found Steve Walker, she said, "he was acting psychotic and making allegations against Ed. He said he was going to urinate on my late husband's grave. So I fired into the ground to scare him off and he wrest the gun out of my hand and took off."

Law enforcement sorted out the two stories and Raynella was charged with attempted murder. Both Raynella and Kaye Walker lawyered up that evening. Steve never really knew why his ex-wife felt she needed an attorney too. He wondered if she was worried that somehow she would be considered a suspect.

Raynella, with her attorney by her side, surrendered to authorities a few hours later, at 1:00 a.m. She was formally charged later that day and released on $10,000 bond.

Given his friendship with Raynella, District Attorney General Randy Nichols notified state authorities that his office could not prosecute her because of the appearance of a conflict of interest. He as well as many of his staff knew Raynella or knew of her from Ed Dossett. To make matters worse, one of the employees, Donna Corbitt, could be called as a witness, since she had spent time with Raynella the afternoon after the incident.

In Knox County General Sessions Court, Raynella's attorney, Steve Oberman, waived arraignment, saying that his client wanted no delay and was eager for her trial: "We are confident when the court and public hear all the circumstances in the case that the truth will be known and Mrs. Dossett-Leath will be acquitted."

Steve Walker shuddered at that thought. What scared him the most was that he didn't understand why she wanted to kill him. After that day he pulled every blind in his house shut tight. Before going to bed, he closed the door to his room and wedged a chair under the knob. He would not mow his yard or drive his tractor around the property without a gun close at hand.

CHAPTER 23

When trouble came calling once again, Dave Leath did the expected: he turned to his good friend Gordon Armstrong. Dave wasn't sure what to think about the charges against his wife, Raynella, according to Gordon. Raynella had told Dave that when she was moving, "the gun went off." Dave called Gordon and asked him to come over and see how well Raynella could shoot. He believed that if she had wanted to kill Steve Walker, she could have hit him. He wanted his friend to test that theory.

Gordon was shocked when Raynella gathered up her weapons: "She had enough guns for a small militia." Armed, Raynella and Gordon went out on the farm a safe distance from the house and the road. Dave did not go up with them telling Gordon, "I don't want to be around her while she's shooting." Was he joking? Gordon didn't think so.

After watching her fire a few rounds from multiple weapons, Gordon determined that Raynella could shoot a handgun or rifle well. It didn't prove that she wasn't attempting murder when she shot at Steve, but it made her story a bit more credible.

Despite the turmoil caused by Raynella's shooting incident, life somehow went on as usual in the Dossett home. Gordon accompanied Dave on a road trip in pursuit of Dave's hobby of collecting old buggies. He'd travel long distances looking for one that caught his fancy. The worse shape it was in when he bought it, the bigger the challenge to refurbish it and the greater his satisfaction when the job was done.

At Gordon's request, Dave decorated a horse and buggy in a holiday theme for 1995 Christmas card photos. Gordon brought his grandkids over and loaded them into the buggy. But no matter what angle they tried, they couldn't get a shot that included the horse and, at the same time, had clear shots of the children's faces. In the end, they unhooked the animal and took pictures of just the kids sitting in the decorated cart.

On July 17, the collision caused by Maggie's careless driving brought more turmoil to the family. Michael Carpenter filed a $15 million civil suit in Knox County Circuit Court citing Maggie as well as Raynella as the oversight person for Maggie's learner's permit and Dave as the owner of the truck.

The next month the courtroom drama continued. This time it was Raynella's action that turned Dave's attention to legal matters. On August 29, Raynella was back in court in Clinton for a hearing to dismiss in the Steve Walker case. Conflict of interest prevented the Knox County district attorney general's office from handling the case. When Steve sat in the witness stand and told the judge his version of the events at the farm, Raynella shook her head and rolled her eyes.

On cross examination, her attorney, Steve Oberman, questioned every little thing in Steve's testimony: "Did you see her aim the gun at you?"

"Yes, when I turned around, she was aiming it at me."

"Were you facing her when you claim she shot at you?"

"No, I was running."

"Did you hear bullets whizzing by your ears?"

"Nope."

After badgering Steve Walker, Oberman argued that the

witness was hostile toward Raynella because he was an il-
legitimate child just like the boy he raised as his son. There
didn't seem to be much relevance in that statement. It was as
if the lawyer just threw that out on the table hoping to offend.

Neither the attorney's theory nor Raynella's drama moved
the judge. He sent the case to the grand jury. The following
January, the panel returned an indictment charging her with
attempted murder and aggravated assault.

On the advice of his attorney, Steve Walker raised the
ante on May 24, 1996, filing a civil lawsuit for mental torment
against Raynella. In the documents submitted, he claimed
that the shooting caused him to avoid strangers, lose sleep,
and become uneasy and anxious both at home and at work.
He sought $350,000 in damages.

Less than a month later Steve requested a dismissal of the
suit, saying that he filed when he did only to meet the one-
year statute of limitations for the civil action. The court complied with his request but left open the option to file again at
a later date. Steve really didn't care. He just wanted it to be
over. He now had custody of his two boys and wanted to
take care of his kids. As a single father, life was challenging
enough without having to drive out of town for court appearances. "I didn't like it. I didn't like any part of it," Steve said.

After a pretrial hearing in mid-August, Judge Buddy
Scott of Anderson County called for a special prosecutor to
examine the overlap in personal relationships among those
involved in the case. The defense expressed their concerns
about receiving any exculpatory evidence uncovered in that
investigation. They were worried about a conflict of interest,
since Marshall's Transmissions, where Steve worked, did
extensive business with the sheriff's office. A trial date was
set for October 14.

Outside of the courtroom, Dave Leath approached Steve
Walker and stuck out his hand. The two men shook and
Dave apologized for what his wife had done. Steve didn't think

that Dave needed to do that, but it made him feel better that he had.

Two weeks before the scheduled date, the defense and prosecution reached a plea deal. Steve insisted that part of the agreement had to be an admission of guilt. Raynella wanted diversion, a sentencing option that would eventually clear her record of any wrongdoing, thus enabling her to return to nursing in the future if she wanted. She agreed to plead guilty to assault in exchange for a dismissal of the attempted murder charge.

Judge Scott placed her on six years of diversion with one hundred hours of community service. At the end of the probationary period, if she fulfilled the requirements, the assault charge would also be dismissed and her record expunged. However, if she did not comply, she would be considered convicted and the assault count would remain on file.

Many were surprised at the sentence. District Attorney General Steve Bebb said, "You can't award diversion for shooting someone in the state of Tennessee. Someone broke the law when the diversion agreement was made."

Another condition of her six-year probation was that she couldn't be around any guns. Dave called Gordon to haul away Raynella's weapons cache, but before he could get out to the farm, Raynella's dad, Dewey Large, came by and picked them up. Gordon wondered if Raynella didn't trust him enough.

CHAPTER 24

Steve Walker started dating Pam Hughson in the fall. Their families fit well together. In fact, both had two sons of the same ages who already were friends. Steve's kids were accustomed to doing what Pam said at the day care center where they stayed after school. That history all made the transition to a blended family much easier than usual when Pam and Steve were married.

The big challenge to a peaceful family life was the girl Pam had adopted during her first marriage. She was seven years old when she moved into the home. Pam's first husband always kept the girl at arm's length. Steve, however, accepted her as his own, problems and all.

During the whole ordeal with Raynella, Steve's boys had given her a nickname: Cruella De Vil, after a character in the Disney film *101 Dalmatians*. That would be the first thing that would pop into Pam's mind when she had a chance encounter with Raynella.

Pam had stopped by a car wash and taken a seat in the waiting area. Raynella strode into the room, looking very much like the cartoon villainess. Pam tried to disappear into the chair; she didn't want to be recognized.

Raynella took a seat and turned her attention to a CNN story about immigration airing on the television. Raynella spoke loudly, giving her opinion of the piece in no uncertain terms. She sprinkled her monologue with derogatory remarks about Mexicans. Pam couldn't wait to get out of there. "It was the longest twenty minutes of my life."

With the threat of his wife's imprisonment no longer hanging over his head, Dave Leath's life went back to normal. For him, that always meant having a project of some sort going: fixing a tractor or lawn mower or making other repairs around the farm. That winter he wanted to do work on the dash of his Corvette, but he needed a place where the car could stay warm overnight while the glue set. Since Gordon had a kerosene heater in his garage, Dave drove his car over there to work on it.

Beside his endless projects, he also had a mulching business on the side. He cut hair during the day and loaded, hauled, and unloaded mulch at night.

That year Dave and Raynella both gave written instructions to attorney Charles Child to destroy the prenuptial agreement. Child requested that they come to the office to do the actual physical destruction of the document in his presence.

On August 12 they did that, and both signed new wills the lawyer had prepared. Raynella took her original document to the bank and placed it into a safe-deposit box that also contained titles to farm equipment, cars, and other important papers.

In Dave's will, Raynella maintained her position as executrix but the successor executor named was Gordon Armstrong. The document created a life estate for the 16.27-acre tract containing the family home for Dave's mother, Mayme. It also provided that if Mayme died before Dave or if she was no longer using it as her primary residence, the property would go to Raynella. Additionally, the remainder of Dave's estate also went to his wife. The new will effectively disinherited Dave's daughter Cindy unless Raynella died first. In that case, all of his estate would go to Cindy except for any property Dave obtained through his wife's death. That would go to "Magdalena Dossett and Nancy Kathalena Dossett to share and share alike."

According to Raynella, Dave went home and put his will in a sock drawer along with the divorce papers from his first two marriages and other important documents. Maggie would claim to have seen the will in that location soon afterward. However, Gordon Armstrong had another story.

Gordon visited the Leath home soon after the new will was prepared. He was in the kitchen when they pointed to a cabinet on the left side of the back door to the garage. They opened the door and pointed to a spot near the midpoint and Dave said, "This is where the will is."

Raynella added, "If we both die at the same time, we want you to be the executor of our wills: we want you to look after the girls."

Gordon never read the will but he never forgot the location. Even though Raynella exhibited this measure of faith, Gordon still didn't think she had a very high opinion of him. When he offered to lend movies from his VCR collection to the Leaths, Raynella asked, "What have you got?"

Gordon handed her an alphabetical list of all the titles. Raynella expressed her amazement. Gordon knew she didn't think he was smart enough to put that long list in alphabetical order. He believed that she thought she was smarter than everyone else, but this was the first time he felt that sense of superiority pointed so tactlessly in his direction.

Nonetheless, Gordon and Raynella got along well most the time and were comfortable in each other's company. On one occasion, when she and Dave dropped by one of Gordon's work sites, Raynella looked over the heavy equipment while Dave and Gordon were chatting. She came back to the men and said, "I always wanted to drive one of those big machines."

Neither man was surprised at that pronouncement. Raynella was always ready for a new experience or a fresh challenge.

"All right. Let me show you how it's done," Gordon said. He and Raynella jumped up on the backhoe and Gordon showed her all of the controls. Then he stepped back to the ground and said, "Have at it."

Raynella jumped down and said, "Oh, no. Not all by myself." Her adventurousness did have its limits.

Gordon got up in the seat and Raynella climbed up into his lap. She worked the controls for a few minutes and was satisfied.

Dave took his responsibilities for Raynella's teenage girls seriously. He and Raynella's oldest daughter, Maggie, got along well. They both enjoyed the outdoors and liked spending time piddling around on the farm together.

According to Gordon, Katie was another story. It's not an unusual scenario that the second daughter or son in a family causes more problems than the oldest child. Katie was no exception as she struggled to discover her independence and build an identity separate from her big sister and her parents.

She usually ate her meals separate from the family, arranging her schedule to avoid being around at mealtime. When she was there, she spent a lot of time complaining about the food and frequently refused to eat it, handing morsels from her plate to the dog.

One day Dave's exasperation with his youngest stepdaughter hit a fever pitch. He grabbed the ends of the tablecloth and hoisted it up with dinner plates, silverware and serving dishes bundled up inside. He carried it out into the front yard and set it down on the ground for the dog.

Dave set aside his frustrations with Katie to focus on Maggie's graduation from high school in 1997. A baccalaureate service for graduating seniors of Karns High School was scheduled for 3:00 p.m. on a Sunday afternoon at Grace Baptist Church. Six days later, on May 24 at 2:00 p.m., Maggie walked across the stage to get her diploma—one of thirteen valedictorians in the class of 270 students.

In October 1999, Maggie married Scott Connaster and no longer lived in the family home. Unlike many who marry in college, Maggie did not drop out. In fact, she went on to earn a BS in chemistry, a BA in history, and a PhD in analytical chemistry.

As Dave rolled through the late nineties, life seemed to be on an even keel. His stepdaughters were growing up and becoming adults. Thanks to Cindy, he had two grandchildren to spoil. Work was going well with both the barbering and the mulch business, and his hobbies and friends filled his leisure time.

Friend Roger Yarnell observed that the relationship between Dave and Raynella was excellent, with frequent signs of affection and no fights or arguments. Dave spoke highly of his stepdaughter Maggie and expressed appreciation for all the help she'd given him around the farm. He never expressed any concern or dislike for his wife or either of his stepdaughters.

Life was good for David Leath—but it wouldn't last for long.

CHAPTER 25

If the courts in Knox County thought they'd seen the last of former medical examiner Randall Pedigo when they sent him off to jail, they learned quickly that he was not through with them yet. Soon civil suits were in full swing both by the doctor and against him.

While Pedigo was still behind bars, he filed for benefits on two disability insurance policies, requesting the $51,492 in annual payments because he was permanently disabled by accidental injury and unable to work as a surgeon. The companies, UNUM Life Insurance Company of America and Union Mutual Stock Life Insurance Company, denied his claims. Pedigo filed a $1.3 million lawsuit against both businesses.

Less than three months after his release from jail on April 27, 1996, Pedigo testified, telling a different story of the day of his arrest. He said, "I didn't at any time hear a command before I was shot. I locked my door and went to the living room to get a pistol between the seat cushion and the armrest." He claimed that he then held the gun to his right temple as he contemplated suicide. He stood there, he said, with his back to the entrance of the room, unaware that TBI special agent Richardson was behind him until he felt the first gunshot.

Richardson's testimony contradicted Pedigo's, but the expert witness guaranteed that Pedigo would not prevail. Assistant Medical Examiner Cleland Blake told the court that the photos, X-rays, operative reports, and all other evidence clearly demonstrated that the doctor was facing and aiming his gun at Richardson when Pedigo received the first two wounds.

Judge Leon Jordan ruled in favor of the insurance companies based on the evidence presented, the lack of proof that permanent disability prevented Pedigo from pursuing his surgical practice, and the fact that his injuries were not the result of an accident.

The case then went to the Sixth U.S. Circuit Court of Appeals, where Pedigo repeated his claims in documents presented to the judges. Again Richardson set forth the version of events that fit with the forensic evidence. He wrote that Pedigo pulled the gun from the chair, faced him, and extended his arms with both hands on the grip. It was then and only then, Richardson said, that he pulled the trigger on his weapon.

The appeals court found Richardson credible and discounted the testimony of Randall Pedigo. They upheld the decision of the lower court.

In the suits filed against Pedigo by six of his victims, his attorneys moved to consolidate the cases to save the courts—and their clients—time and money. Attorneys for the young men objected to this move because of a concern over the privacy of each individual.

State Volunteer Mutual Insurance Company appeared in court before Knox County chancellor Sharon Bell seeking relief from the lawsuits against Pedigo. They argued that the malpractice policy covered the doctor only for administering Versed without consent but did not cover any criminal acts he committed after he injected the drug. Bell declined to prohibit the young men from seeking money from Pedigo's insurers.

Several of the lawsuits were scheduled to go to trial within months. Lawyers for many of the young men sought to negotiate out-of-court settlements. Parents said that they did not want a court fight that might jeopardize the mental recovery of their sons. In the end, only one case would eventually go to trial.

Pedigo complicated his life more by irritating his new neighbors. After selling his condo, he moved into a home in Holstein Hills. He wanted to operate a forensic pathology consulting business office in his home. He requested a zoning exception, stating that the business would generate very little traffic in the neighborhood and that he would not put up a sign advertising the presence of his office in the house.

The neighborhood erupted. They did not want to establish the precedent of a business operating in their residential community. Questions were also raised about the sight distance from Pedigo's driveway to the street: it seemed too short for safe reentry into the public road.

The Metropolitan Planning Commission received six letters and 119 names on a petition against Pedigo's plan. The commission had set the vote for October 8, 1998. Three dozen residents showed up to voice their objections at the meeting. Before it began, Pedigo withdrew his request.

CHAPTER 26

Dave fell into a state of delirium on January 3, 2000. His hallucinations and disorientation were severe enough that hospitalization was necessary. Neurologist Ronald Bryan was called in for a consult because of symptoms of "mental status change, frank confusion, and a diminished level of consciousness." A complete examination revealed multiple conditions. The electroencephalogram produced an abnormal reading. The follow-up MRI showed evidence of a single ministroke caused by the occlusion of a very small blood vessel in the brain. Dave also suffered from high cholesterol and herpes simplex encephalitis.

The latter is a rare but serious disease that kills 70 percent of untreated victims. It strikes at two distinct periods of a person's life, either before the age of twenty or after fifty years of age. In the case of adult onset, the infection affects the temporal and frontal lobes of the brain. Whether the patient undergoes treatment or not, 50 percent of those affected are left with moderate to severe neurological deficits.

Dave's mother asked Frieda to take her to the hospital to visit Dave. When they arrived, Raynella was not happy. She kept trying to get them to leave and let Dave rest. She came straight to the point when Cindy came to visit her dad. "Go home," Raynella said. "I'll call you if there's anything you need to know."

On March 1, Raynella visited Cremation Options on South Peters Road. She met with owner James Safewright. She explained that her husband was very ill and prepaid for his cremation as well as her own.

In March, Dave retired from his position at the Suburban Barber Shop. He turned over his share of the business and his middle chair to his daughter Cindy, who left her job at a shop called Mr. George's to cut hair in his place. She said that her father did not leave his position because of any confusion. He was still capable of working with his hands and paying attention on the job. However, he did have a prostrate problem and trouble urinating that required him to use a catheter on occasion. His prostrate was the reason he retired.

Dave wasn't a stranger to the shop, though. He went to the YMCA just down the road and stopped by two or three times a week between 10:00 a.m. and noon. He often pulled up blowing his horn, rubbing in the many joys of his happy-go-lucky lifestyle as a retired man. And he always kept his tan, visiting the tanning bed as often as necessary to keep bronzed.

Many of Dave's regular customers happily made the transition to Cindy. One of them was Gordon Armstrong. He thought he'd have to pay for his haircuts now that Dave's was gone, but Cindy also refused his money. "Dad wouldn't let you pay and I won't, either," she said.

After retiring, Dave didn't show any serious signs of post-recovery problems for the rest of that year. Now that he wasn't working, he paid unplanned visits to many of the important people in his life. Cindy always knew if he had stopped by the house when no one was home because he'd leave a white barber towel hanging on the doorknob.

He was able to spend a lot more time with his friend Roger Yarnell. They saw each other or talked on the phone nearly every day. Roger usually did most of the driving when they went to NASCAR races together because of Dave's lack of vision in one eye. Roger never observed Dave having any problems with mental confusion.

But on March 8, 2001, Raynella brought Dave to the hospital again. Neurologist Dr. Bryan came in to consult. Raynella described short-term memory difficulties, citing Dave's forgetting to answer the phone or take a bath. She also talked about her husband's emotional ups and downs, short temper, and frequent napping throughout the day.

Dave told the doctor that he believed that his wife was trying to kill him, possibly by smothering. Bryan believed it was paranoid ideation and suspected that Dave had dementia, which waxed and waned. But of course the doctor didn't know about Raynella's recent visit to Cremation Options. Later, when Gordon and Cindy heard about Dave's fears of his wife ending his life, they suspected Dave had been right all along.

Dave began direct, regular care with Dr. Bryan on March 1, 2002. At the time he was on medication for blood pressure, stomach acid, pain, and cholesterol. That day Bryan administered a short mental examination to measure Dave's orientation, memory and ability to pay attention. Dave scored 22 of a possible 30 points on the test indicating mild dementia. At one point he cried when he could not spell a word backwards. Since it was possible that the ministroke was causing mild seizures, the doctor prescribed epilepsy medication. Although he did not discuss Alzheimer's with Dave that day, the doctor was considering it as a possibility.

At a follow-up visit on March 28, Dave was no longer sleeping during the day, his memory had improved, and his mood was better. He talked about activities in his life with greater interest and told Dr. Bryan that he'd gotten a fishing license.

Dave returned to his office for a new mini-test on July 3.

Raynella Dossett Leath upon her arrival at state prison.

(Courtesy: Tenth Judicial District Attorney General's Office)

Officers of the Oak Ridge High School German Club, 1966. A teenage Raynella is on the far left.

(Oak Ridge High School yearbook, 1966)

Oak Ridge High School Junior Key Club. Raynella is seated in the front row on the far left .

(Oak Ridge High School yearbook, 1966)

Magdalena Snodderly Dossett, 1926, a school teacher and the mother of Ed Dossett. She died at the age of fifty from a heart attack.

(Courtesy: Ray Graves)

Ed Dossett graduated from East Tennessee State University in 1969.
(Courtesy: Ray Graves)

Raynella Large and Ed Dossett were married in the summer of 1969 at the Solway United Methodist Church.
(Courtesy: Ray Graves)

Ed Dossett at the podium in the City-County Building being sworn in for his second term as Sixth District Attorney General in 1990. His wife Raynella stands beside the podium with her back to the camera and their young daughter Katie stands between them. *(Courtesy: Ray Graves)*

David Leath in early elementary school, approximately 1952.

(Courtesy: Cindy Wilkerson)

David Leath with his wife Peggy and their only child, one-month-old Cindy, 1963. *(Courtesy: Cindy Wilkerson)*

Suburban Barber Shop where David Leath cut hair for decades and where his daughter Cindy Wilkerson still works.

(Courtesy: author)

The house built by Ed Dossett where David Leath was shot to death.

(Courtesy: Tenth Judicial District Attorney General's Office)

The stringing done at the crime scene to determine the trajectory of the three bullets fired.

(Courtesy: Tenth Judicial District Attorney General's Office)

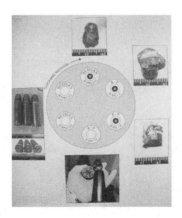

A diagram of the gun barrel showing the fired bullets, the unfired bullets, and a photograph of the barrel from the scene of the crime.

(Courtesy: Tenth Judicial District Attorney General's Office)

The actual barrel of the gun showing the three empty and three unused cartridges of two different brands.

(Courtesy: Tenth Judicial District Attorney General's Office)

At a family wedding in the mid-seventies *(l to r)*, Ed's Uncle Pat Graves, Cousin Ray Graves, Cousin Bob Bailey and Ed Dossett. *(Courtesy: Ray Graves)*

That day, his score went up to 28—clearly above the 22 to 25 point range that indicated mild dementia. Dr. Bryan noted that if his patient had been able to spell a word backwards, he would have gotten a perfect score. The doctor gave him a prescription for medication to improve his memory.

CHAPTER 27

On Monday, May 13, 2002, Randall Pedigo entered the court of Judge Harold Wimberly to resolve the last of several lawsuits brought against him by his victims. In his opening statement, Pedigo's attorney said: "There's no doubt that the victim is entitled to some compensation." He argued, though, that the amount should be just. He minimized Pedigo's crime. "There was no molestation, no rape, no violence, no false imprisonment by Dr. Pedigo."

Sean was one of the last men victimized by the doctor before his arrest. Now 26 years old, he took the stand to relive what happened to him eight years ago. "This event has been the consuming focus of my thoughts for eight years. It hasn't gone away, though I've tried very hard to make it go away by immersing myself in my work. I always wanted to believe that nothing happened," he said.

He worked sixteen to seventeen hours a day, learned to speak a dozen languages, became both a Fulbright Scholar and a Watson Fellow, and was now a doctoral candidate at Vanderbilt University. None of that solved his problems.

In contradiction to the statement of Pedigo's attorney, Sean testified that he knew he could not deny the reality of the intimate assault because "certain parts" of his body indicted that something had happened while he was unconscious. "I have to believe that I was sexually molested by Dr. Pedigo regardless of what he tells me, what he tells someone else. I denied it for a long time."

He didn't report the incident to law enforcement, he said, because he didn't want his family or friends to know what occurred in Pedigo's condominium. "I really wanted more than anything else to forget that evening." But he hadn't been able to do so. The incident left him with an aversion to being touched and caused difficulty in being intimate with his wife of two years.

He hadn't told his wife about it until recently when she needed to go in for a deposition.

"Why didn't you tell your wife?" his attorney asked.

"Because I'm ashamed of what happened."

In his wife's deposition, which had taken place a week earlier, she testified that her husband had to be intoxicated to be able to have sexual relations.

The following day, Dr. James Murray, a clinical psychologist in Knoxville, testified on Sean's behalf. He'd given the young man a mental evaluation in 1996. He believed that Sean suffered from post-traumatic stress disorder from his encounter with Pedigo.

He said that the condition caused the victim to have difficulty in relations with people and to feel that the world was a very dangerous place. He had problems controlling and expressing his emotions. He was suffering, the doctor continued, "from the terrible combination of desperately needing to be close to someone while at the same time being unable to trust people. He clearly viewed himself as weak and vulnerable and damaged."

Sean's wife took the stand that day. She said she often asked her husband about their lack of intimacy. He would tell her he was tired from work. "If I pressed him, he would have tears in his eyes and say he was just tired." She also said that he was terrified of hurting her during sexual intercourse.

"Sometimes, I would think I did something wrong or it was me," she said in a soft, tear-strained voice. "But I knew he loved me very much."

On Wednesday, moments after the court convened, the jury was sent to the deliberation room while the attorneys talked over a mid-trial settlement. The lawyers huddled together for a while. Then they split to talk to clients while the insurance company attorney headed for a telephone.

By 12:30, Judge Wimberley decided it was time to liberate the jury. "It's obvious we had an unusual break this morning," he said. He explained to the jury that the case was now seven years old and everyone involved wanted to see it completed. "But sometimes," he added, "unexpected things happen and sometimes we are not able to proceed straight through a case." He then sent the jurors home with admonishments not to pay any attention to the news on the case and to return the following morning.

When the jurors arrived back in court on Thursday morning, Sean's lawyer thanked them for their service and said, "The plaintiff has agreed to accept judgment for compensatory damages from Dr. Pedigo in the amount of $5 million. Now he and his lovely wife can deal with this and move on with their lives."

Pedigo's attorney told the jurors: "Dr. Pedigo wanted me to say he is profoundly sorry for what has happened. He has basically turned his life around and is doing well and is being a good citizen."

The bargain took punitive damages—the punishment portion of a civil case—off of the table. The $5 million awarded was solely recompense for damage caused. He'd served his sentence on the criminal charges, and now all the civil suits were settled. But soon a 1992 autopsy performed by Pedigo would come back to haunt him and the prosecutors in the attorney general's office down in Cleveland, Tennessee.

CHAPTER 28

September 30, 2002, was a day of new beginnings for Raynella. She sailed through her diversion period and now her record was expunged. Legally it was as if she had never shot five bullets at Steve Walker. No matter what she did in the future, no one could ever point to a previous conviction in a court of law.

Dave returned to Dr. Bryan's office on October 17. Raynella reported a history of mood swings. The doctor discussed with them the frequency with which he changed his mind or moods seemingly without any reason. Bryan requested that he come in again at the end of the month. At that time Bryan was pleased to note that Dave's appetite had improved, he was remaining alert during the day without a need for a nap, his mood was more stable, and he was more interested in his normal activities.

On January 16, 2003, Dr. Bryan saw Dave for the last time. Dave was frustrated and tearful. They did not complete the short mental examinations because Dave did not want to do them any longer. Dave asked the same questions repeatedly. He was often unable to express himself as he wanted and simply stopped talking all together. It seemed apparent to the neurologist that Dave was deteriorating.

However, Raynella insisted that many of his previous problems were no longer occurring.

Nonetheless, the doctor suspected a moderately advanced state of Alzheimer's. He was not completely convinced, though, because there were aspects of Dave's illness that were not typical of that disease.

That month, Raynella was scheduled for a hysterectomy. Dave dropped her off at the hospital and went over to the barbershop. He flopped down in the middle barber chair where he used to cut hair and burst into tears. "I should be there for her," he sobbed.

"Well, go on, Dad. Go back to the hospital," Cindy said.

"She doesn't want me there," Dave said. "And she doesn't want any visitors."

Cindy didn't push him further. Over the years she'd learned that Raynella was the nicest person in the world when you let her have her way, but the moment you disagreed with her or crossed her, she'd turn vicious.

When Dave went back to the hospital the following day to pick up his wife upon her release, he finally got the whole story behind Raynella's surgery. Not only had her uterus been removed but she had cancer in one breast. She had instructed the doctor to perform a double mastectomy. She told Dave that because of the nature of her procedure, it would not be possible for her to have reconstructive surgery. Dave was devastated that she had not confided in him in advance.

Lindsey, Dave's eight-year-old granddaughter, paid a visit to her grandfather and stepgrandmother. Raynella showed the young girl her scars. When Lindsey returned home, she asked Cindy, "Mom, why did she show me that?"

Cindy had no answer. It didn't make sense to her, either.

On the nineteenth of that month, Raynella picked up her appointment book with its blue leather cover and gold-edged pages, resembling a Bible. She wrote: "Dave hateful today. I cried and cried." The next day, she jotted: "Dave not hateful today." On January 22, things were not well again: "Dave paranoid, bad argument. Dave hateful, controlling. His way or no way. I cried."

"Dave fair" was written on January 27. Two days later she noted: "I'm tired of it and everything else. Came home and slept from 3:30–5:00. I feel like not being would be easier than trying."

The only notation on February 4, 2003 was: "Charles Child." On that day Dave and Raynella visited attorney Charles Child to review their will. Both brought along their original documents. Although Dave said, "That's my will, that's what I want," his distress was obvious to Child, who he was not surprised when Dave wanted to meet with him privately afterward.

Raynella claimed the reason for the separate meeting was to discuss the status of his business. She was certain that Dave understood everything the lawyer told him because it was "one of Dave's better days." But Child said, "Dave was emotional. He cried. He was not himself." Dave left the office without requesting any changes to his will.

Raynella waited in the reception area while the two men talked. She said that Dave put his will in his jacket pocket as they left the office. When they returned home, Dave said he was tired and went to bed to rest. Raynella said that she never saw Dave's will again.

Later that month Dave's mother, Mayme, was diagnosed with ovarian cancer. Surgery was scheduled on February 25. For some reason Raynella insisted to all of Dave's cousins that Mayme did not have cancer. Mayme was going into the hospital for a minor procedure, she told them.

The day she was admitted to the hospital, eighty-three-year-old Mayme said that she wanted to return home after the procedure. The nursing staff was not sure if that would be possible.

The night before, Cindy called Mayme and found out that her grandmother was terrified of the upcoming operation.

Mayme poured out her fears and anxieties to Cindy, who did her best to comfort and reassure her. While Mayme was in surgery, Raynella consulted with the nursing staff about her mother-in-law's postsurgical placement.

On Monday, March 3, Frieda went into to see Mayme after her surgery. Dave was there with his mother when she arrived. Mayme freely discussed her cancer, leaving Frieda even more perplexed than ever about Raynella's lie.

Mayme, who never got along with Raynella, told Frieda: "I'd rather stay in your basement than have to go live with them."

Frieda walked out of the hospital with her cousin Dave that Monday and watched him drive away in Mayme's car. She never saw her cousin again.

On March 4, at 4:00 p.m., contrary to her wishes, Mayme was transferred to Fort Sanders Regional Medical Center's skilled nursing facility. Cindy and her mother, Peggy Rowe, knew how unhappy Mayme was with the move. They started looking for a different facility where Mayme had friends among the residents.

Two days later, Raynella turned to her appointment book again. She wrote: "Dave hateful."

On that same Thursday, Dave picked his mother up for a trip to the beauty shop to have her hair done. While she was there, Dave dropped by the home of his former in-laws. Since Peggy's dad had lost a leg to diabetes and was confined to a wheelchair, Dave made it a habit to stop by there for a visit whenever he took Mayme to see her nearby hairstylist.

On this particular day Dave mentioned his plans to go to a street rod car show later that month. He talked about the road trip he planned to take with Gordon Armstrong when Gordon retired in May. He sounded like a man with a future . . . but in reality, his future could be measured in days.

On Saturday, March 8, Raynella jotted down: "Slurred speech. Hateful. Stayed in bed all day."

According to Cindy, however, that day Dave went in to visit his mother. The nursing staff had reported that she'd taken a turn for the worse. Raynella dropped him off but did not come inside with him. She claimed that a liver disease compromised her immune system and she could not go into the hospital because of the risk. Cindy suspected that the real reason was that Raynella and her dad's mother never got along very well.

In the evening, Cindy came by and visited with her grandmother and father. Dave mentioned not feeling too well and his speech was slightly slurred. Raynella called Cindy while she was there, and Cindy asked about her father's speaking problem. Raynella said, "It's just a side effect from his high-blood-pressure medication." She added, "Your father is upset with me again. He didn't like the way I started the tractor. I'm getting tired of it."

At 9:00 that evening, Dave was feeling well enough to go with his daughter to Arby's to eat dinner. They had a great time, laughing, cutting up, and talking about everything that came to mind. Dave did not indicate that he had any problems with Raynella. Cindy thought he was in a great mood.

She went to the hospital to see her grandmother again on Sunday and saw a surprising change in her father. She found Dave was sitting in his car, crying. Cindy pressed him to talk about what was causing him so much distress. Dave said, "It will work out. Everything will be okay," but he would not say anything more.

On Monday, Dave took his GMC Dooley truck with flat bed over to Hardin Valley Body Shop. He was particular about his vehicles. When noticed a small scratch on the fender, he just had to have it fixed. His truck was still in the shop on Thursday, March 13. Dave would never drive it home.

CHAPTER 29

Cindy called her dad on Monday, March 10, 2003, to make sure he was okay. The next day Raynella called her to complain. She said, "Dave and I got into it again."

On Wednesday, March 12, Roger Yarnell and Dave got together and made plans to haul a load of mulch over to Robert's son's place. They planned to meet up at noon on March 13. Roger noticed nothing unusual. He saw no signs of depression, confusion, or slurred speech.

The next day Raynella stopped by Parkwest Medical Center. When nurse Premila Patel spotted her on the floor between 9:00 and 10:00 a.m. that morning, Raynella said she had brought flowers for her mother-in-law—something she had never done before that day. The women hugged and Raynella walked away. A number of people saw her on different floors in that hour but no one really knew why she was there. They assumed it was to visit her mother-in-law, not realizing that Raynella avoided that chore whenever she could.

Cindy could not remember at what time her phone rang that morning, but when it did, Raynella was on the other end. "Have you seen your father?" Raynella asked.

"Not this morning," Cindy said. "Is something wrong?"

"He hasn't eaten his oatmeal and I don't want him working out at the Y with an empty stomach."

Raynella drove back to the farm, where her husband now lay dead in his bed. She called 911 at 11:23 a.m. to report that Dave had committed suicide. While many influential members of Knoxville's legal and political communities gathered in the front yard, investigators, suspicious about the three shots fired, combed the house for evidence of homicide.

Cindy, unaware of law enforcement's suspicions, listened to Raynella talk about her father's suicide, his depression, and the possibility of Alzheimer's or some other form of dementia. None of it made sense to Cindy. She'd seen rarely seen any symptoms that indicated her father's mental capacity was impaired. She'd seen him cry since his mother went into the hospital, but a pervasive depression? It just didn't make sense.

When Dave's cousin Frieda arrived at the house the afternoon of Dave's death, she made a beeline for Cindy. "Cindy, is it true?" she asked.

"Yeah," Cindy sighed.

Frieda walked up to the house and spotted a big white van. According to Frieda, when she asked Raynella's sister, Robyn Randall, what it was, Robyn responded, "When something like this happens, they leave it for the family to clean up, and we just got someone to clean it up."

Later, Frieda learned that it was actually a state-owned truck. It was there to pick up the bed frame, the mattress, the box spring, and a piece of Sheetrock cut out of the wall and deliver them to the lab as evidence.

Frieda continued to watch what was happening around her. She saw an officer come out of the house with a huge freezer bag full of prescription bottles. She spotted Raynella's youngest daughter, Katie, and asked her about her mother.

"Mom's not here. Maggie took her to the doctor," Katie said. "We can't stay here tonight. I think Mom will go to Maggie's house."

Frieda left the farm and went to visit Mayme. No one had

shared the news with her, and Mayme was waiting for her son to visit. He usually came by every morning and afternoon. He'd missed the early visit and now she was waiting for Dave's arrival. Frieda sat with her, chatting, trying to get her mind off of her son. Maybe Mayme needed to know what happened, but Frieda knew it wasn't her place to tell her.

No one was granting any credibility to Raynella's claim that Dave had taken his life. Peggy Rowe, Dave's ex-wife, was at her parents' house when Dave dropped by for a visit just a week before he died. She saw no signs of depression or dementia. He seemed to be in high spirits and was busy planning for events in the near future. Besides, she said, "Dave was a very proud man. He would not have committed suicide—particularly not like that."

Dave's good friend Gordon Armstrong hadn't seen any red flags, either, in the months leading to Dave's death. He, too, thought that suicide was impossible because of Dave's extreme dislike of guns. He talked to Detective Perry Moyers about his doubts that it was suicide.

Perry explained to him that three shots had been fired. Then he said, "Close your eyes."

"What?" Gordon asked.

"Close your eyes."

Gordon squeezed his eyes shut.

"Now," Perry said, "touch your finger to your nose."

Gordon brought up his finger and placed it on the spot.

"See," Perry said, "you ain't gonna miss."

"You don't believe that suicide story, either. Do you?" Gordon asked.

Perry simply smiled.

At the autopsy, law enforcement's suspicions were confirmed. Dave Leath's death could not have been a suicide.

When Gordon attended the memorial service for his friend, he was surprised to learn that Raynella had had Dave cremated. Even more shocking to Gordon was that Raynella had driven to Maryville and prepaid for the cremation while Dave was still alive. Gordon knew it wasn't Dave's idea; in fact, it was in direct violation of Dave's wishes. Dave had often expressed his religious conviction that cremation was wrong and that the cremated can't go to heaven.

Gordon also wasn't pleased by things that Raynella talked about that day. She said that Dave was not well and referred to herself as nothing more than Dave's "hood ornament." In light of the cremation, it seemed more like Dave was the one who was seen as an object in that relationship.

Gordon started collecting rumors about Raynella. The worse the stories made her look, the better he liked it. He said that when Raynella went to the post office, the woman behind the counter said, "Sorry to hear about your husband Dave."

Raynella supposedly responded, "Don't worry about it. I can get me another sucker."

In another anecdote, Gordon said that Raynella had told the receptionist at the doctor's office, "I can have you wiped out in a heartbeat. I'll dig a hole, put your body in it, put a dead cow on top of it, and no one will ever find you."

Although none of Gordon's stories could be confirmed, they clearly demonstrated his attitude toward his deceased friend's wife. He wanted to ask Raynella, "Why did you kill him? What reason do you got to kill him?" But he kept those thoughts to himself when he talked to the new widow.

Right after the funeral, she said, "I know you and Dave were best friends. You can have anything of his you want."

"I appreciate that, Raynella," Gordon said. "I can't think of anything but thanks anyway."

Gordon later regretted that response when he learned that Raynella made that offer to a lot of people but never made it to Dave's daughter Cindy. Raynella gave her a pair of his overalls, a matching jacket, and an old shirt—nothing else. Gordon said if he'd known that, he would have claimed much of Dave's personal property and given it to Cindy.

Cindy returned to work at the barbershop. Her chair now had even more significance with her father gone. She ran her hands across the back of the chair, thinking about the advice her father had always given her: "It'll be all right—just keep working." She was sad but proud to be working in the spot where her dad had taken care of customers for decades. She'd made one major change in the shop. Although Paul and Hoyt still only took care of men, Cindy had a few female customers.

Otherwise, not much had changed since Dave walked through the doors in 1965. They'd gotten a modern Coke machine, removed the once ubiquitous spittoons, and turned it into a nonsmoking establishment. There were still three barber chairs and across from them a line of comfortable brown armchairs where clientele waited their turn, talking about everything from the weather to world politics. The glowing blue ultraviolet boxes still hung on the wall over the sinks. Although the devices were there for the purpose of sanitizing the scissors and other equipment, customers jokingly called them "tanning booths."

Hoyt still told stories about the fish that got away. Businessmen found new clients chatting with others. And the red, white, and blue images of spiral poles were still painted on the outside walls of the shop. The three barbers would have loved to have had a real barber pole to hang there but hadn't been able to find one at a price they could afford.

After Dave's memorial service, there was one new item added to the décor. A cardboard box rested on top of the Coke machine. Inside were the ashes of David Leath.

With Dave gone, Mayme's well-being now rested in Cindy's hands. She and her mother, Peggy, continued to look for a better placement for her. On April 5 the arrangements were finalized. Mayme would move to another nursing home where she had friends. She was scheduled to be transferred there on Friday, April 11, 2003.

After work on April 10, Cindy stopped by to visit her grandmother. She was not allowed to go to her room. Raynella, who a month had earlier claimed she could not visit anyone in the hospital, was now a constant presence by Mayme's side. She blocked all visitors except for herself and the medical staff. Cindy was annoyed, but since Mayme would be moved the next day, she let it go.

But on that day, nearly one month after Dave's death, eighty-three-year-old Mayme Bailey Leath died at Fort Sanders Regional Medical Center's skilled nursing facility. She'd outlived her husband, both of her brothers, two of her sisters, and both of her children.

Cindy was perplexed. Mayme had not seemed all that sick. She had appeared to be improving. Gordon was certain he knew what happened. He convinced himself that, somehow, Raynella was responsible for the elderly woman's death.

Mayme's two grandchildren, Cindy Wilkerson and Bryan Hendrix, and her two great-grandchildren, Tyler and Lindsey Wilkerson, received friends from 6:00 until 8:00 p.m. at the Weaver Funeral Home on the one-month anniversary of Dave's passing. The Reverend Henry Lenoir was called once again to officiate over a Leath family funeral service on April 14.

On April 21, Raynella asked Cindy to meet her in the office of her lawyer, Charles Child. At Detective Moyers's request, Cindy wore a wire. The attorney told Cindy that her father's original will was missing. He said it was standard practice for thirty years for the original to be kept by the client and for the copy to be kept at his office.

However, Raynella could not find the original, and Child possessed the only copy. Child read that document out loud. Cindy and her children were excluded from everything. Cindy was not upset that she was left out of most of her father's estate, but she was surprised that the Leath homestead, which Mayme had deeded to Dave in 1993, was not passed along to her or to her children.

"The lawyer said he would not give me a copy because he could not find the original and no one would get a copy. And he said my father had come by his office a few days before he was killed and that he was upset or concerned about something in the will." Cindy could only wonder if that meant her dad wanted to include her but no record of the will or any activity concerning the Leath estate was recorded in probate court before her father's death. As sole beneficiary, Raynella was the only person who gained financially from David's death.

CHAPTER 30

Law enforcement investigators are fond of following the money trail, because it often leads to the perpetrator of a homicide. They already had suspicions that Raynella had killed her second husband. When they learned about the situation surrounding the will, they looked at the widow with even more scrutiny.

Investigator Perry Moyers began receiving phone calls from Raynella's former nursing students. They didn't identify themselves, not wanting their names mentioned even to law enforcement. They were afraid of their former instructor. They said she was very controlling and everyone knew not to cross her. One past student said, "I'm afraid I'll be next."

The investigators were in an awkward position. They were not able to plead their case to the prosecutors in their jurisdiction. The Tenth Judicial District attorney general's office was an hour away and priorities were not always the same in the two districts.

District Attorney General Jerry Estes assigned Bill Reedy and Chuck Pope to be in charge of the case. In June 2003, subpoenas were obtained for presentation of evidence to a grand jury, but nothing more was done. When Reedy left office to go into private practice and Pope retired, the panel still had not been convened to consider charges.

On February 8, 2005, almost two years later, the homicide of David Leath remained an open case. Frustration mounted. Many wondered if Raynella's social and political influence was protecting her from prosecution.

Cindy called Steve Walker to get all the details about his near-fatal run-in with Raynella. Steve advised her, "If you want to live, you'd better leave it alone."

However, Cindy couldn't just leave it alone. Frustrated with the lack of activity, she wrote to District Attorney General Estes: "My family continues to anguish and suffer over this tragic loss. Our sadness is compounded at each family gathering, holiday, birthday, and anniversary of this murder. My children are now growing up without their grandfather because of this unusually cruel and cowardly act . . . We mark each anniversary of his passing with a tremendous amount of grief and sorrow, knowing that he will never be here to share life's experiences with us.

"As we approach the second anniversary of my father's murder, I need assurances from your office that the case is still a high priority and is receiving the attention that it deserves . . . I seek your commitment, as the people's advocate, that his murderer will indeed be brought to justice . . . I am therefore respectfully requesting that your office provide my family with a current update on the progress of the investigation at your earliest conveniences."

After the *Knoxville News Sentinel* reported that Cindy's letter had gone unanswered for more than a month, Tenth judicial district attorney general Jerry Estes paid attention. He arranged a meeting with his chief assistant Sandra Donaghy and the prosecutor assigned to the case, Chal Thompson, on April 17. In addition to Cindy, Investigator Perry Moyers of the Knox County Sheriff's Office and Cindy's attorney James MacDonald attended the hour-and-a-half meeting.

Afterward, Cindy said, "I feel a little better about it now. They told me the investigation was still ongoing and that it

was not being swept under. I thanked them for getting back
with me." She wished they had provided more concrete information, but for now she was grateful for their assurances.

On May 11, 2005, Raynella, her brother, Marcus, and her
sisters Floanna and Robyn lost their mother, Annie Irene
Owens Large. She died in her home after a short illness.
Three days later, at noon, the siblings stood by their father,
Dewey, to receive friends at the Weatherford Mortuary in
Oak Ridge. They then traveled to the Solway United Meth-
odist Church for Annie's funeral service, which the obituary
described as "a praise and prayer celebration."

The final stop for the mourners was the Oak Ridge Memorial Gardens. There was a graveside service and a sharing of "final blessings" as they bid Annie adieu. She did not
live to see her second daughter turned into a public spectacle.

In early 2006, prosecutor Chal Thompson resigned from the
attorney general's office to run for the office of public defender. The forward progress on the David Leath case once
again ground to a halt. This time Cindy took more decisive
action. On March 2, 2006, Cindy filed a lawsuit against
Raynella Dossett Leath, claiming that she had either killed
David Leath or had him killed. The document stated that
Cindy "maintains that her father, David R. Leath, was feloniously shot and killed by . . . Raynella Dossett Leath, or by a
person or persons acting on her behalf."

It was not a wrongful-death suit, since it did not seek compensation for David's death. Instead, it cited a state law forbidding anyone from profiting from a death for which they
are responsible. The suit sought to void Raynella's inheri-
tance of any of David's property or assets, including the 164
acres at 3031 Solway Road, the Dossett farm property, and
another sixteen acres at 3511 Leath Lane that had been in
the Leath family for some time.

Cindy's attorney, James MacDonald also filed a lien to

block transfer of any of the real estate until the lawsuit is settled. He told reporters, "Obviously, at this point, it is all a circumstantial evidence case. We are just in the beginning of our investigation. We look forward to developing the facts in the case."

Raynella's attorney, James A.H. Bell, fired back, "Raynella Dossett Leath did not kill David Leath; she loved David, and she certainly had no one acting on her behalf to cause his death. The way this complaint is worded, when closely read, is the reason why the public hates lawyers. It's almost scandalous. We will file an appropriate response within the time required by law. A motion for dismissal will obviously be the first grounds for relief."

CHAPTER 31

If James Alexander Hamilton Bell wanted to know why some people hated lawyers, he only had to look at his zealous defense of an unpopular cause. The case that rocketed him into national prominence was one that stirred emotions of outrage against his clients and, by extension, their lawyer.

Bell had represented Deborah Hamilton and her husband, Larry, the minister of the thirty-eight-member Church of God of the Union assembly in La Follette. The religion was founded by Kentucky restaurant owner Charles Thomas Pratt in 1921. They had congregations in Arkansas, Texas, Mississippi, Alabama, Illinois, Ohio, Kentucky, North Carolina, South Carolina, Georgia, and Tennessee.

The church doctrine allowed visits to a medical professional for wound suturing, tooth extraction, and bone setting, but that's where they drew the line at physical treatment. According to Rule 23, "all members of the church are forbidden to use medicine, vaccinations or shots of any kind but are taught by the Church to live by faith." The tenants of their Protestant sect also prohibited sleeveless dresses, coed swimming, drinking, smoking, hair curling, playing cards, and watching ball games or movies.

In July 1983, when the Hamilton's twelve-year-old daughter Pamela broke the femur bone in her leg, they took her to a physician. When, in the course of the treatment, her doctor discovered Ewing's sarcoma, a rare bone cancer in her thigh, the Hamiltons balked at any medical intervention.

They refused to allow treatment for Pamela's cancer because taking medicine was against their religion. They believed that God could heal their daughter on his own. If he did not, then it was God's will that she die.

The Tennessee Department of Human Services sued for custody of the girl in Campbell County Juvenile Court. Doctors testified that she would die without medical treatment—that every day that medical intervention was delayed lowered Pamela's chances for survival. Bell worked with her parents to delay Pamela's treatment as long as he could. "She wants the right to choose between a so-called miracle drug and her faith in God," Bell said.

After a two-month legal battle, the parties to the case appeared in court mid-September. Pamela came to the courtroom on crutches. The tumor on her leg was immense. Since the diagnosis, it had spread to cover her left leg from her knee to her hip.

She testified that she did not believe the doctors who said she would die: "I believe I can be healed without taking treatments and all that"; and besides, she said, she was ready to die "when the Lord gets ready for me."

The Reverend Larry Hamilton told the court, "I don't want her to undergo treatment, based on my religion and my rights to believe and live the way I want to."

Bell asked why he didn't want his daughter to undergo treatment. Larry said, "There's no need of medicine. The Bible plainly tells us that. Only God can heal."

"Will you tell us what kind of soul-searching you've gone through in reaching your decision?" Bell asked.

"She does not want it—" Larry began.

Bell cut him off. "Do you have an opinion yourself in the terms of the medical treatment?"

"Well, if they're going to give you something to make

you sick and your hair come out, it must not be too good for you. If they can't guarantee to heal you, why do it, because if a doctor were to tell me he had a medicine that would heal me, I'd go right there in just a minute, but there ain't none."

In contrast, medical testimony indicated that the child's cancer may have spread while the battle went through the courts. The delay could be deadly.

Judge Charles Herman said, "To allow Pamela Hamilton to go without treatment would be to allow her to die. It is the court's opinion that we have a state interest. Pamela Hamilton was a neglected child and the state had temporary custody."

James A.H. Bell wasted no time in seeking an appeal and preventing the child from receiving the necessary medical treatment. In minutes, he'd obtained a stay from the Tennessee Court of Appeals in Knoxville and a hearing set for the following week. The lawyer was quickly becoming a regular on the national television morning-talk-show circuit.

The appeals court ruling was swift. "Our constitution guarantees Americans more personal freedom than enjoyed by any other civilized society, but there are times when the freedom of the individual must yield. Where a child is dying with cancer and experiencing pain which will surely become more excruciating as the disease progresses, as in Pamela's circumstance, we believe, is one of those times when humane considerations and lifesaving attempts outweigh unlimited practice of religious beliefs.

"We, therefore, designate the Director of the Offices of Human Services in Knoxville or his successor in said office, to act for and on behalf of Pamela in consenting to necessary treatment, which treatment shall be at the direction and under the supervision of St. Jude's Children's Research Hospital and its staff. The Director will accede to and respect the wishes of the parents regarding Pamela to the extent that the treatment recommended by the physicians is not interfered with or impaired."

Again Bell wasted no time filing an appeal with the Tennessee Supreme Court. But this time he did not get a stay, and Pamela was checked into the hospital.

Dr. Frank Haraf addressed Pamela's medical condition at a news conference the following day. He said that her cancer was spreading. "Delay in treatment has definitely reduced her chance of cure." He added that at the time of her diagnosis, she had had a 75 percent chance of long-term survival. Now they placed her odds at 25 percent.

Pamela underwent seven days of chemotherapy to shrink the cancerous tumor on her leg. She was in the hospital for a week of rest and evaluation before the next round of treatment when the Tennessee Supreme Court declined to review the case.

At a news conference on the day of the denial, Bell vowed to take the fight to the United States Supreme Court. "We'll go elsewhere if need be," he said. "We're going to higher briars and bigger bears."

He played an audiotape of Pamela, obviously reading from a prepared statement. In it she said, "I am feeling and doing better, but I feel like it's because of prayers . . . I do not want to take the medicine they are giving me, but I am taking it because of the courts. I wish I could just go home and go to school and live my own life and believe what I believe . . . This is my decision . . . I believe God will heal me when he gets ready to heal me."

Bell declared to the gathered reporters that court-ordered treatment violated the family's constitutional right to freedom of religion and was an unlawful invasion of the girl's body. "It is tantamount to rape."

On January 19, the parents acknowledged that their daughter was improving after several rounds of chemotherapy and thirty-five radiation treatments. They dropped the legal battle. "Pamela assisted in making this determination and Mr. Hamilton concurred," attorney Bell said. "But they believe that God is causing her to get better. They do not believe it is the medicine."

He admitted, though, that with the improvement in Pamela's health, their position had weakened. "It would be a complete exercise in futility from a legal standpoint to pursue it further."

The legal furor reignited on March 29 when the Hamiltons filed a $15,000 lawsuit against the Tennessee Children's Hospital. Pamela's crutches had slipped, causing her to fall and break her cancer-weakened leg earlier in the year. Her bone had healed, but Larry Hamilton accused the hospital workers for negligence for allowing it to happen in the first place. "I'm going to get every dime I can out of them. I didn't ask for this," he told Tom Eblen of the Associated Press. He continued to insist that the experience only confirmed his beliefs about the power of faith and the evils of medicine. Faith had shrunk his daughter's tumor, he claimed. All medicine did was make her hair fall out.

By this time the large tumor had shriveled down to nothing more than a patch of scar tissue. In September the doctors could find no signs of cancer in her body.

However, the news the following January was not good. Pamela came to the hospital for a checkup. X-rays showed the presence of tumors on her lungs.

Pamela lapsed into a coma on the morning of March 29, 1985. The fourteen-year-old girl died that afternoon.

James A.H. Bell and Pamela's parents had engineered the delays that may have contributed to the child's death. With this case Bell made his bones and earned his detractors. Now a prominent attorney, he gathered clients at will. Among them was Brad Renfro, the ill-fated child actor who starred in the film version of John Grisham's *The Client* with Susan Sarandon and Tommy Lee Jones.

CHAPTER 32

The battle over David Leath's estate moved to probate court shortly after Cindy's lawsuit was filed. Raynella's attorney, James A.H. Bell, filed a copy of a 1996 will signed by David along with a petition to confirm it as valid and place Raynella in charge of the estate.

In response, Cindy's attorney, James MacDonald, filed an answer and counterclaim asserting that the inability to locate the will was evidence that the will had been revoked. The document also stated that Cindy should be the exclusive beneficiary and the only appropriate person to serve as the personal representative of her father's estate, since Raynella "comes into court with the most unclean of hands—bloody hands—which should bar her from having anything to do with the estate of her victim. The fact that the original will has not been located is evidence of the fact that it was revoked prior to Mr. Leath's death."

Both sides presented their cases in chancery court before Chancellor Daryl Fansler on August 17, 2006. MacDonald argued that the duplicate will found in Charles Child's office was irrelevant. The missing original created a legal presumption that the will had been revoked.

Raynella told the court that Dave began having health problems in 2000. "There were days where he could not or would not drive because he would get someplace and get lost."

Attorney Charles Child testified that he drew up the will in question, saying that his firm had done work for David Leath since 1973. He informed the court that David had signed two identical will documents and taken one with him. The will presented in evidence, he said, was the most recent one signed in his office. He added that David had returned about six weeks prior to his death to discuss the will. At the time David appeared emotionally upset about something in the will, but that it "was not revoked or changed."

Family friend Roger Yarnell said that Dave had never mentioned the will to him. However, he had expressed concerns about Mayme and the possibility that she might need permanent placement in a nursing home. "Raynella's a nurse, but I don't think she'd be able to take care of my mother," Dave told him.

When asked about Dave's deteriorating mental condition, Roger said, "I've seen or talked to Dave nearly every day after his retirement up till the day he died. I never saw any problems like that at all. I did occasionally notice a little slurring in his speech, but I thought that was because Dave chewed gum—nothing more than that."

Maggie Connaster took the stand and described the relationship between her mother and Dave as excellent. She added, "I knew Dave loved me and was proud of me."

Detective Perry Moyers informed the chancellor about the work in the Leath home after Dave's death. "The crime scene unit catalogues and photographs everything taken from the crime scene. They keep a log of all the people on the scene. Both Maggie Connaster and Cindy Wilkerson were there that day but neither one of them went into the bedroom. I did not see the will when I was there and the room was searched thoroughly. Dave Leath's will was not removed from the home." When asked, he admitted that he could not specifically state that all the drawers had been searched.

The owner of Hardin Valley Body Shop, Mark Ogle, testified that he was a close friend of Dave's nephew Bryan Hendrix but had known Dave since 1983. He didn't see Dave much in those early years but beginning in 2001, he saw Dave every month or so and worked on both his Ford roadster and his Chevy truck. In the last year of his life, Dave came to the body shop every week or two to hang out and shoot the bull. Mark never saw any signs that Dave was confused and never heard his speech slur.

Dave's daughter, Cindy, admitted that she had not been to the house many times after her father married Raynella. She also acknowledged that she was not aware of the will and had never discussed it with her dad.

Cindy's mother and Dave's ex-wife, Peggy Rowe, said, "I saw him at my parents' house about eight to ten times every year. The last time I saw him was a week before his death. I noticed nothing out of the ordinary in his demeanor or behavior. I never saw him confused. He always seemed to know and understand what he was doing."

Gordon Armstrong said that he had visited Dave regularly but hadn't seen him for a couple of weeks before he died. However, they had talked over the phone and made their weekly NASCAR wagers. "I never saw any confusion or memory problems. He was never late; in fact, he was usually early. I thought Dave was on top of it." He added that he believed the will was very important to Dave. He thought that if Dave had destroyed the will, he would have said something to him about it.

Neurologist Ronald Bryan testified next. He went through Dave's medical history and concluded, "David's dementia had advanced to the state where he was losing things and putting things in the wrong place by January 2003. I do not feel David would have been capable of exercising a will or understanding it at that time. There were times when he could not formulate his thoughts and had a blank expression on his face."

Chancellor Fansler said, "The only issue before this court is whether the will has been revoked or not. From a legal standpoint, the fact that the original that was given to David Leath and has not been found creates a legal presumption of revocation." He granted Cindy a continuance on the probate issue and indicated that he would not set a date until he learned more about the status of the circuit court lawsuit.

Back in that other courtroom, circuit court judge Wheeler A. Rosenbalm denied a motion by James A.H. Bell to require a more detailed complaint to be filed in the civil case. The judge ordered that the allegations in the lawsuit be formally answered within fifteen days. "It appears to the court that the defendant can quite easily frame a responsive pleading to the complaint. If she denies that she killed her husband or had someone kill him, she can simply deny those allegations."

He said that the complaint as filed "is legally sufficient to raise the question of whether the defendant has been guilty of such wrongdoing that she has forfeited her rights to inherit or receive property from her late husband. If those allegations are true, then the defendant forfeited all right to inherit or receive property from her husband unless she can show that his death was caused by an accident or an act of self-defense. If the defendant did not kill her husband or have him killed, then she would not be subject to the statue and no forfeiture would occur by reason of her husband's death."

Judge Rosenbaum also denied a motion by Bell to consolidate the case with a probate dispute in Knox County Chancery Court between Cindy and Raynella regarding who should have control over David's estate. "The outcome of this case will have no bearing" on a dispute over the validity of a duplicate original of a will, he said.

With those two doors slammed in her face, Raynella turned aggressive. She filed a countersuit on September 6. In the documents, Raynella "admits that David R. Leath was feloniously shot and killed but the defendant alleges that

David R. Leath was feloniously shot and killed by the plaintiff, Cynthia Wilkerson, or by person or persons acting on her behalf."

As Raynella presented her charges in the circuit court, she was not aware that a new district attorney general was prepared to resurrect the homicide prosecution in the death of David Leath.

CHAPTER 33

The election for a new Tenth Judicial District attorney general happened on August 3, 2006. The incumbent, Jerry Estes, in office since 1982, was not in the running. R. Steve Bebb and Steve Crump battled for the position. Bebb won and took office on September 1.

There were two cases sitting on his desk that Bebb believed needed immediate action. One was a triple homicide that happened on Valentine's Day 1999 and the other was the murder of David Leath. Less than two weeks after taking office, the new district attorney general met with Investigator Perry Moyers and put Richard Fisher in charge of the prosecution. They prepared to present their case to the grand jury in November.

On November 9, Raynella was in chancery court again. Chancellor Fansler conducted a hearing about the estate. He heard conflicting testimony and evidence on several matters, including David's health and mental capacity shortly before he was slain.

Gordon Armstrong, as a longtime family friend, testified that shortly after David Leath was killed, Raynella called him and asked him to retrieve the will from the home. At the time, Raynella was at Maggie's home and the sheriff's office was conducting an investigation at the crime scene. Soon after, Gordon received another call from Raynella rescinding her request.

Fansler said that he found Gordon's testimony compelling and believed that "Mrs. Leath made the call to him on the night of the killing; thus, she either believed the will still existed or wanted Mr. Armstrong to believe she did."

But that wasn't the worst news for Raynella that month. Bebb was having his way with the grand jury. They delivered an indictment in the Valentine's Day triple murder on November 16. On the afternoon of November 28, 2006, they considered the homicide of David Leath and issued an indictment charging Raynella Dossett Leath with premeditated murder.

Ed Dossett's family held their collective breaths. They wondered how long it would be before the investigators would take a serious look at Ed's death. Raynella's classmates at Oak Ridge High were in shock. The Raynella they read about in the newspaper was not the Raynella they knew. "Growing up, there wasn't a mean bone in her body," Jim Campbell said. "Things just don't add up."

The following morning, James A.H. Bell surrendered Raynella to the Knox County deputies. He insisted that Raynella "absolutely denies the offense and denies allegations from any witness that she committed the offenses in this case." He added that, in his opinion, "the possibility of conviction is very, very low."

Bell wanted his client released on her own personal recognizance. Bebb didn't mind a low bond, but he wasn't going to settle for no bond. Criminal court judge Richard Baumgartner set bail at $5,000 and scheduled no court dates.

Out of jail, Raynella turned again to the chancery court for a ruling from Chancellor Fansler. He did not make her day. On December 15 he announced that the copy of David's will was not valid, even though it was an exact duplicate of the original and signed in ink. He also noted that the quitclaim deeds that Dave had executed, thinking he was creating "tenancies by the entireties on his property"—the legal equivalent of "joint tenancy with survivorship" in other states that confer sole ownership on the surviving spouse—had not complied with the filing requirements and were invalid. Those decisions threw the estate into probate court as if there had never been a will, meaning that David's only child, Cindy Wilkerson, could claim at least half of the estate.

Raynella made an appearance in criminal court on January 11, 2007, regarding the charges she faced for the murder of her husband. She arrived at the arraignment with her two daughters, Maggie and Katie, and sat between them while waiting for her case to be called.

She stood before the craggy face, furrowed brow, and downturned mouth of Judge Richard Baumgartner and entered a not-guilty plea. The trial was set for September 10. Both the prosecution and the defense anticipated a weeklong trial.

The next month Raynella's attorney, Bell, subpoenaed telephone records for the month of David's death for the homes of Raynella and David Leath, Gordon Armstrong, and Maggie Connaster, as well as one unidentified cell phone.

Bell asked the judge to prohibit witnesses from reading or watching news accounts about the case because of his concern that media coverage was hampering Raynella's chances for a fair trial. "The media has continued to issue explosive reports regarding this case and this defendant. These reports contain allegations of facts which could greatly influence the testimony of any witness against the defendant. It is the grave concern of the defendant that should one witness be allowed to hear or otherwise learn of the testimony of another, whether in the courtroom or through the press, subsequent testimony will be altered, prejudicing her defense and potentially violating her federal and state constitutional rights."

Bell also filed motions to have prosecutors disclose any evidence that could clear Raynella from complicity in her husband's death and to reveal the names of any "informatives [*sic*] or operatives" the state was using in its case.

On July 6, the attorneys gathered before the judge again. This time the scheduled date of the trial moved ahead to February 4, 2008. The prosecution issued subpoenas to three physicians at the Parkwest Medical Center for Raynella's medical records.

Bell subsequently filed a motion to quash the subpoenas or, alternatively, to order that anything produced by them be squashed. "This request is made in order to protect the defendant's privacy as legislated by the Health Insurance Portability and Accountability Act of 1996. The defendant asserts her right to object to the disclosure of her protected health information pursuant to HIPAA." He alleged that the circumstances required for judicial or law enforcement obtaining these records didn't exist in this case.

In another motion, Bell listed nineteen items he needed to see or have examined for the defense, including the missing portion of his client's personal appointment calendar for his client: the pages for the week of David's death were not in the book. Other items on the list were the Colt revolver found at the scene, the bullet fragments from David's body, and the empty pistol holster and the fingerprint tests for that holster. "We have a forensic report from the Tennessee Bureau of Investigation that indicates . . . fragments of bullets found in David Leath's head were fired from that pistol," Bell said. "But there is no chain of custody documentation for this weapon or for any other evidence . . . We request the gun and bullet fragments for independent analysis" and "we request copies of these latent prints and the holster for independent examination."

CHAPTER 34

Back in August 2006, Dr. Sandra Elkins, the woman who replaced Dr. Randall Pedigo as Knox County medical examiner, met with Knox County mayor Mike Ragsdale, county finance director John Werner, and senior community services director Cynthia Smith. She lodged complaints against the University Pathologists group and requested that an independent audit of the improper use of county employees for forensic work in death investigations outside of Knox County.

They agreed to take action but then everything stalled. Elkins filed a complaint about another matter in June 2007. She alleged that nine-year veteran Trooper Marty Nix of the Tennessee Highway Patrol fraudulently checked out photographs from the medical examiner's office. The death of one of the trooper's friends had been ruled accidental, caused by head injuries incurred in a fall. The son of the deceased had asked Nix to review the file and give him a second opinion.

Nix showed up at Elkins's offices in uniform. He gave every impression that he was there in an official capacity. Later, Elkins learned he was doing a favor for a friend and reported him.

Nix was put on paid leave while the charge was investigated. His cruiser was searched and more wrongdoing was discovered. In the trunk they found photos and negatives of a naked woman and a package of crack cocaine that the trooper had seized in an arrest more than a year earlier. He disavowed the photos and deemed his failure to turn in the drugs as an oversight.

Also investigated was a complaint by a Loudon County deputy who searched the home of Nix's brother Mark and arrested him for resisting arrest and possession of drug paraphernalia. According to the trooper, Nix cursed him out.

In October of that year, after investigations of four violations, the Tennessee Highway Patrol suspended Marty Nix for fourteen days without pay. His attorney, James A.H. Bell, appealed the decision, calling it a "Mickey Mouse case." He told reporters: "It's a sackful of baloney that's spoiled. If it didn't cost Marty so much to defend himself, this case would be comical."

Within months, no one would be laughing when the second Knox County medical examiner in a row ran off the rails of acceptable behavior.

David's demise wasn't the only suspicious death in Raynella's life. Investigators and the prosecutors now looked at the circumstances surrounding the death of her first husband, Ed Dossett. On December 4, 2007, Sixth Judicial District attorney general Steve Bebb filed a petition seeking to exhume the body of Ed Dossett for a "full and complete post mortem examination."

He argued that "since the death of William Edward Dossett, his widow, Raynella Dossett-Leath has been indicted for the murder of her subsequent spouse, David Leath . . . Similarity of evidence in the two deaths, including evidence of drug overdose in both victims; the two deaths under highly suspicious circumstances . . . and similar motives in the two deaths (greed) are reasons that actuate" this request.

Dr. Randy Pedigo, medical examiner at the time, provided a supplemental affidavit. "I went to the scene and was present at the autopsy and signed the death certificate as an agricultural accident. I did so without the benefit of the toxicology report that did not arrive until several weeks after the burial. There was no X-ray of the head and neck and no external appearance of death-causing injuries on the body." He added that "the toxicology report showed a level of morphine that is alarmingly high and near lethal, even for a person who has been on morphine for some time. It has come to my attention that the deceased had an implanted morphine pump that metered a predetermined dosage to the patient. The device was not detected in autopsy and its recovery and examination could help explain the unusual circumstances of how the deceased was killed. Recovery of the morphine pump and further examination of the body, including examination of the head and neck, could assist law enforcement authorities to determine the cause of death of William Edward Dossett. It is my opinion that the interests of justice require an exhumation of the body."

Douglas Wilson, the medical doctor who served as prosector—the individual responsible for the actual dissection—during Ed's autopsy, also filed an affidavit. He concurred that "an exhumation was appropriate under the facts as they exist."

The current Knox County deputy medical examiner, Darinka Mileusnic-Polchan, provided the lengthiest affidavit in support of the petition. In her affidavit she wrote that "Mr. Dossett's demise by being trampled by cattle is not only unusual and bizarre, but is highly suspicious and not supported by the records of the limited autopsy performed at the time of his death." She stated that the toxicology report showed a level of morphine "so extraordinarily high, it is unlikely that any human could walk or continue to live . . . It would be extremely difficult for a person in his state of medication to be conscious, much less able to walk or observe a herd of cattle."

She pointed to the presence of drugs in the body of

Raynella's second husband: "On March 14, 2003, I performed an autopsy on David Leath. The findings clearly indicated that a homicide occurred by a gunshot wound to the head . . . Toxicology reports indicate that Dave Leath had drugs in his system: pethidine (meperidine), norpethidine (normepuridine), doxepin and promethazine. These drugs would have affected his alertness and ability to defend himself. A review of David Leath's medical history, from the records now available, does not indicate that he was prescribed these medications. It is my opinion that a complete autopsy of William Edward Dossett would assist law enforcement authorities to determine the cause of death . . . and could provide evidence of homicide . . . I believe the interests of justice require an exhumation."

CHAPTER 35

Raynella and her attorney James A.H. Bell wasted little time responding to that petition. Three days later she voiced her objection. Bell argued that "the District Attorney General may petition a criminal court judge to order a body disinterred and an autopsy performed . . . [only] when two conditions are met. First, the death must have occurred under circumstances indicating homicide, suicide, a violent, unnatural or suspicious death. Second, the body was interred before an autopsy could be performed. The State's Petition fails to meet either one or both of these statutory conditions."

He concluded: "The District Attorney General has stated that it is his intent to use any evidence obtained from the disinterment of William Edward Dossett to assist in the prosecution of Raynella Dossett Leath for the alleged murder of David R. Leath. As a matter of law, this reasoning is legally insufficient to allow for the disinterment . . . The next of kin further objects to the Petition on the grounds it amounts to an abuse of corpse and is an insult to the dignity of the family to disinter Mr. Dossett fifteen years after his passing when an autopsy was performed prior to his interment."

All parties gathered before criminal court judge Richard Baumgartner for arguments from the state. Prosecutor Richard

Fisher said he understood the seriousness of the request but argued: "It's more important to determine whether Ed Dossett was murdered. We need to disinter him. We need to see."

Bell and Raynella's other lawyer, William Hood, said there was no justification for the disinterment at this late date. Hood said, "We have an autopsy performed by the medical examiner that says the death was an agricultural accident."

Judge Baumgartner asked, "Are you suggesting that even if it's established that this was a partial, neglected, or fraudulent autopsy that closes the door to a subsequent autopsy?"

"Yes," said Hood. "That's a totally separate issue."

Ed Dossett's daughters, Maggie and Katie, were at the hearing with their lawyer, Luis Bustamente. He told the judge, "Leave the body alone. . . . They have ample information to pursue whatever angle they want."

Bell added, "It's unthinkable. It's an abomination. The dead should be left dead unless there is a compelling reason."

Raynella wiped away tears and held on to Bell's hand as she listened to the prosecution's arguments.

The judge said he'd issue his ruling on January 18. He could decide one of three ways: to open the grave, to leave the corpse buried, or to hold another hearing complete with testimony from witnesses.

To bolster the prosecutor's petition, Deputy Medical Examiner Mileusnic-Polchan submitted a supplemental affidavit that went into more detail about the injuries to Ed Dossett's body. "The sternal fracture and several broken ribs are not fatal injuries. As a matter of fact . . . [they] are frequent iatrogenic injuries from resuscitation. Some patients are more prone to this type of fracture such as women, elderly and individuals with chronic, debilitating diseases, cancer being one of them . . . Absence of the external injury associated with this 'trauma' convinces me that [the injuries were caused by the medical treatment he received on the scene] . . .

"Mr. Dossett's blood morphine level of .64 micrograms/

milliliter is clearly much higher than what is reported in the literature. Several other questions need to be answered. What was Mr. Dossett's therapeutic blood morphine level supposed to be? Is such a high morphine concentration in Mr. Dossett's blood compatible with the terminal event and his actions described by family members? Obviously not."

She concluded, "Limited scene investigation describing the terminal event, overinterpretation, and misinterpretation of autopsy findings as well as disregarded toxicology results are all inconsistent with the cause and manner of death as listed in Mr. Dossett's death certificate."

On January 18, the state and the attorneys for the Dossett girls and Raynella Leath stood before the bench of Judge Richard Baumgartner. Special prosecutors Richard Fisher, Joseph "Mac" McCoin, and Cynthia LeCroy-Schemel—the lawyers in charge of presenting the case against Raynella for the death of her second husband, David Leath—told the judge that the two cases bear several similarities. The main medical similarity was the presence of drugs in both at the time of death: morphine in Dossett and, in Leath, several other types of drugs for which David had no prescription and that could affect his central nervous system. As a nurse, prosecutors believe that Raynella would have access to these drugs.

They called their chief witness, Deputy Medical Examiner Darinka Mileusnic-Polchan. Baumgartner asked her to refer to the affidavit she provided to the court and asked, "It shows, as I recall, an extremely high level of morphine within Dr. Dossett's system, basically double . . . the high end of the therapeutic level . . . Is that correct?"

"Actually, that's correct. It's more than double, definitely," Dr. Mileusnic-Polchan answered.

"And also at the original autopsy they were not aware of the fact that there was even a morphine pump implanted in his system; is that correct?"

"Yes."

"Can you tell me how a morphine pump that's actually implanted in the patient's body . . . works?"

"Every pump's different and modern pumps are definitely arranged and set differently than the old pump . . . That's one of my questions: . . . what kind of pump he exactly had because from the medical records . . . I couldn't really gather enough information to tell me . . . and I haven't been able to contact the physician who implanted the pump."

"Even with technological advances with regard to how those things work, are those things that you self-activate or are those things that activate automatically on a given time frame?" the judge asked.

"It can be done both ways."

"If it was set . . . so that a dose was to be administered every thirty minutes, for instance . . . could a patient override that and manually administer a dose in addition . . . ?"

"That can be done," the doctor acknowledged. "It can be the patient or somebody close to the patient."

"So either Mr. Dossett or someone else . . . could have actually activated it manually to increase the dosage to the body?"

"I don't know what kind of pump it was. I assume that to be a yes answer, yes."

"If you were to perform an autopsy today, what would you learn that you don't know about the pump now?"

"The first thing that concerned me when I was approached with the question 'Is there anything in this particular case that could help us with the subsequent case,' my answer was that whatever is in the death certificate and whatever I see in the autopsy and the photographs doesn't really correspond to what I would call the cause of death because the chest trauma was not sufficient to be the cause of death.

"Basically, we had a death certificate that did not reflect the true state of the matter, as far as cause and manner of death are concerned," Dr. Mileusnic-Polchan explained. "Right there, I couldn't really offer much help because, as I said, the cause of death . . . in the death certificate is not what I would call it based on photographs. But the photographs and the autopsy report are not good enough to render a safe opinion to the cause and manner of death. Toxicology's definitely a concern. There's no question about it, and I would lean towards this cause of death being related to the toxicology intoxication of morphine."

"Say that again—that last sentence," the judge requested.

"The toxicology's concerning enough that I would lean toward the cause of death being intoxication of morphine rather than any other cause of death," the doctor said. "But, then again, how the pump was set and whether something happened to the pump and potential use of the pump around the time of death, I cannot answer those questions."

"If you were to do the subsequent autopsy . . . would you anticipate that the pump would be in some form that you could make a reasonable examination of it?" Judge Baumgartner asked.

"I don't know."

Baumgartner considered that forthright answer, then asked, "Of what benefit would a subsequent examination of the body be?"

"One is going to consider the toxicology the main cause of the death, especially if you are going to answer the realm of whether it's accident, suicide, homicide—because we don't have assisted suicide, it's a homicide, basically. Then the safe thing would be to collect any potential residual specimen whether it's bone marrow or anything that is soft tissue remaining still on the body that possibly can be tested and ascertained whether we're dealing with the true positive result because one positive result does not necessarily mean one hundred per cent the cause of death. It has to be confirmed."

"So, in other words, you're saying that you may be able to

find that this level of morphine may be higher or lower than was actually shown on the toxicology report?"

"That's correct," Mileusnic-Polchan replied, nodding.

"Is, in fact, any soft tissue going to be remaining after fifteen years period of time?"

"It really varies. There are cases that are perfectly preserved bodies. There are cases of skeletonized bodies. That's hard to predict. It depends on the soil, on the embalming—how well it was embalmed—on the weather conditions, on many factors."

They discussed the different methods of measuring drug levels and then the judge asked, "How are you going to know by how that level of morphine got into his body . . . whether the pump was operating properly, whether it was activated manually by him, whether it was activated manually by somebody else? I mean, how can you possibly make that determination?"

"The determination—when it comes to . . . who administered and how—would actually be a combination of the autopsy and the investigation. Forensic autopsy does not stand by itself. It has to be linked to thorough . . . scene investigation. Obviously, that really wasn't done in this case."

Baumgartner moved on to a different concern. "Another thing that struck me . . . is that Mr. Dossett suffered from this carcinoma that was terminal. How do we know that it just wasn't the carcinoma that finally killed him?"

"The carcinoma would eventually kill him hadn't the different event intervened. But the probability with this particular cancer—yes, it's locally invasive—but it didn't spread to that extent to prevent all the vital functions, meaning that he had local metastasis in the abdomen but . . . it . . . didn't really spread . . . to the rest of the organs, lungs and heart . . . And then there is another issue with the autopsy. The head was never examined and opened. How do we know really what we missed or didn't miss for that matter? . . . That's why I said there are too many deficiencies for me to give a simple answer."

The judge questioned Dr. Mileusnic-Polchan about the X-rays that had been misplaced and recently found. The doctor said that she'd brought them with her but was not pleased with their quality. "The X-ray's not really gold standard—it's not necessarily good enough to tell us exactly whether there's anything like a base of the skull fracture, easily missed in an X-ray. And the state of the brain? That cannot be ascertained based on the X-ray, and there was not sufficient neck section."

"Do you know from the X-rays now that there's no blunt force trauma to the head?"

"The postmortem X-rays are not good enough . . . I cannot really say with certainty, looking at the X-ray, that there was no head trauma."

"Can you say with certainty that there's no gunshot wound?"

"Most likely, there's no gunshot wound, yes."

"Can you say for certainty that there's no fracture to the skull?"

"No. As I said, the basal skull fractures can be easily missed on the X-ray."

The judge moved on to another subject in the doctor's affidavit. "You said that some of the photographs that were taken of the body, particularly the lower extremities, are not consistent with footprints or foot impressions from a cow. Having been a cow person myself, I'm kind of curious about how you arrive at that conclusion. I mean, how can you tell that a contusion or evidence of trauma to an extremity is not caused by a . . . cow stepping on you?"

"That's an excellent question and I'm glad you're addressing it, because one of the main issues . . . is [whether it's] the trampling or stampede of a cow. Number one, there's not enough chest trauma to kill this person so we have to look for a different cause. Now, the main trauma that has been described in the autopsy report are these different marks on the legs . . . The primary site of the injury are the legs that we all know won't kill the person.

"So now let's look for the pattern . . . Stated in the report, there is a hoof mark on the body. Well, there is really no hoof mark on the body . . . The autopsy photographs were very, very poor quality that I cannot really tell what's there and what's not there . . . In forensic pathology, forensic field patterns are very important. They might seem sometimes silly or unimportant to us, but they are important . . . If we're going to allege a certain mechanism, we better show that it's there, and it's just not there."

"When you say, 'It's just not there,' you mean it's just not there on the upper body or the lower extremities?"

"There's certainly nothing of the upper body that I can say is sufficient trauma to kill him . . . When the autopsy report mentioned hoof mark, then you better show it to me, so objectively, everybody looking at that picture can tell, yes, this is a hoof mark. Well, there's not. And I'm just referring to the presence or absence of the pattern. Therefore, if it's there, show it to me objectively so that whoever's reviewing the autopsy twenty years later can agree with that statement."

The judge had a problem with that statement about the evidence of trauma to an extremity: "It doesn't seem to me that a hoof mark would be distinguishable from the use of a rock or a baseball bat or some other items that could cause the same kind of trauma. I mean, you're not going to have an imprint of a cow foot on your leg," he said.

"I'm glad you're mentioning it, because that's what the original autopsy report mentioned," the doctor said. "I didn't come up with that."

"But doesn't that also come from history . . . given at the time . . . by the individual that—"

Mileusnic-Polchan cut him off. "But see, history has to match the autopsy and if it doesn't, then we have a problem. We have to search further."

The judge questioned the meaning of iatrogenic injuries. The doctor explained that they were not uncommon autopsy artifacts when patients who are older or ill after resuscitation attempts. The judge then asked, "Are you aware of any evidence that there was any effort to resuscitate Mr. Dossett?"

"There was evidence that there was resuscitation attempted . . . in the tracheal tube and there was an IV or intravenous line in place. Now, how much and how intense that resuscitation was, I don't know. The only thing that I can say is that in one of the photographs of the autopsy there was a focus of hemorrhage under the chest bone . . . There's absolutely no description anywhere in the autopsy report to the extent or depth of all these injuries . . .

"So we have discord between what's mentioned in this final diagnosis and what's described in the autopsy report . . . The autopsy does mention that the patient was on blood thinner. That could cause easy bleeding, and therefore, someone on a blood thinner, you would expect exuberant bleeding from serious injury that's going to cause that. But he doesn't have that."

They went back and forth about other superficial injuries, with the judge wondering if the injuries could have been caused if Dossett was grazed by a hoof or leg. "Well, sure," the doctor said, "but then again, is that enough to kill an adult person, given the fact that he does have cancer but he's not dying from the cancer at this particular point?"

"And the morphine level wouldn't affect that, either?"

"Well, the morphine level. He wouldn't be actually walking in the pasture by himself to begin with. So we're going back to the scene. Where the body was placed originally at the scene, is that consistent with what we are finding in his body? Is that consistent with the story given? That's part of the investigation that had to be more thorough."

"If you were called upon to testify, would it be your testimony, within a reasonable degree of medical certainly, that Mr. Dossett . . . was not personally ambulatory and able to walk into the pasture?" Judge Baumgartner asked.

"With this level of morphine, I would say, no," Dr. Mileusnic-Polchan said.

"So it's your position that somebody else had to put him there?"

"Take him, yes."

The judge turned to the Leath autopsy, asking if the doctor had performed that procedure.

"I did do that autopsy and that's why I was asked to see if there's anything in this particular case, because personally, I'm not really interested in the Dossett case . . . However, when I was asked, 'Is there anything in this case that potentially can help us with the Leath case,' I felt obliged to say, 'I'm going to look into it and see how much I can say."

Judge Baumgartner went straight to the point. "What is it that you can do by performing an autopsy on Mr. Dossett at this point in time that's going to aid you in the prosecution of the Leath case?"

Referring to David Leath, she said, "There was some medication present in his body that was not supposed to be." She went on to confirm that she was leaning toward a diagnosis that the cause of Dossett's death was morphine intoxication.

"These drugs in Mr. Leath's body, I want to ask you what they were and what effect they had on a body," the judge said.

Dr. Mileusnic-Polchan described the pharmaceuticals as opiates and metabolites, each with an additive effect causing depression of the central nervous system.

"Do you know how these drugs were administered? In other words, were they taken orally? Were they injected intravenously? Do we know that?"

"No, we don't," Dr. Mileusnic-Polchan said.

"You would not be able to tell by an autopsy if someone had intravenous injection?

"I look for needle punctures, and in this case there was no resuscitation done. I don't recall observing any needle punctures, but [one] can miss some secret needle punctures somewhere in the skull. That's possible, but I didn't find any evidence of that."

"Would it be your reasonable conclusion that these were taken orally?"

"Yes."

The judge then questioned the doctor about the similarities between the drugs found in Leath's body and the morphine in Dossett's body. She said that they all affected the central nervous system but she could not recall the levels in Leath's body; however, she knew that they were not high enough to be toxic. The doctor agreed with the judge that Leath definitely died from a gunshot wound but that Mr. Dossett did not.

"Again, I'll ask you this question," the judge said. "With regard to aiding you in the prosecution in the Leath matter . . . what do you think that you can find by doing a subsequent autopsy of Mr. Dossett that would aid you in the prosecution of Mr. Leath?"

"Can I just clarify something?" the doctor interjected. "Actually, I'm not conducting any kind of prosecution myself. I just happened to be involved in the Leath case as the medical examiner."

"I understand," he said. ". . . But the crucial question today is: What is an autopsy that you do today going to do that's going to aid you or potentially aid you?"

"It depends on the condition of the body."

Judge Baumgartner asked, "So, is it fair to say that it's pure speculation?" The attorneys at the state's table cringed at hearing that last word.

"I don't know the answer, so I guess you may call it speculation," Dr. Mileusnic-Polchan admitted.

The lawyers for Raynella Dossett and her two daughters repeated their arguments that the exhumation would be nothing more than abuse of a corpse and an insult to the dignity of the family.

Judge Baumgartner said, "I'm going to need as much information as I can have before me. I take very seriously a request to disinter a body. You are going to have to convince me that something of substance will be accomplished." But the judge did open another door for the state. He said that if they wanted an autopsy for a purpose beyond David Leath's case—for example, to determine if Dossett's death was a homicide—that "is another matter altogether."

The judge put the prosecution in an uncomfortable catch-22 situation: they suspected a second autopsy would prove something but needed to perform the autopsy in order to find out. Richard Fisher promised the judge that they would provide further legal briefs on their original similarities with Leath in their request as well as file a second petition on the additional basis mentioned.

Baumgartner tabled the exhumation decision until February 15, when everyone would return to the court. While waiting for the resolution of this issue, Raynella's trial, which was set for February, was removed from the docket.

The state wanted an autopsy of Ed Dossett before they took the widow to court. Some of the comments made by the judge that day made them wonder if that would be possible.

CHAPTER 36

On January 2008, medical examiner Dr. Sandra Elkins wrote a letter to the Knox County Commission. "My physical health has degraded to the point I must take a medical leave of absence," she wrote. She blamed the stress of a two-year battle over charges she had brought against the University Pathologists group.

In her letter, she accused Dr. Stuart Van Meter, the president of University Pathologists and chief of the University of Tennessee pathology department, of harassing and intimidating her to drop her complaints. When she refused to withdraw her allegation, he fired her, she claimed.

Reporters resurrected her past abuse of drugs and asked her attorney, James A.H. Bell, if there was any connection to drug use and the need for medical leave. Bell declined to comment on that issue but did have something to say about Elkins's charge that the pathology group was profiteering from autopsies performed by Knox County employees.

"The complaints that have been lodged have been the subject of intense discussions and have been made known to the Knox County Law Department and they have made due diligence in trying to resolve this matter," Bell said. "Dr. Elkins fully intends on resuming her duties upon her return."

Sandra Elkins destroyed that hope on February 18, 2008.

According to local news sources, Larry Vineyard, an investigator with the medical examiner's office grew concerned about Elkins when she "made comments that she would kill herself and threatened the lives of a couple of coworkers." Vineyard got a pair of Knoxville Police Department officers to go with him to the doctor's Cherokee Bluff condominium.

When they arrived, Elkins ran off, searching under her bed and beneath other furniture and objects. Officer Guy Smith asked, "What are you looking for, ma'am?"

"I'm trying to find my gun to shoot you in the back of the head," the doctor said.

The officers immediately put her in restraints and took her down to the patrol car. They suspected mental health issues were at play and drove straight to the hospital. On the way there, Elkins said, "If I was uncuffed, I would shoot you."

That evening the police department spokesperson said, "Obviously, there appears to be some kind of mental issue. She is, in fact, getting treatment, and that's probably where we'll end it. That is typically how similar situations are handled, regardless of who is involved."

Attorney Bell told the *Knoxville News Sentinel*: "There has been ongoing dialogue with my office and the county law department about the Knoxville police report regarding Dr. Elkins. Both offices are trying to puzzle through these matters in order to create a professional path for the future."

A couple of months later, Dr. Elkins failed to show for a hearing with the Knox County Commission about her job. They voted unanimously to terminate her contract. Four weeks later, acting medical examiner Dr. Darinka Mileusnic-Polchan was awarded the contract to replace Elkins.

CHAPTER 37

The same month, the state submitted a new disinterment request focused on the need to uncover how Ed Dossett had died. In their filing, they claimed: "A complete autopsy is expected (a) to establish the cause of death to be an overdose of morphine administered by a person or persons with the intent to kill William Edward Dossett, (b) to eliminate the cause of death to be as designated on the death certificate and the autopsy protocol, and (c) to provide evidence of a homicide with further investigation which will be submitted to a Knox County Grand Jury for consideration."

They also provided the judge with an explanatory memorandum arguing for the inclusion of Dossett's death as evidence in Raynella's trial for the murder of David Leath. In the latter, they listed the similarities in the Leath and Dossett homicides. Both men were married to Raynella and died prematurely. The widow was the only person with known access to both victims at the times of their deaths and the last person believed to have seen them alive. The state maintained that she falsely reported both deaths—one as suicide, the other as an accident. At the time of each death, Raynella did not appear emotional or distraught.

Raynella, they claimed, had a financial interest in both deaths and executed an elaborate, planned cover-up or alibi.

She was an RN, a former head of nursing, with a working knowledge of the Schedule II drugs found in the bodies of both men. Finally, there was a looming, obvious illness in Ed Dossett and a supposed one—Alzheimer's or stroke—in David Leath.

The attorneys for Raynella and the Dossett's daughters submitted a response on February 13. James Bell wrote: "The state has offered nothing other than simple conclusions and speculative theories rather than hard evidence that [Raynella Dossett Leath] profited by the death of both. Moreover, what is glaringly absent from the state's assertion is that [she] had a financial need [that] motivated [her] to kill both Mr. Dossett and Mr. Leath.

"This renewed effort by the state is tantamount to an attempt to disturb the peace and dignity of a well-respected and loved man. The entire family objects to this repeated effort to disinter their husband, their father, their beloved."

Luis Bustamante, representing Maggie and Katie wrote: "Out of respect for the memory of their father and the sincere feelings of his next of kin . . . those . . . interests substantially outweigh the dubious proof that disinterment and a second autopsy will furnish probative evidence that their mother's criminally responsible for their father's death."

Judge Baumgartner handed down his order on the day Dr. Elkins was taken to the hospital. In doing so, he wrote: "There are some similarities" in circumstances surrounding the deaths of David Leath and Edward Dossett "but when you look at the differences . . . there is no way in the world [that] they are similar enough to warrant an exhumation."

The order stated: "The court concludes that even it if could be proven Raynella Dossett Leath was responsible for the death of William E. Dossett, that evidence would not be admissible . . . in the present prosecution of defendant Leath. Therefore, the state's petition to disinter the body . . . and conduct a second autopsy for those purposes is denied."

On the petition to disinter for the purpose of establishing

a cause of death for Ed Dossett, Judge Baumgartner said, "At this point, there is no evidence that Mrs. Dossett Leath has committed any crime." He said that would rule on that matter at a later date.

If Bell's client was as innocent as he claimed, why did she fight so hard to prevent a second, thorough autopsy? Prosecutors suspected that she feared they might find evidence to tie her to the murder of Ed Dossett. But at least two of Ed's cousins had another theory. They did not believe Ed was in the casket. They thought Raynella had removed the body and disposed of it elsewhere to ensure that a second autopsy would never be done.

On February 27, Baumgartner ruled against the state's request. "A grave site is a sacred place and should not be disturbed unless it appears to be absolutely essential to the administration of justice. This court cannot conclude that the disinterment of Mr. Dossett's remains is justified or will lead to information already known or available from other sources."

The special prosecution team immediately began work on the draft for an appeal. They also considered taking the case to the grand jury without an autopsy. On July 29, they did. After hearing from three witnesses—Dr. Darinka Mileusnic-Polchan, Dr. Randy Pedigo, and Investigator Perry Moyers of the Knox County Sheriff's Office—the panel issued the magic words: "Raynella Dossett Leath . . . did unlawfully, intentionally, deliberately and with premeditation kill William Edward Dossett . . . against the peace and dignity of the State of Tennessee."

Raynella was arrested the following morning and released after posting a $25,000 bond at the Knox County Detention Center. Detective Moyer, now head of the new cold case unit, still maintained his role as lead investigator in the Leath homicide and now held that position for the Dossett death probe even though both were considered active rather than cold cases.

Special prosecutor Richard Fisher said that they were tabling their appeal of the denial of an autopsy and resubmitting the issue to the criminal court in light of the new indictment. James Bell filed noticed with the court that he would be representing Raynella against these charges as well. "We intend to, and will, plead not guilty to this charge and this office will fully and completely defend this case to ensure that justice flows like a mighty stream."

Friends of Ed Dossett now stepped forward to state that they never believed that Ed's death was an accident caused by his cattle. Talking to a reporter for the *Knoxville News Sentinel*, Chris Cawood, president of Ed's class in high school, summed up the sentiment of all of them: "Most of us were farm kids, too, and you don't get run over by cows when you know them unless they're in a confined area. So we thought something was probably happening that wasn't reported." He acknowledged that they were aware that Ed was dying of cancer, but the sudden death by an unexpected means shocked them all.

CHAPTER 38

That same month, Raynella's attorney was in federal court representing Johnnie "Bro" Martin, a man accused of funneling cocaine from Atlanta to Knoxville—a half million dollars' worth in one month's time. In a hearing before United States district magistrate judge C. Clifford Shirley, attorney James A.H. Bell pushed for a dismissal of charges against his client, alleging that Assistant U.S. Attorney David Jennings had hidden the possibility that Joe Cofer, a onetime University of Tennessee football star, would be called as a witness against his client.

To bolster this claim, Bell told the judge about a meeting he had in which Cofer revealed information that could impact Martin's case. "It was around ten o'clock in the morning. Mr. Cofer was in my office dressed in a plaid shirt. We talked about his graying hair, how much weight he had put on, talked about his kids. One of his children from Alabama was with him . . . He was wearing brand-new tennis shoes. He was wearing creased blue jeans. He was wearing his leather brown belt and I remember it."

That meeting in Bell's office, however, could not have happened because Cofer was in jail at the time. Cofer filed an affidavit claiming that he hadn't met with Bell since the

1980s, when the attorney had represented him on drug dealing charges.

Assistant U.S. Attorney Steve Cook brought this misrepresentation to the judge's attention, accusing Bell of lying and urging Judge Shirley to punish Bell to protect the integrity of the justice system. "What's epic here is he made a material misrepresentation of the fact. I don't know how Mr. Bell can come in here and do anything but admit it. It could not have happened."

Judge Shirley removed Bell as defense attorney for "Bro" Martin and set a contempt-of-court hearing for Bell the following month on charges that he had misbehaved in the judge's presence, obstructed justice, and made untrue representations in court filings and untrue statements in open court.

At the hearing, Bell said, "When I'm wrong, I'm man enough to stand up here and say so. I made a terrible misstatement of recollection. As your servant and a member of this court, I sincerely apologize and offer that to the court. It's not much, but it's what I have." He urged the judge to accuse him of overzealousness or undue diligence but not to find him guilty of contempt.

Judge Shirley said he would consider Bell's defense and issue a ruling at a later date.

Standing by James Bell, Raynella entered her formal plea of not guilty in the murder of Ed Dossett on September 4, 2008. Her trial for the murder of her second husband, David Leath, originally scheduled for court that month, was now slated to begin on March 2, 2009. No date was set for her trial on the charges that she intentionally killed her first husband.

Prosecutors presented a new exhumation petition to the court on November 21. Judge Baumgartner did not seem pleased with this development. "This appears to be essentially the same issue raised and considered. I am very familiar with these facts . . . It's not going to do any good to disinter the body to determine the level of morphine because we already know precisely what it was."

Special prosecutor Cynthia LeCroy argued that a second autopsy was essential to the case in order to resolve the contradictions between the official cause of death and those morphine levels that were revealed in a toxicology report not received by medical examiner Randy Pedigo until after he'd signed the death certificate.

Baumgartner said he'd rule in December and did so one week before Christmas. In a five-page order, the Knox County criminal court judge ruled once again to deny exhumation, saying that the state had offered "no additional evidence nor presented any new arguments or any additional law."

Matters did not work in Raynella's favor in chancery court that month, though. She'd filed an appeal of the court's decision that she'd failed to present sufficient evidence to overcome the strong presumption that the lost will was revoked by her husband.

Her appeal failed. Judge Sharon G. Lee wrote: "After careful review of the record . . . we do not agree that the evidence presented in this case supports the appellants' contention that the trial court erred." The judge ordered that Raynella, Maggie, and Katie pay the cost of the appeal.

Moving into 2009, the defense and the state prepared for the upcoming trial on the Leath case. But the prosecution team still took time for their exploration of Ed Dossett's death. On January 13, they submitted a motion requesting a Rule 9 appeal on the exhumation request. In other words, the state was asking the judge for permission to pursue the appeal in a higher court, citing the limited existing case law and the unusual issues raised. They also contended that "the State could suffer irreparable injury by the Order denying disinterment in that the jury would be denied the certainty of the medical examiner from a full and thorough autopsy."

Both sides entered the courtroom on January 16 for a

pretrial hearing. The prosecution team of Richard Fisher, "Mac" McCoin, and Cynthia LeCroy admitted that the sample of David Leath's blood had been destroyed. The results of the testing revealed the presence of three medications for which Leath did not have a prescription.

Special prosecutor McCoin argued the admissibility of this evidence in the trial: "Part of our theory is that he was given these drugs the night before by his wife, who is a nurse. It is a vital part of our case." He added that the sample had been destroyed prior to the indictment being served on the defendant and before Bell filed a petition to preserve the sample.

Defense attorney James A.H. Bell indicated that he would submit a motion to exclude that evidence, since it was no longer available for additional, independent testing. The judge agreed to consider the motion *in limine,* or before the start of the trial, and would also rule later on Bell's request to hold the trial in the old federal courthouse at Main and Walnut streets. Bell wanted that location because it was a more spacious courtroom and he intended to introduce as evidence the bed and wall panels from the room where David Leath was shot to death in 2003.

Before the end of the month, the motion to exclude arrived in the judge's chambers: "Ms. Leath requests this Court issue an order excluding from evidence any and all information obtained as a result of the collection and testing of the blood and urine samples, including but not limited to the results of any scientific testing and the effects such chemical test results would have upon the deceased."

Bell's words in the courtroom were more inflammatory than the carefully crafted motion. He said that before his client was charged in 2006, he formally requested that the state preserve the samples but learned that they had already been destroyed. "It is highly doubtful that the blood and urine samples were accidentally spilled or thrown out," he pointed out. "Instead, Ms. Leath submits that someone, either at the TBI (Tennessee Bureau of Investigation) or at the medical examiner's office, intentionally, and with deliberation, disposed of the blood and urine, or allowed it to be disposed."

The deliberate destruction of evidence was a serious charge, and Bell was ready with a reason for it. He argued that the blood and urine might prove "exculpatory theories, such as unintentional over-medication due to the victim's progressive Alzheimer's disease supporting suicide."

When they returned to the courtroom on February 6, the state admitted that the two vials of blood drawn from David Leath and sent to the Tennessee Bureau of Investigation were destroyed after testing, as was routine procedure at the time. The two other vials that reportedly contained blood were stored, perhaps improperly, at Knox County facilities. When they were removed from storage, they were found to contain only swaths of cloth.

Bell went from raising the possibility that the blood could point to his client's innocence to arguing that it was irrelevant evidence, claiming that the amounts were so small that the combined effects were "the equivalent of a glass of wine. It's much ado about nothing. It cuts both ways. It's a red herring."

Judge Baumgartner dismissed the defense's allegation of intentional destruction, saying that he had no reason to believe that happened or that anyone had intentionally tampered with the evidence. He said he would rule later on the admissibility of the test results at trial.

Prosecutors revealed during that hearing that there was no blood on the clothing investigators took from Raynella on the day her husband was found dead. Nonetheless, they believed she had created a "staged scene" in the bedroom where David Leath died.

The state agreed that they would not introduce the tape of a secretly recorded conversation between Raynella and Cindy about Leath's missing will. The judge also ruled that the state could not present evidence pertaining to an incident in which Raynella pleaded guilty to an assault charge after she was charged with the attempted murder of Steve Walker.

In less than two weeks, attorneys for both sides stood before Baumgartner's bench again. They argued their case for inclusion or exclusion of the blood testing results once again. The prosecutors contended that Raynella injected David with drugs the night before his murder to render him unable to protect himself. The defense countered that the drugs were an indication of self-medication in preparation for a suicide attempt.

The judge ruled that the blood test results were admissible at trial. He agreed with Bell that the state had a general duty to preserve evidence but said "that duty must be limited to evidence that might be expected to play a significant role in the suspect's defense.

Because "the defendant's position has always been that the victim committed suicide," he continued, the results could easily support the defendant's position as easily as the state's theory. "The significance of the evidence is limited, based upon the fact that the actual presence of drugs or alcohol in the victim's blood and urine could both be used to support the defendant's position. The fact that the blood and urine samples are missing, either lost or destroyed, will not deny the defendant a fundamentally fair trial."

On February 15, Baumgartner presided over yet another hearing regarding the exhumation of Ed Dossett's body. "I deny the state's petition to disinter the body," he said in his decision on the first request. He then entertained arguments on the second request for disinterment from the state.

"You don't know what's inside the tomb until you examine its contents," special prosecutor Richard Fisher said. "There was a hurry to get Ed in the grave. Whether he was murdered or not, lawyers can talk all they want, but it's not answering the questions. Only medical experts can answer them."

James Bell argued against the exhumation. "Taking a

shovel to Mr. Dossett and trying to disinter him to find what remains are left isn't favorable to the law. Frankly, there are other means the State should use at this point."

"We want this disinterment not to offend anyone's sense but to find out what happened to a girl's father," Fisher retorted despite the fact that Ed's daughters were opposed to the exhumation. "We want to know. The State wants to know what caused his death."

"The information they need can come from University of Tennessee medical records, rather than taking a shovel and digging up Mr. Dossett," Bell insisted.

Baumgartner said he would rule on this request at the end of the month. After the hearing, Fisher told reporters, "The case has been around for a long, long time. There is no need to get into a mad rush. We are moving along at a deliberate speed, and I'm comfortable with that. I think Mr. Bell is too."

CHAPTER 39

Don Carmen, a firearms expert with the Tennessee Bureau of Investigation, prepared to testify at Raynella's upcoming trial. He examined all the relevant evidence, paying particular attention to the Colt .38 blue steel revolver, with six lands and a left twist; the unfired cartridges and the cartridge cases of the fired bullets found in the cylinder of the weapon; the recovered bullet fragments; and the diagrams of the revolver drawn by Investigator Perry Moyers at the crime scene.

The overlooked but obvious drew his curiosity. Someone had loaded two different brands of ammunition in the gun. All three of the casings from the fired bullets were in the barrel when law enforcement arrived on the scene. The firing pin rested on the cartridge case of the final one to leave the gun. It was a brass-colored Winchester Western brand, the only empty cartridge of its kind. The other two cases were silver, manufactured by Remington-Peters.

The brass bullet went into the bed. That meant the fatal shot was not the final one fired. The pressure required to fire that particular revolver exceeded what someone in their death spasms could bring to bear. And, according to the autopsy report, once the silver bullet penetrated the victim's brain, he would not be able to voluntarily pull the trigger again.

David Leath did not fire the third shot from that gun. It

could not have been suicide. It was a gotcha moment that energized the prosecution and made them more optimistic about success at trial.

In the final pretrial conference on February 20, Bell secured permission from the judge to videotape the testimony of an alibi witness in advance because had to be out of town during trial. Prosecutors did not object and agreed to cross-examine the witness, Premila Patel, on tape. A nurse at Parkwest Medical Center, Premila claimed that she'd seen Raynella at the hospital between 9:00 and 10:00 a.m. on the day David died in their home. The defense planned to use this testimony to counter the state's theory about the case.

The judge stated his desire to complete jury selection in one day, on March 2, and begin the trial the following day. He said that because of publicity, jurors would be questioned about what they'd seen or read. The judge hoped to seat the jury that day and to begin the trial on the March 3.

Although it was Bell's idea to question Premila in advance, he had second thoughts. On February 27, he filed a motion seeking to suppress a portion of the cross-examination of Patel. He claimed that special prosecutor Cynthia LeCroy-Schemel had badgered Patel and created confusion with multiple playbacks of an audiotape with several voices.

Bell filed a second motion seeking to have selected jurors to be paid their normal wage or reimbursed the cost of child care, rather than just receiving the regular $10 per day. Bell said that inadequate compensation of jurors could lead to financial strains that "may cause a juror's attention to be diverted" from the proceedings of the case. Raising this issue may have been out of genuine concern for the jurors' well-being and the desire for a fair trial. Or it could have been a gesture intended to ingratiate the defense, and thus their client, with the potential jurors. More likely, it was both: a matter of principle and self-interest walking hand in hand.

CHAPTER 40

Raynella didn't just face the cold reality of being on trial for murder on March 2, 2009. She also received bad news from the Tennessee Court of Appeals on that day. Judge Sharon Lee wrote that although there is no known evidence that David Leath told anyone that he had revoked the will, there remained "the obvious possibility that he might have been prevented doing so by his sudden, unexpected death." That ruling meant that Cindy, Dave's daughter from a previous marriage, was entitled to half of her father's estate, including personal property, cash, and vehicles as well as property—half of the seventeen-acre Leath family property and a half of the 163 acres making up the Dossett family farm. Raynella had sixty days in which to file an appeal. At that moment, she was busy fighting for her freedom.

In Oak Ridge, people who knew Raynella in grade school were stunned, "I thought the charges against her would be dropped because they'd find who did it. I never throught it would go this far because I was always certain she was innocent," Beverly Conner said. "She would not do anything that would make her lose her salvation because she would never see her son again."

She was also disturbed at the public reaction. "The anger in the comments on the Internet shocked me. The psychologists on Court TV talked about her being a sociopath. This was not Raynella." Beverly and many others wondered if the root of Raynella's problems lay in the resentment other area people held against Oak Ridge and everyone who had lived there in its heyday.

A larger-than-usual jury pool was called in for this first-degree murder trial. Five hundred potential jurors filed into a huge auditorium. They were told a major trial was about to begin. More than half of those present were released. The rest went in shuttle buses to the courthouse. First they filled the jury box; the candidates for the jury filled thirteen rows of seating. The remainder stood in the back of the courtroom. However, only twenty of them raised their hands when asked if they heard or read anything about the case at hand.

Judge Baumgartner asked, "Anyone familiar with any of the people in the case? Are any of them friends, relatives, or coworkers?" He excused several people who responded affirmatively to that question.

Then he asked, "Do you believe in the death penalty?" Those who responded in the negative were released.

The judge began individual questioning of the potential jurors, asking them about their education and background. The attorneys for both sides weighed the responses and picked jurors for dismissal. At the end of the morning the judge said," I guess we have our jury. Let's get started."

The jurors went to the deliberation room and took a lunch break. The panel of eight men and six women, including the two alternates, resumed the places in the jury box just before 2:30 that afternoon. Every one of them assured the judge that they would be able to reach a decision based only on circumstantial evidence. Baumgartner announced that they would not be sequestered and that there might be Saturday sessions included in the trial.

Special prosecutor Richard Fisher stood to present the opening argument for the state's case against Raynella Dossett Leath. He was the image of a veteran attorney:

wavy silver-gray hair covering the tips of his ears and brushing his collar, prominent wrinkles lining his forehead, and bags hanging beneath his cool blue eyes. In his quiet, smooth voice, he described a cold, carefully planned slaying based on greed: "Everything from the first arrival of officers to the final turn of evidence will convince you that this murder was premeditated."

He told the jurors that Raynella's planning was detailed, including the staged appearances at the hospital to establish an alibi and the "theatrics of sorrow" she demonstrated when the first responders arrived. What investigators discovered on the scene, he said, was a cold body containing a mixture of drugs that would have incapacitated him.

Fisher told the jury that Raynella murdered her husband because they were fighting over the will for an estate that was worth millions of dollars and included the farm where they resided. "You cannot get shot practically between the eyes and [have] it be anything other than an intentional, knowing killing."

He alleged that Raynella drugged David, shot him, and staged the scene to look like a suicide. "The day after David was shot, she had him cremated and was lining up witnesses to prove where she was at 10 o'clock." The motive, he asserted, was to inherit all the land that belonged to Dave before they were married.

The prosecutors believed that Raynella's motive for killing David Leath was greed. Members of Ed Dossett's family entertained another theory. They believed that David knew something about Ed's death and was contemplating coming forward with what he knew. To prevent that, they theorized, Raynella killed him.

While Fisher spoke, Investigator Perry Moyers sat in a rocking chair next to the prosecution table and close to the jury box. Jury member Lee Stensaker thought he looked "nervous and scared."

Moyers admitted that the presence of Court TV, with

their ever-whirring camera right over his shoulder, did make him nervous. He said he got even edgier when Bell spoke to the jury, because he felt the defense was lying.

Defense attorney James A. H. Bell, a large, lumbering man with a bulldog face, painted a righteous portrait of an innocent widow in his opening. Lee Stensaker said, "He looked right out of central casting with a booming voice, wild white hair, and imposing figure."

Bell asserted that Raynella was not at home when David died. Alibi witnesses placed Raynella at the hospital and later at the school one of her daughters attended. He claimed that the investigation was botched and biased. The Knox County Sheriff's Office, he alleged, dismissed plenty of evidence of suicide. They then "did not just jump but leapfrogged" to the conclusion of his client's guilt. He contended that theory was illogical because of the absence of blood on her clothing and gunshot residue on her hands. "She did not, could not, would not, have killed her husband, the man she loved."

He promised the jurors that he would present forensic evidence missed by the investigators that pointed away from his client. "There is no case at all against this very nice lady." The defense position was clear: it was suicide or, if not, someone else did it.

The jurors' eyes went to the defendant as Bell's finger pointed in her direction. "Her thick, immaculate, wavy hair was always perfectly coiffed and she was elegantly dressed every day of the trial but she was a cool cucumber," Stensaker recalled.

When he returned home that night, Moyers turned on Court TV to catch some of the footage of his day in court. He was appalled by what he saw. Sitting in the rocking chair, he couldn't help it—he rocked. It made him look fidgety. The next morning he got a deputy to replace the rocker with a less comfortable straight-back chair.

CHAPTER 41

Before the jury entered the courtroom on Tuesday, March 3, Judge Baumgartner warned the lawyers that any mention of Ed Dossett during the trial could be grounds for a mistrial.

The prosecution called eleven witnesses to the stand. Knox County Sheriff's Office deputy sergeant David Amburn testified to the "theatrics of sorrow" that Fisher mentioned in his opening statement. He said that when he arrived at the home, Raynella was prostrate on the ground in the front yard, sobbing and wailing. At first he feared that she was a victim.

On cross-examination, Bell pointed Amburn to his written report, filed at the time of the death. Amburn admitted to describing Raynella as being "overcome with grief."

The state called Jeff Crews, a toxicologist for the Tennessee Bureau of Investigation. He testified about the four prescription drugs that were found in Dave's blood and urine after his death. One was Phenergan, a medication used for allergic symptoms and motion sickness. It can cause breathing to slow or stop and should never be taken by someone like Dave who had high blood pressure. Testing also revealed Doxepin, a tricyclic antidepressant. Most troubling of all was the presence of the remaining two drugs, meperidine and pethidine, commonly known as Demerol, a narcotic analgesic similar to morphine. None of the drugs were illegal, but none were prescribed.

Dave's daughter, Cindy Wilkerson, fellow barbers Hoyt Vanosdale and Paul Wilson, and friend Gordon Armstrong all testified that David hated handguns, thought suicide was a sin that would lead to hell, and he did not want to be cremated on religious grounds.

When Cindy was on the stand, the defense confronted her about her possession of the keys to her father's home. She denied having them before her father's death.

When James Bell asked her about the value of her father's estate, she said she did not know what it was worth. Bell yelled at her during the cross-examination, "That's what this is all about, isn't it?" He accused her of knowing that the estate could be worth as much as $18 million. (In reality, the two pieces of property that constituted the bulk of the estate were assessed at a total value of $751,000, according to the Knox County Property Assessor's Office.)

Dave's longtime friend Gordon Armstrong told the jurors that Dave "hated handguns, wouldn't mess with them." He added that when Dave had a terminally ill dog, Gordon had to shoot it for him.

Gordon testified that on one occasion he told Dave that when he died, he wanted to be cremated. Dave's reaction: he "pitched a fit, gave me a lecture, quoted scripture, and said he wasn't going to let me do it."

The prosecutors called attorney Charles Child to the stand. He had prepared wills for the Leath couple. He said that Raynella told him that Dave had disposed of his will.

James Safewright, the owner of Cremation Options, then testified that he never met Dave Leath. Raynella, he said, had power of attorney for her husband, and she had always met with him alone to discuss their arrangements for cremation.

Neither Steve nor Pam Walker attended the trial. Steve was subpoenaed as a possible witness. They did pay close attention to what was happening in the courtroom, though, catching up on the day's events on Court TV, which had sent a camera crew to Knoxville to provide live coverage from the courtroom. Steve even agreed to an interview with the network while the trial was in progress.

After a day of testimony about Raynella's financial motivation for murdering Dave, Steve sat bolt upright in his bed in the middle of the night. *That's why she tried to kill me,* he thought. *She was afraid I'd come after her to get money for Kyle.* With every passing day, Kyle looked more and more like his biological father, Ed Dossett.

CHAPTER 42

The first witness on the stand on Wednesday, was Roger Yarnell, a friend of Dave's since they were teenagers. He clearly recalled the day that Dave died because he was supposed to meet him at noon that day. He was working on his lawn mower while he waited for Dave. He was surprised that Dave had not yet arrived, because he was never late. That's when he heard the sirens and saw emergency vehicles headed up to Dave's house. He told his wife, "I better go see if Dave is sick."

During cross-examination, Yarnell said that he believed Raynella and Dave had a good relationship and that Dave often bragged about his wife bringing him breakfast in bed. He added, though, that Dave was a private person who never talked openly about his marriage.

The state called Barbara Sadler, a registered nurse at Parkwest who'd worked at the hospital for twenty-eight years that included the time when Raynella was director of nursing. She remembered seeing Raynella at the hospital around 9:00 the morning Dave died. Raynella had been tearful and wanted to speak to a social worker. Her mother-in-law was scheduled to go to a nursing home but she couldn't transport her because her husband was home sick with high blood pressure.

Next up was Randall Carr, the hospital's director of human resources in 2003. He testified that there were times when drugs went missing while Raynella was in her position as director.

Dr. Darinka Mileusnic-Polchan, now Knox County's chief medical examiner, took the stand to refute the defense's claim of suicide. "It was impossible for him to have shot himself," she stated. She said that she had reached that conclusion because the fatal shot was from twelve to fourteen inches away from his head and entered his forehead above his left eye, in which he was totally blind. Additionally, Dave had a mixture of unprescribed medications in his system that would have rendered him incapable of getting out of bed that morning. In fact, she doubted that he ever awoke from his sleep before he died. His empty stomach and full bladder supported that contention. Besides, she said, "David was a [mentally] healthy man who didn't have a history of suicide issues."

The possible window for time of death was somewhere in between 6:00 a.m. and 11:23 a.m., she testified. Her professional estimation narrowed that time down to somewhere before 9:00 a.m.

On cross-examination, the defense battered Dr. Mileusnic-Polchan with questions implying bias in her office because one of the employees had their hair cut by Dave Leath. Next, Raynella's lawyers posed questions designed to impugn the doctor's credibility. Mileusnic-Polchan answered that she didn't visit the crime scene but relied on information provided by law enforcement. She also said she did not have the temperature of the room in which he died. She admitted that having that piece of information would have helped.

"You still can't tell us who it was that shot David Leath, can you?" Bell asked.

"I'm not saying who shot him; that's going to be collective evidence that's going to lead to your conclusion."

She didn't contradict the attorney when he pointed out

that gunshot residue was found on David but there was none of that or any blood on his client. When the defense turned to Dave's medical history as an explanation of his suicide, she took exception.

She noted that Dave had had mysterious symptoms for three years prior to his death, and although one doctor diagnosed the possibility of Alzheimer's disease, he was not convinced of his own conclusion because of David's sleepiness, which was inconsistent with that condition. When she performed the autopsy, she told the jury, she could not find any indication of Alzheimer's.

If David had the disease, the medical examiner would have found barnacle-like piles of amyloid beta, a protein fragment, on the brain. Since autopsy was the only conclusive method for diagnosing Alzheimer's, Raynella's claims were clearly unfounded.

Late that morning, Sergeant Perry Moyers, the lead Knox County Sheriff's Office investigator, took the stand as a state witness. He's a forceful man with a passion for justice. "I am the last voice for the victim," he later commented. "The suspect can have lots of people to speak but I am obligated to speak for the victim."

He testified that there were no fingerprints found on the gun that fired the bullet that killed David Leath. The .38-caliber Colt revolver was found in the bed beside Leath, who had died from a single gunshot wound to the head. His hands tested positive for gunshot residue. Raynella's tested negative.

He said that the crime scene appeared to have been staged. "There's three shots: one in the bed, one in the headboard, and one in his head. And he's tucked in and he's got a pillow in between his head and shoulder, which is strange." He added that there was only one person who would know that Dave slept in the nude and always placed a pillow between his legs. Because of the folds in the blanket that were penetrated by the third bullet, it was obvious that Dave's arm had been slipped underneath the covers before that final shot was fired.

The detective also testified that the tray of food that Raynella claimed she brought to him before she left home that morning sat on a nightstand beside the bed, untouched by Dave and not spattered with his blood. Similarly, the glass of milk bore neither lip marks on its edge nor any white line marking a previously higher level of liquid, indicating that Dave had not consumed any of it.

Moyers read entries from Raynella's journal/calendar, a place where she jotted down details for the farm—when a baby goat was born, for example—and important dates for the family, Dave's doctor appointments among them. For the two months leading up to Dave's death, Raynella chronicled the problems between the couple and her claims of his failing health. In talking about the estimated time of death, he said that Katie Dossett's departure from the home to go school at 8:15 a.m. that morning narrowed down the possible time of death. He also told the jurors that the clothes dryer in the house was running when the deputies arrived.

Moyers spent the rest of the afternoon and part of the next morning being cross-examined by the defense. Bell asked why Moyers didn't request fingernails or hair samples from Raynella. The detective said that she was not a suspect at the time.

Everything the detective did at the house was dissected and treated with scorn by the defense lawyer. In a prickly exchange during the questioning about the lack of evidence on Raynella's clothing, Moyers blurted out, "I think she changed clothes before she left the house."

Bell continued to badger the detective, demanding that he reveal state documents and evidence that had been hidden from the defense. He also accused him of conducting a biased investigation. Most of the jurors were bothered by the lack of respect shown to Investigator Moyers.

With Moyers still on the stand, the defense played the

graphic police videotape to the jurors. Bell asked the investigator to explain what was being shown. The camera traveled into the bedroom where David died of a gunshot wound to the head and zoomed in for bloody close-ups of the body and the wound. While the tape ran, Moyers narrated in vivid language that disturbed some jurors and brought Raynella to tears. She turned away from the wall where the video was displayed. "When she cried, it seemed like playacting; it looked contrived," said juror Lee Stensaker.

When the defense finally released the lead investigator, the prosecution called its final witness, Tennessee Bureau of Investigation firearms expert Don Carmen, who testified that of the three shots fired in the bedroom, it was most likely that the second bullet was the fatal one. The evidence of two different brands of cartridge cases in the revolver's cylinder supported that theory, since the third and last cartridge remained in the gun and tests determined that that was the shot that went into the mattress. Defense attorney Bell hammered away at this final witness too. He dredged out answers about the possible ways someone could have tampered with the revolver.

The state rested its case early in the afternoon. As many lawyers often do, defense attorney Bell immediately requested a directed verdict of acquittal. "Based upon what you've heard from Mr. Special Agent Carmen about the various ways that a revolver might have been manipulated by the deceased or in the hands of another person, they certainly cannot clench this lady's hands around the gun at all. It's for these reasons [that] I most respectfully ask the court to enter the judgment of acquittal. Mr. Fisher has utterly failed to put her in that house at 9:00 when everybody in the world knows she was at the hospital when he says the shooting did occur. That's what he told us. And he's utterly failed again to put that gun in this record in Mrs. Leath's hand."

Special prosecutor Fisher responded: "Was there a murder? Clearly, there was. This wasn't a suicide as Mr. Bell has tried to pretend all along and as his client attempted to stage. And the last witness made it very clear: a dead man could not have pulled that trigger the third time. That shot was fired, according to our theory, to get gunpowder residue on David's hands and assist her in her aborted effort to stage an apparent suicide—an effort that fell short.

"Clearly, he was murdered. He was shot in a manner that was designed to kill him. He was shot by someone close to him. No burglary—no sign of burglary. No forced entry evidence. The evidence—all the evidence—points to Raynella Leath as the person who murdered her husband.

"And it's certainly motive sufficient there as well. We would request this court to allow the jury to consider all the evidence that's been presented and that is yet to be presented to come up with a decision on this case," Fisher concluded.

Judge Baumgartner said, "There certainly isn't an eyewitness that puts the gun in her hands, but she had as much opportunity to have that weapon in her hands as anybody else did as far as we know." He denied the defense motion.

CHAPTER 43

The defense began the presentation of its case that afternoon by playing the 911 call made by Raynella the morning David died. At the sound of her own recorded voice, Raynella's eyes welled with tears.

The morning of Friday, March 6, the defense called their first witness, neurologist Dr. Ronald W. Bryan. He discussed his treatment of David Leath, beginning with the first encounter: "He was brought to Parkwest Medical Center in an acute confusional state." He said that David was tested for the cause of this confusion but none were confirmed.

Dr. Bryan testified that David's wife, Raynella, was always supportive of her husband and a good caretaker, even though little things often set off her husband. By 2003, the doctor said, David was exhibiting signs of depression and mood swings. He "appeared to have insight to realize there was a problem, and he just didn't want to deal with it."

On cross-examination, Richard Fisher elicited testimony from the neurologist about Dave's concerns that his wife was trying to kill him. The doctor noted that he wrote in the patient's file that he had paranoid ideation in that regard but did not seem to recall if Dave or Raynella told him about Dave's suspicions, since almost all of the information about

Dave's health and symptoms came from Raynella. The attorneys at the defense table seemed surprised by the revelations that Dave feared for his life at the hands of his wife.

Bryan also acknowledged that blood testing in January 2000 revealed the presence of antianxiety medication in Dave's bloodstream even though none had been prescribed for him.

The ascension of Raynella's youngest daughter, Katie Dossett Butler, to the witness stand brought a respectful hush over the courtroom. It remained in place for the duration of her emotional testimony. The story she told to the jurors directly contradicted the testimony of Dave's daughter Cindy and his friends.

Sniffling, she explained the listlessness and depression that haunted Dave's final days. Her testimony was heartbreaking. She was in tears much of the time, speaking in a soft, trembling voice. She said that she'd known her stepfather for a very long time. While her dad, Ed Dossett, was living, Dave came over to the farm often to work with him.

She claimed that Dave was not working out at the Y with the same regularity as before, that he frequently stayed in bed all day and got lost while driving. She said her mother told her that he appeared to be in the early stages of Alzheimer's disease. "Dave was to the point that he was tired and scared of what was happening to him."

She said for the last two years, Dave had been sleeping later and later in the morning but she never asked him questions about his health. "He didn't understand depression or any other illness and so he saw those as weaknesses and he didn't want me to know that," she said.

She sobbed as she spoke of the love between her mother and stepfather and her own feelings toward him. "I loved Dave. I was like his little buddy. I knew him as my protector, my caretaker, and my buddy."

Bell asked her, "Is there any way that your mother shot and killed David Leath?"

"There's no way my mom would ever kill anybody," a crying Katie insisted. She added that her mom enjoyed her role as nurturer and caretaker, and there were never any signs of violence between her mother and stepfather.

After the jury left for lunch, the defense informed the judge that their client would not be taking the stand. Baumgartner asked Raynella if she did not want to testify on her own behalf. Raynella said, "That is my decision."

The defense attorneys called two more witnesses after lunch. The first was Glen Farr, a professor of clinical pharmacology at the University of Tennessee. He said that the drugs in David's system at the time of his death might have made him a little groggy but not incapacitated. "It would kind of be like a couple of beers," he said. "His reaction time would slow a little." He also testified that the pharmaceuticals could have caused suicidal thoughts.

Dr. Celia Hartnett, a forensic expert with Forensic Analytical Sciences of Hayward, California, took the stand and contradicted the testimony of the expert called by the state from the Tennessee Bureau of Investigation.

She contended, "There's no part of my review, either of the materials that I received in discovery or from my examination of the evidence at all, that I find in any way inconsistent with this being a suicide." She believed that one of the trajectories had to be fired by someone in the bed and that "all of the shots are trajectories that he himself could have accomplished."

She presented a theory that Dave could have fired two shots before killing himself with the third one. Also contrary to the prosecution's witness, she said that the gun was not clean of fingerprints but that all of them were smudged.

She attacked the competence of the investigators, citing the damage to evidence caused by the way they moved the body and because of evidence that was not preserved. She

claimed that her laboratory in California found a bullet still
lodged in the box springs of the Leath bed and strands of
hair on the bullet that went into the headboard.

During a break, the defense set up the actual bed, headboard, and nightstand in the courtroom. They added a flesh-
colored dummy. The jury left the box and gathered around
the exhibit to observe a demonstration by Dr. Hartnett.

She walked them through the defense's version of events
that fatal morning. The first shot went through the mattress
and into the floor. The second one pierced the wall behind
his bed. Then, she claimed, Dave raised the gun, aimed it at
his forehead, and fired the final, fatal shot.

Not one juror found the California forensic expert's testimony credible. Lee Stensaker found her irritating and called
her testimony "a farce."

Judges in Tennessee had the option of allowing jurors to
pose questions to the witnesses. Baumgartner permitted that
practice in this trial. Jurors wrote down questions, attorneys
on both sides reviewed them, and then the judge decided
which ones could be asked and answered.

One of the questions Lee Stensaker submitted to this witness was: "Explain, physically, how it was possible for this
guy to shoot the gun after he was dead."

Harnett stuttered and choked out a convoluted response.
Fisher looked at Stensaker. A brief, involuntary smile danced
across the prosecutor's lips.

The defense rested its case. The judge scheduled closing
arguments for Monday, March 9.

CHAPTER 44

On Sunday afternoon, special prosecutor Richard Fisher called Judge Richard Baumgartner at home. He had to leave town and go home because of his wife's serious illness. He requested a short delay for the closing arguments. The judge gave him twenty-four hours.

That Monday, the jurors filed back into the courtroom prepared for the final words on the case from the attorneys for both sides. The judge apologized to the jury and explained why they would not be deliberating that day. He announced that if Fisher was not able to be present the following day, Cynthia LeCroy-Schemel or Mac McCoin would need to make the closing argument for the state. He sent the jurors back home at 9:27 that morning and told them to report back the next day.

As soon as they were gone, second chair defense attorney Richard Holcomb argued that Celia Hartnett's testimony was cause for the judge to instruct the jury to disregard the statements that medical examiner Dr. Darinka Mileusnic-Polchan made on the stand for the prosecution: "In light of Dr. Mileusnic's testifying that it was impossible for Mr. Leath to have shot himself with a close range shot, Your Honor, the physical facts prove that it was not impossible, so the physical facts negate that testimony."

Mac McCoin responded for the state: "These are intelligent jurors. They've heard two experts. Let the jurors do their job and decide the facts. Let's not interject some pseudoscientific instruction like this."

Baumgartner denied the defense request.

Before the jurors entered the courtroom on Tuesday morning, Bell made a motion demanding that special prosecutor Fisher be forbidden from making any mention of his wife's illness. He argued that such personal information could garner the sympathy of the jurors and influence their decision-making. Fisher did not object.

Since the judge had empowered the jury to consider not just first-degree murder but also second-degree murder, manslaughter, reckless homicide, and assault in their deliberations, Raynella's team had to address that issue as well as the theory of suicide. Defense attorney Bell told the jurors: "She's either guilty of first degree murder or she's not guilty of anything at all. This ain't no assault case . . . [I]f you believe Ms. Raynella murdered him, you have to believe she is nothing but a serpent of Satan" to put her daughter Katie through that ordeal just months before her high school graduation.

Repeating a theme he raised during cross-examination of law enforcement personnel, Bell pointed to the photograph of the bathroom off the Leath bedroom. He reminded the jurors of the Bible balanced on the edge of the sink. It was open to Psalm 69. Bell insisted that tortured chapter displayed David Leath's state of mind. It proved the victim was unhinged, depressed, and suicidal.

Bell concluded with plea for a verdict of not guilty. "It's just impossible. Like I told you on day one, Raynella did not, would not, could not, kill the man she loved. He was her buddy and her best friend."

Lawyer Richard Holcomb also spoke for the defense, reminding the jury that when Raynella pled not guilty, her plea of innocence covered all possible verdicts in the spectrum.

The state, of course, asked for conviction. Special prosecutor Richard Fisher reiterated the state's theory that Raynella drugged her husband, shot him, and staged a suicide scene. He alleged that the defendant missed with the first shot because she closed her eyes when she pulled the trigger. She fired the fatal shot into her husband's forehead. Then she placed the gun in her dead husband's hand and fired into the mattress.

"If she hadn't missed on the first shot, and had realized there were different types of bullets in the gun, she may very well have gotten away with murder," he said. He drew the juror's attention to the lack of blood on Raynella's clothing and suggested that there should have had bloodstains somewhere: she should have touched her husband at least once if she innocently found him dead. Fisher conceded that the case was purely circumstantial and the evidence presented was complex. However, he said, a guilty verdict was supported by "uncontested, irrefutable facts." He urged the jurors, "Please do justice."

The judge turned the case over to the jury just after noon. They broke for lunch and commenced their deliberations when they returned at 1:45 p.m. Their first act was the selection of a jury foreman. One younger juror was eager to assume the responsibility—some thought too eager. The other jurors turned to one of the older people in the room, nominating Lee Stensaker and asking, "Will you?"

"I will if you want me," Lee said. Lee believed he won the vote because of his age.

The man who wanted to be foreman proposed that they take an immediate vote to know where everyone stood. Lee cautioned against voting at this time. "You cast your vote and you can get married to your opinion. Let's run through the facts of the case first."

The same juror, with the support of a couple of others,

kept pressing the point. After an hour Lee relented. In the first polling of the jurors, seven voted guilty, five not guilty.

They discussed the reason for their votes. One "sweet, good-hearted woman," according to Lee, who voted not guilty said she did so because she didn't believe it was possible for a woman to do what the prosecution said Raynella had done. A discussion of the evidence changed her opinion on the verdict as well as that of three other jurors.

The sole holdout argued his theory on Dave shooting the three bullets. "A hesitation shot. A second hesitation shot. Then he did it," he said.

Lee countered, "We know the distance of the gun from his head. He would have had to hold the gun at full arm's length and use his thumb to pull the trigger."

At 6:00 p.m. the jury sent out a request for a transcript of the 911 call. Since that had not been entered into evidence, the judge did not allow it. He also did not permit the tape to be sent into the deliberation room for the jurors to listen to there because the whole tape had not been played during the trial. Instead, the jurors took their seats in the courtroom, leaning forward to listen as Raynella's voice echoed through the chamber. The judge allowed it to be played twice. After that, deliberations ended for the day.

On Wednesday morning at 9:00, the jurors resumed their consideration of the case. At 2:00 p.m. they informed the judge that they were hopelessly deadlocked.

Judge Baumgartner questioned the jury foreman, who told him that the deadlock hinged on a philosophical difference of circumstantial evidence and "a smoking gun." He said that the evidence was not clear and the difference of opinions was very lopsided. "We have been told by the dissenting parties [that] they will never change their mind." He said they needed direct evidence, such as "several eyewitnesses."

In response to the judge's query, the foreman assured him that the jurors had been carefully discussing evidence and had been "mutually respectful" of one another's opinions.

The judge said, "Stand if you don't want to go back and try again." No one rose to their feet. Baumgartner asked them to resume their deliberations and they agreed to do so through that afternoon.

Back in the deliberation room, jury foreman Lee Stensaker used a Magic Marker and the large pages of a flip chart to prepare a probability chart with the facts of the case presented in the courtroom.

The holdout juror said, "The evidence is pretty rough."

"It's all circumstantial, but we've got to look at this realistically," Lee said.

"But you don't have a witness," the other juror countered.

"But if you had to make a guess. What would you say then?" Lee pressed.

"Yeah," the juror sighed, "I guess she's guilty. I just have to think about it overnight and we can vote in the morning."

Shortly after 5:00 p.m., they sent a note to the judge: "We are closer to a decisive verdict but want to leave tonight and come back tomorrow." Above the word "decisive," the foreman scribbled "unanimous."

First thing the next morning, defense attorney Bell submitted a written request for a mistrial. He feared that the juror or jurors who are concerned about circumstantial evidence might be under pressure to cave in just to reach a verdict. He wrote, "The judge went beyond any permissive inquiry in this matter by asking whether 'there were others on the other side of the fence who had a strong opinion the other way.' "

He called the jury foreman Lee Stensaker's comments troublesome, saying that they infringed on his client's right to a fair trial.

Baumgartner denied his request, saying that he was comfortable that the jury was engaged in careful, thoughtful discussion and that no juror was being coerced. "I think the jury is doing exactly what they ought to be doing. If I'm wrong, you have an issue for appeal."

The jury resumed their deliberations, but at 10:41 but they brought the discussion to a screeching halt. The juror who had agreed that Raynella must be guilty the previous afternoon now said, "No. No, she's not guilty."

The panel gave up, deadlocked at 11 to 1 for conviction. That one juror, who like all the others had agreed he could reach a guilty verdict based solely on circumstantial evidence, now found he could not convict under those conditions. He said that he wanted a witness or a confession. Short of one or the other, he could not find Raynella guilty of anything.

"What I'm going to do is I'm going to declare a mistrial in this case," Judge Baumgartner said. Before dismissing the panel, he thanked them for their service. "Sometimes you're not able to come to a unanimous verdict. It doesn't mean you didn't do your job." He warned that they would receive multiple media requests for interviews. They were free to talk but did not have any obligation to do so. "Because this has been the subject of some interest from the local and national media, I know some of those people are going to want to talk to you. It's entirely up to you."

After court was dismissed, the media gathered outside the courtroom for reactions from the participants. Special prosecutor Mac McCoin told them: "We really can't talk about the case. We're going to trial again and for that reason we have to remain silent. It is the intention of the state of Tennessee to try this case again. I can say that with absolute certainty."

Dave's daughter, Cindy, admitted that she was disappointed in the outcome of the trial: "I thought they might reach a verdict. I'm glad they're going to try again."

Steve and Pam Walker were stunned and depressed. Seeing Raynella walk out of that courtroom a free woman breathed new life into their fears about the safety of their family.

Standing beside his client, defense attorney Bell said because of the pending Dossett murder case and the civil lawsuit and despite Raynella's desire to speak, he would not allow his client to talk to them. "This is Raynella Dossett-Leath, the finest client that any lawyer, any person in America, could ever want. I ask you now, let us go now and heal from the torture and torment of the ten days of this arduous trial that this woman has had to suffer. This woman is not guilty of killing her beloved David. She loves him and he lays in her heart and mind."

Raynella made a single, tearful comment when asked if she was pleased with the verdict. "Absolutely. Finally, his soul can rest," she said.

Hearing that, Cindy's mind turned to her dad's ashes sitting in a cardboard box on a Coke machine at the barbershop and wondered if her father ever would know peace.

CHAPTER 45

James Bell filed a speedy-trial motion at the opening of the Ed Dossett murder case to force the state to bring that case to court prior to the planned second trial for Raynella on the charges that she killed David Leath. However, the state filed a fourth petition to exhume the body of Raynella's first husband on March 23. Obviously, they were in no hurry to go to trial.

In the new motion, they wrote, "Because of the revelation made in the David Leath murder trial, it is readily apparent that the defendant, Raynella Dossett Leath, possesses the knowledge and capability to administer medications in a unique and lethal manner." The state claimed that witnesses for both sides supported the possibility that Raynella could have killed Ed Dossett.

On April 8, both sides gathered in front of Judge Baumgartner once again. Special prosecutor Richard Fisher presented a request for the investigation of the jury in the trial that had ended a month earlier. He claimed to have information from a reliable source that someone on the jury was acquainted with a relative of the defendant who was on the witness list for the defense.

Since there was no disclosure of the relationship by the juror prior to the trial, if true, it was a clear case of jury misconduct. "I would like to investigate that to see if there is a problem there," Fisher said.

The judge ordered a probe to be conducted by the Knox County Sheriff's Office and the Tennessee Bureau of Investigation. But the prosecution didn't get everything they wanted. Baumgartner denied their fourth petition for disinterment, saying that digging up Dossett's body would not answer the question of how he had received the morphine overdose or who gave it to him. The prosecutors noted for the record that they would explore the option of appealing his decision. The judge deferred his decision on whether or not to allow that appeal.

Judge Baumgartner also denied the defense's post-trial motion for a directed verdict of not guilty or a dismissal of all charges against Raynella. The written documents submitted by the defense claimed that the judge didn't follow proper procedure after the jury announced they were unable to reach a verdict. Bell insisted that Judge Baumgartner should have polled the jurors on every charge from first-degree murder down to reckless homicide.

On May 1, Baumgartner ruled there was no jury misconduct in the Leath trial. "That investigation has now been completed to the satisfaction of the parties and the court. The investigation revealed no misconduct by any juror and the court has concluded that no further inquiry is needed or warranted."

The judge gave prosecutors verbal approval to approach the court of criminal appeals for an exhumation and second autopsy of Ed Dossett but expressed strong doubts that they would succeed or that the appeals court would even agree to hear the case. "My opinion is not changed about this. There is nothing to be gained by digging his body up." He added, "I would love for them to have a look at this issue. There's not a lot of law on it."

Baumgartner denied the defense request for an appellate review of his refusal to grant a directed verdict of acquittal.

He said that denial of a motion made for a directed verdict cannot be appealed as easily as that for a conviction. "We now know it was an 11 to 1 nonverdict. You got a hung jury. You ought to be dancing in the street."

He set the date for the second Leath trial. Jury selection was scheduled to begin on January 11.

Judge Baumgartner issued an official order on June 9 approving of the special prosecutor's effort to appeal to have the body of Ed Dossett disinterred for a second autopsy. He wrote that he still believed that a second autopsy was "not necessary or essential to the administration of justice in this matter." However, he acknowledged that he would like to see an appeals court decision because "there is a limited body of law on this issue and there will be no effective appellate review at the conclusion of this case."

A year and a half after the accusation that defense attorney James A.H. Bell was guilty of contempt of court, Judge Clifford Shirley finally released his ruling on August 15, 2009: "To describe in detail the clothes being worn by a person who was not even there, and to describe in detail conversations that never occurred, strikes the Court as being methodical, willful and intentional. It is hard for the Court to envision a more methodical and intentional construction of a fabricated meeting that never occurred."

He ordered Bell to pay the maximum fine of $5,000. He stopped short of imposing a jail term on the attorney, writing: "This occurrence appears to be a onetime blemish on an otherwise lengthy and commendable record of legal representation."

The prosecution's hopes were dashed on October 5 when a three-judge panel in the state court of criminal appeals issued a ruling refusing to allow prosecutors to continue their efforts to exhume Ed Dossett: "The State had sufficient evidence to convince a Grand Jury to issue the indictment against Raynella Dossett Leath and presumably feel they have the evidence necessary to proceed to trial before a jury of her peers. While the Court understands and appreciates the fact that the State is always looking for whatever evidence exists, one would assume that any evidence acquired from an additional autopsy would be cumulative rather than essential to establish a crucial element of their case.

"Although we agree . . . that the body of law concerning disinterment in criminal cases is limited, it is by no means inconsistent or undeveloped. The discretion of a trial judge to permit ordering the exhumation of a victim's body when essential for the administration of justice has existed for more than fifty years."

In mid-October, the defense made a request for a delay in the new Leath trial. The new attorney on the case, former prosecutor Paula Hamm, told Judge Baumgartner that she had only recently been brought on board to defend Raynella Dossett Leath. "I have devoted days to just try to familiarize myself with the first trial, the witnesses, the evidence. To say the least, it is overwhelming," she said.

Special prosecutor Richard Fisher objected to any delay. "They have not presented a reason for continuing this trial. It's such an easy thing to do. It's a second trial. They've got a transcript. It's as easy as a case can be."

Defense lawyer Hamm countered that the new trial wouldn't be a retread of first trial. "I've identified witnesses that are not on the defense list or state list. We expect to use experts who weren't used in the first trial."

Judge Baumgartner was not moved. He denied the defense request and added the editorial comment that defense attorneys tend to wait until a trial looms to really roll up their sleeves and get to work anyway. "The most productive part of trial preparation happens when there's a deadline.

The date is a long time down the road. Even if this case is different, that's still a lot of time. I just haven't heard a compelling reason to move this case. We just need to get ready and put twelve people in the box."

CHAPTER 46

Four days before jury selection was scheduled to begin in Raynella's second trial for the murder of David Leath, the prosecutors requested the videotape of the defendant visiting the hospital on the morning of her husband's death. The tape was in the possession of the defense, who said they had no plans to introduce the footage at trial.

Special prosecutor Richard Fisher complained to the judge that defense attorney James Bell refused to let the state view the tape and it was no longer possible to get a copy from Parkwest Medical Center. Prosecutor Mac McCoin expressed outrage: "This is almost like a concealment of evidence."

Attorney Bell insisted he was within his rights to withhold the videotape. He argued that the defense had no obligation to share the fruits of its investigative work with the prosecution.

The judge's decision struck middle ground. The defense was ordered to bring the tape to the courtroom on Monday. Baumgartner would view it in his chambers and then reach a decision on its value as evidence in the case.

Bell brought his own complaints to the courtroom. His main bone of contention rested with the court-approved questionnaire that had been mailed out to five hundred prospective jurors. Of those returned, Bell griped, "Almost 70 percent already believe this lady is guilty one way or another." He asked the judge to sequester the jury.

The prosecution argued against sequestration. Fisher said that since it was not a capital case, the jurors should not face that hardship.

Turning to the defense attorney, Baumgartner assured him, "If someone says they know something about the case and have formed an opinion, we'll kick them off the case." He said he'd announce his decision about the jury on Friday.

The defense also had a quarrel with the testing of a pair of rubber gloves removed from the Leath home on the day of David's death. Bell said that although no gunshot residue was found on the gloves, DNA was found and not identified. He wanted it tested and compared to the DNA of Raynella, Cindy Wilkerson, and several other individuals. The judge approved that request.

On Monday, January 11, at least five hundred people reported to the Thompson-Boling Arena in downtown Knoxville. Out of all the questionnaires received back from them, only forty or fifty wrote that they did not know anything about the Raynella Dossett Leath case.

The judge asked the crowd, "If you are one of those people, it would save time if you would all step forward for transportation to the courthouse. If you don't volunteer in that way, your names would be called one by one."

Some stepped forward with alacrity, others with a heavy reluctance. They boarded an inmate bus. The fact that its windows were covered with bars gave some of them a sharp sense of foreboding.

One of the group, Bryan Creech, was shocked when Raynella walked into the courtroom. He'd seen her mug shot online and thought she looked rough and hardened. When he saw her in person, though, he did a triple take. With her flowing soft gray curls, she looked like the model American grandmother or a Sunday school teacher.

At the courthouse the potential jurors were asked a number of questions including: "Do any of you write books?" and "Does anyone plan on writing a book about this case and getting rich?" All responded in the negative.

When the judge asked, "Does anyone have experience in the military?" a number of hands went into the air.

Then he said, "How about the Marines? Anybody in the Marines?" The lead investigator in the case, Perry Moyers, was a former Marine.

Some arms remained raised, including Bryan Creech's. A self-employed father of seven kids ranging in age from three to thirteen, he was delighted at the thought that he was about to be eliminated. But no, he remained, and the questions continued.

"Does anyone have any connection to the Knox County Sheriff's Office?"

Bryan raised his hand again: he taught Bible study in the county jail once a week. Much to his dismay, after answering that question, he was not eliminated. Now nineteen prospective jurors were being considered, and Bryan was one of them.

"Did you look at anything up on the Internet since you received your summons?"

This was it: Bryan was certain they would not want him now. He raised his hand and was called up to the bench. He was instructed to lean forward and whisper his answer. The judge asked, "What do you learn online?"

"I learned that it might be a sequestered jury and that it was the defendant's second trial on the same charge."

"Is that all?

"Yes," Bryan said, visions of walking back through his front door that morning filling his thoughts. But Bryan was wrong again: he was one of nine women and seven men, including alternates, who were selected to be seated on the jury.

If all went as expected, every one of them would sit

through the entire trial. No one would be designated as an alternate until it was time for deliberations. Then, if all of them still remained, the judge would draw the names of four jurors who would not participate in deliberations.

Baumgartner warned the jurors that only what they heard in the courtroom could be considered in the deliberations: "There's a lot of information out there about this case and a lot of that is not true." But he added, "The mere fact that you have heard about the case does not disqualify you."

He then informed the jurors that they would be sequestered for the duration of the trial and not allowed to have cell phones or other such devices. Since Monday was the Martin Luther King Day holiday, the trial would begin Tuesday, January 19. They were ordered to report to the hotel by 8:00 p.m. on Monday night, January 18.

Before that day arrived, one of the male jurors, a new citizen who was not familiar with the judicial system, realized what sequestration actually meant. He knew he could be away from home for as much as two weeks. He was a teacher, and two of his own children were autistic. The judge ruled that his service would be a hardship and he was dismissed.

Baumgartner brought the problem of another juror to the attention of the attorneys on both sides of the case. During the last trial, he said, one member of the panel had to drop out of school because of a trial. Now someone on this jury needed to continue her online coursework. Both sides wanted to allow her to do the work while she served, but the defense requested that a court officer observe her work to make sure that she didn't surf any other sites while she was online.

On Tuesday morning, the jurors were transported from the hotel to the courthouse. They clustered near the entrance, waiting to pass through the metal detector. As they stood, Raynella and their legal team arrived. It was an uneasy moment. The deputies were not pleased.

A schedule was put in place to avoid any recurrence of

that morning's close encounter. A deputy informed attorney James Bell of the timetable: "We will arrive here with the jurors every morning at 8:30 sharp. Make sure you do not come into the courthouse until the jury has had time to go through security."

After the reading of the indictment and swearing in of the jury, the opening arguments began. Special prosecutor Richard Fisher stepped forward to start the trial.

"He was a short, skinny, gray-haired man who was as smooth as Matlock," Bryan Creech said.

Fisher began by playing the audiotape of Raynella's 911 call. He said that telephone call was designed in advance. It was "part of her plan to make a murder look like a suicide. The evidence in this case will prove to you that she is a killer."

He argued that because of the two different brands of ammunition in the revolver, it was obvious that the second of the three shots fired was fatal, "inescapable proof that this was not suicide," Fisher claimed.

David could not defend himself, the state alleged, because Raynella used her education as a nurse to drug him with a cocktail similar to the combination used to sedate patients before surgery. She wanted him in a state of diminished capacity to make it easier to shoot him. "But she didn't count on missing that first shot, so maybe it wasn't that easy."

Fisher alleged that after firing the second lethal shot, Raynella put the gun in David's hand to pull the trigger for the third shot, because she knew he would have to have gunpowder residue on his hand to make the suicide scenario believable. "She developed a plan, and executed that plan, and executed her husband."

Defense attorney Bell presented a different portrait of the defendant. He insinuated that the prosecution was concealing something from the jury, since the full 911 call was not played. He warned them that they may not hear any defense

witnesses or the defendant at all because the burden of proof
was on the state. He projected a photograph of Raynella and
Dave on the wall—a portrait of a happy couple. Then he
flashed up a shot of Dave dead in his bed. Dave's grandchildren, nineteen-year-old Tyler Wilkerson and his fifteen-year-
old sister, Lindsey, both looked down and away from the
image, brushing tears from their eyes. Tears also formed in
the corners of Raynella's eyes as she sat under the projected
photo.

Bell pressed the button to play the complete emergency
call for the jury, but the audiotape that played had been adul-
terated. The voice of a defense investigator, who was not at
the house at the time, was heard. After a sidebar, the judge
explained to the jurors that the voice was included in error
and was not part of the original recording.

In a line recycled from the first trial, Bell said, "She did
not, could not, and would not kill David. She loved him with
all of her heart." He called the case "an absurdity," since
there was no gunshot residue on her, no forensic evidence of
any kind "matching this lady to this crime, even if it was a
crime."

Bell argued that David's death was a suicide and that
even if it was not, it had to have been committed by someone else. In contrast to his earlier statement that the defense
might not call any witnesses, the lawyer promised that the
defense would present several witnesses who would provide
an alibi for Raynella at the time of the shooting. Many of
the jurors remembered his words and waited for him to deliver.

The state began their presentation of the case by calling
Robert Lee, a former employee of the Knox County Sheriff's Office. He told the jury about finding the body of David
Leath in his bed on March 13, 2003. Photographs of that
scene, entered into evidence, were circulated to the jury
while the courtroom waited in silence.

Bell attacked the Knox County Sheriff's Office investigation, alleging that they didn't have control of the crime scene. Lee admitted on cross that a crowd of people that the investigators were powerless to inhibit gravitated to the barn.

Next on the stand was Sergeant David Amburn, one of the first two officers to arrive at the scene. He testified about finding Raynella on the ground in the front yard. He introduced the Colt .38-caliber revolver into evidence and the state passed it over to the jury to examine.

On cross, attorney Paula Hamm pushed Amburn to admit that he hadn't checked for fingerprints on the phone or lamp beside David's bed, insinuating that someone else was present in the bedroom when David died. Amburn said that there were no signs of forced entry at the scene. Hamm hammered him with another question: "Did you check all the windows and doors to make sure they were locked?"

"There were no signs of forced entry," Amburn said.

"But did you check all the windows to make sure they were locked?"

"No," he admitted.

The defense was determined to plant doubt in the minds of the jurors about the competence and conduct of the detectives and technicians during the investigation.

When the judge stopped for the day, the jury was transported to a restaurant for dinner. They had catered lunches in the deliberation room but went out to dinner every evening before going back to the hotel. "They fed us very well. By the end of the week, I had gained a lot of weight," Bryan Creech said.

That evening, each juror was allowed a five-minute telephone call to his or her family. Several of the jurors, including Bryan, started playing card games together each evening. "It was difficult to meet around that card table every night and not deliberate or discuss the case in any way, but we resisted the urge every time."

When Bryan returned to his room and thought about the evidence presented that day, he believed that everything he had heard from the state's witnesses might be nothing more than coincidence.

CHAPTER 47

On Wednesday, Lieutenant Terry Lee, supervisor of the Knox County Sheriff's Office forensics unit, took the stand. He testified that Dave's fingerprints were not found on the revolver.

On cross-examination, defense attorney Paula Hamm asked Lee if any kind of forensic evidence linked Raynella to the gun or the ammunition. "No," he said. "No usable prints" were found on the gun, and the Tennessee Bureau of Investigation was not asked to conduct more advanced tests for fingerprints.

Evidence technician Aaron Allen was the next witness. He showed photographs from the crime scene to the jurors. One picture was taken in the bathroom off the Leath bedroom. It showed a Bible lying on the edge of the sink. Several jurors took note that the book was open to Psalm 69. They had no idea that Bell had used that to suggest suicide in the first trial, but they thought it might be significant and planned to read the chapter after returning to the hotel room.

Aaron Allen then played the graphic ten-minute silent video he shot at the Leath home on the morning of David's death. The stark, disturbing film held nothing back. The jurors viewed extreme close-ups of Leath's head and the blood-soaked pillow beside him in the bed. The jurors struggled to keep their faces empty of emotion as they watched.

Raynella, who sat almost directly beneath the projected video on the wall, turned her back to it. She cried and her attorneys patted her back and squeezed her hands. Dave's daughter, Cindy, and others cried in the galley. But some of the jurors noticed that, thirty minutes later, they could look out across the courtroom and pick out everyone who had been crying from the redness of their eyes or noses and the puffiness in their faces. Everyone with the exception of the defendant. From the moment she turned to face forward, her eyes, nose, and face were clear of any signs that the tears she shed were genuine.

The state followed up that emotional presentation with scientific fact. The toxicology results were entered into evidence. Jeff Crews, the scientist from the Tennessee Bureau of Investigation, took the stand once again and told the jury that the urine and blood samples taken after death showed four unauthorized drugs, including Demerol, in David's system—all legal pharmaceuticals, but none of them prescribed.

Bryan still thought that everything he heard could be chalked up to coincidence.

On Thursday, prosecutors called chief medical examiner Dr. Darinka Mileusnic-Polchan to the stand to explain why David's death was a homicide. Her testimony was a close duplication of the first time she was on the stand in this murder case ten months earlier. She explained that the muzzle of the gun was farther away than one typically finds in a suicide and that the victim was heavily impaired by drugs to the point of not being able to defend himself. Because the wound was above David's blind left eye, "he would not be able to see the gun or muzzle," she said. "His death was instant when his brain stem was severed by the second shot fired and an involuntary muscle movement could not have caused the double action revolver to fire the third shot."

The medical examiner was Bryan Creech's favorite

witness. "She was a brilliant woman. She was a wonderful teacher. I could have listened to her for days."

Tennessee Bureau of Investigation forensic analyst Laura Hodge told the jury that Raynella had no signs of gunshot residue on her hands following the death of her husband. However, David did have some signs of gunshot residue, mostly on the back of his left hand. Hodge pointed out that an absence of residue does not mean that the person did not fire the gun, because the residue can be removed by washing. She added that the presence of residue does not mean the person fired the gun, only that he or she was close to a gun when it was fired.

Special prosecutor Richard Fisher complained to the judge that the defense was allowing Raynella to display her emotions, a rule of courtroom decorum for those present at the tables of both the prosecution and the defense during a trial. "If she wants to get on the stand and cry, that's fine," he said.

Baumgartner said, "I can't regulate people's emotions." But he encouraged the defense lawyers to make sure there was no "overt reflections" of emotion. "The jurors, like the rest of us, are not fools. I'll leave it at that."

Since Bryan had served on two criminal trials in the past, many of the jurors were already talking about making him foreman. Because of that, he paid particular attention to the others on the panel. One of the women worried him. She didn't seem to comprehend the concept of circumstantial evidence. He was worried she might hang the jury for the second time. He jotted down in his journal that night, "If this woman deliberates, we're in trouble."

After the third day of testimony, the pieces were coming together in Bryan's mind. The weight of the evidence seemed to be becoming too heavy to be coincidental. Bryan remembered the defense attorney's promise to provide an alibi for his client. He looked forward to that testimony.

CHAPTER 48

The female juror who had not seemed to understand the evidence received word that her son had been in a serious car wreck. The judge excused her from duty so that she could go to the hospital. Bryan breathed a sigh of relief. Now fourteen jurors remained on the panel.

The jury heard testimony about the couple's property and wills on Friday. They learned that, in 2001, Raynella made arrangements for both her and Dave to be cremated, but her husband did not accompany her to the cremation facility.

In connection with the testimony about the victim's estate, civil documents of the lawsuits brought by Cindy Wilkerson and Raynella Dossett Leath were admitted into evidence. The point of their inclusion was to demonstrate that Raynella had filed a wrongful death suit against Cindy accusing her of being responsible for David's murder. The prosecution alleged that Raynella's countersuit put a lie to the defense claim that it was a suicide.

Dave's daughter Cindy presented her testimony. On direct examination, the state asked if she believed that Raynella had killed David or had him killed. "I think she did it, I feel like she did," she said.

On cross, defense attorney Paula Hamm asked who would get paid a lot of money if she won the civil case.

"The lawyers," Cindy responded, sending a ripple of chuckles through the courtroom.

The state's final witness was Tennessee Bureau of Investigation firearms expert Don Carmen, who confirmed the earlier testimony of Knox County Sheriff's Office investigator Perry Moyers. Using large illustrations, Carmen demonstrated to the court that of the three shots fired in the bedroom where David died, the third shot was fired after the fatal shot, which killed him instantly. The first two shots fired were Remington-Peters brand cartridges cases found in the revolver's cylinder. The third empty cartridge case, a Winchester Western brand, was found directly under the hammer of the gun, indicating it was the last one fired.

Carmen delivered his expert opinion: Raynella missed with the first shot, killed her husband with the second one, and then fired the third shot in a manner designed to ensure that there would be gun residue on Dave's hand.

On cross-examination, Paul Hamm manipulated the revolver as she questioned his version of events. "Well, couldn't the gun be shot this way, the cylinder rotated, the second shot fired and then the cylinder rotated again to end up here?"

"Yes, it could. But it is not probable and it is not logical. I presented the only logical and probable way it could be done."

On that, the most definitive forensic evidence, the state rested.

That evening, Bryan remembered his earlier plan to read Psalm 69. He pulled out the Bible in the hotel nightstand and opened it to the pertinent page. On the first reading, he thought that the text described Raynella's state of mind. He dismissed the possibility that it was David reading the chapter. After all, the medical examiner had told them that David's bladder was full and his stomach was empty—clear indication that he hadn't been out of bed that morning. It had to have been Raynella who left the Bible on the sink. Bryan read the psalm again, analyzing each passage.

He found meaning throughout the psalm but believed that the most direction correlation to the crime was found in verse 23: "Let their eyes be darkened, that they see not; and make their loins continually to shake."

David was shot over his blind eye. He could not see the bullet coming.

CHAPTER 49

As he promised at the beginning of the trial, Judge Baumgartner held court on Saturday. Investigator Perry Moyers brought his son with him to observe a portion of the trial. Raynella's daughters, Maggie Connaster and Katie Butler, were not present for the state's portion of the trial, but they arrived for the remainder of the proceedings.

James Bell began the morning's defense by requesting a directed verdict of acquittal on the grounds that the state had offered insufficient proof for a jury to even consider the case. The judge denied the motion.

Maggie, plump with a pregnancy that had run past her due date, took the stand to testify on her mother's behalf. She spoke about the difficulty of losing her father and her brother when she was so young. That opened the door for the prosecution to talk about the death of Ed Dossett.

On cross-examination, Richard Fisher asked, "Speaking of your father, how did he die?"

"I don't know," Maggie said.

From the jurors' box, Bryan Creech was perplexed. Here was a very intelligent woman with three postgraduate degrees, including a doctorate, who worked as a scientist, and yet she didn't know how her father had died? It made no sense.

A few questions later, Maggie began to cry and her whole body shook. "I don't remember the question," she said.

"If you don't want to answer the question . . ."

"No. No, it's not that," she said, pointing down at the piles of submitted evidence gathered just below her. "That picture. I've never seen it before. Please take it away."

Lying on top of the pile was an autopsy photograph of David Leath's face. The blood was cleaned away. The stippling and wound stood out in stark contrast to his pale, dead skin. The judge ordered the evidence concealed from view.

The defense called the long-awaited alibi witnesses in the hopes of convincing the jury that Raynella was not at home when the fatal shot was fired. One testified about Raynella coming in with flowers for her mother-in-law that morning. On cross-examination, that witness admitted that on that morning Raynella was not wearing the mask she was supposed to wear because of the liver ailment that compromised her immune system; however, she was wearing it when she returned a couple of days later.

Bryan, meanwhile, deduced that she had not worn the mask during that critical visit on the day of David's death because she wanted to make sure that she was recognized by as many people as possible.

Someone from Katie's high school testified that Raynella showed up at the school to deliver her daughter's medication because Katie had forgotten to take it with her. Then a nurse who worked with Raynella took the stand. After her testimony and cross-examination, one of the jurors read an approved question: "As a nurse in this hospital, would you know how to mix up these drugs and use them to knock someone out?"

"Yes," the nurse said.

The defense team scrambled at their table, shuffling papers, whispering to each other, and looking panicky. The jurors heard James Bell say, "Just tell everybody else out there we won't need them." Then he stood, faced the judge, and said, "The defense rests."

It was an awkward moment in the courtroom. No one had seen this coming. The jurors were baffled. The alibi for Raynella's movements was full of huge holes. Despite the promises in the opening statement, it proved nothing.

Before closing arguments began, the jury broke for lunch. One juror received word that her husband was dying from meningitis. She informed the judge and he released her from service to go to her spouse's bedside. Now only thirteen remained.

Paula Hamm and James Bell divided the time allotted to the defense for closing arguments. Hamm called David's death a crime but insisted that it didn't matter how he had died because Raynella was not at home when David was shot. She reminded jurors that her client willingly gave law enforcement permission to search her home, did not hesitate to give them the clothes she was wearing, and didn't offer a single objection to taking a gunshot residue test. Despite her client's cooperation, investigators could find no forensic evidence indicting her guilt. "No prints, no blood, nothing that ties Raynella to the gun, to the ammunition." She added, "The rest of this woman's life is now in your hands."

James Bell pled with the jury, displaying a passionate conviction that his client was innocent. He mocked the theory promulgated by the prosecutors that Raynella drugged her husband to stage a suicide when she murdered him. "Can't you see how preposterous this is?"

He talked about David's homicide, no longer making the smallest attempt to insinuate that Dave died by his own hand. He, too, insisted that no matter the means of his death, Raynella was not there when it happened. "If you believe Ms. Raynella murdered him, you have to believe she is nothing but a serpent of Satan."

He said the state's case relied on sneaky innuendo and quotations lifted out of their original context and twisted into alien shapes: "The hardest lie to detect is half truth. The state's case is only half the story."

Bell launched into an angry, loud rant against Investigator Perry Moyers. Bell's face reddened. He waved his arms in the air. He accused the detective of being a liar, of being malicious, of having a personal vendetta.

Moyers was stunned. The one day he brought his son to the courtroom was the day Bell chose to vilify his character. His boy, sitting a few rows back, heard every accusation.

Everyone in the courtroom appeared shocked at the level of Bell's vitriol. It sounded personal and vindictive. When jurors spoke after the trial, they agreed that it was so over the top, each one of them felt that there was no basis for Bell's accusations. The state objected, calling the attack unprofessional.

Instantly, Bell transformed. His shoulders slumped. His face dragged downward. From a bold, loud, raging man, he turned into a quiet, weepy penitent. "It was like watching Dr. Jekyll and Mr. Hyde," Bryan said. In one juror's opinion, the entire jury thought that Bell's performance seemed as genuine as a pink dollar bill.

His voice cracked as he wrapped up his argument. "I have been friends with Ed and Raynella for more than forty years, but Raynella has only been my client since 2003. I am now trusting you with my friend. Please give my friend back to me."

Bell collapsed in his chair behind the defense table with tears rolling down his face. Now it was Raynella's turn to comfort him.

Special prosecutor Richard Fisher painted a colder portrait of the defendant and the death of David in his closing remarks. "He didn't have time to say goodbye, to say, 'Lord forgive me,' or to say anything." He reminded the jurors that in the very first call, Raynella told the emergency operator that her husband had committed suicide. As a nurse, she was capable of rendering aid. Had she done so, she would have been covered in David's blood. "But just as her own lawyers have said, there was not one speck of blood on her clothes."

Fisher hammered home the greed motive. "Only one person stood to gain from this, and she did gain. She gained everything."

After closing arguments, the jurors informed the judge that they wanted to commence working on their decision on Sunday. He agreed to their request.

All players in the courtroom drama returned to Judge Richard Baumgartner's courtroom at 9:00 a.m. The judge drew one slip of paper from the fishbowl containing the names of all the remaining jurors. The designated alternate was J. Bryan Creech.

Despite Bryan's reluctance to be selected for the jury in the beginning, after five days of trial and six nights of separation from his family, he was invested in the outcome. "I was upset. I put my job on hold. My family was on hold. And now I was off of the jury but I was still sequestered. I couldn't talk to the others. I couldn't play cards with them in the evening. I could only talk with my guard, Deputy Meredith Driskell."

He opted to ride around in the back of a patrol car that day instead of going back to his empty hotel room, where there was no television, no radio, no telephone, no computer, nobody. He joked that if he saw someone he knew while riding around town, he would put his wrists together, hold them up, and wave, pretending he was handcuffed.

Eight women and four men filed into the deliberation room at 10:12 that Sunday morning to begin their deliberations. They had five days of testimony to consider, more than one hundred exhibits to review, and a wide range of charges to consider: first-degree murder, second-degree murder, voluntary manslaughter, aggravated assault, reckless homicide, and criminally negligent homicide.

The moment the jury was out of the courtroom, special prosecutor Richard Fisher rushed to the airport to fly to Washington, D.C., to handle mediation in another case. He would not return in time to hear the reading of the verdict.

In the jury room, the panel took their first vote. Three jurors thought the state had not proven their case. Foreman Jeremy White went to each juror individually about the reasons for their decision. He drew a line down the middle of a dry-erase board and wrote the reasons for guilt on one side and the reservations about guilt on the other. Then they discussed each point, one by one.

They took a short half-hour break for lunch. Around 1:00 o'clock that afternoon, the jury requested to hear the 911 tape again. After it played, the vote for conviction was eleven to one. Then they dissected the defense's timeline and decided that her alibi simply did not hold up. The person leaning toward not guilty was now uncertain of her vote.

The foreman asked that the .38-caliber revolver be sent into the jury room. Juror Miranda Linkous told reporter Yvette Martinez of WBIR, "Holding that gun really set things in place—like, this is the gun that took somebody's life."

At 4:30 that afternoon, they called it a day. They were taken straight to Calhoun's on the River for dinner.

Deputy Driskell took Bryan to the same restaurant. But he had to walk past the jurors without speaking or acknowledging them in any way. He was seated at a table as far away from theirs as possible.

When they returned to the hotel, Bryan was literally locked in his room. He waited while the jurors made their five-minute calls home. When they were finished and back in their rooms, Bryan was allowed to step into the hall to call his family.

Deputy Driskell said, "I really want to ask you what you think but I can't do that."

"I tell you what," Bryan said. "I'll get a piece of paper and write down the decision I would have made and I'll write down what I think the jury's verdict will be."

Back in his room, Bryan wrote: "My verdict is guilty of premeditated murder. I think the jury will find her guilty, too." He stuck the note in an envelope and sealed it shut.

The jury returned to their deliberations at 8:40 a.m. on Monday, January 25, 2010. Again they spent only thirty minutes for lunch.

Just after noon, they sent word asking to view the ten-minute crime-scene video again. They filed back into the courtroom, their faces grim, their demeanor agitated. While they viewed the crime scene, Raynella turned her back to the projection site and cried quietly. Maggie Dossett Connaster, looking vulnerable in her advanced state of pregnancy, sobbed in the galley.

Cindy Wilkerson slumped as the close-up of her father's wound filled the wall. Surrounding her, family members and friends squeezed her hands, patted her back, and wrapped arms around her shoulders. One juror covered her face at the sight of the murdered man on the wall. Another wiped away tears.

After a total of nine hours of deliberation over two days, the jury walked back into the courtroom to deliver their decision. Raynella Dossett Leath sat behind the defense table, her face stoic. The judge warned the audience not to show any reaction when the verdict was announced. When the foreman uttered the word "guilty," Raynella's jaw dropped. She looked as shocked as if she had never considered the possibility of conviction. This time, unlike the other times she shed tears, her eyes reddened and her face grew puffy as she cried.

At the hotel, a phone call came that afternoon with the news that the jury had reached their verdict. Officer Driskell handed Steve his cell phone; his sequestration was over. He called his wife. She pulled up the breaking news online and gave him word on the verdict.

Bryan shared the news with the deputies at the hotel. Then he pulled out the sealed envelope and handed it to Deputy Driskell. She read the note and said, "Really? I know she's guilty as sin, but she's just a good old country girl."

Steve Walker felt vindicated. He still believed that Raynella had attempted to kill him, even though that charge had been dismissed. Later that evening his phone would ring nonstop with congratulatory calls from family, friends, police officers, and radio announcers. For the first time since May 1995, Steve slept blissfully through the night—all night long.

In the courtroom, sisters Maggie and Katie clung to each other, seeking comfort as they cried out their anguish. Had the jury found Raynella guilty of a lesser charge, a date would have been sent for sentencing. But since they found had her guilty of first-degree, premeditated murder, the judge announced her automatic life sentence.

With this conviction, Raynella Dossett Leath would be eligible for parole on January 13, 2070.

CHAPTER 50

The judge thanked the jurors and sent them home to their families after eight days and nights of sequestration. Before leaving, many wanted to speak to Investigator Perry Moyers to thank him for his work on the case. They did so in the deliberation room while the judge cleared the courtroom to allow Raynella to spend some time with her family to say goodbye.

Bryan waited in the lobby of the hotel for the jurors to return to retrieve their belongings. A special education teacher who had agonized through the presentation of evidence and the deliberations made a beeline to his side. "What would you have voted?" she asked.

"I would have said guilty," Bryan said.

"Well, that makes me feel better."

Judge Baumgartner also allowed attorney James Bell to escort Raynella to the Knox County Jail instead of being handcuffed and led away like most defendants. Bell recounted the experience: "The hardest ordeal to endure was taking her to the dark, dank cell and telling that woman, 'The Lord has a plan.' She's in jail being fingerprinted. We're getting medicines to her, getting the nursing staff to do a clinical assessment."

Many in community say it that those concessions by the judge were another demonstration of the special treatment Raynella received from the beginning.

Speaking to reporters, special prosecutor Cynthia LeCroy-Schemel said they learned a lot from the first trial. "This was a difficult case for everyone. There are no winners and no losers, only justice. I believe we closed the gap as to any question as to whether it was homicide or suicide, and I believe, because of that, the jury was able to see in fact that it was homicide and that she was the only person who had access and motive to commit the homicide. I think Knox County should be proud today. The cup of justice is full."

One of her cocounsel, Mac McCoin said, "We have great sympathy for the children of Raynella Dossett Leath and the hardship they must be going through, but we were called here to do a job." He also congratulated Investigator Perry Moyers for an investigation well done. He said that the defense was harsh on the lead investigator—even having him followed everywhere he went during the trial. "They attacked him in a personal way which was inappropriate and he has suffered long and greatly with this case as all of us have."

Cindy Wilkerson was relieved by the verdict: "Everybody can rest now. My dad can rest in peace. I loved him and I still miss him every day. This is a big burden off of my shoulders and closure for me and my kids. Something needed to be done. He didn't do it. I didn't do it. They chose the right one today."

Of her father, Cindy said, "He was a good person. A good daddy. A good grandfather. He loved us and we loved him. He loved his job, loved working out and loved to help people. He cared about people."

Twenty-year-old Miranda Linkous, the youngest juror on the panel, echoed Cindy's sentiments in an interview with WBIR: "Learning more about Dave, he was an awesome guy. He reminds me so much of my dad."

As soon as Miranda returned home Monday night, she went online and researched Raynella. She planned to continue to follow the story to the trial for the murder of Ed Dossett.

While Miranda surfed the Internet, Maggie Dossett Connaster went into labor and was rushed to the hospital. She gave birth to a baby boy—a newborn grandchild who Raynella could not hold in her arms.

At 8:05 a.m. the day after the verdict, Raynella arrived at the Tennessee Prison for Women in Nashville. The maximum-security prison could be her home for the rest of her days. The only other prison for women in Tennessee is in Memphis. She underwent a classification process to evaluate her physical and mental health, ascertain her other needs, and make an assessment of the risk she posed in prison.

That same day, Cindy returned to work at the Suburban Barber Shop. Her father had not cut hair there for eight years, but for Cindy it would always be his place. She has taken over the family business and still serves some of her dad's old customers. "It makes me feel good that I work here where he did and he's remembered every day," she said. "I think about him standing behind this chair. It felt different coming to work on this morning after the verdict. It felt good. It felt that justice had been served."

Two days after the trial, one of the alternate jurors who sat through most of the proceedings but was not present for the deliberations called Investigator Moyers. She told him which two pieces of evidence most convinced her of Raynella's guilt. One was the fact that Raynella, a nurse, showed no bloodstains or any other indication on her clothing that she had attempted to help her husband. Secondly, the breakfast beside the bed was not disturbed. Raynella had to reach across it to get the telephone to dial 911. She firmly believed that a panicked woman who had just found her husband dead would have moved more abruptly, disturbing if not capsizing the plate or the glass of milk.

Also on that day, Cindy's attorney James MacDonald filed a motion saying that, since the criminal conviction required a higher degree of proof than a civil trial would have, there was no longer any "genuine issue of material fact in dispute." He said that his client was entitled to much of the property "as a matter of law."

If the motion prevailed, Cindy would get any property held in her father's name and half of any property held jointly by her father and stepmother. Raynella would retain her half of the couple's jointly held land.

James A.H. Bell said the appeals process would begin immediately with a motion for a new trial. His two investigators, Shane Cooper and Jim Bradette, began seeking out jurors. Out of curiosity, Bryan Creech agreed to have lunch with them.

"What single piece of evidence made you decide to convict?" one of the investigators asked.

"It wasn't one, it was collective. One thing piled upon another led to my belief in her guilt."

They asked him about a number of moments in the trial, and Bryan mentioned that he was bothered about the case presented by the defense, especially concerning Raynella's alibi. He read panic at the table after the last witness was cross-examined.

"That was planned," one of them told him. "We even practiced that the night before. It was all staged."

"Really? You shouldn't have stopped when you still had holes in her alibi, when you told us at the beginning that you were to present evidence of a solid alibi." Bryan said. "And, by the way, are you recording this conversation?"

The investigators refused to answer the question, trying to steer him away. Bryan already knew the answer to the question. He'd seen the blinking red light of a tape recorder in one of the investigator's pockets.

The jurors and some of the alternates still maintained regular contact more than six months after the trial. They planned a barbecue get-together at Bryan's house in the fall.

On March 5, however, James Bell's attention turned away from the concerns of Raynella and to his own professional survival. The board of professional responsibility of the Tennessee Supreme Court issued a public censure of attorney Bell for the contempt-of-court charge he received in August 2009 for lying to a federal judge. Before the month ended, federal judge Curtis Lynn Collier of the United States District Court for the Eastern District of Tennessee followed up with a harsh reprimand. He'd considered revoking Bell's federal bar license over the violation, but instead he ordered Bell to lecture on legal ethics to Tennessee's five law schools and its bar associations.

On March 12, 2010, Bell claimed to have new evidence contradicting the state's theory that his client had staged a suicide at the scene of her husband's death. He filed an affidavit from former Knox County sheriff's deputy Steve Robinson. Bell alleged that Robinson told him that park patrol deputy Joe Preston came out of the residence holding the murder weapon in his hand, announcing that the victim was deceased.

When questioned, Deputy Preston said that Bell did not accurately represent what he had said. In fact, according to the logbook kept at the scene, Preston never entered that bedroom and left the scene a few minutes after he arrived.

The prosecutors went on the attack with their answer to Bell's motion. "It has been the Defendant's 'method of practice' throughout these proceedings to interview witnesses and then prepare inaccurate affidavits that attempt to summarize their testimony."

They argued that the defense counsel had over three years to interview Deputy Preston and "could have easily determined the falsity of the perjured affidavit; that is, if they were interested in presenting the truth to the court. . . . This is the same 'do anything to win' behavior displayed by defense counsel in their increasing efforts to alter the course of justice."

Judge Richard Baumgartner was not pleased with the attitude of the prosecution. "This is a very, very serious allegation, and I don't know what basis there is for it. I don't like it. I wish you had waited until all the facts were in before implying a perjury scheme." The judge ruled that the defense had no reason to doubt the veracity of the statement when they submitted it to the court.

Bell tried another tricky maneuver for his client. He issued subpoenas for depositions in connection with Raynella's nursing license. He claimed he did so in order to help Raynella keep her license. The prosecution called it a hunting expedition, because no nurse convicted of a felony can retain her license. The prosecutors called the state nursing board and the depositions were quashed.

The state's attorneys moved to drop the charges against Raynella for the death of William Edward Dossett on July 9, 1992. The judge agreed to do so without prejudice, meaning the charges could be refiled at any time.

Meanwhile, Raynella Dossett Leath settled into prison life. The Tennessee Prison for Women, built in 1966, is the main facility for the 2,200 female offenders in the state. It houses all levels of inmates, from those in prerelease status all the way up to death row. There is now only one woman in the state under a sentence of death, thirty-four-year-old Christa Pike. She, too, was convicted in Knox County. She received capital punishment in the January 1995 torture and murder of fellow student Colleen Slemmer. When Christa was arrested, authorities found a piece of Colleen's skull in Christa's pocket.

Raynella is teaching Bible classes to the women in the penitentiary. The other inmates call her Mama Ray.

CHAPTER 51

The air was cool, the sky dark. Light rain fell on the umbrellas of the mourners gathered to pay their last respects to David Leath—seven years to the day after his death. Now that there was justice for her father, Cindy finally felt it was time to remove his ashes from the barbershop and put them to rest in Oak Ridge Memorial Gardens.

The brief service was conducted by Reverend Henry Lenoir, Leath's pastor at Solway United Methodist Church. Family friend John Underwood delivered the eulogy. He began by reading "Joy in Death," a poem by Emily Dickinson:

> If tolling bell I ask the cause.
> 'A soul has gone to God,'
> I'm answered in a lonesome tone;
> Is heaven then so sad?
>
> That bells should joyful ring to tell
> A soul had gone to heaven,
> Would seem to me the proper way
> Good news should be given.

John then spoke words from his heart. "Today, March 13, 2010, marks the seventh anniversary of David's death, though his memories remain as vivid today as they were in 2003. For his daughter, Cindy, his grandchildren, Tyler and Lindsey, and the rest of his family and friends, the road traveled has not been easy.

"Each day over the last seven years has unfolded like a book before us. Though the pages and chapters of the book provided us with many answers, the journey has been long. Today, this family comes together seeking closure, not of David's memories, for they will live on within us, but of a difficult journey.

"So it is fitting that the remains of this good and decent man be placed here in this beautiful memorial park by those who loved him. David will rest beside two people who journeyed with him and provided him their unconditional love.

"This afternoon, somewhere, a bell will toll."

Nineteen-year-old Tyler Wilkerson held a white rectangular box with a green diamond design on its top. It contained his late grandfather's ashes. He carefully and reverently eased the box into its prepared place in the ground. The crowd watched silently as the small hole in front of the memorial plaque was filled and then packed with dirt.

Reverend Lenoir, a veteran of many graveside services, walked with unsteady steps and stooped posture to the graveside. He bowed a bald head fringed with pure white hair and led them all in the Lord's Prayer.

The heavens cried with Cindy, beating a farewell dirge on her upraised umbrella.

AFTERWORD

William J. Stuntz wrote in the *Harvard Law Review*: "American criminal justice is rife with inequity."

I doubt that anyone would deny that reality. Many focus on race-based inequalities. Books written on this subject are filled with compelling and undeniable statistics showing discrimination against people of color.

Others have focued on gender bias, where statistics tend to point in both directions.

Women, responsible for 10 to 12 percent of all homicides, make up less than 2 percent of the residents on death row.

Historically, men have gotten off easy when the person they assaulted was an intimate partner. The abuse of women has garnered short sentences. Women's fears and injuries caused by domestic partners have not been taken as seriously as other crimes.

Yet, when it comes to the ultimate form of domestic violence, spousal murder, the penalty women pay is far less than that of men. A 2009 study found that in 35 percent of domestic homicides, a male is the victim, but that number is not reflected in the judicial outcomes. Of women accused of killing their husbands and facing trial by a judge or jury, 31 percent were acquitted, while men charged with the same crime received a not-guilty verdict only 6 percent of the time. Sentencing demonstrated a similar bias. Men who killed their wives received an average incarceration term in excess of sixteen years, but for women it was only six years. A mere 15 percent of the convicted wives had to serve twenty years or more, but 43 percent of husbands received that level of punishment.

Although the evidence of gender inequality is persuasive, I strongly believe that the worst inequity in the system is created by wealth, privilege, and power. It contributes to racial and gender imbalance and creates inequality of its own. We see it every day on the national level with celebrities who come afoul of the law: Paris Hilton's bust for cannabis possession, Charlie Sheen's domestic violence charges, and the case of New York real estate mogul and multimillionaire Robert Durst, never prosecuted for the disappearance and suspected homicide of his first wife and later acquitted of first-degree murder of his neighbor because the jury believed his claim of self-defense, even though he admitted to dismembering the body in Galveston, Texas. We see the special treatment afforded celebrities splashed on our televisions and filling up blogs on the Internet. But unless it is in our town, we seldom notice how much that scenario is repeated on the local level. In town after town, those with influence, the big frogs in small ponds, get away with a lot—sometimes even murder.

The elite in any community, who can afford the brightest and best legal talent, face less possibility of conviction and, if convicted, a lesser sentence. Those who must rely on the services of a court-appointed attorney take a gamble: they may get competent, dedicated counsel or they may have the luck of Calvin Burdine in Texas. His lawyer fell asleep at least ten times during his trial, and Calvin ended up on death row.

This image of Lady Justice standing on an auction block, ready to accommodate the highest bidder, violates the American precept of fair play and makes a mockery of our vaunted "equality under the law." It should never be tolerated.

Raynella received life imprisonment for the murder of her second husband, David Leath, but even prior to that she'd walked away unscathed from situations that would have destroyed the lives of many of the rest of us. Over the years she seemed to develop an attitude that the rules were made for others—that she was free to do as she wished.

She caused fear in her nursing students and neighbors. Members of both of her husband's families said she could be very charming—unless she didn't get her way. They warned each other not to cross her.

When her first husband, county prosecutor Ed Dossett, died, the first appearance of preferential treatment in the justice system was demonstrated. The medical examiner bowed to her wishes and did not perform a full autopsy. He overlooked the fact that the prime suspect in any homicide occurring at home is the spouse or significant other of the victim. After an incomplete procedure, he issued a full report calling the cause of death an accident before seeing the toxicology results.

That testing revealed an exceedingly high amount of morphine in Ed Dossett's system. The medical examiner passed the report on to the district attorney general's office. Those prosecutors did nothing. Even though many people in that office believed insurance fraud was involved in Ed's death, they made no move to investigate or press any charges against the widow, who raked in a stash of double indemnity cash from the life insurance company.

Raynella's next clash with the law also garnered special treatment for the prosecutor's widow. When her daughter Maggie drove off in the truck with her brother in the passenger's seat, Raynella should have been with her, since her daughter possessed only a learner's permit, which required the presence of a licensed adult in any vehicle Maggie operated. People arriving at the scene said she was not at the intersection at the time of the wreck, but Raynella told the officers that she was there, sitting in the middle seat. No one investigated or questioned what she said. Despite other witnesses on the scene, they took Raynella's word. After all, she was the prosecutor's widow, a woman of great influence in local Republican Party politics and a millionaire since receiving the life insurance payment after the death of her first husband.

Showing even more preferential treatment, the local prosecutor encouraged the state troopers not to bring charges against her daughter and urged them to file charges against the other driver for driving without a license. When they indicted Raynella's daughter despite the prosecutor's wishes, he dismissed the case against Maggie when it came to court.

Then there was the Steve Walker incident. Fortunately, law enforcement did not take Raynella at her word this time. They believed the victim and charged her with attempted murder. But then, no one pulled up to her doorstep, handcuffed her, tossed her in the backseat of a squad car, and made her perp-walk into the jail. She was allowed the privilege of turning herself into the authorities with her attorney by her side.

Throughout the proceedings, she was treated like a delicate flower of the South. Poor Raynella. She lost her husband and then her only son died in an automobile accident. Both incidents are worthy of empathy. After her losses, she did cut a sympathetic figure—but not enough that we ought to lose sight of the fact that if she'd had just one more bullet in her revolver, Steve Walker might well have died in a ditch, shot in cold blood.

Nonetheless, the attempted-murder charge was dropped. She was put on probation and given community service and diversion. In a few short years her whole slate was wiped clean, as if she'd never premeditated murder or terrorized and chased down another human being.

Was it any surprise that Raynella expected everyone to

believe her when she claimed David's death was a suicide? The system had done everything it could to convince her she was untouchable. She was Raynella Dossett Leath, the twice-widowed onetime prosecutor's wife. She was intelligent. She was educated. And with the accumulated assets gained in land and life insurance, she was a wealthy woman. How could they not believe her?

For years it appeared as if she would never be brought to account for the death of David Leath. It took six long years to for Raynella to come to trial the first time. Along the way, the prosecutors tried again and again to exhume the body of her first husband. Every time, the court denied the request. Why was the chief suspect in a man's possible murder even allowed to express an opinion to the court? It seemed a perverse twisting of justice.

If it hadn't been for the serendipitous fact of two brands of ammunition in Raynella's revolver, she might not have been held accountable for David's murder as well.

We can't always depend on these quirks of fate. Unless we work in a prosecutor's office or in law enforcement, we can't directly impact the erosion of justice caused by the influence of power, money, and privilege.

However, we can speak up when we see it happening in our backyard. We can make it clear that we do not find favoritism an accepted practice. We can raise our voices with public statements of outrage and we can make our feelings known at the ballot box when we vote for elected officials like the district attorney and the sheriff.

We can also watch for the red flags in relationships formed by our friends and family. If we see someone involved with a person who is learning the lesson that privilege means there are no consequences for bad behavior, we can issue warnings to others, encouraging them to back away. If we see this situation in one of our own relationships, we need to create distance to secure our personal safety.

Raynella Dossett Leath still could face trial for premeditated murder of her first husband, Ed Dossett. The evidence seems to indicate that she, in some manner, was involved in his death. But how?

Was it a mercy killing? Did the stress of watching Ed suffer and linger in pain make her crack and take his life? Or could it possibly have been an assisted suicide? In either of those cases, many who have cared for a loved one in their final torturous days could understand her motivation. Even if they did not condone her actions, they could empathize with them. If it was assisted suicide, Raynella could admit to that crime, waive the statute of limitations, and not serve any additional time.

However, if Raynella Dossett Leath is guilty of premeditated murder, whether stemming from impatience, loathing, greed, or some other self-serving motive, she should receive the full penalty of the law. If the charge is true, a sentence consecutive to the one she is now serving would be the only way to honor and validate the life of William Edward Dossett.

In this case, as always, my fervent wish is that Lady Justice will assume her classic image with blindfold secured, exposing the truth, and doing the right thing for everyone harmed by an act of violence—without any regard to the bank account, gender, skin color, or social standing of either the perpetrator or the victim. For that is the only true definition of justice.

ACKNOWLEDGMENTS

You hold in your hands my eleventh true-crime book and possibly the most interesting case to date. With this book—as with all of the others—"I have always depended on the kindness of strangers." (Thank you, Tennessee Williams, for giving those words to your memorable character, Blanche DuBois.)

On the top of my list is Steve Walker, who looked down the barrel of Raynella's revolver and lived to tell the tale. Thank you, Steve, for reliving those terrifying moments and sharing your memories with me.

A special thanks to dogged Investigator Perry Moyers of the Knox County Sheriff's Office cold case unit. His insight into the cases was invaluable. Perry, I've added you to my Favorite Lawman list. Thanks, too, to Detective Ray Treece of the Sheriff's Office and Sergeant Gary Moyers of the Knoxville Police Department.

For memories of David Leath, thanks to his daughter Cindy Wilkerson, his first wife, Peggy Rowe, his fellow barber, Hoyt Vanosdale, his cousin Frieda Jo Brock-Miller, and his good friend Gordon Armstrong and his wife, Gail.

For memories of Ed Dossett, thanks to Norman Jackson, Chris Cawood, Elizabeth Perril, Ray Graves, and James McMillan.

And thanks to Jim Campbell and Beverly Conner for their recollections of Oak Ridge and Raynella Large and to Mildred and W. C. Large.

For those of you who shared your memories but didn't want the world to know your names, I have honored your request but wanted you, too, to know how much I appreciated your assistance and enjoyed talking to you.

Thanks to these legal eagles: Assistant District Attorney General Cynthia LeCroy-Schemel and her boss, Tenth Judicial District attorney general Steve Bebb; Eighth Judicial District attorney general Paul Phillips; Knoxville attorney James McDonald; and my friend, New Braunfels, Texas, attorney Ron Friesenhan.

I have much appreciation for jury members Lee Stensaker and J. Bryan Creech for sharing their thoughts and recollections of Raynella's trials.

A big thank-you to my favorite private eye, Dan Phillips of Mission Investigations in New Braunfels and to Ronald Lee at the Tennessee State Library and Archives.

Thanks also to Michael Rogers of Jupiter Productions, producer of *Snapped*; Lynn Brownell at *Mountain Press*; and Betty Bean, reporter for the defunct *Knoxville Journal*, who now writes for the online edition of the *Knoxville News Sentinel*.

For local hospitality, my gratitude to Cleveland Kendrick and Robin Carter of the Hotel St. Oliver, a temporary residence that truly felt like home; Coffee and Chocolate for terrific lattes, unbelievable Chipotle Carmel Chocolates, and their friendly staff; Earth to Old City for fun shopping and excellent conversation; La Costa with its comfortable ambiance and incredible food; Shonos with its yummy sushi; Peggy Thompson and all the fine folks in the Knox County Courthouse; the helpful librarians at the Lawson McGhee Public Library; and Shelley Wascom at Community Shares of Tennessee.

For research assistance, a big thank-you—and a promise

of chocolate—to my good friend Sue Russell, author of *Lethal Intent*.

As always, there are four people who make it possible for me to write these tales of true crime: the unsurpassable Charles Spicer at St. Martin's Paperbacks; Yaniv Soha, the terrific editor who improves every manuscript I send to him; my fabulous agent, Jane Dystel—I'd be lost without her; and the person who never seems to mind accommodating a sometimes crazed writer, the one and only Wayne Fanning, the keeper of my heart.

FULL
MOON

FULL MOON

The Amazing Rock and Roll Life of the Late Keith Moon

Dougal Butler

with Chris Trengove and Peter Lawrence

WILLIAM MORROW AND COMPANY, INC.

New York   1981

Library of Congress Cataloging in Publication Data

Butler, Dougal.
    Full Moon.

    "Morrow quill paperbacks."

    Previously published as: Moon the Loon.
    1. Moon, Keith, 1946-1978. I. Title.
ML419.M66B9   1981   789′.1′0924 [B]   81-38416
ISBN 0-688-00759-7   AACR2
ISBN 0-688-00757-0 (pbk.)

Printed in the United States of America

    2   3   4   5   6   7   8   9   10

BOOK DESIGN BY MICHAEL MAUCERI

CONTENTS

Get a Job 9

You Better Move On 25

Roadrunner 75

You've Got a Friend 125

Don't Throw Your Love Away 167

I Can't Help Myself 185

Act Naturally 217

Who's Sorry Now? 245

Glossary 263

FULL MOON

Get a Job

At the time I first meet up with The Who they are not quite the most famous rock and roll band in the world. It is roughly 1966/67 though you will find that exact dates are not this history's greatest strength—this is partly on account of I have a memory like a sieve and partly on account of being somewhat disorientated by medicines of one sort or another—a time when I am working as a Customs & Excise clerk at Heathrow Airport, London, England. This is by no means the most exciting job in the world and it is especially unappealing to an immaculately suited, short-haired Mod, which is what I am at this time.

However, operating as a Customs & Excise clerk does earn me a small amount of cash money each week and each week I take this to various clubs where Mods and other dudes of similar interests to my own meet to drink, dance, fight, take pills and, occasionally, practice sexual intercourse upon the various chicks present. The Ricky Tick, The Starlight Ballroom (Wembley), The Blue Moon, The Georgian at Cowley and Burton's Dance-hall are some of the more popular of these clubs and may be familiar to any of you who are sensible enough to be Mods at this time. Such Mods will also remember that it is around this time that The Who begin to make their breakthrough, for it is in 1965 that they release their first hit, *I Can't Explain*, and it is in 1967 that they go on their first American tour which, incidentally, leaves them the thick end of £50,000 in debt—despite its pulling American kids in all over the place.

Well, it is in Burton's Dancehall that I meet Bobby Pridden who is a fairly small, nothing sort of geezer famous only for feet that are inclined to produce a particularly dire pen and ink, and which cause many of the punters at Burton's to leave him a great deal of space in which to dance about. The reason that I am familiar with Bobby Pridden is that I know him from when we are kids, and he is the boy that everyone takes great delight in beating up when there is not much else to do. I am probably one of the few people who rarely join in this pastime because, when it comes to fisticuffs, I am not a keen sportsman. Not, I add, because I am in any way a pacifist or unable to take care of myself, but because I prefer to leave such exercise until it is seriously necessary and inevitable. But this is all by the by, except that it is how I originally know Bobby Pridden and, when I see him at Burton's, he is The Who's roadie. He achieves this distinction, despite the smell of his feet, by being the only one of all the prospective roadies who offers to buy John Entwistle, The Who's bass guitarist, a drink. So that is a lesson for anyone inclined to be near with his money; buy your round and it may get you the job.

Before he joins The Who, Bobby works with The Alan Bown Set and Cliff Bennett and the Rebelrousers which, in case you are never privileged to hear it, is once a very wonderful showband indeed. So Bobby knows more or less which end of a bass guitar is which.

When I nod to Bobby at Burton's we commence to bunny.

"What you up to?"

"Fucking Customs & Excise clerk down the airport," I reply. "Fucking boring."

"Good money?" he asks.

"Not bad, but I ain't putting the deposit down on me Roller just yet."

Well, at this stage a little chick with a very hot ass and neat Playtex-pointed tits gives the come-on and, feeling a tingle in the cricket set, I leave Bobby and jump about with this little chick until she makes similar come-on gestures to a huge geezer with a scar running from his eyebrows right down inside the neck of his Ben Sherman button-down. Suddenly the cricket set ceases to tingle and, in the absence of anything better to do, I return to Bobby Pridden. Now, whether he wishes to impress me or what I do not know, but the next thing Bobby Pridden says to me is:

"Fancy a gig with The Who?"

"I don't mind," I answer, being very cool and thinking to myself that it can't be worse than Heathrow Airport, London, England. "What sort of dough?" I ask.

"Fifteen quid," says Bobby. "If you're lucky."

"OK."

"Come down the office, then. Monday. End of the week we've got a gig in Scotland."

With that I leave Bobby Pridden and his terrible feet and continue my search for available gash.

All these years later, I cannot recall whether this search is fruitful but, the next day, I find myself in Old Compton Street, in London, which is where Track Records, the recording company handling The Who at this time, has its offices. It is in these offices, smartly suited up in a Hepworth's three-piece, that I have my first encounter with the band and the man who has such an effect on my life. I have to admit that my first sight of The Who, close up, is quite a surprise.

Of course, I often watch the band perform before I actually meet them, but it is one thing to watch them playing and quite another to speak to them. My first impression is that they are four very flash geezers indeed, what with all wearing fur coats. Their hair is too long for my Mod tastes but I see straightaway that Daltrey is small, quiet and a bit of a hard nut; Entwistle seems even quieter and sort of looks into himself; Moon has a mischievous good-looking boatrace with a million laughs tucked in behind those dark eyes; and Townshend, well Townshend has an extremely large hooter. I do not mention this observation to Townshend because I know that he has a reputation of being handy with his fists when necessary and, anyway, he is generally thought at this time to be the driving force behind the band.

I do not have time to notice more than this because I am only a few moments in the office before the band agrees to Bobby's suggestion to employ me as a roadie, at least for the duration of the Scottish tour, and once this decision is made nothing will do but we must all go down to The Ship Inn, Wardour Street, and have a few bevvies.

It is on the way to this pub, comfortably ensconced in a very smart two-tone Bentley, that I realise that the reason for my rapid and casual employment is not so much my magnetic personality as the fact that the geezers who are well on their way to becoming the most famous rock and roll band the world ever sees are further out of it than a handful of cardinals at a Bar Mitzvah. Of course, this is no great surprise because The Who are practically a religious experience for all good Mods and, in turn, all good Mods are firm believers in communion with medicines of many types and colours.

Once in the pub, I sink a couple of light-and-bitters and soon find myself in a considerably inebriated state—and if that seems a relatively small amount of alcohol on which to become olivered I can only say that at this stage I am more accustomed to take medicine in pill form. Through this quite ordinary introduction I find myself one week later at the wheel of a Hertz rental truck loaded with the band's equipment and headed for the first gig in Scotland—the first gig of my time with Keith Moon.

From the start, this must be made clear: what I am telling you is the story of my ten years with Moonie. Ten years as Moonie's personal. Moonie's man, that is. During that time, no one knows Moonie better than me because no one, not even his wife, spends as much time with him as me. No one sees him in the trouble I see him in. No one sees him in the states I see him in. I doubt, too, whether anyone has the laughs I have with Keith Moon, this geezer that some journalist with not much imagination but a sure eye for the quick buck, quick copy and sod the truth calls: MOON THE LOON.

Of course, I do not have Moonie entirely to myself but it is true that no one has such intense contact with him as I do for the ten years up to 1977.

Please do not think this is the story of The Who. It is just the story of Moonie as I see him and, as far as it goes, it is true. OK, here and there the incidents from several trips or tours are rolled into one big incident or trip. Like making one giant spliff from several butt ends. But that doesn't mean that each incident is not true—any more than the roaches that die for the cause of the giant joint are not smoked before they become butt ends. What is more, this story is not a chronological narrative simply because it cannot be either described or remembered like that. Life with Keith Moon is not a simple progression from Monday to Sunday, waking to kipping, paypacket to bank, breakfast to dinner. It is much more a glorious bugger's muddle of laughs and madness, highs and lows, jolly-ups and shout-ups—all interspersed with spells of boredom and depression. During these spells I creep away to my old haunts, to my family and to my mates, sane islands in a sea of madness. Moonie, however, simply retires to his bed and blasts himself to oblivion with Jan & Dean at 200 watts per channel. This erratic ten-year roller-coaster ride is fueled by great quantities of medicines washed down by greater quantities of other medicines—mainly brandy and champagne—which is, of course, why no prolonged time with Moonie can be remembered as a simple and straightforward narrative.

I am sure that if Keith Moon lives now, his memory of this time will be equally episodic.

However—to return to the Scottish gig—Bobby Pridden and I set up the equipment so that the band can commence playing at the time for which it is booked, which is nine o'clock. It is a good thing that I have Bobby to guide me because what I know about electronics and electrics and musical instruments you could stuff into a gnat's piss-pot and still have room for the piss. Even while I am wrestling with the intricacies of the wiring I begin to grow concerned that, though it is quite late, there is little sign of the audience. When I mention this to Bobby he just tells me that the concert is Sold Right Out and not to worry. Yet when nine o'clock comes and the band kicks off with *My Generation*, with Daltrey revving up very strong, my worries are well founded because I can see that there are approximately ten people in the hall and ten people in a hall that holds at least a few thousand is by no means SRO.

What transpires is this: this concert is held in some obscure Scottish dorp with a name that sounds like the title to a tedious folk song and is surrounded by many sheeps and many dogs that all look something like Lassie. Most of the inhabitants of this place with the folk song name are not Who fans. In fact very few of them even hear of The Who. All they can take is a couple of bars of Jimmy Logan and as far as they are concerned Kenneth McKellar borders on punk. Mind you there are very few people in this world who can take more than a few bars of either Kenneth McKellar or Jimmy Logan, but that is altogether another kettle of fish. So there is no way that these inhabitants will be able to mob out a Who concert, even in a hall that only takes a few hundred. What the tour promoter does, therefore, is to hire coaches which drive around outlying districts, scouring the hovels, farms and villages to pick up many Scottish youths most of whom are characterized by red hair and spots dotted around their beezers. Along with such youths, the coaches also collect many Scottish bints who, as far as hair and spots go, are about identical to the youths but are partly distinguishable on account of having lumps fitted here and there.

Of course, the concert promoters, being tighter than a ring snake's arsehole, which is very tight indeed, do not give the job of audience transportation to efficient, dynamic, and therefore relatively expensive, operators. No, what they do is hire a couple of down-and-out no-hopers with a few vintage Bedford vans that are last used about the time that Hitler is mixing whitewash. The natural result of this policy is that when Roger is stuttering through *My Generation* not even the first-bussed section of the audience is present. Which, when I learn the cause, is all equal to me because I figure that the carroty kids can pursue the matter with the tour promoters.

Unfortunately the concert hall, which is more accustomed to flower shows than it is to rock and roll riots, begins to fill up just as the band completes the final number. And instead of taking the matter up with the tour promoters, and maybe their lawyers too, what the carroty kids and their bints proceed to do is to take the matter up with such innocent parties as me by hurling Coke bottles and whatever else they can get hold of onto the stage. Because I am up there on stage dismantling the equipment, many of these missiles score direct hits upon my body, forcing me to take shelter behind the amplifiers. So I find myself crouching down and wondering whether I am entirely sane to swap a nice Civil Service number complete with inflation-proof pension, for a post as assistant Who roadie, at £15 a week, which I do not yet receive despite the fact that I am already ten days on the payroll.

This is a question that raises itself frequently during the ensuing days while I haul equipment from one toilet to another, surrounded by idiots, encountering considerable hostility on the way and very rarely receiving the promised ackers, to wit £15 per. In fact, the only way I manage to eat, and this applies to Bobby too, is to diddle the petrol money so that we can afford the occasional egg and chips.

During this Scottish tour, which lasts a couple of weeks, I spend much time with John Entwistle and Keith Moon, mostly because they are where the action is. Daltrey has a tour routine very much his own and relatively private, and, even at this stage, Townshend spends much time inside his own head. What is quite interesting to me, and it seems to occur in many bands and with many individuals, is that very few rock stars behave consistently. What they do when they are at home is very different from what they do when they are out on tour. At home, for instance, John Entwistle is a very quiet sort of bloke and he and his Mrs. are constant targets for vicars and other similar worthies who are looking for new ways to increase the gate at their fêtes and local events. Being easy-going in this respect, John agrees to be used as a crowd-puller. So he is nicknamed The Mayor of Ealing, which is certainly a great knock to his touring reputation as the life and soul of whatever party is going on. But I suppose that rock and roll musicians are no different from any other sort of person who is most polite at the PTA, shakes hands with church wardens and loves small animals but will make Jack the Lad seem like a Trappist monk when he is away from these civilising influences.

The exception to this rule of schizo behaviour is none other than Keith Moon himself, who is consistently unpredictable no matter where he is or who he is with. Moonie simply behaves like a lunatic virtually all the time.

But to get back to Scotland: after two weeks it seems that I am invited to become a full member of the band's road crew. Almost immediately after I make this discovery, I am laid off the job while The Who undertakes its first American tour. The reason for the enforced rest is that the band cannot afford me, all £15 a week of me. However, because I do not know what I miss at the time, I am not especially disappointed and, anyway, make up for this initial absence on many subsequent visits to America. On the band's return from the USA I am promoted to £17 a week, still paid somewhat erratically. After a few weeks rest and recreation, The Who undertakes a grand circuit of Great Britain, along with The Tremeloes, Traffic, Marmalade and The Herd—which then includes Peter Frampton, a rather wet geezer at whose expense we have much fun. It is during this tour that Moonie and I get to communicate for the first time and begin to realise that we have a very similar sense of humour. The first incident leading to our alliance revolves around the

Mini Opera, during which Moonie seizes a tom-tom and plays it upon his lap. When he completes this sequence of playing on the tom-tom, he hurls the entire apparatus up in the air and over his head, where I am standing to catch it.

Now this is a fine piece of theatre which always has the kids screaming and shouting. The only problem with its first performance in my presence is that no one actually bothers to tell me exactly what role I am to play. So when Moonie hurls this heavyweight drum in my direction I find myself clocking a tasty little chick in the front row of the audience and the heavyweight drum hits me right upon my crust—BOFF!—and I do an immediate Cyril Lord, spark out on the carpet.

When I eventually surface and reappear in the late twentieth century, I am no little annoyed with Moonie, figuring, as I do, that he executes this manoeuvre deliberately. So I go looking for him to repay this beaning with a knuckle sandwich. But when I find him and draw back the elbow he simply backs off and says, laughing:

"Steady on, dear boy. An accident. A mere bagatelle. An omission of communication. Have a large brandy, old chap." Quite soon I am sufficiently wrecked to forgive and forget the lump upon my bonce and the spell of dizziness which goes with it.

From this event Moonie and me become as thick as thieves and inflict many merry pranks upon the other bands in the tour. Most of these jests are centered around The Herd, perhaps because it is a rather precious outfit with pretensions that outstrip its talent.

At this time the drummer of The Herd is an old guy who, despite the fact that he is not far off the state pension, is not a bad performer. One of his star turns is in a number called *From the Underworld* during which a bloody great gong is lowered from the beams above the stage so that this pensioner can whack it at the appropriate moments. It all makes for quite a dramatic effect, but that effect becomes extremely comical when Moonie and Entwistle attach wires to the gong and lift it up out of the geriatric drummer's reach just as he goes to make his big play.

So at the end of this highly serious piece, there is the wizard of the timpani leaping up off his drumstool and flailing wildly at the steadily ascending gong, while desperately trying to keep the rest of his drum kit going at the same time. Keith, John, and I nearly fall out of the stage roof with laughing. In fact, The Herd proves to be an endless source of amusement and innocent entertainment to us, and I dare say this daft band gives us a lot more fun than it ever gives any of the kids in the audience. On the last gig of the tour, we wire firecrackers, complete with electronic detonators, to Andy Bown's keyboard, so that his star turn sounds more like a rerun of Pearl Harbor than an Ava Gardner rock number.

But, of course, The Herd is not the only band operating on this tour and everyone else comes in for the Moon treatment too. Traffic at this time play with timpani upstage and to one side of the band, and it is not long before me and Moonie attach thin wires to this equipment so that we can pull it offstage just when it is being used to its fullest effect.

Why do the victims of these little jests and japes not complain to the management, or at the very least beat the living daylights out of Moonie, Entwistle and the boys? Because The Who has a fair reputation for being hard nuts and not many musicians, or anyone else for that matter, are prepared to take their chances.

Capers like these first throw Moonie and me together, making each of us realise that the other is of a similar mind when it comes to mayhem and jolly-ups. But despite all this entertainment, I decide at the end of this tour to curtail my career as a roadie. The work is arduous and boring. The money is fucking dire. Watching the band smash up thousands of pounds worth of equipment and then being told by the management that there is no mazuma with which to pay my weekly £17 is not my idea of a job with a future. And to drive non-stop from Glasgow

to London and back to Glasgow just to pick up some skins for
Moonie's drum kit, on a Sunday, with no thanks and no reward
other than the half-hearted offer of a beer, is not my idea of a
vocation. I mean, just being in Glasgow is bad enough, leave
alone having to drive back to the fucking place from London.
So I think to myself *sod this for a game of soldiers* and decide
to find a proper job where I can win friends and influence people
and, maybe, make a few dibs at the same time.

This decision is further encouraged by the fact that Christmas
1967 sees me absolutely cleaned out. No ackers whatsoever.
Not even a penny. For two weeks preceding this Yuletide no
one pays me any wages, and when you are on £17 a week you
cannot go a day without wages. Two weeks without is like being
sent to cross the Kalahari desert on a unicycle with a flat tyre
and a bottle of neat meths for drinking.

What with seeing many houses with illuminated Christmas
trees, lovers holding hands and exchanging gifts, saucepans with
eager and overexcited faces, and even the odd geriatric smiling
here and there, this state of poverty at Christmas makes me
somewhat desperate. I do not feel festive at all. So when The
Who management of the time tell me about not having received
payment for the last gig and therefore being unable to spring
me even a turkey's leg, I go to touch Peter Townshend for a
few bob. He not only hands over £30 wages but also gives me
a £30 Christmas bonus. But for Peter's generosity, the season
that celebrates an immaculate birth will be also celebrating an
immaculate death. Mine. From starvation.

So, at this time, I cease to be a roadie and commence to hustle
about. You may wonder how anyone can give up the chance to
work with people like Moonie, Entwistle, Townshend and Daltrey. But I can tell you that most bands look on most roadies
as being little more than marginally useful dog shit.

It is true, of course, that most roadies know about as much
as the average piece of dog shit—and I am not saying that I am
too well up on Einstein and the interaction of space and time—
but I do have enough brain not to enjoy being treated like the

average roadie, and at this stage I do not know the boys in the band well enough to be treated as anything else. In fact, just about all I get out of this period is a nickname: Dougal.

This comes about on account of having the same handle as Townshend, which is Peter. We're in De Lane Lea Studios, Kingsway, on a session and Townshend and me keep getting confused whenever anyone calls out:

"Peter!"

So Townshend insists that I have another monicker. When I asked why *he* can't have a nickname, he just looks at me a bit mean and says:

"Because I don't have one. That's why." Fair enough, I think —though this is news to me because Townshend is known by a whole list of names and aliases, the least offensive of which is Big Nose. But I do not mind having a nickname, especially as it is thought up by Moonie's little girl, Mandy, who names me after the little dog in a television programme called *Magic Roundabout*. This name is Dougal and it is given me on account that same canine and I have long blond hair.

Like I say, I am not close enough to any member of The Who for them to think of me as anything other than another member of the Union of Grovellers, Lackeys and Allied Toadies but, when I leave the band, I do keep up with a couple of them— Moonie and Entwistle. Sometimes, when I have time to spare from hustling about on my own behalf, I go to recording sessions with them, or visit The Speakeasy or just go to a pub and have a few bevvies with them. John and his Mrs. are inclined to telephone me now and then to encourage me to drive them to The Speakeasy. They pay for my meal and give me a quid or two for petrol, so that I can drive them home afterwards. It may seem surprising that someone as up and coming as John appears to be paying for his company, but the rock and roll business is so full of creeps and arse-lickers, fakes, frauds and fuckers that perhaps it is safer to pay for someone you know and think you can trust rather than to go along with one of the great circus of hangers-on.

As this time The Speakeasy is a very wonderful place, full of musicians, their wives, other people's wives, bints, groupies and assorted star-fuckers. You can be sitting there and you will clock McCartney and Lennon, Jane Asher, Eric Clapton, Ginger Baker and so on. One time, when I am there with John and his Mrs., waiting for my steak and french fries, there is an unearthly howling at the door and Moonie appears swinging from the ceiling and treading in all the punters' grub. He leaps from table to table, bellowing:

"Hello, hello, hello, dear boys! Hello, my old darlings! Large brandies all round, what?"

Surprising to say, very few of the stars present seem to mind that their steaks are trodden on and their glasses up-turned. Even the bints do not seem to mind being groped. Everyone accepts that this is simply the way that Moonie is. On the other hand, Lennon flees extremely geschvinn indeed when Moonie appears in front of his table, absolutely stark bollock naked and waving his wanger. But then, it is well known that Lennon is unpredictable and, perhaps, is not in the mood to have a dubious prick flashed about in front of his hooter.

One day, after just such a night, I meet up with Moonie and John Entwistle at a *Top of the Pops* recording at Lime Grove, planning to have a few bevvies after the session. I discover that, for some reason best known to himself, John Wolf, at that time the band's driver, does not appear with the Bentley to take Keith and John home. At this time I am driving an exceedingly knackered TR4, which is a sort of two-seat sports car when it is operating, which is not very often on account of being well buggered, and I arrive at the rendezvous to find Moonie leaning up against the railings outside Lime Grove, pissed as a rat and generally somewhat uncoordinated. Entwistle is sitting gloomily on his guitar case and when I ask him what is what and why does he look so glum, he replies thus:

"Wolf's got the fucking Bentley."

"Well where is he?" I ask.

"How the fuck should I know?"

At this stage, Moonie focuses one of his eyes on my tatty jam jar. With no further ado, he leaps into the passenger seat and points forward.

"Highgate, dear boy. Take me to Highgate." Then John slings his guitar in the car and stretches out on the bonnet.

It is quite clear that I cannot drive like this first to John's place and then on out to Highgate. For one thing, the coppers in this country are apt to disapprove of rock and roll guitarists lying about on the bonnets of moving cars and, for another, Entwistle might fall off and sue me. And, anyway, who knows what medicines Moonie has inside him, and any one of these medicines may land me in the pokey for a night or two. So what I do is to creep along to a bus stop, where I leave perhaps the best bass guitarist in the world to catch the 207 bus home to Uxbridge, and then I drive on to Highgate to drop Moonie off.

I do believe that it is my action this evening that later causes Moonie to request me to become his personal assistant.

Well, after nine months of hustling about on my own account, I find that I am no nearer taking over J. Paul Getty and I begin to wonder exactly what the purpose of life is—or even if there is life on earth. If so, how does it finance itself? After much thought, I come to the conclusion that there is life of a very low sort and that, by and large, it finances itself by performing such invigorating tasks as Customs & Excising at Heathrow Airport. With this remarkable discovery in hand, I am about to think of some painless, or even pleasurable, way of knocking myself off, rather than resign myself to such a drab existence. The only problem is exactly where to find the wherewithal to invest in such a method.

Then, out of the blue, after yet another night of lunacy and inebriation at The Speakeasy, John Entwistle telephones me and suggests that I become the driver of the new Citröen DS21 Pallas that he recently buys and is unable to fathom out for himself. As I say, this is nine months after I leave the band and the memory of my time as a roadie—especially of the ball-breaking universities tour that makes me realise just what an abject existence roadies live—is fading. Moreover, this job seems to be more than just a simple roadie's employment, or so I tell myself, and, anyway, I am fond of John and his Mrs.—even if they do open fêtes here and there and discuss the price of fish more than interests me personally.

It does not take John long to discover that, although I am a pretty fair DS21 pilot, I am hopeless at the other half of this job which requires that I should understand which string goes where on a bass and which wire enters which amplifier at what point. I am not a technically minded dude and tend to make the wrong connections. What is worse is that I cannot tell the difference in sounds when I do manage to make the right ones. So what with John's nagging me about this incompetence and his frequently referring to me as a cunt, which I resent, we fall out. Not in any disastrous way—not with fists and boots and knuckles. But we agree that my employment should be terminated and I begin once more to think about alternative methods of raising scratch.

While I am thinking about this, Moonie's personal assistant has a total freakout. This happens to such an extent that even Moonie finds him too much to have around the place, so he gives him the old heave-ho, the tin-tack and the bullet too. When none of this gets through, Moonie tells him to fuck off out of it —but it takes a great deal of time for this message to sink in and the unfortunate geezer hangs around for a surprisingly long time.

Then Moonie calls me up on the telephone and says like this:

"Dougal, dear boy. Hear you're a bit pissed off with the Mayor of Ealing."

"More like he's a bit pissed off with me, Keith."

"Come and work for me, old chap. Sixty quid a week, a room in the house and use of the Roller whenever you fancy it. All right?"

"Aaaaarrrrgggghhhh!" I reply.

"Only thing is, I need to know by tomorrow, dear boy."

This is Saturday.

Sunday I go round to Keith's large house in Chertsey, the house he shares with Kim, with whom he is just together again after a spell apart. I take a gander at my room in the house, then I pick up the Roller and drive down the pub for a drink.

Right, I think, this'll do me.

That's how I come to work for Keith Moon—the start of what is, for me at least, a great friendship. The beginning of ten quite extraordinary years.

You
Better Move On

Much of Moonie's time is spent hurtling from one part of the globe to another because, of course, any rock band which gets past the stage of playing local gigs in bars and pubs spends a great deal of time touring. Now, the definition of "touring" can range from a quick three-weeker taking in various seedy toilets like Sunderland and Wick (or Akron and Millersburg, Ohio), or it can mean a four-month tour involving the whole schmear of private planes, five-star hotels, six trailer trucks for the equipment and a complete rolling entourage of assistants, assistants' assistants, record company people, publicity people, dopers, gropers and all-round no-hopers. Most of these tours on the grand scale take place in the USA and when I arrive on the scene with Moonie, The Who are well past the toilets in Wick (or Akron). In fact, it is not long before they are very much on the five-star level and spending much of their time in the States. It is well known to one and all that, while it is possible to garner a few bobs and a very nice living in Britain, for the really big moolaw it is necessary to crack the Stateside market.

The reasons for this are very simple. First off, the States is quite a large piece of real estate such as would easily accommodate dear old Blighty in one corner of one of the larger states. Thus there are many more people who wish to see rock and roll bands rocking and rolling, and there are also many more people who are happy to fork out the hard-earned in favour of albums that liven up their home life. Second off, it is a strange thing but these people seem to have more of the green and folding stuff about themselves than the average citizen of the UK.

As a result of this the venues where rock and roll may be heard in the States are very different from the halls to which Brits are accustomed. There are stadiums and such like in the States which accommodate perhaps eighty thousand persons, or even more for all I know, whereas even the largest venues in Britain, which are the football grounds, are lucky if they get fifty thousand—apart from Wembley, of course. Mounting a concert in a venue like Earls Court, London, which holds, perhaps, twenty-five thousand punters, is difficult enough but organising a similar concert in the States takes on most of the attributes of a military operation. Except, of course, that those engaged in the business of rock and roll do not normally display the qualities of discipline, reliability and rigidity of upper lip such as are associated with successful military types. Indeed, just about the only items to display rigidity tend to be the roadies' dicks and they are not much use even for fucking, let alone organising a rock and roll concert. Consequently, the average performance on any large scale tends to proceed in what might be called organized chaos. This applies to rock concerts anywhere, but in the States the chaos is on a larger scale and the problems, lunacy and aggravation multiply so that it is quite amazing that any concerts are successfully completed at all.

Naturally, there is a lot more to touring than simply arriving on stage and playing. For a start, the road crews have to be at the venue hours beforehand to complete the setting up, the sound checks, etc. Often there are massive distances to be covered between venues because the one thing the tour organisers never think of is how the road crews should get the equipment from Miami, Florida, to Seattle, Washington, in twelve hours. People often remark:

"Dougal, you are indeed lucky to travel with the most famous rock and roll band in the world and to see so much of one country and another." The truth is that it is quite surprising just how little you do see, on account of you are either on a plane, in a hotel, at the gig or on the job, and the last thing you feel like after a gig involving fifty thousand raving kids is a guided tour round the historical monuments of Baton Rouge. What you feel like is consuming as many medicines as possible in the shortest time possible, then making a beeline for one of the bints that hang around rock and roll bands at all times, in order to perform permutations of screwing the bint/wrecking the hotel/falling senseless upon the floor. All this is much easier to achieve, of course, when you have several people encouraging you in this behaviour and, indeed, competing with you in the matter of causing mayhem.

It becomes very difficult to answer the question "What is it like to tour with Keith Moon?" because my memories of touring become all scrambled up, until it seems sometimes as if all The Who tours are one big tour. Of course, various incidents stick in the mind, and various people have various ways of making the best of touring. Daltrey is perhaps the most consistent and he has a routine which pertains to gig after gig. Townshend and Entwistle sometimes opt in and sometimes opt out and, though they are both masters in the art of mayhem, they cannot hold a candle to Moonie who makes merry in the accepted fashion— that is, with many medicines and a variety of ladies of not completely impeccable character. While Townshend and Entwistle may involve themselves in these celebrations if the mood takes them, Daltrey's routine—at least before his marriage—is to return to the hotel, often with a selected bird, and retire to his suite. There he orders up a nice pot of tea, a toasted muffin or two, and maybe a few cucumber sandwiches. He drinks the tea, eats the muffins, pokes the bird, then it's everybody out and a good eight hours of the dreamless. Fair enough if you like that sort of thing. The other lads in The Who take their pleasures in somewhat more boisterous fashion. John Entwistle is apt to become quite a different character when he is out on the road and, when stimulated by the magic ingredients, will jump about quite considerably. Pete Townshend, too, although he is of a philosophical bent and is liable to commune with various divine presences that are not entirely visible to me, is quite capable of competing with Moonie himself for the title of King of Hotel Wreckers.

But, of course, it is Keith who really relishes life on the road. It is a whole act that might be invented just for him, combining as it does the opportunity to indulge in every kind of excess and then move on. To put it another way, on tour you can shit a lot and never shit in your own nest. Furthermore, there is a built-in audience at all times: backstage staff, hotel and restaurant staff and many other varieties of menials who can be wound up, stitched up and generally fucked up at relatively small personal risk or cost—for this is the thing about menials: they are menial. So, on the road, Moonie is like a dynamo, always buzzing and humming with new schemes and pranks. Maybe this incessant energy is generated because on tour he's playing virtually every night and this keeps him very fit indeed. In spite of the amount of malicious damage that Moonie commits upon himself he is quite remarkably healthy, which is no bad thing, for drumming—and especially as it is practiced by Keith Moon—requires great physical effort. In full flow Moonie puts out as much energy as Battersea power station (assuming it is not on strike, of course). Some university geezer once calculates that in one night on stage Moonie uses up more energy than the average lumberjack does in a week.

Personally, I have some of the best times in my life when I am on the road with Keith Moon but this is partly because I am Moonie's man and do not become involved in all the hassle of setting up gear, driving trucks, organising soundchecks and so on and so forth. There are many who will say that keeping

Moonie together is a greater task than all these things put together and multiplied by seven. However, it is a job to which
I am accustomed and it dictates that I am always where the action is too. No, give me a job as Moonie's personal any day. An
equipment roadie's life is a misery. For a start he is by no means
overpaid, even if he does get first shot at any left-over dope and
surplus groupies. He is the geezer who receives the platefuls of
shit that are thrown around if anything is wrong with the gear
—or if anything goes wrong with anything else for that matter.
And it is certainly not unusual for the equipment roadie to arrive at his hotel completely knackered and starving only to find
that all the grub is in other people's stomachs and several of
those other people are now using his bed.

No, once I am working for Moonie everything is pretty much
plain sailing when it comes to essential life support systems such
as Dom Perignon champagne, Courvoisier VSOP, high class dope
and large porterhouse steaks. Moonie stays in the best hotels,
eats in the best restaurants and travels first class at all times and
I will look after him until the cows come home in exchange for
a good slice of same lifestyle.

It is peculiar, however, that although Moonie flourishes in
America and is well into the big cars and the flash life, he never
really feels at home in the States. Maybe this is because, for all
his fame, he always remains a kid from Shepherds Bush or
maybe it is because he simply finds Americans intimidating, but
all the time that he is in the States, including the time he lives
in Malibu, he generally hangs out with expatriate Englishers
and makes few efforts to fraternise with the natives.

Most of my time on the road is spent trying to get Moonie to
where he is meant to be and trying to prevent him from taking
so much medicine that once he is there he is incapable of performing whatever it is he is meant to perform. Surprisingly
enough he rarely gets so out of it that he cannot do a gig, although it is true that on two occasions I know of it is necessary
to cancel gigs because Moonie is present in body but absent in
the brain department. And, strange to relate, this giant of ex-

hibitionism is actually stage-frightened! Before gigs, before filming and even before a recording session, Moonie is quite often
sick. By which I mean that he indulges in full scale technicolor
yawning and has to take large doses of kaolin and morphine to
soothe his stomach. More often than not, of course, he steadies
his nerves with liberal doses of brandy or similar fluids and this
steadying process usually starts well in advance of the gig. In
fact, the steadying up process often seems to commence several
weeks before it is necessary and it is when it goes on an exceptionally long time that the gig is threatened.

When this happens, it is a most disastrous thing what with
the remainder of the band being all hot to trot and many thousands of kids wishing to hear some rock and roll. Under these
circumstances, the hall management will concoct a plausible
excuse, such as:

"Unfortunately, one of the band is ill." Or

"It appears that the Fire Department is not satisfied with our
safety arrangements."

The kids are then advised that they should retain their tickets
which will be valid for a concert to be arranged at a later date.
In the case of opera or ballet lovers such advice will be met with
a few genteel moans and groans and a high degree of acqui-
escence, leading to a general dispersal toward the exits. But
rock and roll fans are not known for their tolerance of sudden
illness amongst their heroes, and what they tend to do when
they are deprived of an evening's rocking and rolling is to go
raving mad. They cause a great hullaballoo and seek to cause
damage to anyone and anything which is within swinging distance. Naturally, the tour promoters are not keen on this kind of
behaviour as it gives them a bad name and hits them in the
pocket book too, so you can bet your grandmother's pension
that as few gigs as possible are cancelled at the last moment.

One time in LA, in 1973, I go into Moonie's room to pack
him up and drag him off to a gig. The problem is that the gig is
not in LA. It is in San Francisco and we will have to do a bit
of a hurry-up, being as that is a distance of some 400 miles and

Moonie is due on stage in just three hours. Now Moonie is not a very tidy geezer at the best of times and on this occasion there is a certain amount of revelry the night before. A bit of a jolly-up. Nothing too strenuous. A few Buffalo Bills. A spot of brandy. Anyway, Moonie's room is in pitch-black, which is not surprising as he blows out all the lights in the chandelier the night before by hurling the 30″ Hitachi, remote control, spot focus, super deluxe, colour TV set at them. All over the floor, there's glass, bedclothes, broken bottles, tipped up ashtrays and so on and so forth. In fact, the room is a right khazi and right in the middle of it is Moonie, stretched out on his back, completely out of it and stark bollock naked.

Will he wake up? Like fuck, he will.

I shout at him. I shake him. I hit him. I kick him. I roll him over and jump up and down on him a bit. Like someone coming out of a deep anaesthetic, eventually he stirs.

"Ah, dear boy, what is the matter? What's the time? Get me a brandy, there's a good chap."

"Oh no. No brandy. I mean, listen man—you're on stage in three hours and we're not even packed up yet."

"Never mind, dear boy," replies Moonie. "Just throw me over a few pick-me-ups." This means even more aggravation because I have to find Moonie's pill box. Moonie carries his pills around in an 8-track cartridge box on account of it's the right size for a couple of hundred assorted uppers, downers, blues, reds, greens, purples and, probably, even a few aspirin if anyone cares to look. Plus, this box is a perfectly reasonable thing for a musician to be carrying. If anyone asks, that is.

Eventually the box is found. It is hidden in the first place any narc agent will look; behind the cistern in the john. I sling the box over to Moonie and he grabs a largish handful which he downs in one. Then he begins to get his act together. But Moonie's idea of getting himself together for a trip is not everyone's idea of same. He is not over concerned about his toothbrush or the whereabouts of his pyjamas (whatever they are). No. He is more worried about his buffalo horns which he buys a few days back at Nudie's, the western shop. He is not about to go anywhere without these fucking horns.

At last we find them, stuffed down behind a sofa, and Moonie fits them to his head.

Today Moonie starts off by being sleepy and out of it. Now he is awake and out of it, behaving in a manner very odd and unpredictable, even for him. He talks in fits and starts. Sings. Moans. One second he comes over all speedy. The next, he's all glazed. But, eventually, he's more or less dressed, buffalo horns and all, and we get into the limo and off to the airport.

Of course, by the time I get Moonie to the plane he is practically a basket case, flopping about all over the place, joints like jelly, completely incoherent. Fortunately it is only a short trip to San Francisco so we just remove his horns and leave him to it. He's leaning forward, half out of his seat, like a puppet.

By this time, what with one thing and another, I am fairly well out of it myself, being as it seems to me that I deserve a brandy or two during the flight, what with getting him onto the plane in the first place and then stopping him from groping the stewardesses and removing the wig from off the head of an old bint who is sitting up front. So, on account of being well out of it, I have more than a little difficulty getting Moonie out of his seat when we arrive at SF. I pull him. I push him. I heave on him. I haul on him. All to no avail. But then the captain, who is waiting to shut up shop, ups and shows me that Moonie's seat belt is still done up tighter than a dog tick's blood sack. Once this problem is sorted out, removing Moonie is comparatively simple. Comparatively, because the only way Moonie's leaving this plane is by wheelchair, which the captain kindly organises for us. I think to myself that this is a captain who deserves a medal. Or at least a couple of willing chicks. I make a note to organise same.

One thing about Who tours, they certainly have the wheels well sorted. I mean, one moment I'm pushing Moonie in his wheelchair and wondering how I arrive at this strange pass in my life and the next moment this guy who is built like a Green

Bay Packer linebacker hurtles down the ramp, heaves me out of the way and wheels Moonie off to a big black Caddy. Moonie, well he's still moaning and groaning with handfuls of oval, round, square, oblong, hexagonal, purple, green, blue, black and white pills coursing through his system on an ebb tide of champagne and brandy. I mean, he is making like he is taking the Japanese water torture. Just when I am thinking this, the Caddy pulls up outside the St. Francis and tumbles us out into Reception. And who should be there but half of Tokyo on its annual works outing, all flashing Pentax and bad teeth.

Joey the Doorman has only to take a quick squint at the wheelchair with Moonie leaning out of one side and a pair of four-hundred-dollar buffalo horns dragging along behind to know that this can only be the drummer of the world-famous Who rock band.

"Hey, Mr. Moon! How're you doing, man?"

"Ooooooooorrrrgggghhhhhh . . ." replies Moonie.

"That's good, man. That's cool."

The tide of Japanesers parts in amazement as Moonie is wheeled into the St. Francis. There's the sound of "Ahhh so's," and the old Asahis are flashing away like it's Pearl Harbor all over again. Then, wallop, Moonie is behind enemy lines and we're in his suite.

Now here's a problem: over at the Civic Center the gig is starting and Moonie is further out of it than fucking Skylab. And not only that, but while I'm making him half-way decent, Moonie is at the brandy. So here's the most famous drummer in the world, late for the gig and legless with uppers, downers and booze.

Well, to make a long story short, Moonie arrives at the theatre and, not more than half an hour later than billed, on come The Who, Moonie and all.

The band plays.

The kids scream.

But, suddenly, Moonie doesn't know what he's meant to be playing. I mean, Big Ben could chime in his ears and he wouldn't know what time of day it is. Just as I realise what is happening, Pete Townshend spins round and screams at Moonie:

"Play faster, you cunt. Faster!"

So Moonie plays another 30 seconds at a passable clip. Then his head starts to go. His feet stop. He drops one of his sticks and I can see that he is about to do a diver into the biggest of his floor-standing Premier tom-toms. Townshend? Well Townshend's gone fucking raving:

"Faster, you fucking cunt. Play faster . . ."

I look round for a phone because what I think we need is a doctor, and fucking quick at that. But, stone me if every phone backstage isn't either ripped out of the wall or jammed with something that isn't a dime. So the next thing I'm doing a legger down the theatre's aisle, running between rows of screaming kids who aren't going to stay too long before they turn riotous.

Then I'm out in the street and phoning the Free Doctor Service.

On most tours and at most venues we've got a long list of doctors, lawyers, peddlars, fixers, heavies, whores and God knows what all else. But just this once we've got no doctor and I'm thinking to myself *what the fuck happens if this Free Doctor turns out to be some Quaker from Kansas?* I mean, the guy could have us inside in two seconds flat. But then I remember that this is America and that this is the Free Doctor Service, and anything in this country that is free must be run by Commies or by Heads—and probably both—so that's cool.

The phone rings maybe three or four times before it is answered by a young-sounding voice.

"Hey, listen, man," and I'm shouting so loud that he can probably hear me from where he is without the benefit of Alexander Graham Bell. "Listen, man, I'm with The Who at the Civic Center and the fucking drummer is right out of it, freaking out, and I don't know what he's on!"

"Far out, man."

"Oh man, you've got to get over here."

"OK. Hey, has he been mixing it?"

"Mixing it? Jesus Christ, he's like a Waring Blender!"

"Hold it right there, man. I'll be over."

And with that he hangs up.

Hold up, I'm thinking. *This sounds a bit too easy.* First off, he believes me straightaway and I could be any of several thousand loony freaks who inhabit San Francisco at all times. Secondly, he sounds dead keen to get on over right away. *What if he's a plant?* What if he turns up with a dozen narcs in tow? That would come in really handy, what with Moonie higher than the World Trade Center, three-quarters of the band and entourage nearly as elevated and about fifteen thousand kids who between them must be carrying enough to put the entire Sixth Fleet out of action.

But it's either wait for the doc or blow the gig out. And if it's blow the gig out, then it's every man for himself. So I stand outside the main entrance to the hall as we arranged and wonder how long it will be before the doc turns up. From here I can hear "Pinball Wizard," which sounds all right except it seems to be going at variable speed, like it's an album being played on a record player with a dodgy turntable. I pace up and down and a couple of patrolmen begin to look at me somewhat suspiciously, but because I am totally straight for once I just stare back at them and they leave me alone. Then a couple of bints come up and hassle me for tickets, with that whiney voice that's the American street hustler's stock-in-trade:

"Hey, maaan? You got any tickets?"

I tell them to fuck off.

Then suddenly this old wreck of a Chrysler, like something from an old Bogie movie, comes belting up onto the sidewalk and pulls up with the brakes screeching and smoking. The cops look vaguely interested but there's a big sign that reads *Doctor* in the front windscreen, so they let it go. Then out jumps this guy who looks like one of the Fabulous Furry Freak Brothers. I mean, he is the real thing. The genuine article. 100% Al and kosher. Patched up jeans with a huge flare on them. Sweaty Grateful Dead T-shirt. Afghan waistcoat. And hair well down below his shoulderblades. So I leap over to him feeling quite well cheered up, reckoning that if he is a plain clothes cop he is certainly the best I ever see in my life.

"Hey, man, you the doctor sent to fix up Moonie?"

"Yeah, man. Got the stuff right here in my little old bag."

"Right! Follow me!"

So we sprint through the front entrance and, luckily, I remember to pin on my backstage pass to avoid any aggravation with the promoters' muscle. We shoot on down the aisle, through the wings—and I can see that Moonie is just about on his last legs, swaying about while he's playing and generally looking just like the lights are going out. The doc is peering about too and looking quite professional with it, considering as how he looks more like something out of Haight Ashbury, and then he tells me just what we have to do. It seems like there's only one sure way of getting Moonie well set up enough to finish the gig and that's with this special stuff which we have to inject into both his ankles at the same time. Now I can see that this is quite a problem, but the next thing I know the Furry Freak Brother is shoving into my hand a huge great syringe that is certainly large enough to ice the President's daughter's wedding cake, and telling me to take Moonie's left ankle while he takes the right. Well, of course, I can handle a syringe as well as the next man, and maybe better—though don't get me wrong, I am never on any of the hard stuff. That is strictly for loonies and fruit cakes.

I give the doc the OK.

What we have to do now is crawl out on stage, up behind Moonie's drum riser, and crouch down beneath him while he is playing. Then somehow we have to let him know what is coming off, which is not easy bearing in mind that The Who once have an entry in the Guinness Book of Records as the World's Loudest Rock Band, and that Moonie plays a very large drum kit indeed, including double bass drums. I jump up behind him, just like an apparition in *Macbeth,* and shout in his ear:

"Don't play the bass . . ." But Moonie doesn't even notice me and just carries on, head lolling about over the place and looking like the drummer in *The Muppet Show*. I try again:

"DON'T PLAY THE FUCKING BASS DRUM!" This time he does notice me but seems to think that I am just fooling around because he starts wailing and carrying on, making noises like:

"Wwwwwaaauuuggghhh" and "Woooooooaaaaaarrrrrr!" and "Yeah, yeah, yeah." So eventually I really have to turn up the decibels and I bellow in his ear:

"FOR CHRIST'S SAKE STOP PLAYING THE FUCKING BASS DRUMS, YOU CUNT. BECAUSE WE'RE GOING TO HAVE TO INJECT YOU IN YOUR FUCKING ANKLES! RIGHT?"

Moonie looks somewhat surprised at this proposition, but he is never known to turn down the opportunity to have something new introduced into his bloodstream, however obscure the method. So he stops playing the bass drums and hangs his ankles down ready to receive the blessed sacrament. Meanwhile, Pete Townshend looks round at us with a "What the fuck?" expression on his face, but, otherwise, the band just carries on playing as if this is something that happens most times they play together.

By now the good doc tells me that what we have to do is inject both ankles at exactly the same time, otherwise the two halves of Moonie's body could go out of alignment (or something). So we lurk under the drum riser, syringes at the ready, until the doc mouths "One, two, three . . . GO!" and boff! It's into both ankles right on the button.

Moonie? Well Moonie makes like some old bag who's being goosed for the first time in thirty years! Startled, but pleased with it. The doc and I creep away into the wings and by the time we're behind the side curtains I can see that the Fabulous Furry Freak Brother's medicinal compounds are beginning to do their stuff and Moonie looks pretty well cheered up. He's got both feet working away at the double bass drums and pretty soon he's drumming up such a storm that Townshend turns round and screams at him:

"PLAY SLOWER, YOU CUNT. SLOWER!"

There's no pleasing some people.

Once this little crisis is over, Moonie finishes the gig OK. In fact, he plays as well as ever before. In the dressing room afterwards, even Entwistle, who doesn't often say too much about the rest of the band's playing, is telling Moonie that it certainly seems as if he is starting to get the knack of this drumming caper, and that if he keeps on in this way, why then with a bit of luck, he might even get a gig or two at it. But poor old Moonie is starting to suffer again and his head is falling about and there is plenty of moaning and groaning going on.

Fortunately we still have the Furry Freak Brother with us and from the size and general appearance of his eyes, I'm pretty certain that he is at the black bag himself. The next thing he does is to stuff a couple of pills that look big enough for a fair-sized carthorse down Moonie's face. Then he turns to me and he says:

"Listen, man, whatever you do, do not let him drink alcohol. Right?"

"Right," I say, but my heart bounces right down somewhere round about floor level on account of trying to stop Moonie drinking alcohol is like trying to cross the English Channel on a pogo stick.

"I mean if this guy drinks alcohol," continues the Furry Freak, "then, man, he is going to die." But then he must catch the glum look I give him, so he adds: "It's OK, man, those pills I give him will knock him out for maybe ten-twelve hours." Then he turns to Moonie and says:

"Listen to me, man. No alcohol." But Moonie just laughs ha ha ha in his face and before any of us can do anything he hurls down a quick tumbler of brandy. The doctor goes absolutely crazy. He snatches the glass from Moonie's hand and hurls it across the room.

"No man! No! Like I say. No alcohol. If you drink now, you

die. I mean *die*. Like *dead*. D-E-A-D. Dead. You dig?"

I have to say that this is indeed quite an impressive Furry Freak because Moonie looks exceptionally hang-dog.

"Yes, doctor," he says and he sounds just like the small boy who's caught with his hand in the cookie jar. But the Furry Freak doesn't give up that easily and there's plenty of mugging on the ears—especially Moonie's. And Moonie's only reply is to nod his head *yes doctor* and shake his head *no doctor* a few times. By now the pills must be working anyway because Moonie's eyes are starting to go and his head is beginning to loll and he can't hold anything in his hands without it slipping to the floor. So I turn to the Furry Freak and say to him:

"How much do I owe you, man?" forgetting for the moment that this is the Free Doctor Service. He replies:

"Nothing, man." I ask him if he wants to come back to the St. Francis, if he wants me to fix him up with a couple of chicks. Or three. But he says no to that too.

Then I give him a hundred dollars, which is all I have on me at the time, a stack of albums and a few tickets to the next gig. I take his phone number and tell him that whenever we're next in town we will look him up. He says that'll be fine, man, but somehow he doesn't seem too pleased at this suggestion, so I figure that maybe this Fabulous Furry Freak isn't such a Fabulous Furry Freak as I originally figure, and perhaps he is not cool at all. The next thing anyone knows is that he's on his way.

Moonie is absolutely out of it by this time and we have to heave him into the back of the limo. To do this I enlist some help from Chalky, who is one of the many geezers that hang around rock bands and whose function is not entirely clear because, by and large, such geezers are so dumb that they cannot discover which way is East with two compasses, a geography teacher and a praying Arab to help them. However, Chalky is able to provide the muscle necessary to aid Moonie back to the St. Francis. It must be said here that Joey and his mates, who run the doors at the St. Francis, are pretty good fellows, because there's Moonie, in and out of what must be one of the best hotels on the West Coast, and every time he is in or out he is invariably out, if you see what I mean, but all Joey and his mates say is:

"Hey there, Mr. Moon! Good to see you, man."

Once Moonie is safely cleaned up and in his bed, I return to my own room to take a shower. Then I get the smart gear on and go on down to John Entwistle's room, which is where the party is due tonight. When I get there, all the boys are there except Roger Daltrey. But he is probably laid out with the tea and cucumber sandwiches. After an hour or two I am well away and wondering which of several bints I will get to tonight. I glance around and most people seem to be doing OK too, what with Mick the Roadie, who is famous for being the operator that has to light Arthur Brown's helmet when Arthur Brown is all the rage, leaning very heavily over some old boot with huge lungs. Huge lungs is what this Mick is into. I'm grinning to myself and starting to feel the old mouth go numb, which is always a good sign for me, when there is an unbelievable crashing and smashing on the door to the suite. Well, I am nothing if not a sucker for doors, so I go to open it and who should be standing there but Moonie!

"Ah, dear boy," he says. "Thought I heard a little party. Where's the brandy?" No one can believe this. The guy has enough sleeper inside him to put down a horny buffalo and here he is looking for a jolly-up. I am unable to cope, so I say to him, very seriously:

"Listen, man, I really do like you. I don't want you to die. You know what the Furry Freak said. Drink and you're dead. Right?" He looks at me with a straight face, so I continue. "So, if you want to die, the brandy is over there."

Moonie stands in the doorway for a few moments. Then he says:

"Ah, fuck it."

But he does go back to bed.

* * *

One time we do cancel a gig is also the time we nearly find that Moonie himself is cancelled and has to return his ticket to the Great Promoter in the Sky. We are booked in to a place called the Cow Palace, which is not a luxurious home for ruminants but a very large stadium near San Francisco which stages some very large rock and roll concerts. It is true that on this occasion a great deal of medicine is prescribed before the gig. It is all medicine of the liquid kind, but there are some quite considerable dosages. Although the local constabulary will not consider us fit to drive upon the highway, there seems to be no reason why this medicine should form any obstacle to the performance of rock and roll songs. In fact, it is well known that liquid stimulants can have a highly beneficial effect on the performance of same, though it is somewhat out of order to throw up on stage—or even over the first couple of rows of the audience—which is what I once see Joe Cocker and one or two others achieve.

By the time The Who are due on stage, Moonie is certainly staggering about, but this is more or less de rigueur, and certainly commonplace, so the playing begins. The band thumps along in fine style until about the fifth number, in which Townshend, first, and then the others, notices that Moonie is slowing down. With a resigned and angry look, Townshend rounds on Moonie and screams his musical directions for the evening:

"PLAY FASTER, YOU CUNT!"

So Moonie speeds up some, but quite soon slows down again, so much so that the more perceptive members of the audience begin to boo and jeer, directing their abuse at Moonie. They are very subtle and their musical education allows them to make such sensitive suggestions as:

"GET YOUR ASS TOGETHER, MOTHERFUCKER!"

It is quite clear by now that Moonie cannot act on this advice and is not able to follow the basic rudiments of drumming as set out in the Eric Delaney Drum Tutor. Seconds later, however, he launches on a most spectacular drum break as he gracefully does a nosedive into one of his floor-standing tom-

toms. At this juncture, the rest of The Who cease to play and I and a couple of other geezers rush onstage and cart Moonie away.

The kids, of course, are going potty and it looks as though we have a blown-out gig on our hands, along with all the associated rioting that takes place under these circumstances.

In the dressing room I commence to administer oxygen to Moonie. This is just one of the many means usually at the band's disposal for this type of emergency and while I am holding the mask over Moonie's boatrace and generally coming the Florence Nightingale, he begins to recover. During the treatment I bellow at Moonie:

"What have you taken? Tell me, man! What are you on? What have you had?" These questions are necessary as it seems unlikely that Moonie is reduced to this pass simply by an excess of Courvoisier—unless, that is, Monsieur Courvoisier and his colleagues decide that after dinner tipplers nowadays need the sort of extra boost that may be achieved with a soupçon of heroin or a gram or two of STP. Moonie, of course, does not answer my questions but merely wrestles away from me, all the while claiming that he is perfectly all right, thank you very much, and what the fuck is going on? Moreover, he is determined to get up on stage and continue playing for his loyal followers. There is not much anyone can do when Moonie is in this kind of mood. He is virtually unstoppable and, to tell the truth, most people will be pleased if he can recommence the rock and roll songs as this may soothe the savage punters who are about to take the theatre apart, brick by brick, seat by seat.

In due course, therefore, Moonie and the band take the stage once more and truck into another number. I station myself close at hand because I am not convinced that Moonie is fully recovered and I believe that my services will once more be required. On this occasion I am right. Halfway through the second number, Moonie does another swallow dive into one of the many tom-toms before him.

The band jacks it in. Moonie is once more carted off. Various doctors materialise and it's off to hospital in one of the big black limos that seem to be provided wherever The Who play.

In the hospital, it's out with the stomach pump and into Moonie's stomach and out with various appalling looking and smelling liquids. Syringes get stuck in here and there and many geezers and bints swarm about like Dr. Kildare on piece work. I lurk about close at hand because it seems to me that, this time, Moonie does himself irreversible mischief—though I am not too pessimistic or hysterical because during my time with Keith Moon I see him get out of many scrapes that would put the average bloke several yards beneath the sod.

Nevertheless, when the verdict is delivered I have to admit that I am more than somewhat taken aback. It appears that in Moonie's bloodstream there is circulating a large quantity of stuff that is used for tranquillizing. OK, you may say, so what is so tough about that? It may well be a good thing that Moonie becomes tranquillized. True. There are even occasions when I would like to see him tranquillized into oblivion. But the problem here is that the tranquillizer circulating in Moonie's bloodstream is not the sort that is normally used to pacify boisterous rock and roll drummers. It is the sort of tranquillizer that is double double strong and is designed to put down huge gorillas and orang-outangs who, despite their pacific and vegetarian habits, when they are riled up require a great quantity of pacification before they will adapt to air transport or zoo life.

At this stage it becomes quite obvious that Moonie does not lose his marbles and suddenly consume this great quantity of monkey knock-out drops, but that some berk spikes Moonie's drink with same drops. At this, one and all curse Moonie for not obeying Rule Number One in the Rock and Roll Survival Guide: Never leave a drink lying around and then pick it up again. Always get a fresh drink. The reason for this is that there are many candidates for the funny farm around the place who think it a great hoot and a laugh, and perhaps even a favour, to introduce outrageous chemicals into any unguarded drinks. Many bands and many individuals suffer from Moonie's fate and some of them do not recover so well. They wind up knocking on the door of the great pusher in the sky, the one who is never required to take a rap.

What they say of war and making movies, both being days of intense boredom interspersed with moments of intense shitting yourself, is also true of life with Moonie and not everything is as traumatic as episodes like the large monkey drops. Come to think of it, it is a strange life. Tell me what other businesses there are in which the entire working outfit of thirty-odd operators must be injected as a precaution against the spread of clap? This is exactly what happens after a gig in Boston when there is not a totally fastidious attitude in the matter of who commits sexual intercourse upon whom, and the lady in question turns out to have a round of applause from somewhere. A photographer is present who takes a team picture of everyone clapping and it is indeed a great tragedy that I cannot obtain this picture to show it to you. However, it is destroyed at a later date, otherwise I dare say that it would be regarded as an heirloom by the descendants of those concerned.

Another time, one of the roadies, who is not generally regarded as a suitable candidate for *Mastermind* (though in my experience very few are), is selected to sort out our supply of uppers, downers and what have you. This supply comes from a tame doctor in Denver, Colorado, who deals out a prescription for everyone in the unit, including the retinue of lurkers and assistants' assistants. Of course, many people will think it strange that such a large quantity of relatively able-bodied geezers should simultaneously be struck down with depressive diseases, but that is the way it is in rock and roll. The tame doc accordingly lashes out thirty-odd prescriptions which he gives to the chosen roadie—who goes to cash them in. But, whereas anyone with two cents of sense will take each prescription to a different pharmacist, this twat, being as he is tangibly stout between the ears, takes the whole fucking lot to one chemist. And this chemist certainly does think it strange that there should be such an outbreak of melancholia in Denver, Colorado. He immediately hollers copper. Exit crestfallen roadie.

Sometimes it seems to me that life with Moonie is too hectic for my raspberry to take the strain and I envy the schoolmates who go on to become accountants, minicabbers and window cleaners. I reckon that the one or two guys who enter the criminal life also have it somewhat cushier than me. These thoughts come to me especially when we are hotel-wrecking, which is the highly specialised and destructive sport that Moonie pursues. In fact, though there are many rock bands (and sports teams, I believe) that practise this sport to professional standards, I am quite prepared to bet my entire boodle that Moonie is by far and away the World Champion of Hotel Destruction. He is the Jesse Owens, the Muhammad Ali, the Stirling Moss of this activity. If there is ever a Nobel Prize to be won for consistent performance above and beyond the call of normal duty, no question but that it is Keith Moon who will have to travel to Nobel to receive it.

It is frequently reported, in this newspaper and on that TV station, that this or that rock band/sports team is in the pokey, or nearly so, for wrecking the Hotel Expensive, riding motorcycles up and down the corridors, blowing up the lavatories, leaving sharks in the baths, floating dining tables down the nearby brook and so on and so forth. You ask yourself why these hotels allow this to happen. Why do the managers not say to these barbarians:

"Fuck off out of it and do not come back, thank you very much."

The answer is, of course, doh re mi, moolaw, ackers—money. For it is an undeniable fact that this mayhem can be very profitable to the hotels, their management and their staff. It works like this. The damage is caused. The rock musicians pay out large sums of cash money to the hotel/manager/staff to compensate for same damage. The hotel/manager/staff say thank you very much—then make a huge insurance claim. The insurance pays up. The rooms are renovated, which is necessary on a regular basis anyway. Much money is made by all—except the insurance companies who can only recover, presumably, by screwing everyone concerned for higher premiums. The amount of money to be made is greatly magnified by the fact that the musicians are usually in a hurry to move on to the next gig and are not inclined to hang about while detailed negotiations take place along the lines of: "One occasional table, $120. Two knives and a teaspoon, $17." What usually happens is that the hotel negotiator says:

"Give us a thousand dollars and we'll forget it."

The thousand changes hands and that is that. This explains why some hotels will repeatedly put up with the most outrageous behaviour. I am not saying that any particular establishment indulges in this type of sharp practice. No. All the establishments we patronise are purer than the driven snow, but there is one example of a watering-hole that is very tolerant in its attitude to the likes of Moonie. In fact, it is so liberal that it has a nickname: The Riot House.

It is quite amazing how much a larger-than-life figure like Moonie can get away with, even in hotels that do not have much experience of rock musicians. This may be because rock musicians are, in fact, very little worse than any other type of hotel guest, and better in so far as they are prepared to spend large sums of cash. Unfortunately, where Moonie is concerned, such hotels come off worse in the deal and usually end up with egg on their faces, and in their carpets too, not to mention champagne all over the walls and television sets in the swimming pools.

When Moonie is recording *Pussycats* with Harry Nilsson, he finds himself staying in the Beverly Wilshire Hotel, on account of the lease of the ex-Kennedy beach house, which is where he starts off, runs out. We are all sitting in the suite one night and Moonie decides that it is time for a surfing evening.

This involves large piles of Beach Boys and Jan and Dean albums and a stereo system turned up to 10 on the dial, plus endless supplies of brandy and ginger and champagne. So here we are, Jan and Dean at a couple of hundred watts and Moonie capering about like a caricature of Noel Coward on LSD, when suddenly the phone rings.

"Hello, hello, hello," sings Moonie down the phone.

"Ah . . . Mr. Moon? Ah . . . we have a complaint. Ah . . . about the . . . ah . . . noise. The . . . ah . . . noise . . . Mr. Moon . . . on the . . . ah . . . stereo."

"Ah," replies Moonie. "Ah . . . why don't you . . . ah . . . fuck off? Mmmmh?" With that he turns the unit up a notch or three and then continues to caper.

But not for long.

With no warning, the disc ceases to rotate on the deck. The lights are extinguished. Darkness descends, as does silence. It is but a moment's thinking to work out exactly what gives.

The management are confiscating our electricity.

Fortunately, they are only able to do this as far as the power points are concerned and I am able to turn on the overhead lighting. But the restoration of vision does absolutely nothing for Moonie's temper.

"You fucking dumb Yankee bastards!" he screams. "Five hundred dollars a fucking night and you cut off the fucking electricity. What sort of shithole is this?"

Then he calms down a bit and paces up and down. It is clear from the gleam in his eye that he is hatching some devilish plot. He stops pacing.

"Right, Dougal, give us a hand with the telly. If we can't amuse ourselves in the comfort and privacy of our own rooms, why then, dear boy, we shall do so in the fucking corridor. Right?"

"Right!" I reply.

So we hump this bloody great television set out into the corridor, find a power point where the cleaners energise their vacuum machines and so on, and plug in the television. Moonie sets the volume to very high indeed and, while the television's amplifier is not able to deliver anywhere near 100 watts per channel, it certainly does make a fair showing. This demonstration, however, is quite insufficient for Moonie, and the next thing he does is to spring up and hurry off toward the lift shafts. There he searches about for a while, looking behind curtains and doors that are marked *Private*. Then, BINGO! He discovers what he wants and returns to the television clutching what looks to me like an extremely important set of fuses. They are not the corridor power because the television remains there booming away.

While I am wondering what these fuses belong to, there is the sound of pattering footsteps and a highly flustered manager appears before us. He has sweat beads on his upper lip and his hands are wringing themselves dry.

"Oh, Mr. Moon," he wails pathetically, "what have you done? What have you done to our fuses? The elevators won't work and we've got a convention of Monte Cassino veterans stuck between the fourth and fifth floors. Now, Mr. Moon, please, please let us have our fuses back or I will simply have to report this entire matter to the police. Please, Mr. Moon . . ." His voice tails off and he is a sight that even the most hard-hearted should feel sorry for. Moonie draws himself up to his full height and speaks most witheringly:

"Ah, dear boy, so you have some trouble with the electricity, do you? A spot of bother with the lifts—or elevators as you most quaintly call them. A little difficulty with the operation of the hotel. Mmmm? Well, let me tell you something, dear boy . . ." and now he really turns up the decibels, *"the fucking electricity in my fucking room doesn't work either. And that's the fucking room that I'm paying five hundred fucking dollars a fucking night for. And when I pay for a suite I expect it to come complete with fucking electricity, dear boy."* Now his voice goes all soft: "A suite in which I can relax and enjoy myself, listening to records, if need be, without some miserable fucking little worm like you horning in every five minutes and complaining about the noise. *If the fucking rooms are too fucking noisy then get some fucking soundproofing in!"*

The manager is somewhat nonplussed by this tirade and he is drying his hands quite frantically and making shushing noises with his mouth. He is especially put out because a small crowd is gathering around us, and this scene is by no means a boost to the reputation of the hotel.

"Well, Mr. Moon, I'm sure we can come to some arrangement over this matter. Yes. We can. I'm sure we can. Can't we?"

"But of course we can, dear boy. Of course we can. It's really very simple. You take the sofa and the television set back into my suite. Then, when you have done that, you reconnect the electricity to my rooms. At this stage I, in turn, will ensure that there is adequate electricity supplied to your elevators, to ensure that the survivors of Monte Cassino can get to their rooms in peace, and we will consider the matter closed. When, of course, some silly twat complains about the noise from my suite, you will simply offer to move them further away. Right?"

The manager scurries away.

The next thing is that a handful of minions arrive and carry the television set most respectfully into the suite, where they arrange it and the sofa in a position quite convenient for viewing.

We continue with our surfing session. The guests disperse from the corridors. I assume that the Second World War survivors attain their rooms.

In the morning, Moonie receives a bottle of champagne and a bloody great bunch of flowers from the management. Which all goes to show why some hotel suites cost several hundred dollars per night.

Oh, yes, hotels are a wonderful source of amusement and the scene of many entertaining sexual escapades—like for instance, the occasion on which Moonie does all the screwing but I get the clap. You may think that this is a medical miracle, but it is true and this is how it happens.

At the time, Moonie is staying in Malibu and he hears that

Led Zeppelin is in town to do a gig at the LA Forum. So, of course, nothing will do but we must go and visit them where they are staying, which is the Beverley Hilton. We arrive at about five o'clock in the afternoon, get a very big hello from the Zeppelin lads and commence to down a great number of bevvies for, when it comes to it, Zeppelin are not slouches in the matter of taking their medicine. Moreover, they have a great deal of readies to ensure that the supply is fairly constant and, by and large, of the Dom Perignon and Courvoisier class, to mention but the least exotic. When it comes time to move on to the gig, we find ourselves in John Bonham's rooms and it is Bonzo who suggests Moonie and I should nip along with him and watch the gig. Which is what we do. Although this is a digression from the tale of how Moonie does the screwing but I get the clap, a most extraordinary thing happens at this gig. It demonstrates the affection that rock and roll fans have for Keith Moon. In their set, Zeppelin have a spot where John Bonham has a long solo which involves him and his massive drum kit rising up in the air via a hydraulic drum riser. And just as he is about to elevate, he calls on Moonie, who is watching from the side of the stage. Somewhat hesitantly, Moonie steps out and joins Bonzo and, suddenly, we have the spectacle of two of the heaviest and most exciting drummers in rock flailing about Bonzo's kit like a pair of Bruce Lees on speed. Naturally the kids go crazy because they can see that it is none other than Moonie who joins Bonham. They carry on and holler as if Our Lord himself descends to bang about on the skins whilst singing *My Way* at the same time. Next thing, aboslutely everyone is standing up and then they begin to light up cigarette lighters and matches and wave them about until all that anyone can see from the stage is an undulating carpet of lights, thousands of pinpoints of fire all making up one big starburst. These kids give Moonie and Bonham a standing ovation that lasts five minutes and when Moonie comes off stage I can see he is quite affected by this vote of approval.

When the gig is finished and we are all milling about backstage, as the handbook dictates, Moonie does not take long to latch on to some chick who, though she is not the most tasteful tart in the world and does not match Ann-Margaret—or even Princess Margaret—for looks, is sufficiently well equipped with anatomy to cause Moonie to wish to take her back to the hotel and practise his medical knowledge upon her. (I should mention that in an excess of camaraderie, Bonzo books a suite in the hotel for us before we go to the gig.) Now this suite is only equipped with one room in which to sleep and that room has two beds. Selfishly, I try to dissuade Moonie from taking this bint back because I well know that he is quite noisy when he is practising gynaecology. This tends to interfere with my own performance, even if it is only sleeping. But, needless to say, my objections are overruled and Moonie drags the boot over to the hotel and commences to writhe upon her. I stay away as long as I can and when tiredness and nowhere else to go overcome me, I bury my head under the pillows, just a few feet away from a sort of four-legged, four-armed, two-headed monster that does plenty of panting and heaving and makes many noises such as:

"Eeeeeeeeuuuuuuaaaaarmrrrrgggssssssssss," and

"Wwwwwaaaaaaauuuuuuuurrrrrrrruuummmpphh."

It is only the brandy, well known to be most efficacious in curing insomnia, that enables me to kip.

This kip lasts only a few hours before another desperate Moon attack on the fur pie, round about nine o'clock in the morning, rouses me from my dreams. As I surface, I notice that the night's activities already cause a couple of legs to drop off Moonie's bed and the force of the couplings moves the lopsided bed some two feet from the wall that divides this room from the next bedroom along the corridor. Just as I notice this, Moonie gives, and the bint receives, such an almighty thrust that the bed is driven—rammed—into this dividing wall— BOFFFF!!! A split second later there is a terrible scream from the bedroom next door and I am sure that someone is murdering someone else, which occurs with distressing frequency in the USA. We find out what happens very quickly, because there is a furious hammering on our door and, when I answer this hammering, I find a large dude with a red face and a crew cut hairstyle like a lavatory brush. This turkey bellows:

"What the fuck is going on here? I'm in bed getting some sleep when there's noise like a fucking earthquake and a fucking picture falls off the wall, smack dab on my fucking head. What is going on?" Although I am about to piss myself with laughter at this outrage, I employ the diplomacy for which I am paid and the turkey shuffles off muttering to himself.

Moonie, of course, is still thrashing around and his bint is thrashing around even more so. It is clear that she is greatly enjoying the exercise and she communicates this enjoyment by making a noise like a rhino with a tent peg wedged up its bottom. I figure that this is my lot as far as the deep and dreamless is concerned, so I stroll out onto the patio for a spot of early morning sunshine. To do this, I do not bother with any item of clothing other than a pair of leather trousers, which I am zipping up as I pass through the french windows from the suite to the patio.

Well, I cannot believe the sight that greets my eyes. There, out on the patio, in a neat semi-circle, is a group of old boys and old biddies sitting in chairs just like they are in a theatre. And the focus of their attention is the french window through which I come, securing my dong within the leather trousers. When I appear, this group of geriatrics commences to clap and I realise that not only must they be sitting around here for some time listening to the soundtrack of Moonie's porny performance, but also they believe that it is me who is the star turn and perpetrator of the act. *Bloody hell*, I think to myself and I dart back into the bedroom where the bint is working up enough steam to launch herself upon Moonie once more.

"Christ, Keith," I shout. "Pack it in. There's a whole bunch of pensioners outside who think they're judging a talent show. They're bloody listening to you making all that din!" But, of course, he doesn't care. He just laughs and laughs.

"Never mind, Dougal. Even if you haven't had the pleasure of screwing this delightful young thing four times in the last couple of hours, at least there's a fan club who think you have! I'd watch out if I were you, they might drag you off for a repeat performance."

Outside, I can hear the geriatrics applauding and shouting "More, more, more!"

Which is how I get the clap while Moonie does the screwing.

For sheer destructive power, Moonie excels himself in Europe—perhaps because he feels safer. One time, around 1973, when The Who is gigging around Europe, we are staying in a very expensive and plush hotel in Copenhagen, Denmark. Most of the outfit is there, including, as I recall, Kit Lambert and Chris Stamp, the band's early managers, and Bill Curbishley, who becomes the manager later on. Moonie gets bored and things commence to happen, and the focus of what Moonie causes to happen is a group of American tourists bent on visting every country in Europe in seven days. The guys all wear cameras like other people wear watches and most of them have those appalling sports jackets with large and loud checked patterns. The dolls all have fat ankles and polyester dresses in Dayglo colours. Now, though Moonie adores many American individuals, he is certainly wary of the race and he is definitely antipathetic to this type of late-middle-aged, early-middle-class caricature. He is apt to send up such folk as often as possible.

We are sitting in Moonie's room, where there is a giant waterbed such as are quite common at the time in American establishments, but quite rare in European ones.

"Here!" exclaims Moonie. Everyone turns to him. "I've just had an idea." Everyone groans and jeers. "Dear boys! Observe this giant waterbed. We will place it in the lift, leaning it against the doors and when the doors open, hopefully to admit some of those bloody tourists, the waterbed will fall on them and maybe crush one or two to death. That'll liven up their holiday. 'Gee, Molly, do you remember? Where was it? London? Pareeee? No, somewhere up in Scandinavia. That goldarned waterbed crushed Ivor and Miriam to death.' " Naturally, there are several objections raised to this scheme, such as it is slightly illegal to crush American tourists to death despite their dress sense, and also a giant waterbed such as this one in question must weigh at least a couple of tons and we do not have a crane to lift same couple of tons. We might all get hernias. Moonie rounds on me quite affably.

"Don't be a bore, dear boy. Who pays your wages?"

Well, there is no answer to this, even if it is illegal to crush American tourists, even if the bed does weigh a couple of tons and even if I do get a hernia.

We grab at the waterbed and tug it here and there. I even release my grip on an excellent glass of Danish lager in order to give the waterbed the undivided attention of my two hands.

We pull. We push. We heave. We grunt. We groan. We sweat.

We rip a fucking great hole in the waterbed.

A million gallons of rather smelly and greenish water squirts out all over the tasteful Danish carpet. In ten seconds the entire room is under three inches of this water. Everyone except Moonie finds this development a touch distressing. Moonie sees the catastrophe as the cue to dive onto the floor and commence practising the breaststroke around the suite. While he is swimming about in this manner, everyone else but me takes it on the toes out of the disaster area. How am I going to explain to the management, liberal and Danish though it may be, that this beautiful suite resembles nothing so much as Atlantis, the well-known Lost City?

Moonie, as ever, has an answer.

"Tell you what, dear boy, we'll pretend someone else did it. Right? We'll say we've just come in, found the room under water and demand another immediately." The only flaw in this plan that I can see is that when Moonie says "we," what he means is "me." That is, yours truly, Dougal Butler. However, I know that it is no use suggesting any modifications to this grand plan, so I get on the blower to the management.

"Now, look here," I say. "There has been a major disaster in that Mr. Moon and I have just arrived at our suite only to find it under several inches of water. The waterbed has burst and not only has it ruined your rooms, it has also ruined our luggage and Mr. Moon's stage gear. Kindly tell me what you intend to do about this and how will you compensate us for the catastrophe?"

It occurs to me, while I am delivering this outraged English *milord* act, that I will very soon get an earful back because anyone who knows of Moonie's reputation will surely twig that it is Mr. Moon himself who causes this flood of biblical dimensions. Fortunately, the Dane does not suss this out and, in fact, virtually shits himself in his efforts to grovel at and appease us. He apologises for the shocking inconvenience to which we are put, especially as he does not have another suite in which to site us because the water is seeping down the three floors below our rooms, which puts a large number of accommodations out of order.

"Can you leave it with me for half an hour, sir?" he asks.

"But of course, dear boy," replies Moonie, reassuming command now that I have prepared the way.

Once the Dane is out of the room, Moonie and I celebrate another victory over the hotel and catering trade by downing several large medicines and by holding a boat race with little boats that are made out of paper, floating them in the sea from the waterbed. Sure enough, in half an hour, the Dane makes his next announcement:

"Mr. Moon, Mr. Butler, please do not be worried about anything any longer. We have found alternative accommodation for you. We have made available the Royal Suite, which is normally only opened for the Royal Family and Richard Burton. If you would care to make yourselves at home there, we will ensure that your luggage and stage clothing is attended to. We will then have it sent up."

A couple of minutes later a lackey arrives to escort us in the general direction of this suite of myth and legend and when we clock it we are most impressed. It is not very much smaller than

Wembley Stadium and it is packed very full of antique furniture—or if it is not antique then it is the type of reproduction
that you will not find in Woolworths, or even H. A. Rods, which
is a large London department store well-known for its high
prices and general snottiness. There are many crystal chan-
deliers which throw their shimmering light upon the many oil
paintings dotted about the walls. The appointments are most
tasteful and what is more on one of the occasional tables there
is a note from the management apologising for the upheaval.
Better still, this note is prevented from blowing away by a large
bottle of Dom Perignon and a huge bowl of fruit.

Unhappily, this tale of Danish destruction does not end here,
for it is Moonie's birthday, which requires us to down the Dom
Perignon extremely rapidly, dump our toothbrushes in the bathroom, get the gig over as quickly as possible and then return
for the celebrations. As it happens, the gig is most successful
and all lads in the band are in very high spirits as a result.
Naturally, it being his birthday, Moonie invites one and all back
to his room.

"I have got the Royal-fucking-Suite, dear boys and it is only
fitting that we celebrate our success in the royal manner." With
that, everyone piles into the Royal Suite and in no time at all it
looks like any other khazi that is inhabited by rock musicians.
There are butt ends all over the floor, empty bottles here, there
and everywhere, plenty of half-eaten food scattered about and
enough smoke of various types to provide an effective screen for
the advance of the Sixth Army.

Particularly because it is Moonie's birthday, things soon start
to become a little hectic. The conversation grows louder and
louder. The laughter gets increasingly hysterical. Several bints
emerge from somewhere. It seems that it will develop into an
all-nighter. Most of the entourage look forward to occasions
like this because The Who are certainly not short of funny men.
When Pete Townshend and Moonie get together, the rapping is
quite hilarious. It is clever, very sarcastic and usually based on
in-jokes which the world-at-large finds hard to understand.

Moonie is thriving on all the attention and is becoming drunker by the minute and, because he is getting drunker, he is getting more and more boisterous. Someone then flicks a sandwich at him and gets three flicked back in return. A stream of peanuts takes wing and goes *ping ping ping!* against various crusts. Then an ashtray or two commits levitation and I realise that all I can do now is to sit back and wait for the really big explosion. Sure enough, the explosion comes.

Moonie: "Now ladies and gentlemen, seeing as it is my birthday I wish to make a speech to mark the occasion. First, I must thank you all for being here. Then I should point out that we are occupying the Royal Suite and I suggest that we comport ourselves accordingly. So, dear boys, I give you a toast: raise your glasses . . . and chuck them at the fucking wall!" With that, Moonie hurls his heavy crystal goblet at a beautiful gilt-framed mirror above the open fireplace. A million slivers of glass scatter the area. Then he grabs a half-empty champagne bottle and slings that at a chandelier, which comes tumble-tinkling down. All the while, Moonie is screaming:

"Royal Family? Richard Burton? Fuck the lot of them! Who gives a fuck about any one of them? I'm Keith fucking Moon and more people know me than any of that fucking lot." This and similar hysterical gibbering is the cue for Moonie to dismantle the entire suite on his own. Ornaments fly out of the windows, which are shut at the time. Elegant tables are reduced to matchwood. Sideboards which are once lovingly assembled by master carpenters suddenly take on a somewhat two-dimensional appearance. Everything that will burn is stacked into the fireplace and doused in brandy.

Everything movable is moved—either through the windows and into the street, or through the doors and into the corridors.

The odd thing is that no one else joins in. Perhaps they feel that as it is Moonie's birthday, he alone should have the fun.

Why does Moonie behave like this? Why do many, many other rock musicians behave like this? Maybe, because after a really good gig with thousands of kids screaming, stamping and waving, it is a bit of a comedown to be just another guest in just another hotel. Maybe, because while the gig is on, you feel as if you could rule the world, but when it is over there is only anticlimax. What it is all about is adrenalin and excitement, energy and entertainment and these things just do not wear off the second the gig is over. Also, rock and roll musicians are not quiet and respectable people—or they will not become rock and roll musicians in the first place. It takes a sort of looneyness to become a rock musician and that looneyness remains even when you've become successful. After all, whether you're successful or not you still make your living by producing levels of noise that are otherwise only the preserve of jet airplanes at close quarters.

But maybe the most important reason is this: when a musician is struggling, he does not have too much cash money and he has to sleep in vans, on floors and, on tour, sometimes in shitty little doss-houses that are happy to take his dough but not too happy to have him there. And when he does scrape enough loot together to pay for a luxury room, the chances are that the hotel in which the luxury room is located will turn him away from its doors with words such as:

"Get out of it, you long-haired/short-haired/black/yellow/smelly/dirty little bastard/pooftah/junkie/arsehole." Then, maybe years later, the musician becomes successful—by which we mean he has a lot of cash money to fling about. He may be no better musician. He may still take dope. He may still smell, be long-haired, short-haired, black, yellow, dirty or a little bastard. But now he is welcomed by the hotel with open arms. It is not entirely surprising then, if, when he is pissed up and high after a gig, he turns on the hotel and beats the living shit out of it.

No doubt there is, at this moment, some geezer doing a Ph.D. on the Psychology of Rock With Special Reference to Hotel Wrecking. No doubt he will provide answers to these perplexing questions and, at the same time, save the world for the rest of us. He will surely devote several chapters to Keith Moon.

But, although Moonie causes much mayhem in his time and a great deal of embarrassment to a great number of people, and although he is by no means the easiest person in the world to cater for, he always, as far as it is in his power to do so, pays for the damage he causes. And he certainly does not wish any harm to fall upon the lackeys, grovellers and victims of his japes. On this subject, I recall a stay in a hotel in Manchester, England, when Moonie wakes up in the middle of the night and requires a chicken. Not a live chicken, I hasten to add, but the dead sort that are possible to eat. He goes down to the Night Porter, who is an inoffensive sort of old geezer with only one arm, which means that the hotel can pay him less, and he asks him if any edible chickens can be rustled up. Well, of course, the old geezer cannot do anything about this and he is probably not even allowed into the kitchens himself. Moonie then waits for a chance to sneak down into the kitchens, where he opens up a giant-sized fridge. There he discovers not one, but a dozen freshly-cooked dead chickens of the edible kind, all ready to be dismembered and served up as chicken salads such as the denizens of Manchester are known to enjoy. He takes every one of these birds up to his room and when he and his companion of the moment decide that they are full up with chicken, they use the remaining chickens that they do not wish to eat as footballs, so that ultimately every chicken is pretty well knackered.

The long and short of it is that Moonie replaces all these buggered-up chickens in the giant fridge in the kitchen and the next day the old one-armed geezer is nowhere to be found. It turns out that he gets the bullet and the old heave-ho for failing to guard the hotel fowls. When Moonie discovers this, he grabs the hotel management and speaks as follows:

"Listen here, dear boy, I nicked your chickens. And, in fact, the old geezer was very anxious to preserve them from my depredations. I had the devil's own job to break into the kitchen and it is clear that the old boy would have laid down his life to prevent me. So what I suggest is that you give him back his job. In fact, I will go so far as to say that my patronage of this hotel—and of the entire chain to which it belongs—depends upon your reinstating him. To encourage you in this course of action, here is one hundred pounds with which you can go out and buy yourself some replacement chooks . . . or whatever else it is you feel the hotel needs. You will notice," adds Moonie, "that this one hundred pounds is in real cash money and I am not demanding a receipt for it. In fact," he says, thrusting the bundle into the management's hands, "what cash money?"

In due course, the geriatric one-armed bandit reappears behind the night security desk at the hotel, though no one will ever know how many chickens Moonie's one hundred pounds buys or what the denizens of Manchester receive the following day when all that can be found in the giant fridge in the kitchen are a few violently kicked-about chicken carcasses.

The truth of the matter is that Keith is most at home when he is in transit from here to there. He is a rootless sort of geezer with no special friends in any one locality and though he is undoubtedly very fond of his family, he is not a family bloke in the accepted sense. For much of the time that I work for him, he has no real home to go to (though even when he does, he treats it like an inferior sort of hotel anyway) and spends much of his time in hotels. What is beyond question is that Moonie spends so much dough in hotels that, deep down, they welcome him—even if they do have to rebuild his rooms now and then.

But, of course, not all the mayhem Moonie is involved with occurs in hotels and at concerts. Imagine the effect it must have on him to be kept waiting for several hours at an airport—especially as the bars are mostly open at such locations . . .

One time, after a spot at The Apollo, Glasgow, which is a sort of public convenience on the left hand side of Scotland (Glasgow, I mean, not The Apollo—the Apollo is not a bad venue considering that it is located in the middle of such a toilet), a great fog descends upon this part of the world and we have to fly from Prestwick airport instead. This type of fog is quite common in Glasgow, Scotland. Some claim that it is the result of closing time when all the bars eject paralytic Scotsmen into the streets and, in doing so, allow millions of cubic feet of cigarette smoke into the upper atmosphere. Others claim that such fogs are the true signs that there is a God in Heaven and that he does not wish to look down upon the unwashed and gnarled midgets that crawl around this city grunting *Hrrrrnnnn Jimmeh*! at each other. It is a scientific fact that language, the ability of one human to communicate with another, developed only quite recently in Glasgow and it is not yet perfected.

This diversion from Glasgow to Prestwick takes the form of a luxury coach which, of course, is full of fellow passengers. Unfortunately, by the time that the coach is prepared, Moonie is well into his second bottle of Courvoisier and he spends much of the coach journey stomping up and down the aisle calling out such witticisms as:

"Any more fares, please?" and

"Move on down the cars, please," and "City Center! Next stop City Center."

When these jests cause nothing but irritation to the would-be air passengers, Moonie retaliates by trying to grab the wig of an old lady who is dozing in the front seat and then interfering with the driver, pressing him to take a few swigs from the rapidly-emptying Courvoisier bottle.

While I confess that these antics amuse me, the rest of the boys are fairly well pissed off and are trying to have nothing to do with us at all. But there is worse to come because, earlier, while we are all waiting for the bus that takes us to Prestwick, Keith and I stumble across a joke shop in which we buy many items such as itching powder, sneezing powder and toy guns that look most realistic but have no internal mechanisms other than a small flag which pops out and reads BANG! when you pull the trigger. Well, before long we have all the passengers in this coach either itching, sneezing, or cowering before little flags reading BANG! and one and all are very pleased indeed when we finally reach Prestwick airport and they can escape from the dreaded Moon. By now he is completely arseholed and is becoming quite violent and even I am a little tired of the antics. But I figure that we will soon be on the Trident aircraft and then I can strap Moonie into his seat and have an hour or so's kip.

Wrong.

Once we check in and are inextricably enmeshed in the workings of British Airways, we discover that there are no Trident aircraft at Prestwick—or any other type of aircraft—and that we must wait indefinitely until some intrepid ex-Battle of Britain ace manages to find his way to this airport in order to evacuate us. Moonie's reaction to this delay and the management's suggestion that we form an orderly queue is fairly predictable.

"Fucking hell," he says, and "bollocks!" Then he disappears, taking with him only a small and very expensive Japanese cassette player. Just before he vanishes from my sight, I see him insert a cassette into this machine and from what I hear I know that Moonie is going into a Beach Boy mood.

Just as I am flopping down on one of the couches that the Prestwick management thoughtfully provides for delays such as these, Pete Townshend says to me:

"You better go after him, Dougal. Christ knows what he'll get up to." While I recognize the wisdom of this advice, I just do not have the energy.

"Oh listen, man," I reply. "I'm too knackered. He'll have to look after himself." But after a few moments I remember that Moonie is never able to look after himself, so I wander off after him, deciding that all I will do is keep him more or less in my sight. It takes a while to find him because, momentarily, I forget the first rule of Moon-hunting, which is to find the largest group of punters congregating with their eyes glazed and their mouths open in amazement. At the center of such a group, you will find Moonie up to some extraordinary activity. In this case, he finds himself a wheelchair in which he propels himself at great speed around the airport. I must say that he looks most professional and might well be a kosher invalid. But, of course, Moonie has much practice in wheelchairs all over the world, though usually he has a lackey to push him in these wheelchairs. The next moment I think to myself that he will need the wheelchair permanently because I see a couple of airport security guards take off after him and he is only able to avoid their pursuit by wheeling himself straight down a staircase. I push past these guards, who are standing at the top of the stairs, gawping after the wheeled Moonie, and arrive at the bottom of the stairs to find that Moonie manages to remain in the chair throughout the entire descent and, moreover, still has the Beach Boys playing good and strong, the cassette player jammed against his ear.

At the bottom of these stairs, Moonie staggers from the wheelchair and discovers that he is quite unable to walk in the approved manner, but this does not disconcert him at all. He simply lies down, leaning back against a pillar, his head resting against the cassette player which is now belting out *Don't worry baby*. Several small children who are also waiting for their plane are most intrigued by this prostrate figure which is wrapped in a most expensive fur coat and is listening to the Beach Boys. But then it is unlikely that saucepans this young ever hear the Beach Boys before, so they are entitled to look surprised.

Thinking that Keith is relatively safe for a while, I retreat to a nearby couch and prepare for some shut-eye. I am not exactly sure what wakes me in the end, but when I look toward Keith I can hear that the Beach Boys tape is now finished, and I can see that Moonie is getting his kicks by pointing his toy gun at anyone in uniform who passes him and is making very loud *Bang Bang!* sounds to accompany the appearance of the little flag that also reads *Bang!* As I get to my feet, Moonie spots me.

"Ah, Dougal, dear boy," he slurs. "Give me some money. I need some cash, dear boy. I feel extremely dry."

"I haven't got any fucking cash," I reply diplomatically.

"Bollocks," says Moonie and with that slings his cassette player toward a little tobacconist and confectioners stand which is nearby. To his amazement, and certainly to mine, the Japanese electronic device bounces off the kiosk glass and returns to Moonie, hitting him smack dab on the top of his pimple.

"Bollocks!" he says and I can tell from the brevity of his vocabulary at this time that he is very far from sober, for Moonie has to be extremely inebriated indeed for his usually flowery turn of phrase to desert him.

"Must have some money, dear boy," he says and with that he staggers to his feet and heads in the general direction of the kiosk that he just assaults with the combat model cassette player.

The kiosk is manned by a dried up old bird who cannot be more than four-and-a-bit feet tall. Her hair is very white and very frizzy and she has a boatrace like a dried up prune that is in the sun too long. When she sees Moonie approaching, her mouth, which is anyway not much bigger than a tom cat's arsehole, and is so disguised by the lines around it that it is virtually invisible, this mouth grows even tighter and more disapproving.

"Are you the hooligan that's been making all the noise and trouble round here, young man?" she demands most aggressively.

"That's me, you miserable old boot," replies Moonie. "Give me some fucking money!" And to support this request he draws his toy gun and sticks in right in the old biddy's face.

"Arrrrgggghhhh!" remarks the old biddy and faints, dropping down out of sight behind the counter. Her disappearance confounds Moonie because he can see no way of extracting cash from the kiosk without her cooperation, so he wanders off, vaguely waving the gun at anyone who ventures too close.

Next time I spy Keith he is lurking behind a very fat pillar. He is hiding and his collar is pulled up around his ears as if he doesn't want anyone to clock him. What is worse is that he has in his right hand the realistic looking toy gun. He is holding it with his finger on the trigger and the barrel is pointed toward the sky. The whole thing is very close to Moonie's face, which makes him look just like one of those gangsters that appear three times a night on all channels of every TV service in the civilised world. He seems as if he is about to step out from behind the cover of the fat pillar and stick someone up.

With an inward groan I realise that that is exactly what Moonie intends to do and that all he is waiting for is a suitably uniformed victim. At most airports of the world such victims are freely available, for there are usually many pilots, navigators, engineers, radio operators, stewards, and stewardesses about, to say nothing of all the desk crews and the car rental girls. But amongst all these uniforms and potential victims, the uniform that Keith Moon has to choose is that of the police sergeant who is summoned by the old kiosk biddy to arrest the young hooligan who tries to commit armed robbery upon her kiosk.

Moonie springs from behind his fat pillar, rams the gun barrel against the sergeant's temple and screams: *"Gotcha!"*

The police sergeant deftly takes Moonie's arm, twists it up behind his back and calmly speaks: "Oh no you haven't, son. *I've got you.*"

Well this is a pleasant interlude, to be sure, and is infinitely better than queueing for the Trident and its veteran pilot, who must think that he is back in the war and is en route for Bremerhaven to unload a few tons of TNT upon the Nazis living there. We all troop down to the police station after Moonie and we are compelled to amass quite a large quantity of cash before we can spring him from the cooler. But it is all to no avail because as soon as we return Moonie to Prestwick airport, he becomes even further out of order and, when the airport security force attempt to put the collective arm upon him in order that he may offend no more users of the British Airports Authority facilities, Moonie becomes so violent that he pushes over one of the check-in desk computer terminals. It falls to the floor with a splintering noise and, just before the screen goes dead, it books thirty-two Mormons on a massage parlour tour of Bangkok.

Of course, this type of destruction cannot be tolerated and Moonie is thrust back into the slammer with no further ado. And, no matter how much cash money we raise, this time the forces of law and order are not prepared to release Moonie into our care. For, while it is quite all right to scare an old kiosk biddy out of her thermal underwear, and for this offence you can be bailed out quite simply, it is altogether another thing to commit grievous bodily harm upon a computer terminal, though, personally, I cannot believe that this terminal suffers the damage that the airport people claim it does. After all, Moonie's cassette player survives a short violent return flight to Moonie's bonce via the kiosk window—and this device is built by Japanesers.

The next step is to summon a lawyer who will argue our case for us and, no doubt, claim that Mr. Moon is an upright and sober, responsible member of society (though he will not mention which society) and that he is under a great deal of business pressure and so is entitled to one slip and very sorry he is, your worship.

Now, the lawyer we find is most surprisingly hip and the next thing we know is that he, John Wolf and I are indulging in much exercising of the elbow and gullet muscles, for it turns out that this lawyer is quite ill and requires satisfying quantities of liquid medicine to be applied. John and I, greatly sympathetic to such illnesses, cannot leave him to take his doses by himself.

The long and short of it is that we become partially paralysed and the last I see of the lawyer is around three in the morning as he makes his way homeward wishing us good night and claiming that he will see us in court first thing tomorrow. Mind you, I have to raise my eyeline somewhat to spot him on account of I am progressing homeward on all fours.

The next morning I am waiting outside the court when a geezer in Cuban heels and long hair, but who looks vaguely familiar, approaches me with a cheery:

"Morning, Dougal, and how are we today?"

It takes me several moments to recognise this hip type as our lawyer friend of the night before—though I feel I have a right to be confused as, firstly, my eyesight is not functioning too well the night before and, secondly, who will expect a lawyer to look and dress like this? While I'm thinking this, I'm also wondering how on earth the geriatric judge will react to this lawyer who, if the truth is to be told, looks more like a young hooligan than Moonie.

But my fears are groundless because, just as he is about to enter the court, this lawyer dons a large gown and a small wig and, hey presto!—he is the image of Rumpole of The Bailey, only younger, or even Marvin Mitchelson, the famous American lawbooks.

Moonie is bound over and released into our care and on the flight back to London in a private plane, I regret that the term *bound over* is only a bit of legal jargon and is not a description of someone who is tied up tight with many ropes and knots. For Moonie remains almost unmanageable throughout the flight and the other lads will have nothing to do with him—even to the extent of claiming that he is 100% entirely my responsibility.

Yes, you may say, it is all very well for these miscreants to miscreate on account of they have large wads of moolaw with which to mop up the ensuing aggravation. And that is true, I suppose, though I can prove that cash money is not everything in these matters, as is demonstrated by the fifty pence piece that flies me, Moonie and two bints halfway round Europe and back. It happens like this:

One night I am sitting in John Entwistle's gaff and feeling a trifle bored. Don't get me wrong. John is an extremely nice geezer and, when he is on the road at least, is good for many laughs here and there. But at home he prefers the quiet life and there is apt to be far more discussion as to the price of fish in the Entwistle household than there is in the Moon household. All this makes John's place excellent for a few hours rest and recuperation, even if it is not exactly a Roger Corman movie. But while I am sitting there and listening to John and Alison discussing the price of fish and wondering what to do with myself, the phone rings and I am very pleased to hear that it is Moonie on the blower.

"Ah, dear boy," he says, "what I need is a break—and so do you. Fancy a quick trip somewhere? Won't cost you anything."

Then, before I have a chance to formulate a reply, he goes on: "We're off tomorrow at nine. Meet you at the airport—Gatwick. But don't be late, there's a good chap." I don't even have the chance to say yes, no or maybe before he hangs up. *What the hell?* I think to myself, *what have I got to lose?*

So the next day I find myself at Gatwick and not very long after that Moonie and I climb aboard a Fokker Friendship and head for Tangiers via Malaga. For once, I am not very well organised and do not have very much on me in the way of cash or clothing. In fact, all I have in my pockets is an American Express card and a fifty pence piece such as will not purchase even 20 cigarettes in England. Moreover, the only clothes I have with me are the clothes in which I am sitting in the plane. But I do not have much time to reflect upon this state of un-readiness because Moonie is well geed up for this gig and has a great deal of spending about his person and he is always most generous with such spending. Much of it is laid onto me during the flight, mostly in the form of brandy and ginger ale. The flight to Tangiers via Malaga is very long indeed and the supply of liquor also appears to be endless so that by the time Tangiers comes round we are both out to lunch and to dinner too.

Because we are so far out of it, when we clock into the local hotel, it does not take the local operators more than a few seconds to realise that here are a couple of very easy touches. Within these same few seconds, same operators relieve us of about 800 dollars in return for the promise of vats of booze and flocks of hookers.

Needless to say, neither the vats nor the flocks materialise and the next thing we know is that we are all alone in this North African khazi with no money whatsoever and only a small Kodak Instamatic to trade.

Fortunately, Keith is highly effective when he has no ackers about his person and within a very short time he persuades the hotel to lend us the necessary folding to provide me with a few threads and both of us with enough to put us back in action.

Moonie is able to get into and, more importantly, out of virtually any jam in the world. If ever you find yourself in a last ditch and facing a million Chinesers all armed with Chinese version Kalashnikovs firing nuclear-headed dum-dum bullets and attempting most enthusiastically to kill you, the person you need in that last ditch with you is Moonie, because if anyone is going to cause these Chinesers to suddenly commence firing upon one another, then that someone is Keith Moon.

This is Moonie's first time in Tangiers, so nothing will do but we must see and experience the famous Casbah. We set off and within five seconds flat of our hitting the Casbah perimeter, there is a scruffy little Herbert running around after us and muttering many words in both Arabic and English. The clearest of these words are:

"Dop'? You wan't dop'?"

"Not half," I say, but this sally must be incomprehensible to the scruffy Herbert because he simply repeats himself:

"Dop'? You wan' dop'?"

"Got any coke, dear boy?" Moonie asks and for all the world he sounds like he is in a posh bar in a posh hotel and is ordering up the internationally famous fizzy drink rather than the real thing.

"Eh," says the kid.

"Coke, dear boy," says Moonie.

"Coc . . . coca . . . cocaine," I translate.

"Ah, coca," twigs the urchin.

"Yeah, coca," I reply.

"Coca," adds Moonie, just in case anyone misses the point of the conversation.

"You wait," says the kid, shoving us into what looks like a dive of some iniquity, and with that he scoots off faster than Willie the Shoe bringing one in.

As we look around this iniquity den it becomes quite clear that it is such a place as has customers that like to toke upon the pipe of peace filled to the brim with opium. And in this opium parlour are many chocolate coloured geezers with eyes like golfballs, and these geezers are filling themselves up with smoke from an extraordinary array of devices like pipes, hookahs and spliffs as long as your arm and twice as fat—unless you are a Japanese arm wrestler, that is. Even Moonie is somewhat nervous here and we are both feeling as conspicuous as a ham sandwich at a Bar Mitzvah. But not too much later, we are feeling even more obvious because the scruffy little Herbert enters complete with a bloody great polythene bag absolutely full of what looks like top grade coke and what does this small person do but plonk this sodding great bag right down in front of us in full view of the various stoned citizens. All we can say is:

"Fuck me!" But Moonie recovers very quickly and heaves the bag down and out of sight.

"How much, dear boy?" he asks.

"Come on, man," I protest. "We'll never do all that."

"Shut up, Dougal. How much?"

"Five hundred pounds," says the kid, whose English is certainly improving by leaps and bounds.

"Do me a favour, fuck off," I remark.

"You are joking, dear boy, of course," adds Moonie.

Anyway, to make a long story short, we bargain with this miniature tycoon and eventually the coke changes hands for ten dollars and my Instamatic. As soon as the kid has his loot, he scurries away like a hungry ferret and we too are quite pleased to be able to leave the chocolate coloured dopers and return to the (relative) luxury of our Tangiers hotel. Of course, as soon as we are back in our rented car and under way, we both reach for the bag and take a mighty snort of our top grade coke.

But the next thing we know is that our eyes begin to water like Niagara and our hooters commence to burn as if someone thrusts a red hot poker up them and then wiggles it about some. We are coughing and spluttering like regular tuberculars but, despite all this aggravation, we are by no means stoned.

No, we are not stoned at all—until we run over the chicken, which we achieve on account of not being able to see where we are going what with the Niagara Falls taking place in our eyes.

Then we are most comprehensively stoned with many mini-ature boulders and full-sized building bricks being hurled at the car by a variety of punters who seem most unreasonably incensed that we run over and mortally damage this fucking chicken. I have to confess that this is quite the most unpleasant case of being stoned that I ever experience and I will rather suffer the delusions and hallucinations associated with some of the weirder chemicals than ever go through this Casbah aggravation again.

It is, therefore, a greater relief when Moonie and I reach the hotel, eyes still producing waterfalls, and are able to retire to our rooms to examine the coke in great detail. Of course, when we come to make this close examination what we find is by no means high grade cocaine but simply sweet sherbert. High grade sweet sherbert, but sherbert nonetheless and, as anyone will tell you, sherbert is not apt to do the trick in quite the same way as cocaine no matter what grade it may be.

At this stage, Moonie decides that he has Tangiers up to here and maybe further, and that he is most disillusioned with the chocolate people present. So we decide to move on to Gibraltar which is, at least, British. But when we arrive in Gibraltar we are suddenly very pleased that our cocaine turns out to be sherbert because, for the first time ever, we are most thoroughly searched by the customs people. When I say thoroughly, I mean *thoroughly*. It's bend down and touch your toes while some dago in British uniform takes a good squint up our arse-holes to ensure that we do not conceal joints, coke, diamonds or maybe even hookers in these private regions of our bodies. The entire episode is very depressing and I tell Moonie that I intend to fly a chick out from England to meet us and console us, or more especially, to console me. When she arrives, I take her to the hotel to meet Moonie and we spend the last of the cash we con out of the Tangiers hotel by getting well-blasted in various Gibraltar bars.

Whether it is all the Casbah aggravation, whether it is the

bending down and having foreigners peer up my ring piece, or whether it is a combination of both of these things, but whatever it is, on this particular night, I am out of my box before Moonie and my chick are even dizzy.

Which is all right by me except that the next thing I know I wake up with a strange whistling in my ears. It is a very high pressure type of sound and what do I find but that I am thirty-two thousand fucking feet up in the fucking air in a fucking Trident on the way to fucking Malta. I still have the fifty pence piece in my pocket but not much else, and Moonie and my chick are leaning on each other and giggling at me.

When we land at Malta, the old American Express card comes out once more and it secures us accommodation in one of the island's top hotels.

"Let us explore the location," says Moonie, but my chick decides that she is tired after the flight and that she requires a shower and a rest. Which is very unfortunate for her because Moonie and I go off into the night and very quickly discover two dusky bints who claim to be princesses. We return with these princesses to their hotel, which turns out to be even more luxurious than our hotel and there we remain for several days screwing until we are unable to screw any more, though the dusky bints maintain their enthusiasm and grow quite impatient with us when we suggest that a couple of hours of tiddly-winks might be fun.

At length we decide that it is time to return to good old England and we go back to our hotel to collect the ever-loving girlfriend. It turns out that she is no longer especially ever-loving, which is not entirely surprising since she is forced to spend all her time in the hotel, eating in the hotel restaurant and unable to go out and enjoy Malta because she has no money whatsoever and we are elsewhere. Moreover, she does not take kindly to Moonie's explanation that Malta is a dead-and-alive place anyway and there is nothing to see even if she does have some money.

The flight back to London is distinctly frigid and very quiet indeed. Even Moonie does not have the energy to bunny and it is a most silent trio that passes through the British customs and catches a taxi home. When it comes to pay off this taxi I feel in my pockets but all I find is the fifty pence piece that accompanies Moonie and me on our travels to Tangiers, Gibraltar and Malta. This is certainly insufficient for the cab driver and he is most unhappy at my suggestions that we should pay by American Express.

The whole episode is so tiring that I am very pleased to be able to return to John Entwistle's gaff and listen to him and his Mrs. discussing the price of fish which, it seems, soars quite distressingly during the time that Moonie and me are frigging about in the Mediterranean. In fact, fish is now so expensive that my fifty pence piece will only buy me a very small piece of cod, and an only marginally bigger piece of huss, which makes fish a most luxurious commodity indeed when you consider that this fifty pence piece sees me and Moonie through a great deal of flying, a great deal of liquor, some phony dope and more screwing than we can cope with in three different countries of the world.

Roadrunner

If anyone ever puts together all the machinery that Moonie owns during his lifetime, they will have a pretty comprehensive museum of exotic cars. Moonie and cars are like bees and honey. When he sees one he likes, then he just has to have it. On the spot. With no delay whatsoever. This attitude results in him running through several Mercedes, two or three Rollers—including a Corniche—a couple of Lincoln Continentals, an AC 428, at least two Hot Rods, an old Chrysler limo, two Excaliburs and a milk float.

This is not a comprehensive list and this alone is enough to make the average geezer in cavalry twill trousers, the sort that specialises in gawping at concours competitions and saloon car races, wet his shooting stick.

Most people lucky enough to own exotic machinery like this—not to mention the motorbikes and the hovercraft that Keith purchases—will spend many hours breathing on the bodywork, buffing up the paintwork, cleaning out the ash-trays, painting the tyres and, perhaps, tweaking up the engines. But not Moonie. He treats his cars as if they are slightly less expendable than a fourth-hand bicycle nicked from outside the local pub. He drives them into solid and often quite immovable objects. He capsizes them. He leaves them around in such unsuitable environments as ponds and generally treats them in such a way as will have the editors of *Motor, Road & Track* and *Classic Car* reaching for their smelling salts.

Part of this propensity for motorised mayhem may stem from the fact that Moonie is perfectly unable to drive anything. Technically, he is aware of the purpose of the steering wheel and the pedals, but he is violent and inaccurate in his efforts with these controls and is not at all bothered with the niceties of signaling and occasionally glancing in the rear view mirror. In fact, he completely ignores all the things that many policemen agree are most necessary to conduct a motor vehicle in safety. If anyone ever hears of a driver as bad as Keith Moon coming anywhere within fifty miles of where they are standing, the best thing they can do is to discover the whereabouts of the nearest air raid shelter and dive into it double geschvinn.

This lack of talent in the matter of piloting autos means that Moonie is very rarely, if ever, in possession of a driving licence and this means that whenever he is actually behind the steering wheel he is not only putting many people's lives in jeopardy, he is also behaving in a quite illegal fashion. What is quite extraordinary is not so much that he is always crashing cars and causing aggravation for all concerned, but that he nearly always gets away with it. But, of course, this is all part of Moonie's practically miraculous ability to survive.

His attitude to economy in the matter of motoring is certainly not in accord with the advice currently dished out by Her Britannic Majesty's government. No, he does not believe in Austin Allegros, Honda Civics or Ford Pintos. His requirement is for something very large and very fast—and preferably both. This device must also contain enough gadgets and gimmicks to entertain a California apartment block. The finish should be well lacquered and/or polished, at least during the honeymoon period.

These necessities are best exemplified in one motor car, the Lincoln Continental Cartier model, otherwise known as The Pimp's Motor. It is, perhaps, twenty feet long, has an intensely powerful sound system (at least, as owned by Keith Moon), an engine with enough litres to power the *Titanic* and is generally fitted with so many extraneous items that it closely resembles a Christmas tree. It is exactly the sort of car that Moonie will cherish for ever and a day, or at least until he discovers something even flashier.

One day in Malibu we are out and about in the Pimp's Motor, after a lengthy and enthusiastic bevvy-up with Harry Nilsson, Ringo and Micky Dolenz. (The same Micky Dolenz who is once the drummer in a diabolical band called The Monkees; despite this drawback he is not a bad geezer who is by no means averse to buying his round. Moreover, he is quite snappy on the one-liners, though inclined to be a bit sixties-ish, which is not surprising because this is the period when fame and fortune strike him.) Moonie suddenly turns to me and speaks:

"Fuck me, Dougal, those bastards have got some money. I mean, look, here I am, meant to be the man in The Who, and what have I got? I'll tell you what I've got. Fuck all! That's what I've got. I mean, Christ, who the fuck is Micky Dolenz? Tell me that, Dougal. Who is Micky Dolenz? But he's the one with the readiest and the last beer I bought was on your fucking American Express card!"

Well, of course, this is a language that I understand very well because it is only my American Express card that saves me from vagrancy charges on more than one occasion and the dealings between me and American Express are not far off the Nelson Rockefeller league. It seems that however much Moonie earns, he very often seems to have little or no cash money about his person. Moreover, his bank balance is always seesawing alarmingly between very healthy credit figures, indeed, and overdraft on the scale of the British national debt. But as long as he has me along with my trusty credit card, he tends to behave like the Queen of England in the matter of cash. That is, he doesn't carry any.

Anyway, this time when Moonie complains about the state of his finances, I can see that he is genuinely dejected but, what is more worrying still, is the fact that he is quite clearly dreaming up some scheme to raise the necessary. I am desperately hoping that he will not dream it up before I can drive the Pimp's Motor back to the hotel and catch up on my kip but, unhappily, while I am navigating in the general direction of bed, we drive right past what must be the most exotic car showroom in Malibu. And even though it is only seven o'clock in the morning, nothing will do but we must stop so that Keith can press his hooter up against the showroom window and take a gander at the most exotic car in this most exotic showroom.

The car is a brown Excalibur SS, which is a replica of a 1930's Mercedes sports tourer. This is a veritable picture of automotive perfection, with huge flaring wings and many yards of chromium exhaust pipe around and about—the kind of car that even Hermann Goering would find a bit flash.

When Moonie turns back from staring at this vision, it is clear that he will stop at nothing until he possesses this car. The prospect of having it gives him new verve.

"Right, dear boy," he says very briskly. "Home."

So we drive home, me wondering what evil plan he has in his mind. When we arrive home, what he does is to call up his lawyer, Mike Rosenfeld. What transpires during this conversation is that Rosenfeld is negotiating Moonie's visas and all the paper work this insane world requires before it is possible to get down to the business of earning a living. Part of this negotiation involves convincing the proper authorities that you are a worthwhile human being in all respects and that, in particular, you are able to take care of all the bills involved in staying more or less alive. To do this, Rosenfeld arranges for a well-known company of accountants, who are called something like Greenback and Schtum, to hold a large sum on Keith's behalf. It seems that this large sum will help to convince the government of the good old USA that Moonie is upright and worthy at all times. The sum in question is 40,000 dollars, cash, and why Keith wishes to contact Rosenfeld on the phone is that he wishes Rosenfeld to instruct Greenback and Schtum to release the cash so that he, Moonie, can spend it. But, as is the way of these things, it proves impossible to raise Mike Rosenfeld on the Alexander Graham Bell. I heave a sigh of relief and prepare to put myself to bed, but Keith will have nothing of it.

"Wait, dear boy," he commands. Then he leaves the room but, before I can sneak away, he returns, complete with Rommel cap and a large aluminium camera case that he somehow manages to padlock to his wrist.

"Right, Dougal old chap, take me to Greenback and fucking Schtum."

We arrive just as the office is opening. I do not think that the chick who is the receptionist there is used to seeing rock and roll stars in Rommel caps, complete with red eyes and plenty of verbal, enter the office and demand to see the guvnor, that is Mr. Greenback or Mr. Schtum. However, she puts up a pretty fair fight and claims that Mr. Greenback is out of town, if not deceased, and that Mr. Schtum is with an extremely important client and cannot be disturbed even if the Japanesers are commencing to attack Pearl Harbor once more. But it takes much more than this to stop Moonie. He just looks at the gallant bint and then marches straight by her and on into the building.

Then what he does is to open every office door in sight and behind each door there is a very surprised accountant and to each very surprised accountant Moonie addresses this question:

"Schtum?"

And when the very surprised accountants just shake their heads and manage to stutter:

"Nnnnno, sir!"

Moonie says:

"Terribly sorry, old chap," and moves on until, eventually, he does indeed come across Mr. Schtum who is clearly in conference with someone who looks as though he might be extremely important.

"Schtum?" asks Moonie once more.

"Yes?" says this Schtum, not a little surprised and quite angry with it. "You are . . .?" he begins to ask but, before he has time to add anything else, Moonie screams:

"Give me my fucking money?"

Well, whoever this geezer is with Mr. Schtum, he has at least got the brains to realise that this wild-looking person in a Rommel hat who interrupts the meeting is not about to be fobbed off with an appointment for next Friday week, so, while Schtum is beginning to break into a bit of mumbling, the important-looking bloke takes it on his toes as quickly as possible, if not before. Schtum is left on his own to face Moonie who is just beginning to get into his stride. What he says is something similar to this—a completely gratuitous attack on the innocent Mr. Schtum:

"Now listen to me, you cunt. I know you and your pinstriped lackeys have got forty thousand dollars worth of my readies. I haven't come here to fuck about, so get on over to the safe, dive into it and hand over my money—preferably in nice, new, clean notes. Then I'll be out of here before you can say profit and loss already."

By now poor old Schtum must work out who this Nazi-hatted maniac is and, of course, he is put upon the spot. On the one hand, he knows that Moonie represents a considerable slice of income to himself and his partners. On the other hand, he is not used to being called a cunt. And on the third hand, he knows that the money he holds for Keith ought not to be spent if the necessary paperwork is to be forthcoming from the immigration branch of the government of the good old USA. He is undoubtedly in a difficult position and, although he handles himself quite well under the circumstances, what he comes up with is not suitable for dealing with one such as Keith Moon, for what Mr. Schtum comes up with is an attempt to initiate a conversation of a more reasonable turn.

"Now, Mr. Moon," he says placatingly, "let us not be so hasty. It is indeed true that I hold some forty thousand dollars on your behalf, as you and your managers instructed, but you must understand that these monies are held and retained for eventual payment against taxes, so what I suggest is . . . BOIIIINNNGGGGG!!"

Of course, Mr. Schtum does not so much *say* BOING! as *go* BOING! and the reason that he goes BOING! is quite simply that Moonie strikes him over the crust with the handy aluminium camera case which is still attached to his wrist and in which he hopes to carry off his 40,000 dollars. What Mr. Schtum actually says when he is struck by this weapon is:

"Mmmmmnnnnnneuuuuurrrrrgggggg."

He follows this statement with a clear manual indication that he is not in favour of this treatment and does not deem it the approved kosher method of dealing with professional advisers. My own view is that if more people bonged their professional advisers on their beans with more aluminium camera cases, then the quality of professional advice would improve and the world become a better place. In double quick time, Schtum and Moon are having a rare old barney, but Keith does have the edge right from the start on account of his age advantage and his possession of the deadly camera case. Schtum points out that if Moonie has it away with the dollars, he will wind up up the pictures when the IRS comes poking around for its share of the take. But Moonie will have nothing of this. His argument is neither as well constructed nor as cogent as Schtum, but his one irrefutable point is that the money does actually belong to him and not to Schtum—or even to the IRS for that matter. If he, Moon, wants to buy a car with the cash, then that is his affair. This discussion is carried on at full volume and with much gesticulation involving the camera case. Finally, Schtum just shrugs in a very resigned manner and despatches one of his minions to the bank to get Moonie's mazuma out.

Later, Schtum refuses to handle Moonie's financial affairs ever again. In the circuumstances, that is not very surprising.

One of Moonie's great problems is that he believes the supply of cash is never-ending and that however much he spends there is always more to come. In a sense, of course, this is true and he is possibly one of the highest earning individuals in the business, providing that he continues to work gigging and recording. Because he has no writing royalties, Moonie has less income than the other members of the band, yet he spends more than anyone else because he lives a faster and more frenetic life. There is, therefore, a hell of a lot of outgoing to match the considerable income. Moonie, of course, keeps no record of either flow. As I say, he spends much of his time in debt and at one point, to my certain knowledge, that debt reaches forty thousand dollars, which is a lot of the folding to borrow against the dubious collateral of being the world's most spectacular rock and roll drummer.

Moonie exits Greenback and Schtum's with his money, but with very little in the way of fond farewells. No one says to Moonie that they are grateful for his business and look forward to seeing him again soon. But this does not bother Keith and he demands that we go immediately to the showroom and buy the metallic-coloured Excalibur. I make a feeble attempt to dissuade him from spending this money, not only because of the IRS but because we are particularly boracic at this time and need the cash to live on. These protests are about as much use as sunglasses half a yard up a chimney in the middle of the night. We wind up in the showroom. Moonie marches up to the salesman, his suitcase full of dollars. He speaks:

"How much for the Excalibur?" He is so keen to buy that he cannot even be bothered to make with the Noel Cowards. The salesman, fairly typical of dumb salesmen everywhere in so far as he is filled with that self-importance that blinds him to all else but his preconceptions of how wealthy Excalibur owners should appear, raises his eyebrows and virtually says: *more than*

you can afford, you scruffy little rat. But then he remembers
that this is California and in California you never know your
luck. So he buttons down his sneer and turns on an ingratiating
smile.

"Twenty thousand dollars, sir. Exclusive of delivery, of
course."

"Of course," says Moonie, suddenly cheerful. "How much
will you give me for the Lincoln?" He nods towards the Pimp's
Motor which is parked just outside and this does wonders for
the salesman. He figures that we are not timewasters after all if
we have a Lincoln Cartier to trade. So he takes a stroll outside
and gives the Pimp's Motor the once-over, tutting and humming
and ahahing as he goes. Eventually he returns to us and makes
his offer:

"I think we can probably let you have 10,000 on this car
against the Excalibur, bearing in mind that it does seem a little
. . . ah. . . *used* for its age. You understand what I mean?"

This geezer never makes an easier deal in his life.

"Right. Done," says Moonie. "I'll take it now. For cash."
With that he plonks the aluminium case down in front of
the salesman and commences to count out the greenbacks. The
sight of this cash excites the salesman no end and he is jumping
about like a mosquito on mescalin. In no time at all, he has the
Lincoln and we have the Excalibur and we are trucking down
Sunset Strip in this fabulous motor.

Under normal circumstances I will be very pleased to be
cruising about in such a car as this, bearing in mind that it is a
kind of extra-flash, all mod cons, Cinemascope and Todd-AO
replica of a 1930's Mercedes tourer. But right now I am very
worried about the finances and also find that it is about thirty
hours since I last shut my eyes. I am very knackered. Moonie,
however, is far from knackered. He is on a great high and is as
pleased as Punch with his purchase.

"Come on, man," he says, "let's drive down the beach." It is
more a command than a suggestion.

"Christ, Keith," I reply. "Leave it out. I mean, I am absolutely fucked." But nothing will do except we must drive up and down the beach in the new car. This machine is fitted with an extremely loud sound system—even more powerful than the special unit fitted to the Pimp's Motor—so even if no one notices the car on account of their being blind (and this is the only way they will not notice it), they will certainly *hear* it. And when these innocent sun-seekers and beach bums and holidaymakers and bathers turn to see where all this noise is coming from, what they see is the flashy Excalibur with me hiding as best I can behind the steering wheel and Moonie leaning two yards out of the passenger seat and very nonchalant with it. In this respect he is exactly like a small boy with a new toy, which is precisely what it is.

This motorised promenade up and down the beach takes up the best part of two hours and the only thing that keeps me awake during this time is the knowledge that if I whack up this particular model, we have nothing to exchange for wherewithal. But, thank God, Moonie eventually drops off to sleep, still leaning precariously out of the passenger seat. So I drive very steadily back to the house. There I park the car with Moonie still fast akip in it, and creep off to my bedroom for the desperately needed hitting of the hay.

That is all there is to the metallic Excalibur—except that it does not last very long, and the reason it does not last very long is that Moonie spots the legendary Liberace Excalibur, which is even flashier than the metallic one and is more conspicuous than an Italian pimp in a Swedish nunnery. When Moonie clocks this device, he must have it. So it's out with the first Excalibur and in with Liberace's gaudy monstrosity.

Before Keith Moon discovers the joys of the West Coast, Excaliburs and extracting cash from Greenback and Schtum, he has a love affair with an AC Frua 428, which is a car that AC produce to replace the one and only Cobra. It is very fast indeed, what with being equipped with a very large American V8 stuffed into a lightweight and quite elegant Frua-styled

aluminium body. This particular car virtually breaks the manufacturer's heart because Moonie requires that it be rebuilt so
many times after assaulting many gates, pillars, cars and other
solid items with it.

AC, the manufacturer, is like many small British companies
that treat their customers as members of the family. Each car is
hand-built and its records are kept as carefully as any horse-
breeder documents his stud. Of course, in the old days when
the only people able to afford such machinery are Hooray
Henries of one sort and another, a pain in the arse but well up
the social register, it is very easy for a company like AC to deal
with its custom (except that Hooray Henries do have a marked
propensity not to pay their bills). But once the good old rock
and roll business rears its ugly head, fame and especially fortune
can strike any obnoxious little berk and people like AC are
forced to deal with same obnoxious person, like it or no.

While I am certainly not saying that Keith Moon is obnoxious in any way, he is certainly not the sort of person that the
grovellers at AC will wish to deal with if it is not for the fact
that he is flush with spending money and that each time the 428
has to be reconstructed it costs him many of these readies.

The first time the 428 requires radical surgery is as a result
of Moonie driving along Chertsey Lane, which is not a big road
and definitely no racing track, at somewhere in the region of
150 mph. As I previously mention, the Frua 428 has a gigantic
American engine and this engine enables it to accelerate very
rapidly indeed. And to make the very most of this acceleration,
the best thing to do is to drop a gear or two in the automatic
gearbox, which is achieved by simply pulling the gearshift back
a notch or two. Obviously, this is the sort of manoeuvre that
must be executed at specific speeds and is not the sort of thing
one can do at 150 mph. For one thing there is very little acceleration left in the car at this speed. And for another the maker's
handbook advises drivers against such an action very strongly
indeed.

However, there we are at 150 mph in Chertsey Lane with me

driving. We are both very wrecked. Moonie turns to me and speaks:

"Come on, Dougal, let's see this fucking thing go." There is nothing that Moonie prefers to slipping the AC into its lowest gear and then having me tramp on the accelerator as hard as possible, because this is the best way to experience the AC's acceleration to the full and imposes the sort of G-forces that are usually only encountered in Phantom jet aircraft. When Moonie makes this suggestion to make the car go I omit to point out to him that it is already going somewhat anyway, probably on account of the difficulty entailed in keeping my eyes focused on the road ahead. So the next thing I know is that Moonie has his hand on the automatic gear shift, which is sticking up between us, and is clearly about to operate it. I immediately ease up on the accelerator and shout:

"Leave off, Keith! You can't change gear now! We're going too fucking fast!"

But that is all I have time to say and, somewhere down in the region of 120 mph, Moonie heaves the gearshift down to Drive 1, which is the lowest gear on the car and should never be engaged much above 30 mph.

I do not have the time to exclaim:

"I love you mother!" before the rear wheels lock solid, which affects the car's handling in a most adverse manner. It departs from Chertsey Lane despite my best efforts on the steering wheel and then crashes through at least three fences, skidding and sliding along the fields enclosed by these fences. Somewhere during this crashing process, the car turns over—but there is nothing simple about this manoeuvre. No. It does not undertake the movement from side to side. It somersaults end over end.

But, happily, all the time this poor roadholding is going on, the AC is slowing down and finally it comes to rest three feet away from a sixty foot drop down a bank into an enormously wide and deep reservoir.

Once the car is stationary and it seems to be safe for Moonie and me to alight, we climb out—me from the passenger door (although originally I am driving the car) and Moonie via the rear window. And once we are outside and enjoying the fresh air, we commence to laugh most heartily and I believe we will still be laughing to this day if it is not for the fact that we spy cycling toward us on his black, heavy-duty pedal cycle, the local copper.

When PC Plod arrives on the scene, which requires him to dismount and push his heavy-duty machine across the fields, he simply looks at the wreck and says:

"Hello, Keith. I knew it was you."

Then he sighs a trifle sadly to himself and cycles away into the evening.

One thing that I must say for the AC is that it is basically a very strong car indeed. Each time it comes back from the people at Thames Ditton, Surrey, whose responsibility it is to rebuild the car each time Keith destroys it, it is as good as new. In fact, I believe that it is now the pride and joy of some Carburettor Charlie who no doubt rejoices in the fact that the late Keith Moon once smashes its nose into more cars, banks, walls and houses than the average driver can shake a stick at.

Of course, the thing about Moonie and cars is that cars provide him with an excellent method of demonstrating his one-hundred-per cent madness. I mean cars are a strange item. All they really represent is a method of getting from here to there without having to hang about waiting for buses that never come. Cars are just lumps of metal and plastic and this and that, slung together by some poor bastard who spends forty hours a week waving a pneumatic screwdriver about. They're sold by some smartarse in a shiny suit and expensive shoes and each time they break down they cost plenty of bread. That's cars. Of course, I do not say that there are not a few very special types that are built by geezers who fancy themselves latter-day Chippendales. The AC is that kind of car. Yet these bits of machinery, from your crappy Cortina, through your manky Marina to your expensive Eldorado take on a life of their own which causes their owners to worship them. I mean, these cars get polished and

shone and loved and talked about from the time they are bought
to the time they are very old and sad indeed.

So every now and then when someone comes along who obviously doesn't give two monkeys what he does to his jam jars,
this is very impressive and horrible to the great public that
spends several hours every month bulling up its own autos. And
it is especially impressive if the motor car being treated in this
way is very expensive or desirable, such as a Roller or a Ferrari.
Or an AC.

Moonie's attitude to cars is well summed up by the Ferrari
Dino 246. Now this is a very pretty sort of car, a little Ferrari
that goes like the clappers and is highly thought of by all sorts
of punters, whether they can afford same Ferrari or not. It is
conceived by old man Ferrari in memory of his son Dino who
is killed in an accident—and the very sad thing is that when the
company Ferrari is taken over by Fiat, the old man is forced to
drop the name Dino on account of the Fiat management claims
that people—and especially Americans—buy Ferrari cars for
the name Ferrari and not for the name Dino. Which is a bit sick
if you think about it. Anyway, Moonie takes delivery of one of
these little gems and virtually the same evening I drive it, with
him, down to the local pub. We leave the car parked outside
and commence to down a few brandy and gingers.

In this pub are some very young guys, probably under age,
who clock Moonie and sidle over to talk to him. They are most
starstruck and dead chuffed to be able to have a private audience
with someone they clearly believe to be a god of the rock business. This is the type of situation in which Moonie absolutely
revels—if he's in a good mood, that is, and tonight he is. He is
very expansive and funny, buys drinks left, right and centre and
dispenses these drinks with many a:

"Dear boy!" and "Old chap!"

I have to admit that the great quantity of booze that appears
from over the bar—and barmen are always pretty prompt when
it comes to serving Moonie—and the speed at which it is dis-
appearing is beginning to make me feel distinctly Brahms and

Liszt, so what it is doing to the young guys I cannot imagine.

This particular evening is a warm summer evening such as arrives once every ten years in England, and after a while it becomes too hot inside the pub to be comfortable. So we all move outside the pub and that is how the youths come to see Moonie's brand new Dino 246. There is plenty of:

"Oooooooooh" and even more "aaaaaaaaah."

Again, Moonie is dead chuffed, though not unpleasant with it. He is generous in that he likes to share his pleasure and he is honestly pleased that they like his car. He turns to me and utters the words that I dread to hear:

"Dougal, give me the keys, dear boy."

I dread these words because in my experience to date they presage mechanised disaster. But, to tell the truth, during the last few days Moonie is on a high and is giving me plenty of work in the matter of looking after him and keeping him out of the local jail, hospital and lunatic asylum. So I am somewhat tired, as well as being olivered, and I cannot be buggered to stop what I know is likely to happen.

"The keys, dear boy, the keys!"

I take the Ferrari's keys out of my pocket and give them to Moonie who only goes and throws them to the lads who are glomming the car.

"Go on, chaps. Take it away. Have a spin in her."

Needless to say these kids are amazed at this opportunity. They cannot believe their luck and before he has a chance to change his mind, three of them squeeze into the cockpit, fire up the engine and accelerate off down the road, engine screaming, tyres squealing, clutch slipping and the car hopping about like a kangaroo with a lit cigarette end in its baby box.

"You're crazy, man," I say. "Absofuckinglutely crazy. You ain't going to see that again."

"Ah so what, Dougal. It's only money. Who gives a fuck?"

Of course, the kids do not come back with the Ferrari, but we come across it, smashed up in a ditch, as we are walking home. It is never insured for the kids to drive, so Moonie loses several thousand on the evening. But he does not seem to mind because the evening gives him a few hours of pleasure.

But, to return to the AC, we drive to Shepperton in it one time, soon after the reservoir incident, and park it near a bar/canteen place. Once there, we commence to have a few bevvies and eye the talent that is there eyeing anything that might employ talent. Pretty soon we are in a group that includes several quite tasty little starlets and a quite tasteless, but inevitable, PR man. Now this PR geezer is clearly pissed off that the starlets are giving Moonie plenty of action, and me some, but seem to be ignoring him altogether. Nevertheless it takes the PR man quite a while to work up the courage to start getting out after Keith. As is so often the case, this courage appears after a large amount of alcohol, mostly bought at Keith's expense, is consumed. The PR man then starts making such remarks as:

"Of course, most of your publicity is bullshit." And:

"I know you never do half the things people say you do." And:

"I can't understand why anyone publishes that crap. I mean, who cares?"

I try to explain to this dude as simply as possible that while some of the publicity is cobblers, it is by no means all cobblers. But he will have nothing of this explanation and simply continues to rant and rave about how it is all lies—the implication being that Moonie is just another little dick who owes everything he has, including his giant talent on the drums, to some PR guy like this one who is doing all the mouthing.

Sometimes Moonie can display a great deal of patience in circumstances like these but, inevitably, this geezer really gets on his tits and he is eventually faced with three choices. He can give him a good belt in the vestibule. He can ignore him. Or he can prove he is as mad as his publicity suggests. Of these choices, the first is dependent on mood and Moonie clearly does not feel violent enough to enjoy giving the PR guy a good punch in the gob. The second is too tame. So he is left with something to prove. He turns to me and utters the doomed words:

"Dougal, give me the keys, dear boy."

As usual, I give him the keys. Then Moonie jerks his head at one of the more stunning looking starlets and they go out together to the car park and climb into the AC.

Just a few seconds later the car roars into life and Keith begins the manoeuvres necessary to extricate the car from the metal parked all around it. This causes quite a few minor contusions to vehicles all over the parking lot but, finally, Keith frees the AC and accelerates off up the driveway. This is a very narrow driveway indeed and we can all see that the car is weaving alarmingly from side to side, gravel and dirt spurting up from behind its rear wheels. Then, with no warning at all, the car turns sharp left and enters some studio premises via a large, white five-barred gate.

This is a most spectacular move indeed, because the gate is firmly chained shut. There is a great explosion of splintered white wood which afterwards settles like a heavy fall of snow. This is followed by a stupendous crashing and smashing as the AC comes to rest in a garden, surrounded by shattered dry stone walls, plants, earth, young trees and I do not know what all else.

Naturally, the PR guy, who sees everything, is standing there open-mouthed in amazement.

But Keith is not finished yet. With engine screaming and roaring, he manages to extricate the AC from its resting place and, even though it now has three flat tyres, is smashed in from nose to tail and leaks more smoke and steam than the average power station, he turns it round to drive it back and park it in the lot. As he approaches the remains of the gate, he stops and the starlet gets out of the car. She handles the episode very well indeed.

Keith says to her:

"Open the gate, there's a darling."

And she makes as if to open this totally demolished gate so that he can drive through. Which he does, stopping the other side to pick the chick up. Then and only then does he drive back to where we are.

He parks the wreck and walks back to the bar, which is now quite surprisingly silent. He turns to the PR guy, who is a very strange shade of white and grey all mixed in together, and says:

"Thank you, dear boy. Mine's a large brandy and ginger. And hers," he adds, indicating the starlet. "Is champagne. A bottle."

Which of course the PR toad buys.

While Moonie's automotive capers put the shits up himself, me and any bystanders standing by, they rarely put the shits up any passengers because Moonie very rarely has any. There are many people prepared to put up with Moon's antics in clubs, restaurants and, maybe, even in their homes, but it is common sense to try and avoid being a victim of these antics in a tin box that is only too likely to impress itself on the nearest tree, evergreen or deciduous, because the driver's hands, instead of conducting the steering wheel, are clamped around a large bottle of brandy.

However, there are exceptions to the no-passenger-rule and one of these concerns a local Chertsey taxi driver who goes by the name of Ted. This guy does a fair bit of taxiing for Moonie and, being a regular sort of bloke who is quite prepared to buy his round when the matter arises, Moonie takes a shine to him. Consequently, if they meet up in the local pub, they may well spend the evening drinking together and, like as not, Moonie will give Ted a lift home. Most sensibly, Ted, being a professional driver, leaves his car at home when he is out on the booze.

One evening, we run into Ted in the local pub and have more than a few drinks with him. When chucking out time comes and it is time for us to go home, Moonie is totally legless and can hardly walk, let alone drive a motor car.

Now this geezer Ted is legless as well, though not quite as legless as Moonie on account of he has one leg missing in the first place, which leaves him only one leg to get legless in. What I mean by this is that Ted is a hopper and must make do with one wooden leg, a modern version of the same item worn by

Long John Silver and other piratical types. The long and the short of it is that, if anything, Ted is now steadier on the wooden article than he is on the real one and Moonie decides to give him a lift.

"Come on, dear boy," he says. "Hop into the motor and I'll run you home."

Well, Ted is not so legless that he cannot see that Moonie is by no means in the condition recommended for the safe conduct of motor vehicles by the British School of Motoring. He demurs:

"No thanks, Keith, it's a nice night. I think I'll walk. It'll do me good. Just the job for me sinus trouble. And, anyway, I don't want to put you out." While he makes these excuses, Ted is trying to sidle off, but Moonie will have nothing of it and persuades Ted to get into the motor, where he sits looking most apprehensive.

This is not surprising because, quite aside from the fact that Moonie is determined to drive and is obviously drunker than a skunk, this particular car is the sort of car that will make most people apprehensive if they are about to become a passenger in it. It is a Bucket T Street Rod—that is one of those jobs that looks as if it is once a nice sedate Ford such as doctors and suchlike drive around in during the nineteen-twenties, but is fitted with an engine bigger even than the one in the AC 428. It is also equipped with big, fat grabber tyres and has many air-brushed murals painted on it. It is the sort of car that will race up to 100 mph quicker than you can say it though it is not very good at going round corners—or at stopping, for that matter.

Moonie fires up the motor, which makes a noise only slightly quieter than the Concorde close to, because this car is not fitted with baffles in its exhaust pipes. This terrible din alarms Ted considerably and, from where I am sitting, in the back seat, it looks as though Ted is going to jettison right away. But, before he has time to bale out, Moonie slips the clutch. This motor is so powerful that it will sit up on its back wheels when it accelerates and this is what happens all down Chertsey High Street.

The banshee wailing of the motor is only equalled by the banshee wailing of Ted.

I then see that the reason for Ted's banshee noise, what with being hurled about all over the place, is that his artificial leg comes right off and he is forced to scrabble about to recover it. As he recovers it, I notice that we are on the wrong side of the road and making rapid progress toward a large trailer truck whose progress towards us is not being appreciably slowed by the loud hissing of airbrakes that comes from it.

Moonie, of course, is pissing himself with laughter and shows no signs of making the sort of movements with the steering wheel that will result in evasive action and salvation for us all. I also start in on the banshee wailing and am convinced that at last my number is up, I am about to meet the Great Roadie in the sky. I am just contemplating leaning over and grabbing the steering wheel geschvinn, when I observe that Ted takes matters into his own hands. More accurately, what he takes into his own hands is his leg and what he does with this leg is give Moonie a mighty BOFF! over the head with it. This does not seem to me to be a wise move because the BOFF on Moonie's napper can only contribute to the dizziness that is already present in Moonie's head and may make him stray even further into the path of the trailer truck. But, in fact, Ted's action seems to do the trick after all, and the hot rod does a neat four-wheel-drift which ends up with the car facing toward the pub, on the pavement on the wrong side of the road. The truck thunders by with its driver's eyes tightly closed and his lips moving very quickly and vehemently indeed. Once we are immobile, I have to restrain Ted who is administering further powerful BOFF's to Moonie's crust. Eventually he straps his leg back on and stumps off into the night, all the while screaming that he will get The Law, his solicitor and maybe even the Royal Marines, with whom he loses his leg in the war with the Germans, to deal with Mr. Moon.

    ❊   ❊   ❊

At one time or another, Moonie owns several Rollers, such as are known as the Best Car in the World and such as engage the talents and best endeavours of about five hundred wizened British craftsmen to assemble. What some wizened craftsmen do not realise, perhaps, is that the hours and days of skilled labour that they put into each vehicle can be undone in a matter of moments by the activities of one Keith Moon. And Moonie's inherent desire to smash things up is anyway heightened if the things to be smashed up are held in awe and esteem by the general public and anyone else looking on.

It is very rare for Moonie to be involved in fisticuffs as a result of his hooligan behaviour, but the nearest he comes to such violence seems to occur when he damages, destroys or otherwise abuses his motor cars.

On these occasions there is no shortage of dudes who wish to distribute knuckle sandwiches in Moonie's general direction. Strange to tell, these turkeys are not often fellow drivers whose machinery is suffering damage from Moonie's cars. No, they are much more likely to be bystanders taking great exception to the sight of expensive and (to most people) unattainable machinery wantonly destroyed by the drug/drink/sex depraved rock and roller. There is no question but that most people cannot bear to see destruction on this scale—unless, of course, same destruction is by order of governments and executed in the form of warfare.

Of all the vehicles caused injury by Moonie, the one that excites the most indignation is the Rolls-Royce, and it is Rolls-Royce wrecking for which Moonie is most notorious.

One time he is returning from a Christmas party at Ringo's and is in company with a model whose monicker is Patti Bygraves, relative of Britain's least entertaining, but probably richest, entertainer. She is a most pleasant-looking bint with the long, blonde hair and the faintly-vacuous expression beloved by many photographers. This is a look that is particularly favoured by Moonie, but Patti is by far and away one of the best of her trade and is happily in possession of brains as well as everything else. So when Keith fails to negotiate a roundabout that appears with little or no warning in the Roller's path, it is Patti who telephones me with the news of the accident.

"He's in trouble, Dougal," she says.

"Again," I reply. "Bollocks." But this is said more in irritation than surprise, for it is Christmas and I wish to be fast asleep when Santa Claus places his gifts in the stocking which I pin to the foot of my bed. I do not wish to be running about all over southern England in search of phantom Rollers whose road-holding fails at the sight of each gentle bend. But, of course, this is what I am paid to do, Santa Claus or no Santa Claus, so I speak as follows to Patti:

"I will be over."

Then I rouse out a mate who is staying at the house with me. His name is John Heath and I ask him if he will accompany me to the scene of the crime. Seeing as he is awake, after I shake him about a bit, he agrees and we eventually discover the Roller inextricably mixed with a heavy-duty wire mesh fence such as is used to provide safety barriers here and there and also as 'Keep Out' material by germ warfare and other similar establishments. John Heath agrees to stand by the desirable jam jar just in case any passers-by take the Christmas spirit too literally with regard to its accessories. I return to the house with Moonie and Patti and the first thing I do upon reaching the house is to arrange for Keith to have a large tumbler of brandy at hand so that when the police arrive, which they do remarkably quickly, we are able to claim that Moonie's lack of coordination occurs only after the accident and is only acquired in an effort to calm himself. Despite the brilliance of these tactics, Moonie is in no mood to comply.

"Say you did it, dear boy." He illustrates this distasteful suggestion by waving one hand airily about.

"Bollocks!" I reply. "I ain't losing my licence!" This argument continues in desultory fashion until the law arrives. As usual it is me who opens the door to these guardians of public morals and I am relieved to find that the gentlemen before me are quite genial and not over-enthusiastic to hang Moonie for his offence. So I take them to the room where Moonie is waiting.

When he sees them, he springs from his chair, sending the strategically placed brandy, or what is left of it, flying about all over the place.

"Ah, come in, come in, dear boys!" he cries to the coppers. "Have a bacon sandwich . . ." This quite inappropriate invitation can only be explained as the result of a rush of Christmas spirit to the brains, displacing the other spirits that are coursing around that venue. But the coppers do not wish to eat bacon sandwiches and are far more interested in obtaining the answers to such searching questions as:

"Do you own a Rolls-Royce Corniche, registration number BTO 722K?" and "Where were you on the night of December 24th, to whit, tonight?" and "Where is your alibi?"

Moonie's jovial and unanswerable retort to these and many similar copper-type queries is:

"Have a drink, dear boys!" When endless repetition of this reply eventually stills the coppers, Moonie makes as if to get them a drink, but he pauses in the middle of the room and confusion spreads across his features. He turns and looks at me uncertainly.

"Christ, Dougal, I've forgotten where the fucking drinks cabinet is. Be a good chap and pour these chaps a glass or two."

The two coppers are quite amazed at the insanity taking place concerning their enquiries, but they seem to realise that it is not a case of deliberate obstruction to the course of justice. So they suggest that they should return tomorrow, complete with reinforcements and maybe an interpreter, too, not to mention any other police equipment that will enable them to tell which end of this story is its head and which its tail. As they are about to leave, however, Moonie bounds to his feet, totters about, recovers and then staggers off in the general direction of the staircase.

"Wait a moment, chaps!" he calls.

I hustle the coppers off toward the door and instruct them to ignore Moonie but just as I am about to close the door upon these protectors of the innocent public, Keith reappears carrying in his arms a small and expensive Japanese television set.

"Here, chaps," he shouts, "a token of my friendship." Naturally enough, the coppers are truly amazed, though whether this is because they believe that Keith Moon has the audacity to bribe them, or whether it is because they do not figure that it is time yet for Father Christmas to make his annual appearance and, anyway, if Father Christmas looks anything like this paralytic idiot, then the coppers will no longer believe in same Father Christmas—and will certainly not instruct their children in the delights of this legend, I cannot tell.

The matter is taken out of their hands before they can refuse Moonie's generosity, as we all know they will, on account of their being British coppers and highly incorruptible, for the next thing that happens is that Moonie falls flat on his beezer, still hanging on to the small miracle of Japanese technology. Though he manages to bear the brunt of this fall, the TV set takes quite a tumble too and, as we occasionally find with such examples of the Japanesers' economic miracle, it explodes into minute fragments. The few fragments which do not appear to be damaged beyond repair are then comprehensively destroyed when Keith staggers to his feet, walks about upon the fragments, swears, and collapses on to them in a most determined fashion, his vertical hold temporarily maladjusted.

Surprising to tell, this scene only amuses the coppers and, in fact, it must do the trick for, as far as anyone recalls, Moonie is never prosecuted for the accident.

But, although it is truly amazing how often Keith manages to get away with such capers, he is by no means immune to prosecution. One morning, at around eight o'clock, I am once more rudely awakened whilst akip (this time at my parents' house). Before I can collect my senses fully, my mother is giving me plenty of assault and battery upon my ears as to how a geezer from Smith's, the TV repair shop in Chertsey, wishes to speak to me more immediately than sooner. As I am stumbling to the blower, I try to remember whether I am behind with my TV rental, or whether Smith's finally takes delivery of the new all-powerful in-car stereo systems such as they know Moonie is extremely partial to. Either way, I resolve to give them a good bellowing down the dog-and-bone because I do not believe that either case justifies them dragging me from the sack at this hour of the morning.

"Ah, Mr. Butler," says the man at the other end of the phone. "I have Mr. Moon here for you." In two shakes the man himself is there and talking to me.

"Ah, good morning, dear boy," he greets me and I realise that it is not likely that I will be able to return to the Land of Nod.

"The price of meat has just shot up," continues Moonie.

"Ah, don't fuck about, Keith, it's too early." I feel like there is a wasp's nest in my brains. "What do you mean, the price of meat has just shot up?"

"Well, the thing is, dear boy, I've just smashed the Roller into a Tesco meat truck. Woke up bright and early, you see. Thought I'd take the motor for a spin and the next thing I know, the Roller is closely attached to this fucking Tesco truck." *Here we go again,* I think to myself.

"What do you expect me to do about it?" I ask.

He then explains that once he attaches the Roller to the truck, he flees into the TV repair shop, where he is known on account of over the years he represents a considerable slice of income to this shop what with investing large sums in TV sets, stereo systems and the like (not to mention the cost of repairs to these items which are not designed for aerial usage). Because of this investment, Smith's do not tell Moonie to piss off out of it, as they might anyone else in a similar predicament. No. What they do is to sit him down with a cup of tea, make his phone call for him and generally treat him somewhat better than they would Mr. Smith himself. Well, the long and the short of it is that Moonie wishes me to come and collect him, so I drive down there as quickly as possible and when I get to Smith's I find

Moonie there, wearing a black and gold caftan, a crochet hat such as are not worn by blokes unless they wish to cast grave doubts upon their sexuality, and the sort of soppy grin that is indicative of large medicinal doses. However, he appears to be quite calm and gives me a large hello:

"Terribly sorry to wake you from your slumbers, dear boy, but I thought it would be better if you were to see about the car."

"Why's that, man?" I ask, though I have a pretty shrewd idea that it is because he bunks off from the scene of the crime. This turns out to be exactly the case, and that he only gets away with it so far because the sole witness to his overenthusiastic parking is an old dear who is under the impression that the driver of the Rolls is an old woman. Apparently, when she sees the accident occur, she calls out:

"Look at that silly old cow who's just smashed her car up!" She gets this impression, of course, because of Moonie's eccentric caftan-and-crochet-hat combo. Clearly, the best thing I can do is to get Moonie away from the scene of the crime as quickly as possible and to see to the coppers myself. But Moonie will have nothing of these tactics.

"No no no no, dear boy," he says, "while I am here I might as well buy a few things I need—especially as this gentleman here has kindly provided me with a few Valiums. I could definitely do with a new portable telly. Joan needs a replacement for hers, and these speakers are really something special. Listen, man . . ." With that, he's off, the shop manager trailing along behind him. Moonie indicates virtually every type of device in the shop and insists that this dude writes down the orders, though, to give the manager his due (for he stands to make several thousand out of this ranting), he tries to dissuade Moonie from these purchases.

Eventually, however, I manage to pack Moonie into a minicab and then I go to interview the coppers who are crawling all over the Roller and the meat lorry. Naturally, the first thing these coppers discover is that it is none other than Keith Moon who owns the car and when they discover that I work for Keith Moon, they ask me many questions which I do my best to fend off. But, even though these coppers do not shine the famous third degree Anglepoise lamp directly into my eyes, I cannot prevent them from taking up the enquiry with Moonie at a later date and as a result he is well and truly nicked. Maybe that is no bad thing because it does keep him off the road for a while —though why this should be I am never sure, for Moonie does not care much of a fig whether he has a licence, and so on, anyway. This nicking, incidentally, is also the occasion when Keith offers to pay the fine that is imposed upon him by American Express, an offer which is rejected most haughtily by the magistrate, thank God, for it is my American Express card which will suffer in the unlikely event of the court agreeing to be paid in this manner.

The best-known tale of Moonie and autos is one which never occurs and if this seems altogether too much to swallow let me expand upon it. Wherever you read anything about Moon the Loon, King of the Jokers, Madman of Rock, in such bladders as *The Sunday Express*, *Newsweek* and maybe even *The Pig Breeder's Weekly*, you will also read about the Rolls-Royce in the swimming pool. Like so much of the stuff written about Moonie, it is a lie. Maybe it stems from the day that Moonie has a terrible ruck with Kim, in the house at Chertsey. Now, of course, this is not an unusual occurrence even though it leads him to a momentous decision, which he communicates to one and all present, to commit suicide. But one and all present are used to this and make many useful suggestions as to how he might achieve this end. There follows a highly intellectual conversation as to the relevant merits of gun, knife and rope and the only thing on which all present agree is that to achieve suicide by medicine is a sin and a shame and a terrible waste of same medicines anyway. Naturally everyone assumes that Keith will use his regular monthly method of suicide—emptying a bottle of aspirin down the john and then showing the bottle to Kim and telling her that he is now full to the brim with aspirin and will she save his life, please, if she loves him.

But this time it is different, and Keith is definitely about to commit suicide and is most aggrieved that no one is taking his threat seriously. He storms out, screaming:

"That's it! That's it! I've had enough! Fuck the lot of you! I'm going to end it all right now!"

Vaguely wondering why he needs to go into the garden to perform this harm upon himself, we follow him out and take a gander. What he does is to leap into the Roller, rev it up as if he's at Sebring, slam it into Drive 1, and hurtle off in the general direction of the ornamental pond.

This ornamental pond is a very horrible pond indeed. For a start there is hardly any water in it whatsoever and what water there is in it barely supports the rotting varieties of weed and water lily that repose in the thick bed of slime that accumulates there over the years. In fact, just about the only ornamental thing about this pond is the large number of empty brandy bottles, demijohns of champagne, drumsticks, beer cans and so on which find their way into it after parties and piss-ups. This pond is, indeed, a pain in the neck as Moonie and I often find to our cost when we are returning from the pub on our monkey bikes and inadvertently plunge into it. It is true that there are occasions in the past when the water in this Black Lagoon, which will be top of the charts with any Creature that happens upon it, is maybe up to chest level, but that is a historical situation and, anyway, this year sees such a hot summer that the slime is even tackier than usual.

Suddenly Moonie jams on the Roller's brakes, heaves the gearshift into reverse and hurtles backwards into this Black Lagoon. Naturally, being as this car is intended for luxurious travel upon relatively even blacktop and is not designed for cross-country expeditions in glutinous bogs, the Roller barely gets five feet into the ornamental pond before it sticks fast, rear wheels spinning very angrily indeed. Next, the engine stalls and Moonie is heaving and shoving upon the driver's door. Though I am by no means an expert lip-reader, I have no difficulty in calculating that what Moonie is screaming is:

"Bollocks!" and "Fuck it!" and "Shit!" and "Jesus Christ!" The slime in the ornamental pond is well up over the door sill and is making it extremely difficult for Moonie to open the door and, when he does so with a massive effort, he steps directly into same slime, which is at least two feet deep. I step forward to commiserate with Moonie as he is prostrate in the mud, still cursing and swearing.

"Fucking typical, isn't it?" he says when he sees me. "I try to drown myself and all the fucking water's gone." With that, he rolls over onto his back and lies quite calmly in the ooze. Eventually, of course, he returns to the house for a few bevvies, and stinks the whole place out most effectively. In fact, the pen and ink from the ornamental quagmire is so effective that Moonie could not be more alone even if he succeeds in committing suicide in the first place. It is several days before anyone can approach within ten feet of him.

And *that* is the story which gets embellished into the *Status Symbol In Rock Star's Swimming Pool* episode.

Even though there are very many incidents in Moonie's life which revolve around cars and other such things mechanical, it may come as a surprise to you that Moonie is quite well into car racing and rallying. As into it, that is, as anyone can be who is out of it most of the time. But Moonie is sufficiently enthusiastic about it all to be asked on one occasion to start the RAC rally, which is a big event in the European racing and rallying calendar and is not the sort of event which you might expect to involve drug-crazed rock and roll drummers.

On this occasion, and for all I know about it, on many other occasions too, this rally is taking place in Wales, which is a small country tacked onto the side of England. It is very beautiful in spots, what with much green grass, many silver streams, pretty valleys and even a mountain or two here and there. In fact many people are heard to remark that Wales is a place they would like to live if they can find any way of earning a living that does not involve burrowing down into the ground and heaving lumps of coal around. But, speaking personally, no matter how many valleys and rivers it has, I find that Wales is far too full of Welshmen for my liking and for this reason have to admit that I can either take or leave Wales and, by and large, am quite happy to leave it.

It may also surprise you to hear that Moonie numbers a considerable quantity of coppers among his acquaintances. They are not what you or I might call mates, but then Moonie has very few of these. It is true, however, that not every copper thinks that Keith Moon is an asshole and there are several who do make considerable efforts to cultivate his friendship. And Moonie himself is not against speaking to policemen, although I have to say that I myself am not entirely in favour of this habit because every policeman I ever meet is on the lookout for something with which to either further his career or his bank balance. By which I mean that the day I can offer a copper a quick snort and he can take same without making several notes in his little black book, then, maybe, I will have a policeman for a mate. Until then I prefer to treat such persons as large and possibly dangerous dogs which may be played with from time to time but on which it is wise to keep a severe eye and a very strong chain.

Anyway, this time we travel to Wales via Bristol, where we pick up an XJ6, which is a large, fast and comfortable sort of Jaguar, and from Bristol we drive straight across the river and into Wales. Now I cannot remember the name of the place we stay in Wales, not because I am any more out of it than usual, but because this place has a name which has more letters in it than a Post Office van and is harder to pronounce than that volcano in Mexico. When we arrive at this place we meet up, as arranged, with a little chick from Track Records and a geezer known as Barry the Poof and his boyfriend and, because this Wales is not as advanced as San Francisco in these matters, Barry the Poof and his friend have to check into their bungalow as Mr. and Mrs. Smith. For once I find myself in a different bungalow from Moonie, for which I am very thankful but, as usual, we meet up in the bar and proceed to inhale considerable quantities of brandy before we drive off into the nearest town, which is spelt something like Llandudno, to continue the merry-making. While we are in this strange Welsh town, we meet up with John Field, who is the Track Records accountant, and we pick up one or two Welsh bints who, considering they are Welsh and consequently have extremely low foreheads indeed, are quite passable in such areas as the legs and lungs.

Also at this time we bump into one or two members of the local constabulary and they join in this jolly up in such a way as you will not figure them for policemen at all until you remember that they do not show much inclination to buy their own drinks.

Now in Wales, as in most of Britain, the drink licensing laws are not a little eccentric and it is not very long before we are no longer permitted to become drunk in the local bars and must return to the bungalows if we are to complete the mission successfully. So we all cram ourselves into the XJ6 and drive back to the place with a name like that volcano in Mexico. And once we are there what do we do but drink several drinks and attempt to interfere with the female Welshers who seem to arrive at the bungalow with us.

It is not long before the famous drummer of the famous Who rock and roll band has inserted himself inside one of the Welshers, who clearly has no great objections to this occurrence, and is heaving up and down upon her in a most surprisingly energetic and satisfactory fashion. In fact, everything is going very well indeed and those of us present and capable are keeping an eye on the proceedings, in case we pick up any good tips, as well as making considerable efforts to insert ourselves here and there in the various places that appear to be available when there is suddenly an appalling scream and this scream almost certainly emanates from the Welsher on whom Moonie is performing. This scream has such an intensity and such a pitch that for a moment or two it throws even Moonie in mid stroke and he ceases to heave up and down upon the Welsher and looks quite surprised. But this has an extraordinary effect upon the girl and she shrieks:

"Oh, give me a real good fucking, Keith bach! Don't stop, look you. I want more, more, more."

And then she lets out with something that sounds like:

"OooooaaaaaaRRRRRGGGGGGGHHHHHHHHHH!!!!"

For a moment these noises lead me to believe that the Intercity Express between Cardiff and Newport must be passing this way, but then despite the brandies and various medicines that are acting upon our bodies, we come to the simultaneous conclusion that this small Welsher is indeed responding to Moonie's heaving up and down upon her and is enjoying it no little and that these noises she makes are noises of encouragement and endearment. So, of course, Moonie continues with a will and the more he heaves the louder the noises, until they are so powerful that the rest of us are unable to concentrate upon what we are doing and cease attempting to perform upon the Welshers with us, but stand back to watch the show. It is not long before Moonie's Welsher has a nickname: Howling Wolf.

Now, the manager of the bungalows, in which we're staying, is a short and fat man whose straight name is Gilbert Mylchreest but who goes by the nickname of The Stoat on account of he has an extremely large nose and is always very dirty. Moreover, wherever he goes he is accompanied by large quantities of cigarette ash and a dingly dell that is probably connected with the stains that characterize his trousers front and back. His stomach wells up over his belt because for every cigarette he smokes he consumes a large gin and tonic and, for every gin and tonic he consumes, he eats an egg sandwich, a shortcake biscuit or anything else that he finds lying around and which will spring from his mouth in a not-so-fine-stream if he talks while he eats— which is invariably his habit.

But, for all this, as hotel managers go—and despite this unpromising start—Gilbert Mylchreest is not entirely despicable because he does allow whoever stays in his bungalows to do exactly what they like provided that he, Gilbert, can join in, too. This is in great contrast to the very many hotel managers I come across in my time with the band. Most of them are exceptionally tedious, what with their disapproving of our smashing the place up, breaking the furniture, scandalising the guests, throwing food about and generally behaving in a manner some people might consider controversial. I well remember one time in New York being threatened by a hotel manager with a gun for no other reason than I inadvertently drop a colour television set upon him from the second floor balcony of my room.

But the point of this digression on Gilbert Mylchreest, The Stoat, is that he hears Howling Wolf from several bungalows away and, before anyone knows any different, sprints into our room trailing a plume of cigarette ash and producing sufficient sweat to fry a large quantity of chips. And as he enters the room I think to myself *this is it. It's all up. He's sure to call in the coppers.* But then I remember that, anyway, there are several coppers present and, of them, several are attempting to commit grievous bodily enjoyment upon the Welshers present. Moreover, The Stoat does not seem to be about to call in a copper at all because the next thing I see is that he drops his tarnished trousers and, without so much as a by-your-leave, thrusts Moonie aside and himself into Howling Wolf.

As far as anyone can tell the little screaming Welsher does not even notice this substitution of a scabrous hotel manager's dick for the more illustrious, but probably equally dubious, rock star's plonker because all she does is to continue her impression of the Cardiff to Newport Intercity Express.

Well by this time none of us can raise much enthusiasm for the continued molestation of the Welshers, not least because the sight of Gilbert Mylchreest's besmirched nether regions humping up and down is a touch off-putting—even to those of us accustomed to the sort of coupling that seldom appears in romantic literature such as the late Dornford Yates creates. So we decide to leave the revolting Stoat to continue his exertions upon Howling Wolf and, gathering up a few of the coppers, we pile into several cars and drive off in the general direction of Llandudno once more. And, whenever we pass a dwelling of any sort, we wind down the car windows and call out to the sleeping citizens:

"THIS IS YOUR CONSERVATIVE CANDIDATE SPEAK-ING. HERE IS A MESSAGE ON BEHALF OF THE LEADER OF THE CONSERVATIVE PARTY. IT HAS JUST BEEN ANNOUNCED THAT THE CONSERVATIVE PARTY HAS OFFICIALLY ADOPTED A POLICY OF COMPULSORY PURCHASE IN ORDER TO FACILITATE THE RESET-TLEMENT OF THE ENTIRE BLACK POPULATION OF GREAT BRITAIN IN THE LLANDUDNO AREA."

This message is communicated via one of the policemen's loudhailers, so it has considerable volume and force—and not little authenticity too. Of course, it may not seem very convinc-ing to you but you must remember that it is now 3 o'clock in the morning, when no one's brain is too clear, least of all the brain of a Welsher who spends most of his time grovelling about in the depths of the earth. And you must also remember that Moonie's hooray accent is just about perfect. Close your eyes and you could mistake him for Norman St. John Stevas or several other leading members of the Conservative and Hooray Party. So I am not entirely surprised when I read some months later that in the local by-elections this area returns a socialist candidate with one of the largest majorities in the history of politics.

Now one of the coppers who is with us—the one who lends us his loudhailer—and who is a great distance out of his box, de-cides that this political message is becoming boring and anyway remembers that the Conservative and Hooray Party is more likely to up his salary than the Heavy Socialists. So nothing will do but he must have a go on the loudhailer. When we pass the next set of houses he commences to bawl, very loud and authen-tic:

"THIS IS AN EMERGENCY POLICE ALERT. EMER-GENCY POLICE ALERT. THIS IS AN OFFICIAL POLICE MESSAGE. A LORRY LOAD OF POISONOUS SNAKES HAS OVERTURNED IN THIS AREA AND YOU ARE

ADVISED TO SIT IN A VERY COLD BATH UNTIL FUR-
THER NOTICE. THANK YOU."

Now this message has the most remarkable effect on the local
people, especially when the coppers then proceed to knock upon
the doors of these local people and very sincerely warn the various Welsh geriatrics that the only known protection against such
poisonous snakes as these is to surround oneself with as much
cold water as possible and, if same geriatrics are unlucky enough
to be bitten by same snakes, they must immediately remove their
dentures and suck the poison from their bodies, no matter where
the snake bites are situated. It later transpires that the casualty
ward of the local hospital is inundated with geriatrics twisted
into quite grotesque shapes as a result of their practising this
sucking in anticipation of the poisonous snake bites.

Thus we continue generally behaving somewhat inconsider-
ately in the streets of this area with the name like the volcano in
Mexico, and warning the citizens about the imminent resettle-
ment of blacks and the proximity of poisonous snakes, until such
time as we start to feel somewhat knackered. The coppers in
particular begin to moan about how they have to start the day
early, what with arresting people who make too much noise and
helping old ladies across the streets and so on. So we sling the
coppers out of the car at their various residences with many remarks such as:

"See you later" and "Good luck" and "Don't do anything I
wouldn't do!"

Moonie and I decide to make tracks back to the hotel for a
short kip and we figure that by now Gilbert Mylchreest, The
Stoat, has finished his horrendous acts upon Howling Wolf and
that Barry the Poof and his mate should also be back in their
own rooms to do whatever it is such people do when it is time to
hit the sack.

So there we are making excellent time back to the bungalows,
especially as the XJ6 is ideal for doing four wheel drifts and
travelling very rapidly indeed, when suddenly Moonie screams:

"Stop the car, Dougal! Stop the fucking car!"

Of course what I assume is that Keith wishes to regurgitate some of the evening's intake, possibly over me and certainly over the Jaguar's sumptuous Connolly hide seats, which would be a shame—specially over me—so I heave on the anchors and the car stops in remarkably short order. But it transpires that Moonie does not wish to have a liquid laugh but sees various items with which he wishes to instigate various jolly japes before fully retiring for the night. The items in question are a number of road signs of one kind or another which are scattered around the road in preparation for the RAC rally which Keith Moon is starting tomorrow, and these signs say such things as:

START, FINISH, CHECKPOINT and *TURN LEFT HERE.* The plan that occurs to Moonie is very simple: to collect same signs and attach them to the roof of Gilbert Mylchreest's hotel which may well cause Gilbert to have a mild coronary when he sees them and a major coronary when he has to arrange for their removal from the roof of his expensive and desirable holiday home.

Now the hotel part of the bungalow complex is at least five stories high and it is in this section that the poorer members of the holiday-making public are forced to stay, while those of us who are richer (or at least attached to richer persons) stay in the very luxurious bungalows. Fixing the rally signs to the hotel's roof seems to me to pose various complications, not the least of which is the fact that neither Moonie nor I are too steady on our feet at this time, what with the various medicines that are acting within us. In fact we both appear to be prone to the occasional Cyril Lord, which means that we are crashing to the carpet with distressing frequency. However, what with one thing and another, we succeed in carrying these signs, which weigh probably about a hundredweight altogether, up to the roof and we suspend them between the various chimneys that we find up there.

If you are to ask me how we achieve this act I cannot give you a convincing answer. All I remember is that we are forced to heave on many ropes, to prop many ladders here and there, nearly fall off the roof several times and generally scare ourselves

shitless. What I do remember very clearly is that when the tasteful display is discovered the next morning, Gilbert The Stoat can
get nobody at all, including the local fire brigade, to remove the
signs. Which indicates, perhaps, that these Welshers are not
quite so stupid as I previously am led to believe.

So the signs stay up on the hotel roof until we depart and
may, for all I know, still be there.

But all this is by the by. After a good night's kip, Moonie and
I are up good and early the next day and make our way to the
start of the rally for Moonie to wave the starter's flag and generally get things off to a good beginning. I have the distinct impression that the local society has mixed feelings as to the
propriety of the famous drummer of the famous Who rock and
roll band, the drummer who is well-known to one and all for
stuffing things up his hooter and down his gob and for stuffing
himself into other things too, come to think of it, performing the
opening ceremony of this serious motoring event. And I am sure
that many of the Carburettor Charlies present can think of many
people they would prefer to conduct the start, because at this
time the serious racers and rallyers are not generally in favour of
long hair, drugs and rock and roll.

Of course, these comments refer only to those people connected with the world of four wheels; it is well known that those
who prefer to risk life and limb on two wheels are heavily in
favour of long hair, drugs and rock and roll.

However, everything passes off OK. Moonie behaves himself
in a manner which is surprisingly civilised and issues a great
number of "Dear boys" and "Old chaps" and for all I know the
Carburettor Charlies believe that he is required to pay a great
deal of money for his education and his accent and, of course,
this is always very impressive to Carburettor Charlies. Once the
cars are well under way, vroom-vrooooming off through the
Welsh forests, we leave the four-wheel enthusiasts to their entertainment and commence the search for light relief once more,
for we are now hot to trot again.

Moonie, I, Barry the Poof and his boyfriend (who is especially bored with the motoring types) drive about looking for a congenial hostelry. Our search does not take too long because, although the licensing laws in Wales are most eccentric, there is no shortage of pubs, possibly because, apart from heaving coal about and playing Rugby, there is nothing to do in Wales other than visit the local pub, unless you include taking long scenic walks and screwing sheep. We pick on a hostelry that seems to have an extraordinary number of black people hanging about its entrance, making me wonder whether the Conservative Party takes heed of our broadcast messages of the night before. Then, as we enter the establishment, I realise that these are not true black people, such as come from Africa, the West Indies and Brixton, but are coal miners who are still covered with dust from the mines.

What I forget to mention is that by now Barry the Poof's boyfriend is wearing a dress, a fetching little number in cashmere, suitable for day wear and sporting events, and the ensemble is completed with high heeled boots, a fairly convincing brunette wig and plenty of Max Factor face paint. Now while it is true that Barry's boyfriend is not up to much as a fellow, he is certainly not up to much as a bird either, on account of he has a heavy five o'clock shadow and a generous selection of pimples which even Max Factor pancake cannot hide satisfactorily. In short it is a toss up as to whether he makes a better chick than he does a geezer. Whatever else, you would need to have very short sight indeed not to realise pretty geschvinn that this is in fact a bloke and not a bint. And shortly after that you would also realise that this is an extremely poovy chap who is wearing a chick's outfit—all of which occurs to me just as we are entering this pub which is chock full of tough looking miners who are drinking large glasses of extremely strong-looking ale and are generally looking grim, as miners are apt to do.

Now I have to admit that the episodes which follow make me revise my opinions of Welsh persons in general. I am expecting these heavy gentlemen to give Barry and his boyfriend plenty of verbal on account of being a poof. I am also expecting that they will then commence to give Moonie plenty of verbal too because, all of a sudden, Moonie takes it into his head that today he is a poof too. This is nothing new to Moonie, I might add, since he frequently takes it into his head to act the ginger beer, especially if he can get hold of a dress or two. On this occasion, fortunately, he does not have a dress and I personally consider it most inappropriate that he should suddenly decide to act completely bent, what with plenty of the cocked wrist, hand on hip, pouting and mincing around.

While it is true that Moonie makes a good start by ordering up drinks for everyone present, I can see that our general demeanour and behaviour is causing a certain amount of comment among these underground burrowers. Then Moonie discovers that the pub has a juke box and that this juke box, while it has a number of dozy country songs on it such as *The Green Green Grass of Home* along with a few Welsh favourites such as *Men of Harlech*, also has a very early Beach Boys disc on it—to whit *I Get Around*. Now, as I mention before, surfing music is Moonie's favourite kind of music and it is the only sort of music, apart from rock and roll, that he listens to at home, so he jams a tanner into the machine, slips the guvnor of the pub a couple of quid to turn up the volume, and commences to leap about like all the members of Sha Na Na rolled into one. Then, before you *can* say Rudolph Nureyev (if you *can* say Rudolph Nureyev), he grabs one of the blacked-up miners and gets him capering about too.

Fortunately, the miner Moonie grabs hold of is one of the local top-notchers because, although at first he looks as if he is going to land one on Moonie—and even on the rest of us too— he then gets into the swing and in no time at all is performing an extremely creditable jitterbug. Then, on account of they can see that the head lad puts the seal of approval on these goings-on, the other miners start putting in some fancy footwork too.

In this pub, by the way, are absolutely no women whatsoever —not that women are banned in any way, but it seems that Welshers generally frown upon the presence of ladies in pubs like this where somewhat grimy burrowers ease off the tensions of the day. Pretty soon, then, we have a scene like something out of *Jailhouse Rock* where all the prisoners are doing the rocking and rolling while The King is belting out the title song. The only difference is that this time we have Moonie screaming his head off somewhat untunefully, backed by the Beach Boys. In fact, Moonie is by no means the best singer in the world. You will even find those who claim he cannot pitch a note in tune, but he has plenty of heart as anyone who hears his solo album will testify.

Time goes by and pretty soon we're having a right old jolly-up with these miners who decide that perhaps we are not such a bad lot of pooves after all. Naturally Barry's boyfriend loves it all, what with being surrounded by butch geezers with bulging biceps and pectorals and he commences to become very coy with one and all. Now the funny thing is that, although only Ray Charles and possibly Stevie Wonder, will think that Barry's boyfriend is a dame—and even then they will have some suspicions, especially if they are unlucky enough to remove his dress—these miner geezers act as if he is the most desirable bint in the universe. They are extra polite. Ease up on the swearing. Provide chairs for him to sit upon and buy him drinks too. I do not mean by this that they make any attacks upon his body or they appear to fancy him in any way. Far from it. But they do behave as if he is a girl that requires some looking after.

I suppose that on the whole these dudes, who are compelled to spend most of their waking hours making like moles and/or earthworms, do not see many guys dressed up as dolls in this place and so they decide to give him the benefit of the doubt and treat him like some rare and endangered species. Another funny thing is that I am sure these mining dudes have no idea that Moonie is a member of the world famous Who rock and roll band, although they do know he has something to do with show biz. So their behaviour toward us is not influenced in any way by Moonie's fame and affluence.

I have to confess that I and the others with me are considerably impressed by the spirit of these Welshers—these particular Welshers at least—and by the time we decide to leave, around about mid-evening, I am beginning to think of them as Welshmen and not Welshers and am inviting them to gigs and offering them free tickets and I do not know what all else—and they are inviting us all home and practically suggesting that we give their wives one too. But after many hand shakes and such statements as "See you soon" and "Nice to meet you" we split and head back to the hotel.

Even now, Moonie's Welsh mayhem is not complete and more jollying-up ensues in the hotel. Not for the first time in my ten years with Moonie am I amazed at his extraordinary stamina and tenacity. I think of myself as a fairly tough geezer with plenty of get-up-and-go and, although I am frequently out of my tree, I am seldom as far away from the branches as Moonie is.

Once we are back at the hotel we find that Gilbert Mylchreest, The Stoat, has many of his cronies with him and is practically cleaning out the hotel bar to keep the company filled up with liquor. Moonie starts doing his bit for the cause too, handing out the medicine.

Finally we collapse into our beds at around four in the morning, by which time The Stoat is a rather alarming shade of purple and seems more like a panting bullfrog than a stoat to me.

The next day we are due to return to London so, at about noon, I begin to organise Moonie and I have to say that if David Livingstone ever has more trouble organising his expeditions than I do organising Moonie, then David Livingstone deserves every bit of posthumous fame he ever achieves—and perhaps more too. Not that I am implying that my trips with Moonie are quite as highly motivated as those of the late Dr. Livingstone. All I am trying to convey is that the running of

Moonie's life is only marginally simpler than persuading the local blind school to see the light.

At about lunchtime we meet Barry the Poof and his boyfriend, now in his civilian drag and looking more like a chick than he ever does in his dress, down in the bar. And just as we're all about to take it on our toes, who should appear, all fag ash and long pointy nose, but Gilbert Mylchreest. He insists that we must partake of his hospitality before we leave and although, because I am driving, I make one or two comments about the drink and drive laws of the land, I am overruled. Luckily, Barry the Poof's boyfriend, who is clearly exhausted by the evening's activities with the Welsh miners, and perhaps by Barry himself, confesses that he does not fancy any more to drink and he is deputed to drive us all back, which leaves me free to quench my thirst with the rest of them.

So pretty soon we are all well Brahms and Lizst, which is another way of saying arseholed up to the hilt.

At four o'clock we make another attempt to hit the road and it is at this time of day that The Stoat makes one of the worst mistakes of his life.

"Listen," he says, "is it true that you lot smash places up? I mean is it right that you like to create damage and chaos? I mean, you know, I read in the papers that you do places over—hotels and so forth. But you stay here for three days and all you do is drop a couple of brandy glasses on the floor—and one of them is empty anyway." I cannot believe what I hear—especially as it appears to me that Gilbert has an almost wistful tone in his voice, but Keith is onto him like a cat on a cockroach. He turns to me.

"Dougal, dear boy," he commands somewhat imperiously, pointing at the nearly new XJ6 that is waiting to carry us off to London, "the car, the french windows, the bungalow." And as he mentions each item, he moves his hand to point at it. Of course, I know Moonie well enough to suss him immediately and I depart toward the car giggling to myself. Once in it I have some difficulty locating the ignition device, but once I have achieved contact I fire up the six cylinders, bang down the loud pedal with considerable force and unleash the best part of 250 brake horsepower upon Gilbert Mylchreest's hotel.

BOFF! We're through the hedge.

KERPLONNGGG!! We're through the french windows.

CERRRUNNNNCCCHHH!!! We're neatly parked well inside the bungalow.

What does Gilbert do?

Inevitable.

He shits himself.

He hurtles across the lawn like a drug-crazed warthog sweat and fag ash spraying all over the geraniums and screaming:

"I can't believe it! I can't believe it! No! No! No! You bastards! You fucking bastards—look what you're doing to my lovely hotel! Oh you crazy bastards! You bunch of fucking crazy bastards!"

Unhappily for Gilbert, Moonie now has the taste, and a genuine destruction derby ensues.

"Come on, Dougal," he shouts, "let's finish off the job, dear boy." And with that he indicates the wardrobe.

Now, the thing is that Gilbert's bungalows are not particularly well built, whereas Mr. Jaguar's XJ6 is. So it is quite simple for me to back up the motor and slam it into Drive I. All it takes now is a not-too-subtle application of the right foot to produce considerable acceleration directly into the wardrobe, which subsides in a most cowardly and satisfactory manner. A quick three point turn, a touch more pedal and the sideboard is efficiently reduced to matchwood.

Poor old Gilbert is virtually deceased by now. He is no longer berserk but is standing there with his hand over his mouth watching us take his best bulk-buy G-Plan to pieces. The fact that he will never have to buy another cocktail stick as long as he stays in the hotel and catering trade does not seem to bring him much consolation.

If nothing else, Moonie is a genius for seeing how things should develop before they do and he is now looking at Gilbert with a shrewd glint in his eye.

"Gilbert, dear boy," he says, and he looks more like the devil than I ever see him, "why not have some of this fun yourself?" And so saying the hands Gilbert a bloody great plant pot complete with bloody great plant. He then passes me similar and takes one up himself. He nods at me, like as if we are Siamese twins, we hurl our ammunition at the wreckage of the bungalow. Gilbert is not slow to learn. His potted plant hits the wall with great force and explodes all over the place. And before you can say even half the name of that place that sounds like the volcano in Mexico, Gilbert picks up another pot and slings it into the mess so that in no time at all what is once a luxury bungalow holiday home is not very different from the wreckage of Kew Gardens after a small nuclear arms attack.

It is quite clear that Gilbert, who is now revving himself up like an ancient Fokker triplane, is commencing to enjoy this destruction and is searching for anything with which to further the damage caused to his once lovely hotel.

The only thing that causes us to cease this orgy of destruction is the fact that Barry the Poof and his boyfriend commence to whinge about the necessity for us to return to London.

So we climb into the car and return to The Smoke, leaving Gilbert Mylchreest in a rather peculiar state of mind. On the one hand he is dead chuffed that he participates in a bit of wanton damage. On the other hand he is by no means happy about the cost of the damage.

But then Moonie tells him to bung the bill down to The Who's accountant and instantly Gilbert can see how he can square himself away with the senior management of the hotel and bungalows. So he ends up very cheerful and even asks us if we contemplate returning to the area.

But, sad to tell, the rock and roll lifestyle does not suit The Stoat very well. Two weeks after we leave Gilbert, his heart ceases to beat and this is a situation that leaves Gilbert Mylchreest extremely brown bread. I do not know whether it is the overdose of shortbread and egg sandwiches that kills this pleasantly unpleasant geezer, or whether his raspberry gives up on him as a result of delayed shock and the general exertion required to keep up with Moonie.

But whatever the reason, the result is the same: the demise of The Stoat.

Well, that's show biz. Sing as you go.

We now hit the route for Bristol airport, Moonie and I in the back of the jam jar and, I think, Barry driving. What I forget to mention is that we are filled up from floor to ceiling with spare cans of booze, believing that we may become somewhat parched in this land of strange licensing hours. Of course, we waste no time in opening this spare booze and applying it to our systems.

What I also omit up to now is that Moonie and I are wearing those plastic bow ties that go round and round like an old-fashioned airliner's propellers, and on our heads are kids' plastic helmets of the pattern that is worn by many butch construction workers. We find these items in a Welshers' joke shop, although what Welshers find to joke about is quite beyond me.

Accompanying these silly items is a large bell which we nick from Gilbert's hotel, believing that it may come in handy for a bit of extra mayhem.

So there we are bowling along in the Jaguar, enjoying ourselves greatly with the booze and the occasional bong on the bell—and even the odd piece of witty and amusing conversation —when suddenly Moonie spots a security van, which is a sort of armoured vehicle used to transport large quantities of potatoes from bank to bank and company to company. As this heavy piece of machinery approaches from behind us, what does Moonie do but decide to hold the fucking thing up.

It does not occur to me, and certainly not to Moonie, that the attempted hi-jacking of a bullion van is liable to carry a sentence of umpteen years in the pen, and maybe even the amputation of a hand or two, and even if this does occur to us, I doubt it will make much difference because we are all so out of it that to commit mobile burglary seems to be an excellent idea all round.

Here is where the hotel bell comes in very handy because I lean out of the window and commence to shake same bell up and down with much vigour, which makes the bell produce a great deal of "BONGS!" I can see the dudes in the armoured van are looking excessively alarmed at this intrusion and the van appears to slow down somewhat, perhaps so that the guards can loosen their coshes up a bit—and maybe even load up their artillery. I will say this, that if I am anywhere near sanity I will never agree to this caper as it is well known to one and all that there is nothing these private security guards prefer to bludgeoning half to death anyone who seems as if he might come within three hundred miles of even touching their vehicles, let alone attempting to remove any of the potatoes therein.

But, of course, when you are a famous rock and roller, or even only attached to one, you begin to feel quite immune from the law and all that being a straight citizen entails. Before I join up with Keith, I am fairly naïve about these things, my only experience of the law being when the coppers break up the scooter runs to the south coast, or raid the dancehalls to see what medicines they can find. But later I discover that many of the types you would expect to be extremely fussy when it comes to complying with the letter of the law, I mean such types as policemen, lawyers, security guards and so on, many of these people are quite fond of the occasional toke, the odd snort and a bit of molestation of underage girls. Now, I am not saying that they will join in with these activities if they are being undertaken by a bunch of Mods on scooters in Brighton, or by a chapter of Angels in California. No, what I am saying is that if same illegal activities are being undertaken either by respectable or very rich people—and the entourage of world-famous rock bands certainly fall into the latter category—then suddenly they do not seem to be illegal any more but all part of life's rich tapestry. Moreover, there are many occasions on which we are arrested for various misdemeanours (probably because we do not have the foresight to invite the arresters to join in), only to be released a short while later because we are able to draw upon large sums of ackers with which to mobilise plenty of legal muscle and even more publicity. In this respect, it seems that someone like Moonie is similar to the old time feudal lords who are effectively above the law unless they do something very naughty, such as raping and pillaging the king's Mrs.

Well, this is probably why we do not think it is very unwise to attack a security van. It just seems to be another jolly prank. So when the van begins to slow down, we swing the Jaguar round, Barry the Poof doing a very fair impersonation of Ryan O'Neal in *Driver*. As a result, the van screams up onto the side of the road, narrowly missing a telegraph post. We are trying to work out what to do next, but because we are pissing ourselves so much with laughter we cannot agree on the right course of action. The general consensus seems to be that it may be unwise to leave the safety of the Jaguar as that may encourage the security guys to hit us about the head.

"Fuck it," says Moonie. "Let's piss off out of it."

So we do.

Twenty minutes later, we are all somewhat surprised to hear the shocking din of police sirens and we find no less than three cop cars converging on us with many policemen leaning out of the windows and commanding us to pull over. They seem to be quite excited and not a little angry about something. It seems clear that the policers mean business and we just about reach the conclusion that they are not about to put up with any nonsense when we hear a sort of WHOP-WHOP-WHOP-WHOP-WHOP noise above us. Moonie sticks his head out the windows and peers upwards.

"Fuck me, Dougal," he says, giggling, "it's Hawaii Five-O!"

Naturally, we pull the motor over and the law swarms all over it, bundling us out of the Jaguar and into the cop cars. We seem to be being arrested and it is clear that what happens is

that the potatoes van radios the fuzz that it is being attacked
and help, please. What makes it worse, we find out later, is that
this particular armed mazuma motor is carrying no less than
one million pounds in used notes. Which makes Moonie say
that if he ever realises that there is one million in green ones
inside the security van he will make sure he holds it up good
and proper and will not fuck about with just getting a few
laughs out of the incident.

As we are speeding toward the cop shop, the Old Bill is
growing extremely annoyed because we still do not realise the
gravity of the situation and are pissing ourselves with laughter.
Remember that it is now about six in the evening and we are in
a state of complete leglessness. For all we care we could be in
a flying saucer, whisked away by little green men wearing green
horns and tin ears. So we are cracking funnies as we roll along
and when we are actually locked up in a room which appears to
be the copper's messroom, this is absolutely hilarious. Moonie
really comes into his own here because we find many items of
coppers' clothing, such as boots, helmets and capes. We all put
on coppers' helmets and nothing will do but Moonie must don
a cape, a pair of boots about eight sizes too big for him and a
helmet. Then he parades up and down the messroom saying
such thing as:

"Evening, all," and " 'Ello, 'ello, 'ello," and "What's going
on 'ere, then?" which, of course, are all the things that coppers
in Britain are meant to say. Personally, I find this all extremely
funny and the tears are streaming down my face and plopping
onto—and into—the coppers' boots that find their way onto
my feet. Barry the Poof is very excited too, what with all the
butch, if somewhat flat-footed, manhood around. Being that
we're locked in the mess, every now and then a copper has to
enter to collect his hat, his club or his sandwiches, and each
time a copper does this he has to run the gauntlet of Keith's
antics and Barry's winks and nudges.

To be quite honest, I can never work out how we get out of
this place but I think it is probably because the coppers become

so pissed off with Barry making suggestions as to what can be done with coppers' truncheons that they cannot be bothered to hold us any longer. It also must be quite clear that we have about as much chance of holding up an armoured van full of cabbage as we have of being elected to the Synod of the Church of England.

But perhaps what really causes the rift between us and the coppers is the darts match. What happens is that we find a darts board in the mess but the only place we can find to hang it is on a coat hook fixed to the main door in and out of the mess. I have to say here that Moonie, though he shows plenty of enthusiasm and panache with the darts, is by no means the world's best player. In fact, he is probably the worst—or will do until the worst comes along. His darts are about as good as his singing. So if he is looking for a double twenty when he hurls an arrow, what he is likely to hit is a nearby lamp. And if he is after the bull's eye, he is liable to stick the dart into the ceiling behind him.

So when he aims for a double, which is what he needs to start off with, what he hits is the helmet, just above the left ear, of a copper who sticks his head round the door to see that we are not misbehaving. Now this copper appears to be quite a top-notcher and is fairly high up the management structure of the bunch that is responsible for arresting us and he is excessively displeased when the missile hits him in the sombrero. His temper is not improved when Moonie grabs him by the shoulders and says very casually:

"Dreadfully sorry, dear boy." Then he follows up this rather weak apology by leaning up against the counter in the mess and asking:

"I say, you don't know where we can get a couple of large brandies, do you?" The copper does a very slow burn indeed and I am beginning to wonder whether he intends to summon a few of his mates to give us a bit of a working over. But then he subsides slightly and just says, very quietly and through tightly clenched teeth:

"Right. Out. The lot of you. Just get the fuck out of here and don't come back. Right?" With this he grabs hold of Keith and frogmarches him out into the street, Moonie all the time going on about the necessity to find a few large brandies, and continuing with much talk about police brutality. The rest of us decide that this incident yields up just about all the laughs it is likely to and, by and large, we are quite pleased to regain our freedom.

Which is just about the final word on our participation in the RAC Rally in Wales—except that when we return to the car we find that it is still in the process of being thoroughly searched for drugs. Many cops and many trained dogs are crawling all over it and I can see that the dogs are most excited. They can obviously smell the medicines but cannot find them.

This is because although we start the jaunt off with enough medicines of one sort or another to provide the entire British Medical Association with research material for five years, we haven't even got a single tab left by the time we are arrested. Not a grain nor a phial. And this entirely because in these places with names like that volcano in Mexico, if you ask anyone for dope they think you are after something to finish off your model aeroplane with.

So on the whole we have to thank the Welshers for not ending up on a dope charge. Maybe Welshers are not such a bad lot after all, even if they do have extremely low foreheads.

You've got a Friend

It is strange how most of Moonie's friends are celebrities in their own right (apart from me of course). There are plenty of other musos, film people and show biz types who have a close clan around them of people they know from way back. And these are the people they can rely on, who they know aren't interested in them just because of the fame or the money. In the time I know him, Moonie appears to have no one like this and, apart from the other geezers in the band, does not seem to have anyone from his childhood or his schooldays. For a time I consider that this is on account of Moonie has such a large ego that he can only rub along with bigshots, but eventually I come to the conclusion that it is not quite as simple as that.

Moonie's rise to fame and fortune does isolate him. It's no use the average punter saying:

"I should be so lucky! All that money!" But the average punter can no more handle this situation than Moonie can. The reason why there's such a high casualty rate among stars is that most of them start off as average geezers—or bints—and they are just not equipped for the job, nor for the life they are just about forced to live.

Once they make it to the top they are expected to live in a certain kind of way. They can't win. If Moonie decides to stay quietly at home with the Mrs., not that he ever does, he will be accused of being a skinflint and boring. If he goes out, and about a bit, taking a few bevvies here and there, it is very hard not to go over the top and end up with a booze problem. Say he decides to knock off at midnight and go on home to kip. Then everyone will moan:

"Ah, come on Moonie, don't give us all that going to kip bollocks." Bearing all this in mind I soon see why it is possible for Keith to rub along only with people who have a similar probem, i.e. they are rich, famous and slightly bananas.

The main two of these people are Harry Nilsson, the singer, and Ringo Starr, former drummer with a popular singing act. There is a period, around 1973, when these three are virtually inseparable and go around everywhere like the Three Musketeers. Most of the time I go along too, on account of Moonie must have someone along to drive him, plus he seems to like to have me around at all times in case he runs out of money. Then he can use my American Express card.

Moonie first becomes friendly with Ringo when they are both involved in the movie *That'll Be The Day*. Ringo's part in this movie is to play a Teddy Boy, and he is most convincing in this role, what with the drape jacket, the thick crêpe-soled brothel creepers, the bootlace tie and the slick greased quiff in the barnet. Of course, Ringo is old enough to be a Ted first time round and for all I know this is exactly what he is when he is younger. Moonie, as I mention elsewhere, plays the drummer in a rock and roll band. I play a guitarist in the band, which is faintly hysterical as I am more likely to pick out a tune on a tennis racket than I am to understand the workings of a guitar, and another roadie who goes by the name of Mick Double, who has similar musical ability to my own, pretends on bass.

The pianist is a geezer called John Hawken, who is once with The Nashville Teens and who is quite a red-hot whizz of the keyboards. Graham Bond, formerly boss of the Graham Bond Organisation, is on saxophone.

Now this Graham Bond, who very sadly later checks in his clogs and is part of that great rock and roll band in the sky, is a very weird, funny and interesting dude. He is a huge fat fellow who is most influential in British rock around the mid-sixties and is one of the few players who really can play. He is primarily an artist of the keyboard, although he starts his career as a jazz saxophonist and is highly regarded in that sphere.

Not only is he double fat, but he is also well into dope, black and white magic, mysticism and one thing and another. He takes up these interests like other people take up hobbies and at the time we are filming *That'll Be The Day*, Graham Bond is considerably into Buddhism.

One morning I go with Moonie to get Bondie ready for the day's action. Now, on this movie, Moonie has a ball acting as roadie for the make-believe band that features in the film. He has many laughs organising everything and generally behaving very much unlike the superstar and very much like the runaround. He makes a great show of getting everyone, with equipment, to their places on set and fairly straight in the head.

So we hammer on Bondie's door at seven o'clock in the morning, which is not the time to be rousing up a rock and roll musician but, to our relief, Bondie shouts out:

"Come in!"

So we go in and find him sitting in his bath. However, he is making very little use of the soap and the face flannel. No, what he is doing is reading a giant book which I later discover to be the Buddhist equivalent of The Bible. Moreover, Bondie is taking large tokes on an ornate opium pipe. Well, for all I know this may be a large and integral part of the Buddhist religion and if it is, it sounds to me as if this Buddhism may be a lot more fun than Christianity as purveyed by the famous Church of England, well-known landlords and businessmen.

Mind you, there are not many things that are less fun than the C of E.

While we are standing there in Bondie's bathroom, the conversation goes something like this:

"Hi, man, how're you doing?" asks Moonie.

"OK, man, OK. Yeah, I'm just doing my religion, man," answers Bondie.

"Yeah," says Moonie. "Want me to scrub your back while you're doing it?"

"Hey no, man," says Bondie, all indignant. "Don't fuck about man, I mean like I'm in serious trouble. Like I've got to pray to the East, man, and I don't know which way is East!"

"Well," says Moonie, "I tell you what—I do know that East Kilburn's over that way." And he points vaguely toward the corner of the bathroom.

"Wow, man, that's great. That's fantastic. East Kilburn. I never knew that, man." And with that, old Bondie starts heaving himself out of the bath. What with being pretty hefty and not too slim around the derby—in fact Bondie would walk the finals of the Buddha look-alike competition—he needs both hands for this extrication. Consequently his Buddhist Bible book drops—PLOP—right into the bathwater where it disappears under the somewhat murky surface. At this Bondie seems quite upset and crest-fallen.

"Oh shit, man, now I'm *really* going to have to do some praying!"

Anyway, like I say, Ringo is on this movie and although he is quite quiet for the first few days it soon turns out that he and Moonie are kindred spirits, not to say blood brothers. It is not entirely surprising that alcohol of one sort or another is connected with the start of their friendship, which begins one day on the set when we all have to hang around for an entire day to shoot a couple of scenes with the movie band. It is extremely taters, brass and all round very cold indeed, and as soon as each take is done and we have a few moments to spare we shoot off to try and warm up in the dressing room. One time, Ringo walks in and starts on the first of what seems to be an endless supply of miniature brandies and I have to say that Ringo is most generous with these miniatures and they are dealt out all over the place. This is the time that Moonie and Ringo start to get into each other, rapping away like two old biddies at a flower show. What transpires is that they both have a similar sense of humour —and here I am referring to words rather than carrying on— which is weird, offbeat and very British, not to say English. Ringo is very fond of Monty Python, a television programme that is much in demand at this time, and Moonie finds this very pleasant because the Python team are his favourite comics. So Moonie and Ringo sit there bunnying like there is no tomorrow and though I cannot recall the detail of this bunnying I do remember pissing myself with laughter at their loony sayings.

The movie is concerned with the early days of rock and roll in England and during this period many punters dress in the Teddy Boy or Rocker style. It is strange that both these styles still survive and all around Britain there are active groups of Teds and Rockers—especially Rockers, probably because Rockers' gear, leather jackets, jeans and big boots, is still the best gear for motorcycling, which is what Rockers love to do above everything else. Naturally there is a ready supply of Rocker gear all around the film set. Moonie, Ringo and me proceed to don same and sally out to the local pubs and high spots, which are not very high at that.

What I neglect to mention is that this movie is shot, or at least this bit of it is shot, in the Isle of Wight, which is a small island off the south coast of England and is famous on account of it is said to be exactly the right size to accommodate the entire population of the world, if you will give each member of this population just eighteen square inches in which to live, which is not large enough for me and certainly several sizes too small for the likes of Ringo or Moonie. It is on this island that, a few years ago, Dylan stars in a rock festival. But I have to say that even though this little island is the venue of several rock shows, the Isle of Wight is by no means the swingingest place in the world.

It tends not to be very lively at all and, in fact, in the liveliness stakes this island is liable to come in behind Oshkosh, Wisconsin, and just ahead of the suburbs of Peking. So, when all three of us appear in the local hostelries and watering places, all done up so that we look like Marlon Brando in *The Wild Ones* in triplicate, the local citizens are not delighted.

In fact, they seem about to shit themselves. And they do this to such an extent that our exercise turns out to be not very entertaining. As soon as we walk into any place, the locals are suddenly schtum for a few moments, before breaking into extremely agitated and private bunny. But they make very sure that they do not make any comment about the three bikers who appear to them to be the worst incarnation of a trio of Hell's Angels. We have a good, but certainly not legendary evening, but by the time we get back to the hotel Moonie and Ringo seem to cement a friendship very firmly and this friendship last until the day Moonie ups and dies.

Through Ringo, Moonie meets Harry Nilsson, a meeting that leads to the three of them becoming a legendary bunch of loons. It is strange, really, to think that although Moonie always has the reputation of being a major prankster and Ringo's exploits reach the public's ear from time to time, no one thinks of Harry Nilsson as anything other than a singer/songwriter with a leaning toward romantic and even slightly soppy songs. After all, one of his biggest successes is *A Little Nilsson in the Night*, which is his version of many standards such as *Makin' Whoopee* and so on.

But, as I later find out, Harry Nilsson is not only a lunatic of the first order but also a highly intelligent geezer who knows a great deal more about what is what than the average singer—let alone the average rock star. Later, of course, he gets into writing plays and films and all sorts of other things that are generally reckoned to display the presence of brains in the head. A while ago he had a musical entertainment named *The Point* running at the Mermaid Theatre in London, which is not a place known to put on anything knocked up by the average moron.

Early Who. From the left, Pete Townshend, John Entwistle, Keith Moon, and Roger Daltrey. COLIN JONES

At work. TRINIFOLD LTD

Kim, 1973. PETER BUTLER

Keith and a small bit of his girlfriend Annette. TERRY O'NEILL

His Majesty the Queen. BRIAN ARIS

At play.

(ABOVE) *Moonie and Dougal in Phoenix, Arizona, at the start of his last tour.* JOHN ENTWISTLE

(BELOW) *A typical appeal following a barney in April 1973.*

GPO ● GREETINGS TELEGRAM

```
DM9 GTG 1.15 LONDON T PRIORITY 27 PRIORITY GREETING

MR PETER BUTLER 16 PRECINCT RD HAYESMIDDX =

PLEASE COME HOME ALL IS FORGIVENLOVE MOTHER
PHONE CHERTSEY 60893 AS SOON AS POSSIBLE
EVERLASTINGLY YOURS = KEITH +
```

Keith and Annette, the night before he died. REX FEATURES LTD

BRIAN ARIS

Ringo introduces Moonie to Nilsson at a time when Apple Films are producing a movie called *Son of Dracula*, which has Nilsson in it plus, of course, he writes the musical score. By an amazing and original stroke of casting genius, Moonie is roped in to play the part of a drummer in a rock and roll band, which, of course, he is able to do fairly convincingly with just a little rehearsal. When Moonie and Nilsson meet up it does not take them very long to discover that they both have a taste for hard liquor and for anything else that may be going—especially if laughs are also involved.

In the beginning, though, Moonie does have a further and ulterior motive for hanging out with Harry Nilsson and this reason is that Moonie fancies Nilsson's bird. This is about the time that Moonie splits with Kim, and though he is knocking off some model bint this liaison is not sufficiently exciting to prevent him from attempting to parlay his way into Nilsson's chick's knickers at the earliest opportunity, if not before. This is one of the rare occasions that he does not get his wish, and he gives up the attempt because he gets to like Nilsson too much and does not wish to interfere with his love life.

Speaking of love life, Moonie, Nilsson and Ringo have this in common, that they each have plenty of problems on the domestic front. Ringo is parted from his wife, Maureen. Harry is divorced from his first wife. And Moonie, well Moonie is not only split from Kim but does not have anywhere to live, either. This last problem is taken care of when Nilsson invites Keith to move in with him in a very nice pad in Mayfair, very handy indeed for the Playboy Club, the Inn on the Park and many other watering places.

Over the course of the next few years, Moonie, Ringo and Nilsson inspire memorable evenings and I have to confess that I never see three guys who are more on the same wavelength. I, myself, am by no means the slowest person in the world, but I have to admit that Moonie, Ringo and Harry Nilsson frequently leave me behind in the bunny stakes—especially when they get into the Monty Python schtick. But the great advantage to

Moonie is that Ringo and Harry are perfect foils to him. Moonie is always full of mad ideas of one sort or another and whereas most people react to such ideas by saying "Oh yeah?" or even taking the piss—assuming they are either very fast runners indeed or have a car with its engine running waiting outside for them—Ringo and Harry encourage Moonie to develop these ideas because they are very funny and demonstrate Moonie's quite extraordinary imagination.

One evening at Nilsson's, Moonie stops the proceedings with this remark:

"Dear boys, I wish you to know that one of my latest inventions has just been patented." Now the thing is that when Moonie makes a statement like this it is very hard to disbelieve him. He seems perfectly logical and calm and is very, very convincing. Many people are taken in and there are many instances when Keith enthralls audiences with stories as to how he makes himself a zillionaire in mining shares, how he owns hotels up and down the country, how he invents various devices that will solve the problems of the world, how he has films in production and so on and so forth. So when Moonie mentions this latest invention, Ringo and Harry, though they do not necessarily believe it, are very happy to have Keith describe same invention. They know that at the very least they are about to be entertained. So Ringo replies:

"Yeah? What's that, then, Keith?"

"It is a hovercraft," says Keith. "A hovercraft that carries 1600 people. It's got a swimming pool, a billiard room and a cinema. Now, as you know, the problem with billiards on board a ship, or in a hovercraft like this, is that as the ship moves the billiard balls tend to roll about. But the point is that my invention, dear boys, my invention eliminates the rolling billiard balls by means of an intermittent magnetic force field that is linked to wave sensors. As the hovercraft approaches the waves, the sensors measure the exact movement that the waves will cause. Do you follow me, Dougal? Then, by means of a real time computer link up, the magnetic force field is applied to the billiard table in such a way as to automatically compensate for the movements the waves will cause. Thus," finishes Moonie triumphantly, "the billiard balls stay in position while the table moves."

Naturally, we are all struck dumb by this description and while we are silent Moonie's eyes gleam, just like the mad professor in all those B movies. Before any of us can speak, he continues:

"Ah, you will say, if the force field holds the balls still, how do you play them? The point is, dear boys, that in the end of the cues I have placed a small microswitch that—just for a fraction of a second—cancels that part of the force field holding the ball about to be played. Simple, when you know how."

Moonie is truly hypnotic when he carries on in this manner though, of course, he is not world famous for inventing hovercrafts, or even automatic toasters or electric mousetraps. When Moonie gets an idea like this, he is forced to attempt to convince everyone in sight that it is strictly kosher and very serious. And if there is no one in sight, then he will telephone anyone in the world who he thinks of and will start to give them the blag, even if these people live on the other side of the world and it is their night-time. On one occasion when we are in an airport hotel near Manchester and are rather depressed at the quality of the two hookers we line up for the night's entertainment, Moonie has an idea for a film and nothing will do but he must telephone Steve McQueen, Zsa Zsa Gabor and Tony Curtis about this idea. Now if you or I attempt such telephoning, we will not even get through to Hollywood, let alone to the name stars. In fact, if you or I are phoning from Manchester, we will be lucky if we even manage to get out of Manchester. But Moonie is somehow able to talk his way right into these stars' homes (though of course he knows Steve McQueen vaguely even at this time, which is before he winds up living next door to McQueen on Malibu Beach). And when he gets through to them, he makes them listen to his script and despite the fact that he has the best part of several bottles of champagne inside him, Moonie is able to be most articulate and convincing about the project and Tony Curtis, Steve McQueen and Zsa Zsa Gabor are most interested indeed in the scheme— especially Zsa Zsa Gabor, but then I suspect she is hankering after further diamonds and is a bit short of a bob or two to purchase such.

Well, of course, Moonie does not have to make a telephone call across the Atlantic to rev up Nilsson and Ringo about his hovercraft but the same principle applies and they are most fascinated even if they do not understand too much about the intermittent magnetic force field. Eventually, however, they manage to escape from their own silence and begin to ask Moonie for further details. Ringo asks, in that peculiar accent which people brought up in Liverpool, England, are liable to obtain:

"Well, Moonie, what sort of uniforms are the crew of this hovercraft going to wear?" And Moonie can answer this one without batting an eyelid.

"My dear boy, I've already signed up Ossie Clark and he is designing the uniforms even now." It never occurs to us to question all this spiel.

No, we ask for more and more information, which Moonie is able to provide—right down to the cost of the billiard balls, who will supply the cut glass decanters, which company is contracted to do the catering and what the menus will have on them.

Eventually Ringo asks:

"What about a group for the ballroom?" Moonie stops for a moment.

"Ah, dear boy," he says. "I must admit that I had not thought about the group for the ballroom. We'll just have to form our own. You and me on drums, Harry on vocals. We'll see if Elton can sit in on keyboards. Eric on guitar and if we pull in Entwistle, as well, that'll be about it. Right?" And the next thing we know is that Moonie is all set to phone Elton John, Eric Clapton and John Entwistle right away. But while he is looking for the telephone, he sees that his glass is empty and, by the time he discovers the bottle and tips the contents into his glass, the hovercraft scheme is completely forgotten.

The point is that Moonie makes us almost believe him when he talks of such things simply because while he is talking about them *he* really believes in them. This is maybe why he can do things that must kill anyone else. He believes that he is indestructible and because he believes this he can perform stunts that most people cannot even contemplate, *and* come away unscathed.

Like, for example, when he walks through a plate glass window at the house in Chertsey. At the time he is carrying a gun and the hole left in the window exactly fits the silhouette of a man with a gun—rather like those Warner Bros cartoons. Or another time when he has a row with the band and jumps off the end of Brighton Pier, smack dab into the sea, which is by no means calm at this time. Now Moonie is certainly not Mark Spitz when it comes to swimming and when he leaps into the English Channel, which is extremely cold, the rest of the party with him shit themselves and rush off to find the nearest lifesaver.

Well, these two lifesaver guys, who are most butch indeed, have some trouble struggling out to where Moonie hits the briny and when they get there they can find no trace of him. So they plough their way back to the beach and they find this quite a struggle too—but, when they arrive back on Brighton Beach, who is waiting there to greet them but Keith Moon, himself.

"Most kind of you, dear boys. Most kind—but I'm perfectly all right, as you can see."

During the time Moonie, Ringo and Harry Nilsson are together they have a great deal of free time to booze away, dope away, have it away and generally behave like juvenile miscreants—which, I may say, I join in with with plenty of enthusiasm of my own. I doubt if at this time Moonie is working more than sixty days a year and, having no hobbies whatsoever, other than abusing his body, he is usually quite hot to trot. The daily routine that becomes established is this: rise between noon and one o'clock. Make breakfast (in Moonie's case, of course, it's usually me who makes it). Off to the Inn on the Park, or

somewhere, for champagne cocktails. Round about this time, we
meet up with Harry. Then it's off to the Apple Offices in Savile
Row, and there we spend the afternoon with Ringo, boozing,
fooling around and generally shooting the breeze.

It is now about five-thirty in the evening, which is when the
pubs in the West End of London open their doors for business,
so, of course, we repair to the nearest one of the several hostelries
we use, and indulge in a game of darts and a few bevvies. Especially a few bevvies. Then it is time for something to eat, so we
find a restaurant, at which we stay till somewhere about one in
the morning, by which time we are ready for an expedition to
Tramp.

It may occur to you that this is indeed a tedious routine, but,
of course, bouts of raving in this manner are interspersed with
bouts of doing nothing much at all. At these times Moonie takes
to his bed with endless Beach Boys and Jan and Dean, and I
take my rest and recreation by nipping off to see my folks,
spending time with my girlfriend and catching up on the news
of my various mates.

When we do hit the town, believe you me things get to be
mighty expensive. For a start, at the time of which I speak, three
or four people cannot entertain themselves properly at Tramp
without spending three or four hundred pounds. And that's without the rest of the day's food and drink quota. Mind you, there
are degrees of entertainment. When Ringo, Nilsson and Moonie
are together, the correct degree is to be able, when time for the
champagne breakfast comes round, to just about see enough to
propel a forkful of scrambled egg to a region somewhere round
about the mouth.

But the five or six hundred pounds a day that we consume is
money well spent in so far as it buys us a very good time indeed,
especially in Tramp—though I admit that that place does
operate a somewhat exclusive and biased policy when it comes
to its treatment of those punters who try to wander in off the
street. But Tramp tolerates the bad behaviour of rock stars and

is particularly liberal toward those who are prepared to spray their money around the place.

If you do not know Tramp, let me explain that it is a club in Jermyn Street and, for a while, it is certainly the place to go if you are rich and famous. Or at least rich. Some people, such as George Best, the famous footballer, practically live there; and if you are someone who likes to be thought of as someone, the day you look in the scandal sheets and do not see yourself entering or exiting Tramp with some flashy bint attached firmly to your person is the day you seriously consider two final tequila sunrises and sticking your head in the gas oven.

When I look back on it, I cannot understand why this place is so popular. It is dark, sweaty and very cramped. At all times it contains a very high proportion of extremely tedious people of low intelligence, most of whom have voices that cut diamonds quicker than any laser beam.

However, there you are. Such is the way of fashion, and who am I to say that Hooray Henries and Hangers On of one sort or another cannot have fun in the way in which they wish to have fun, even if they are being ripped off left right and centre, and especially centre. And, like I say, in my time I enjoy many a good time at this peculiar place.

In Moonie's case, many legendary things come off in Tramp— mostly his clothes. One time I arrive there with Moonie absolutely stark bollock naked and spreadeagled on the bonnet of his Corniche. This particular evening starts off in The Pheasantry, which is another club but this time in the King's Road and Moonie decides that it is my place to drive the Roller to Tramp with him naked on the bonnet. Now this is a distance of some couple of miles, right through the West End of London, which is by no means under-populated. But, of course, I begin the drive, aiming the car by lining up the two most prominent things I can see, which are the car's silver mascot and Moonie's hairy asshole, and pointing them in such a way that I hope to avoid most other drivers on the road at this time of night.

Moonie keeps himself from rolling off the bonnet by clinging on to the silver mascot and wedging his feet against the windscreen, so that we are able to arrive before the doorman at Tramp in reasonable order. Not unnaturally, he is quite surprised to see two of his clientele arrive at the club in this way but he recovers his composure rapidly and, when I slip him a couple of quid, he scoots off to park the jam jar. Moonie then enters the club, where he is at least persuaded to don a pair of underpants. The first person we see upon entering the eating section of the club, which is off to one side, is Mick Jagger who has with him, as far as I recall, Bianca. Moonie strolls over.

"Hello, my dears," he says and with no further ado he rips off the underpants. Thus the king rock star of them all and his dusky spouse are treated to an extreme close up of the Moon dong waving about their Steak Dianes. Well, I am not saying that I never see anyone move faster, but Mick is up and out of the place in 10 seconds flat—though not before he has to put up with a great deal of assault and battery on his ears from La Bianca. Personally, I believe that this show of shock is somewhat unnecessary and that Bianca seems a very snotty lady, but I concede that the Moon dong is not everyone's first choice in side dishes.

One of the best periods of this friendship between Moonie, Ringo and Harry Nilsson is when Nilsson requests Moonie to play upon his album *Pussycats*, to be produced by John Lennon. This is before Keith sets up the house in Malibu and the gig necessitates flights to California, where Harry arranges a suite in the Beverley Wilshire hotel in L.A. We take the suite over directly from Bob Dylan—though I only mention this because I am a Bob Dylan fan and get quite a kick out of sleeping in the same bed as this hero . . . but only after the hero has vacated the bed, of course.

Meanwhile, Nilsson, John Lennon and Ringo hire a beach house in Santa Monica, a house which is extremely well appointed and comfortable in every room. It once belongs to the Kennedys, of presidential and large sums of moolaw fame, and it is apparently where they invite Marilyn Monroe, among others, to view their etchings and indulge in private performances. This probably accounts for the comfort in every room. I do not mean to imply that I necessarily believe in the mud that people sling at Marilyn and the Kennedys, but if there is any truth in this mud at all, then this house is where it sticks.

It is not long before Nilsson, Lennon and Ringo invite Moonie to stay in the house with them, which suits me because I am left with the entire Beverley Wilshire suite and I find this much to my taste.

A daily routine now begins whereby I drive out to the studio every day to meet Moonie and his mates. We complete the session and then we repair to the beach house for epic partying. Moonie is perpetually out of his box, and also his tree, and is generally quite starry-eyed every single day. It is just as well that he is not the only drummer on the session and, for all I know, this is the main reason Nilsson has Jim Keltner, one of the best respected session rock and roll drummers in the world, performing alongside Moonie. Sometimes they alternate and sometimes they play together. On one track, which is *Rock Around The Clock*, they play together along with Ringo too, and this punishment of the skins is really something to hear. In fact, the entire track is something to hear, and this particular version of *Rock Around The Clock* is a very high speed version indeed; here is the reason:

It all starts because Moonie is a very flash geezer. Whereas Jim Keltner plays an ordinary, standard size drum kit, and Ringo too, as anyone who ever watches The Beatles will confirm, likes a very standard kit. Moonie likes to play on a kit that is just about twice the size of anyone else's and, of course, it is me that has to provide this oversize unit for him. In fact, he tells me to find the biggest fucking drum kit in the world—bigger, even, than his usual array. So I phone around the place and the third call is lucky. They will do an eighteen drum unit and, moreover, they are able to deliver it right away, free of charge. No payment is involved because it is standard practice in the business for famous rock stars to be provided with their instruments free of charge—provided they consent to a couple of publicity shots, which most of them do—many of them being so out of it anyway that they do not know that these shots are being taken. They probably think that the flashlights are in their heads, and try to remember not to have that particular medicine next time round.

Well, here is the set up, with Moonie sitting behind a drum kit large enough to house a colony of midgets, Ringo in the middle and Jim Keltner off to the other side. Now, Moonie is, as everyone who has half a brain, one eye and an ear will tell you, one of the greatest drummers of all time, but even Moonie becomes tense and nervous if he feels that he is up for comparison with anyone else, and Keltner and Ringo are fair competition. So Moonie orders up a couple of Amyl Nitrates to help him along. It so happens that in my medicine box I have a very large supply of Amyl, supplied by our friendly and understanding doctor in LA—the one who needs the money—so I snap one phial under Moonie's hooter and he inhales the fumes gladly. Of course, Ringo clocks this treatment and speaks:

"Hey, Dougal, what about us then?" So I zip round to Ringo and snap a phial for him. Then it seems to me that it will be rude to ignore Jim Keltner, so I give him a quick blast. Then I realise that the other musicians may well be offended, and not able to perform to the best of their ability, if they do not have some medicine too. So I snap a phial for Jesse Ed Davis, who plays the guitar on this session, and then hurry around everyone else in sight doing my best impression of The Flying Doctor.

Recording another album in the great rock and roll myth is no longer a matter of into the studio, wham-bam-thank-you-mam-here's-another-hit-already-give-me-the-loot-and-let's-piss-off. No, what with the synthesisers, the oscillators, the vibrillators, the scintillators and I do not know what all else, there is so much technology around that something is bound to go up the pictures every two seconds. And it does on this session. Which means that the entire recording is held up a few moments. Which, in turn, means that I have to snap another Amyl for Moonie, and yet further Amyls for everyone else present.

So, by the time they get to play, there is more speeding around than in the Indianapolis 500.

And when the one-two-three-four comes, well there is no holding these dudes. They play like they all have just one minute to live. Moonie thrashes away at his giant kit, looking like nothing less than Bruce Lee putting down a pack of thugs. Ringo is hammering away like the mad carpenter in that Swiss fairy tale, and Jim Keltner is committing rapid machine gun fire on his skins too. Of course the rest of the band is forced to keep up with this trot, and their fingers are working at their instruments quick enough to set the sparks flying. In fact, to hear them you will think that each musician must have at least four hands, and on each hand he must have at least double the usual complement of fingers and digits. *Rock Around the Clock* is operating faster than *The Flight of the Bumble Bee* and it seems to me to turn out pretty well.

I can see that Lennon, up in the control box, is loving every minute of it, laughing and smiling, and he eventually decides to leave the track as it is on the final album.

Personally, I think that Dr. Dex and The Amyls ought to have a credit on this album, but maybe this is a dangerous idea at that.

I have to digress briefly from Moonie here, to say that *Pussycats* is one of the high spots of my life, because it is through this album that I meet Lennon. Now John Lennon, for me, is one of the all time heroes and legends. However you look at it, and no matter whether you hate the whole rock scene and everything it stands for, there is no question but that Lennon and McCartney, and Lennon especially, influence an entire generation.

And from that original influence the waves and ripples spread far and wide until practically everyone in the world who isn't deaf, dumb and living in a concrete box three yards thick, is affected. Of course, I exclude those who are unfortunate enough to be locked in behind barbed wire in the depths of Siberia and also those who are more concerned with what they will eat for the next few days than which record they will buy. But that's show business. Sing as you go. Lennon and McCartney are not responsible for the design of the world.

So for me to meet John Lennon is similar to a genuine and devout Catholic meeting The Pope. I am nervous at first, though it soon turns out that he is a nice, relaxed, sort of bloke and quite one of the lads. I personally never see him awkward or hoity toity such as many people claim he is. Far from it—he is a great laugh in the studio and a considerable hand in the partying afterwards. He loves Moonie's drumming and rates Keith as one of the all time greats. In fact, he and Keith strike up quite a friendship and spend some time together. Later, The Who play a gig in New York, which is where Lennon lives, and he intends to attend the gig. But then he phones up to say he cannot make it but can we meet up later—which we do. We go round to his hotel suite and there we meet Chris Charlesworth, the *Melody Maker* journalist. This evening is very special because Lennon spends much time talking about the early days of The Beatles in Liverpool and Germany.

Well, there is no doubt that of all Moonie's mates, Harry Nilsson and Ringo Starr are two of the best. But as I say, Moonie really does not have that many proper friends, perhaps because he does not show such people that he needs and rates them as much as they like him. I recall one time in LA Ringo sets up a Thanksgiving Dinner and invites Moonie, Harry and me, among others. Now this is an event that me and Moonie greatly look forward to but at the last moment Moonie decides he is just not in the mood. He won't go. So I have to tell Ringo that when Ringo telephones to ask just where the hell we are. And, naturally, Ringo is most upset. The point is, though, that people like Nilsson and Ringo, are like co-stars in Moonie's personal movie. That is how he sees them, not just as friends who may give and may need help. Certainly, they measure up to him in general craziness, capacity for stimulants of one sort or another and the ability to put the shits up normal people. Maybe that is all Moonie ever wants in a mate.

There are times when Moonie even manages to piss Nilsson and Ringo off—quite aside from incidents like the Thanksgiving Dinner. On several occasions I see them shy away from some particularly outrageous Moon prank, perhaps because Nilsson and Ringo have at least some—however minimal—capacity for embarrassment.

Personally I think that this is one of the keys to Moonie: he is impossible to embarrass. I cannot recall ever seeing him embarrassed, whatever the situation. No matter how much disapproval is showered upon him.

Mind you, there are several people who can match Moonie when it comes to being un-embarrassed. One of them is Viv Stanshall of the Bonzo Dog Doo-Dah Band, another great eccentric and another of life's unembarrassables.

Moonie always loves the Bonzo Dog Band and if you ever hear their records or catch their act, then you will instantly know why. In many respects, they are the forerunners of Monty Python type humour. Stanshall is one of the band's originators, and in his own way is quite as extreme a lunatic as Moonie. He has a similar and total disregard for domestic arrangements. At this time his lounge contains nothing whatsoever in it except a sofa, a television set and a fish tank full of tropical fish. One time I am sitting there with the television on, but watching the fish because they are infinitely more entertaining than ninety per cent of television, when Moonie and Stanshall burst in wearing Nazi uniforms, complete with medals, armbands and the whole thing. For a second or two it gives me the fright of all time, and the tropical fish do not seem too happy either. But after a while, they sally forth into the streets. At first, they cause very little comment, for it is well known that the great British public tend to turn a blind eye to eccentricity, mugging and rape. This apathy makes Moonie and Stanshall feel quite unloved and dissatisfied and they decide that what is required for their uniforms to be properly appreciated is a Germanic atmosphere. Now it is really quite difficult to find Germanic atmosphere in London, England, where you do not find many geezers hanging around in lederhosen. Or if you do they are by no means German but are perverts who like to wear tight leather shorts and are looking for people of similar mind in order to exchange slaps upon each other's bottoms.

At this time, German bierkellers have a short vogue in London, and this is where Moonie and Viv Stanshall go in their Nazi uniforms. They shout a few *Sieg Heils* and *Donner und Blitzens*, which do not go down too well with either the punters or the barmen. But what gets them turfed out effortlessly is when they rant on about *Englisch Schweinhunds*.

However, they are still not satisfied with the effects of these uniforms and so they go right over the top and decide to visit Golders Green, which is an area of London well-known for having a great many front wheelers living there. Many of these Jewish persons are such as Hitler and loonies force to flee from Germany, Poland and elsewhere. It is not an area of rich people either, and there are many shopkeepers, bakers, delicatessens, that specialise in the Jewish way of life and they are horrified and appalled when two high-ranking Nazi officers appear in their shops and demand goods in heavy German accents. But they overstep the mark when they descend on a little bakery and scream for German bread. The proprietress, who is a Jewish lady of quite impressive density, especially around the hips and in the forearms, scurries from behind her counter and chases them up the street, screaming at them and inflicting considerable damage on them by boffing them with various heavy duty baker's products.

This may seem to be a somewhat tasteless performance and you may feel that they deserve all the damage they get from the heavy duty bakeress. I agree, but add that Moonie is not motivated in any way by malice. I do not think that he considers even for a second that Jewish ladies will be deeply offended by his appearance in Nazi uniform. It is just another way of sending up the straights, and he is reckless as to the implications.

This is, in fact, one of the very few times that I ever see anyone delivering, or attempting to deliver, physical violence to Moonie's person. He has an uncanny knack of avoiding retribution. A way about him which disarms virtually all of the victims of his pranks and japes.

In fact, I only recall one time that anyone really puts Moonie down and that person is Peter Townshend. What happens is this. Moonie is taking the piss out of Townshend and he won't let up. At first, everyone laughs. But then, one by one, the people standing about—and there are a lot of them because we are about to go into a recording session—go quiet and only Moonie's voice breaks the silence. He is really lacing into Townshend and is sneering at many of the things that Peter Townshend holds quite dear. Eventually, Townshend simply stands up and lands a massive swing right on Moonie's button. Moonie does an immediate Cyril Lord, out flat on the deck and Townshend marches off to the studio as if nothing happens at all. Moonie clambers up and scurries after him and, to tell you the truth, I am expecting him to spin Townshend round and give him a good boffing. But no, far from it. What he does is sidle round Townshend and rather abjectly apologise.

"Sometimes you just go too far, Keith," is all Townshend says and that is the end of it.

But apart from this, like I say, Moonie is never, never embarrassed. He really doesn't give a rabbit's fuck what anyone thinks about him.

When you're like that, well then you're really on your own. And I reckon that this is what Moonie knows and lives with.

No one can deny that Moonie has a soft spot for anyone who is really in the crap. Tramps. Bums. Oldies. Inadequates of one sort or another. I remember one time when we are driving back from a Rock Festival at Crystal Palace and we are in the AC 428. As we are zipping into town and about to cross the river, Moonie naturally starts to consider where we may partake of a few bevvies and enjoy a shindig. After all, Moonie is the compère at the

Rock Festival, and these things are hard work, especially when they require a certain amount of laying around on the grass and sampling various stimulants, so what with one thing and another we are ready for a spot of alcohol. The next thing I know, Moonie turns to me and says:

"Here, man, I know a good pub round here."

"Yeah?"

"Yeah. At Waterloo. It's where all the down-and-outs go."

Terrific, I think.

Anyway, nothing will do for Moonie but we have to go there, although I try to persuade him to call into at least half a dozen healthier places en route. Not that I have anything against winos and such but, firstly, they make me think too much for comfort— I mean I could be like that one day—and, secondly, after a hard day at a Rock Festival what you need is somewhere to sit in comfort and get the head together. A nice middle-class gaff with a few stockbrokers sipping at their Martinis is about right for me. But, of course, Moonie is the guvnor and I am his man, so it's off to Waterloo we go.

Just as we pull up to the pub, we see these four geezers sitting by the railway arches. And these are really bums. I mean, they are fucked. Meths bottles in brown paper bags. Red eyes. Plenty of filthy beard. Matted barnet. Stinking clothes. Man, these guys are really evil. Prototype winos. And I am feeling very uncomfortable indeed at the sight of them. But Keith looks out at them and the next thing I know they are shouting:

"Hey, Keith! How are you doing, Keith?" and suchlike, although much of what they say is unintelligible to me and sounds more like a traveller in the desert dying of thirst. But Moonie really perks up:

"Hallo, chaps," he says, "just the chaps I was looking for. Come on in for a few bevvies." So then the prototype bums all come and cluster round the car and what emerges is that they are all banned from this pub.

I brighten up at this, but then I feel somewhat sorry for the bum geezers, being as this pub is once one of the few places where they can buy a quart of cider when they have a few bob, which is not very often. So when Moonie says "Oh, fuck them. Come on, lads, I'll sort it all out" I go along with it and feel quite righteous about the whole thing.

So we all stroll into the pub and I suppose we do appear a right crew, what with Moonie in a £2,000 fur coat, I with long fair hair and immaculate denim gear and these four derelicts who look like something out of a TV documentary on the deprived. At this time of day there are quite a few suits scattered about, and some of these suits are with their wives or whatever, and they seem somewhat less than overjoyed to see us come into their little snuggery. In fact, I am beginning to feel as welcome as Attila the Hun, but Moonie doesn't give a damn. He just marches straight up to the bar, hails the barman, who is also the landlord, and slaps a hundred green notes on the bartop.

Now the landlord is in a real quandary. I mean, here we are with four definite undesirables—but what makes them desirable is one hundred very desirable green notes which are obviously heading toward the till if the landlord plays his cards right. At one stage, I think that the disgust is going to win especially as our four mates are all sniggering and rolling around and are already making themselves quite offensive. But in the end, of course, the mazuma talks and even though the landlord stands there looking like someone repossesses his truss only a few seconds back, when Moonie orders treble brandies all round he springs to the optic like a good one. Mind you, I do not particularly care for the way he slaps the glasses down. There seems to me to be a touch of the petulant strop in the gesture.

We park ourselves at a table and start getting stuck into the brandies. The winos are all well chuffed and they're chatting away to Moonie and he is chatting back and everything in the garden is hunky dory. Of course, Moonie is often in this pub and frequently buys this crowd of sad cases drinks, so they think that the sun shines right out of his drumstool. Now what you must understand about this number is that there is no patronising going on. When Moonie is with these geezers he is absolutely

natural and unselfconscious. It's as if they are just another bunch
of average guys meeting for a few ales and it seems to me that
Moonie is genuinely interested in these geezers. I do not mean
interested in the social worker's way, with all that goodness leak-
ing from every pore. No, once we move on, Moonie will forget
these geezers until the next time we are passing near to the pub.
But while he is actually talking to them, it appears to me that he
is interested in them as people and that is why the conversation
flows so freely, with me, to tell you the truth, feeling a bit of a
spare prick at a wedding.

Now, of course there, may be very many other elements in
this little episode—which, anyway, is not ended yet. It may be
that Moonie is enjoying putting the wind up the straight suits
and their little ladies but, by and large, the act seems quite
straight to me and, I recall, Moonie frequently says to me that
he is more likely to end up on the Embankment, which is where
all the down-and-outs kip, than see his fortieth birthday live.

Half an hour isn't past before we knock off the first lot of
brandies and are well into the second. This injection of relatively
pure liquor into the winos' meth-riddled systems is having a quite
remarkable effect and, quite soon, the winos are blowing rasp-
berries at the stockbroker suits and making remarks that are not
entirely in keeping with the style the brewery wishes to project in
their pub. But, because they are good solid middle-class Brit-
ishers, these stockbroker suits ignore the down-and-outs and
make like they do not exist in the slightest. They just continue to
gab about stocks and shares and bulls and bears and all this and
that. So then Moonie leaps up and orders yet another handful of
very large brandies, but the landlord is now looking like thunder
and he says to Moonie:

"After this drink, I want you lot out. Understand?"

Now this is a very grave mistake and I am sure that if he knows
whom he addresses, the landlord will not speak in this manner
at all.

But Moonie does not say anything, although the entire pub is
now quiet and it is more like a bad scene from a Western than

it is an English pub. However, I can see that Moonie's eyes are suddenly very beady and that they are fixed upon the tray on which the landlord is placing the drinks as he draws them from the optic. And just when the round is sitting there, all neat and wonderful and ready to be downed our gullets, Moonie lifts the tray, catapults the full glasses against the wall behind the bar, which is very full indeed of bottles and glasses and suchlike, and then bongs the landlord over the head with the tray, which makes a very satisfactory metallic "DING" indeed.

Instant chaos.

The winos all stamp and cheer. The landlord commences to shout copper. The suits set up a considerable beef, too, with their ladies saying such things as "Disgraceful" and "Disgusting." One of the larger suits approaches Moonie and attempts to apprehend him but Moonie, though he is by no means a large man, threatens to commit grievous bodily harm upon the suit's brain, if he has one, and emphasises his point by waving an ice bucket at him. So the suit backs off muttering.

Of course, I'm over to the bar like a shot, anticipating big trouble because you never can tell with Moonie. Sometimes he makes a very big issue out of things, and wishes to see it through come what may. Other times, he just lets things go. On this occasion there's a few moments when we stand by the bar and everyone is frozen. Moonie has the ice bucket to hand and I am quite prepared to commence throwing a few knuckle sandwiches if necessary. The landlord is making vaguely threatening sounds about the police being called, but even he does not seem overenthusiastic.

Then Moonie just says:

"Bollocks. Let's get out of here."

Funnily enough, in all the confusion, the pile of one hundred notes is still up there on the bar, tucked up by the cash till. So, looking the landlord straight in the eye, I reach across and grab Moonie's money. Then we gather up the entourage and leave the Hole in the Wall. As we leave, the derelicts have the time of their lives, hurling abuse at one and all and shaking their rather puny fists at the suits and the landlord. I do not suppose they often have the chance to make themselves felt in this way and especially not with a famous rock star on their side.

Once outside, the winos are all for slinging a few bricks and what have you through the window, but Moonie says to them: "No, fuck it, lads. Those bastards aren't worth it." Then he gives them the rest of the cash that I rescue from the bar and we slide into the 428 and leave the area.

Well, of course, the next day I'm fully expecting to see in the papers as how four trambos are arrested trying to break into the Playboy Club waving bundles of fivers, but when I flick through the dailies there is nothing in them at all so I figure that the trambos must just spend the money on medical alcohol and I hope that they are not completely dead by now. On the other hand, Moonie and I only run out of gas on the way back to Chertsey—and, of course, neither of us has got any dough on our whereabouts thanks to Moonie giving it all to the winos. So what we have to do is leave Moonie's extremely expensive fur coat at the gas station as collateral. And even then the geezer there only lets us have a gallon.

Still, that's how it is with Moonie. Money and him stick together only marginally longer than it takes an Arab to cycle through Golders Green. He gives it away, throws it away, loses it and, for all I know, wipes his arse with it if there's nothing else handy. It is the same with all his possessions, in fact.

Now, when he wants something, he has to have it immediately. Like on the spot. Even if it means borrowing the mazuma from whoever is unluckly enough to be within grabbing distance at the time. On the other hand, once he gets hold of whatever it is he wants to get hold of, he is only interested in it for a few days. He plays with it, then he forgets all about it. I do not mean by this that he is like a small child at Christmas, spoilt with too many toys—although obviously something like this does enter into it. No, what I mean is that he really does not need much to live on or with. Because this is a geezer who, if he is not out on the piss, or wreaking havoc here and there, spends most of his time at home in bed watching TV and listening to Jan & Dean on the stereo. And this is certainly not the high life as I understand it. I am sure he does not ever stop to think about it, but what I believe is that the experience of things is far more important to Moonie than the possession of things. True, this is very easy to say when you are talking of someone who has enough ackers to buy virtually anything and anyone in the world. Nevertheless, I think it is the truth, and, in his own way, Moonie is an ascetic.

To show you what I mean, let me tell you about one time in Atlanta when Moonie buys a really gorgeous Rolex watch and has to pay at least 5,000 dollars for it. It has diamonds set all around the dial and all in all it does look a picture. What happens on the afternoon he buys it is that nothing will do but he wants to go ice skating, and the next thing we know it's off down the ice rink, hire the skates and fall flat on our bums. At this stage, Moonie realises that on his wrist he has 5,000 dollars worth of wristwatch, so what does he do but find the nearest chick and give her the watch to hold for him and what does she do, of course, but take it on the toes with same watch. What is more, Moonie is quite aggrieved that this bint should disappear with his watch because all he does is to trust her. It never occurs to him to ask the receptionist to take care of it for him.

All right, you can say, that is just a flash rock star with more money than sense. But Moonie reports this loss to the local cops and they, all credit to them, find the chick and the watch after a couple of days. But Moonie asks them not to take any proceedings against the bird which, I suppose, does count for something.

More than that, I several times see Moonie giving things away when he does not know that anyone is witnessing the giving and from this I deduce that his giving under these circumstances is 100% genuine and is not done so that everyone will say what a truly wonderful person he is. After all, no one who wishes to be thought of as truly wonderful behaves in the manner of Keith Moon.

There is a time in London once when Moonie and Kim and me and my lady, Jill, all go out to the movies one night. It is a double horror bill at the Odeon in the King's Road, Chelsea. We clock the first movie, which is all about bints who turn into lizards at the drop of a hat and who, quite honestly, are better looking as lizards than they are as bints. Next, we're half way through the second movie when I look round and realise that there is no sign of Moonie. I do not worry at this stage as I calculate that he goes to take a leak but, when after half an hour, there is still no sign of my employer, then I begin to feel concerned. Mind you, I still would not do too much about it but for the fact that Kim is starting to become somewhat agitated, so we all decide that we should abandon the movie and find Moonie.

Once we are out of the cinema, we split up after arranging to meet back outside the foyer. Each of us goes to a different pub because it is a pound to a pinch of shit that Keith is in a pub—assuming, that is, that he is not in the slammer. I am assigned in this plan to check the Six Bells, which is a pub with a bit of a disco attached to it and is quite famous in the fifties when traditional jazz is all the rage.

I stroll into the Bells and have a good look around, checking out all the punters as carefully as I can without appearing too nosey and, of course, I take a special interest in the birds present because, although Kim is with Moonie tonight, that is not a guarantee that he will not look elsewhere for a bit of pulling, especially if he has a few bevvies. But on this occasion I cannot see Moonie anywhere and I am about to call it a day when I see a very scruffy geezer indeed wearing three overcoats and sitting in a dark corner. And who is with this scruffy geezer but Keith Moon, just returning from the bar with a couple of drinks. Now this is a fairly surprising sight, what with the scruff's boots being tied up with string, his cap being greasier than a Greek salad and his beard full up with last year's Salvation Army Christmas dinner. So I decide not to make myself known as soon as I see them but to watch from a distance, and this is what happens.

Moonie and the scruff are chatting away about the government and politics, although what Moonie knows about politics you can write on a midget's shirt button. As they're talking, the scruff starts to rummage around in his pockets, which takes a fair effort when you consider that he has three overcoats in which to rummage. After some time, his eyes take on that triumphant look and he eventually comes up with a filthy old sock which he holds up to his face. I think to myself *bloody hell, he's going to blow his nose in it* but what it is is not a sock at all but one of those very old-fashioned rope lighter things, with a piece of rope passing through a gunmetal tube with a wick and a flint attached. What happens is that you twirl the flint-wheel, and with a bit of luck the rope eventually catches fire and you can light your cigarette with it—if, that is, you still have the energy to smoke the cigarette once you've got the rope on fire.

The scruff starts to twirl the flint wheel and a few feeble sparks fly here and there, none of them too near the rope which is meant to be ignited. I can see, and Moonie can see, that there is no way this lighter is going to light the scruff's cigarette and the entire operation is somewhat pathetic to behold. After a decent interval of time, Moonie outs with his lighter, which is solid gold and Dunhill and must be worth at least a couple of hundred quid, and gives the old boy fire for his cigarette.

Well you can see that the old scruff is quite taken by Moonie's Dunhill, so what does Moonie do? Only grabs the scruff's mitt, presses the Dunhill into it and says:

"Look, I don't give a fuck whether you keep this or flog it. I don't mind what you do with it." Then he reaches out and takes the old scruff's rope-and-flint contraption and continues "Let me take your lighter. It is worth more to me because this is a memorable evening for me."

I have to confess that I am somewhat ashamed to be earwigging on this conversation because this is one of those private moments that are nobody else's business. So I sidle away and then go back to Moonie pretending that I only just enter the pub and am very pleased to find him. By the time I do this, the old scruff stuffs the Dunhill away as quickly as possible, hardly daring to believe his luck, and Moonie says not a word to me about the exchange. He just drinks up, says goodbye to the scruff and leaves the pub with me.

A similar happening to this, but not nearly so private, occurred when we once run into an American guy in Old Compton Street, Soho. This is in the very early days when the band's managers have a small office in Curzon Street. Now there are no decent pubs near Curzon Street so what you have to do for a good bevvy is wander off toward Soho and this is something we find ourselves doing fairly regularly. This time we're in a pub called the Admiral Duncan and in comes this American guy who is dressed entirely like a tramp. I say that he is dressed this way because despite the clothes, it does not seem to me that he is a tramp proper. For a start he is quite young—about 30—and he does not have that hopeless look about his face.

He comes up the bar where we're standing, that's me, Moonie and the geezer who is doing all Moonie's chauffeuring at the time and he orders up a drink. Moonie, hearing the guy's strong American accent, asks him where he is from and, before we know what is happening, there is a conversation going on. This geezer explains to Moon:

"No, I am not a tramp. I am a hobo." It seems that he spends many years travelling the world and whichever interesting place you can think of, this hobo is there one time or another—or at least says he is. You may gather by now that Moonie is quite a romantic at heart and he is genuinely impressed by all this talk of foreign parts and it is clear to me that he really takes a shine to this hobo.

I take quite a shine to him too, not least because he does pay for his round of drinks, even if he is paying for it with what seems to be like his last few quid in the world.

By the time chucking-out time comes, we are all having a great time and do not feel inclined to return to the office in Curzon Street, and Moonie wishes to visit the Playboy Club and to take this hobo geezer with him. Despite his protests, and it does seem that he does not wish to seem like a hanger-on, we all jump into the limo and drive up to Park Lane. At this stage

I can hear you ask how we are going to get a bloke dressed up like a tramp into the Playboy Club because although the Playboy Club is by no means the most exclusive place in the world it does not encourage tramps among its members. But, of course, the only reason that the Playboy Club does not encourage tramps among its members is that tramps are not apt to have too much ready spending cash and if they do tramps will be most welcome to become Playboy Club members and, no doubt, the bunnies too will grow accustomed to the smell of trambo clothing—and even get to like it.

Yes, it is quite remarkable what the judicious application of relatively small sums of cash money can achieve and within no time at all we are well inside the Playboy Club, complete with American hobo. And once inside the disco, we proceed to give our friend an extremely fine meal which includes a great deal of champagne and not a little brandy to help it down. From what I recall, which is not entirely crystal clear, there is also a vast quantity of Turkish Delight involved and all this is served by very enthusiastic bunnies who flutter around and give the famous rock star much attention, despite his scruffy friend.

During the course of our conversation it turns out that our newly found mate plans to sleep out rough tonight on account of having nowhere to stay and no money to purchase sheets and blankets, let alone a bed. So Keith has a quiet word with the limo chauffeur, who glides off with hardly a cocked eyebrow in Moonie's direction.

When the times come to split and our hobo is saying thanks very much and so on and so forth, but goodbye all the same, Moonie suddenly says:

"No, no, dear boy. You're coming with us. A few brandies, that's what we all need." And nothing will do but we must follow Moonie down the street where the limo and the chauffeur are waiting for us. We pile into the car and drive all of three hundred yards down the road before pulling up at the forecourt of the Inn on the Park, which may not be quite the most expensive hotel in London but will certainly do until the most expensive has a few free rooms. Whatever else, this is not a hotel in which you will expect to rub shoulders, or anything else much, with hobos such as our American mate.

It transpires that what comes off here is that Moonie only goes and sends the chauffeur to this hotel to book a room for the scruff—and not just any room at that, but the Wellington Suite, so called on account of this is the room in which the management would like the Duke of Wellington to kip if they can find him, which of course they cannot as he is dead several hundred years.

Now, just in case you're wondering how easy it is to get a real A1 genuine trambo into the Inn on the Park, especially remembering that we have some difficulty in same manoeuvre at the Playboy Club and require the distribution of several dirty notes around the place, let me tell you that I am truly amazed at the civility with which Moonie and the scruff are greeted by one and all at this rather ugly modern hotel. But then it only takes me a few moments to remember that Moonie and his mates stay many times at this Inn and, although they destroy the fixtures and much of the fabric each time they stay, what they do do well is to lubricate the palms of the flunkeys with great efficiency and always pay for whatever damage and mayhem they cause. Readies in the pocket have a most wonderfully soothing effect on all types of groveller and flunkey and Moonie only has to poke his hooter round the door in Reception to be surrounded by many uniformed greeters, mostly Irish and Spanish, making with the:

"Tis yourself Mr. Moon and very good to see you to be sure, to be sure. And that." and:

"Mr. Moon! Is very hood to see you ahain. I ope you are estay long?" Then the manager himself appears and he adds:

"Mr. Moon, sir. What a pleasure. How is your good wife? Your mother? Dog? Parrot? Cat?"

The upshot of all this crawling is that a flunkey is summoned to take the American scruff up to his room, though the flunkey is marginally surprised that the hobo has no suitcases with him.

We all follow and I have to tell you this, that I stay in some of the best hotels in the world in my time with The Who, but I do not stay in many accommodations that beat the Inn on the Park for sheer expensiveness. There is plenty of super luxury in the Wellington Suite, with no little period furniture and a giant four poster bed that even impresses Moonie, and I can see him eyeing it as if to say:

"How can I get this bed out of here and down to my gaff in Chertsey?"

This bed is not much smaller than the USS America and at each corner there is a bloody great brass cannon, presumably to make the Duke of Wellington feel at home when and if he clocks in.

We put the hobo into this bed and that really is all there is to this particular episode in Moonie's life—except that, about a week after these events, the office receives a letter from the hobo, and this is quite likely the only thank you letter Moonie ever receives in his thirty-odd years—though many people who should know much better owe him a fucking sight more than thank you letters. In the letter the hobo says that he writes to the *Daily Express*, which is a large and ailing British daily newspaper, but the *Daily Express* does not publish this letter or follow it up in any way, which may be because the newspaper is about dead on its feet or may be because no one at the *Daily Express* can believe that the story is true.

Which, of course, it is.

Don't Throw Your Love Away

There is no question at all but that Keith Moon only ever loves one woman in his life and that this woman is Kim. The only real question is whether there is anyone else he treats worse than Kim —apart, that is from some of the scrubbers whom he passes through in the course of his career. But then such scrubbers expect short shrift and do not know how to behave if anyone shows them anything other than a very bad time indeed.

Of course, there are some who will say that Moonie loves Annette, whom he takes up with after Kim leaves, just as much. But it is my opinion that he feels differently about Annette, and the fact that he is altogether more civilised toward her, and more together with her, than ever is the case with Kim is on account of Kim's leaving teaches Moonie a most severe lesson. He does not wish that Annette should repeat this lesson, namely that it is extremely cold out there without a woman to lean on.

One thing I notice about women in rock is that many of them have similar characteristics. For example, large numbers of rock women come from what you might call middle class, or at least comfortable background, with mothers and fathers who have considerably fixed ideas when it comes to dope, screwing and fraternising with undesirables of inferior classes. Now this does not only apply to Britain, though I confess that the class definition is more significant in this country than it is elsewhere—because that is the sort of country Britain is. I do not know whether these chicks get to hang around rock stars because they like the music mainly, or whether it is because same stars are forbidden, exciting and liable to fuck indiscriminately. Maybe they are so used to being treated as little women at home that it is attractive and desirable to be treated like a piece of shit by some Herbert who makes a million teenies wet their knickers and probably doesn't bath too often either. I concede that many rock women must stay with their respective men for many different reasons, and, while some are ever loving wives and mothers to the rock stars' sprogs, others are girlfriends and yet others scrubbers. But if you examine all these women closely you will see that many of them have similar backgrounds—and not the sort of background you will normally associate with the sort of life up-and-coming rock stars indulge in before they up-and-come.

Moonie's Kim is no exception to this tendency. She is the quiet and respectable daughter of a quiet and respectable family and you will quite easily mistake her old man for a retired major or naval commander. Her mum, at least, is more of a suitable mother-in-law for Moonie because, anyway at the time I know her, she is quite partial to a few bevvies herself.

What Kim does have going for her in addition to being quiet and respectable—if you like that sort of thing—is that she is extremely beautiful and very nice with it. She and Moonie get together when they are very young indeed and when I first meet her, they have a baby, Mandy, who cannot be much more than one year in age, and they are living in a small flat above a car showroom in Highgate, North London. This is not at all the sort of flat you will associate with a rock and roll drummer who already has two smash hits to his credit. It is more the sort of flat you will think is lived in by a family of alcoholic badgers engaged in the manufacture of pasta and tomato sauce. But then Moonie's money is being used at this time to support The Speakeasy, and it is well known that The Speakeasy is a very worthy cause indeed, if somewhat demanding when it comes to moolaw.

The night I first experience this flat, and meet Mandy and Kim, Keith insists that I accompany him after a night out. By the time we arrive at the front door, Keith loses his door keys and leans upon the doorbell, which makes a very pretty BING-BONG sound until the door is opened by a stunning blonde with a turned-up nose. This apparition looks like it just calls in from St. Tropez, and I begin to wonder how I am going to tap this supply of French au pair girls when Moonie says:

"Dougal, dear boy, this is Kim. Kim . . . Dougal," and he accompanies this grandly-spoken introduction with an expansive sweep of his arm.

So this is Kim, I think and I am most impressed—though I do wonder what such a delightful-looking bird sees in such a geezer as Keith Moon.

We go into the flat and Keith starts to show me round. In her bedroom, Mandy, who as I previously mention is around the one mark, is standing up in her cot, grinning and shaking the cot's structure wtih a great deal of malice aforethought. In fact, the cot is rattling so violently that it must fall right over if it is not for the electrical flex with which Moonie previously ties the cot to a central heating radiator. I can see that in the matter of destruction, this is a little girl that takes after her father.

In Moonie's bedroom, I see that there is very little in the way of furniture. The bed is flat on the floor and what serves as a wardrobe for Moonie and Kim's threads is a piece of wire strung across a curtained-off alcove.

"Listen, Moonie," I ask, laughing, "what's the bed doing on the floor?"

"That," says Kim, "is when he came in feeling fruity and jumped on me."

"Yeah," adds Moonie. "The legs all broke."

As we approach the living room, on the next leg of this guided tour of Moonie's stately home, I become aware of a strange smell, and when we enter the living room the smell is quite overpowering. It does not take me long to work out that this smell arises from the many piles of animal droppings dotted around the place and it is quite clear that these droppings are the efforts of a small fox that peers out from behind a speaker. This is by no means a large fox. In fact it is a small fox; a baby fox which seems to be most endearing, and which Keith explains lives in the loudspeakers of the sound system. But what I believe is that no matter how endearing the fox is, it cannot make up for the dreadful smell of fox shit that permeates everywhere.

It is clear that Kim does her best to keep the place as respectable as possible, at least to look at, but, what with supporting The Speakeasy, she is losing the battle accounting for most of the housekeeping, what with the spaghetti stains on the chaise longue and what with the miniature foxy creature squatting down here and there.

For all I know, it is the cold looks I give this place that cause Keith to decide that with all his money in the world he will set us both up as second-hand car dealers. The total of all Keith's money in the world at this time is £2,000 and it is this sum that we take down to the car auctions, where Moonie's flower power fashions cause several rude comments and many turned lips amongst the car sharks present. After the auctions, at which we fail to spot the car that will make our fortunes and so enable Moonie to decorate his flat, I take Keith home to my mother's house and she is so taken by him that she gives him a large gilt picture frame, with no picture in it. Keith accepts this gift courteously and returns to his flat in Highgate, where a considerable ruck ensues. At the height of the ruck, Moonie picks up a champagne bottle and hurls it at Kim. She ducks and the bottle ends up embedded in the wall of the living room. Whereupon Moonie cements it firmly into the wall with Polyfilla, then carefully nails the gilt frame around it. This champagne bottle and Polyfilla masterpiece shapes up better as a piece of art than many of the things that may be observed in modern art museums around the world, and it is always much admired by visitors to Moonie's gaff.

It must be clear from this that the Moonie/Kim domestic set-up is not such an arrangement as recommended by marriage guidance counsellors and other such people who have expert advice to offer on this and similar subjects. The home is by no means as fastidiously maintained as those in the TV commercials. Not many cosy evening are spent playing draughts. Not much Ovaltine is served up around bedtime at ten thirty. Moonie does not spring through the front door at the appointed hour, just in time for a delicious gourmet meal as dictated by the editors of women's magazines. In fact, during the time I know Moonie and Kim they lead a very haphazard life indeed, in which all the rules for a stable and successful marriage are bunged right out of the window. For a kick-off, they spend a great deal of time apart—not least because if Moonie takes it into his head to go on a binge, it will never occur to him that he should take Kim along too. And even if he does, it is probably the last thing that she will wish to do anyway. Nor is she likely to wish to accompany him when he is jumping about dressed up as Adolf Hitler or walking across other people's tables in restaurants.

Moreover, they have very different temperaments. While Moonie is a complete lunatic, Kim is bascially shy and quiet—though I am not saying that she doesn't enjoy a jolly-up as much as the next bint when the occasion calls for it. She is quite partial to parties and clubs and a lively social life—but she is normal about it. She talks to her friends and does not throw beer at them.

So, if she is so shy and normal, why does she marry Keith? The answer to this is that she marries Keith when they are both very young and do not know any better, and when Keith does not have a reputation to live up to. At the time, he is just about opening his account as a great rock and roll drummer and she is making early inroads upon the modelling game in Bournemouth. Now Bournemouth, while it is not the dullest town in

Britain—especially in the summer when it is filled to overflowing with foreign bints all learning English and various other things too—certainly does not rival New York or London in the excitement stakes. So when the young Bournemouth model meets the up-and-coming rock and roller, who at this time has plenty of looks, personality and charm, it is practically love at first sight. At this time, Moonie is not as outrageous as later, partly because he does not have the dough to be outrageous with and partly because he is not famous enough to get away with the sort of stunts he is able to pull later on in life.

Whatever anyone says, there is no doubt that they love each other and it seems to me that this is the case throughout their married life. As time goes on, however, they find it increasingly difficult to live with each other and this is basically Moonie's fault. Most of the time he does not regard himself as married or as having any connection with anyone else that requires him to consider their feelings. He fails to execute the most basic courtesies—such as telephoning to say that he will be late. Three months late. Many's the time Kim produces a meal that must be thrown out some two hours later—only for Moonie to stroll in and ask:

"Where's my fucking dinner?"

And, because of the sort of girl she is, Kim usually cooks up something fresh.

One time I remember Moonie taking Kim out to The Speakeasy. What usually happens under these circumstances is that she quietly sidles off to chat with her mates while he commits embarrassing mayhem elsewhere in the club. In The Speakeasy, there are usually people Kim knows, whether they are modelling mates, musicians' wives and girlfriends, or whatever. On this occasion, Moonie becomes totally out of his bonce with liquor and winds up hurling his dinner, and everyone else in sight's, up in the air. At this time, which is the Swinging Sixties, when we all never have it so good, such dinners cost approximately a fiver, which in those days is some dough.

Around about five o'clock in the morning, the management

and staff of the club decide that all they wish to do is slide between the sheets, so they suggest to Moonie that he should gather up his cohorts and direct himself homewards. When we arrive there, everyone is as knackered as the management and staff of The Speakeasy, and I am just about dozing off into dreamland when I am awakened by a great shouting and carrying on. It is emanating from the region of Moonie's room and it sounds something like this:

"Kim! Wake up! I want something to eat! I'm fucking hungry. How about grilling us a steak . . ."

And she does it. She has to. Because it's just not worth the refusal and its ensuing chance that Moonie will wreck the place, wake Mandy up and so on.

This may lead you to believe that this Kim is nothing more than a sort of female doormat and that she deserves everything she gets if she will not stand up for herself. But it is not as simple as that. She is a spirited girl and on many occasions she stands up for herself most effectively. Remember what we are talking about here is real physical danger. For his size, Moonie is impressively strong and when he is out of control—either because he is angry or because he is out of it—he is perfectly capable of inflicting great hurt on all and sundry.

Kim copes with this well, but she has the disadvantage of having to worry about Mandy, who is by no means large enough to stick up for herself.

This is well demonstrated by the Great Spaghetti Aggravation. Now I notice this before—that grub and aggravation often go hand in hand—not only in the Moon household, but elsewhere too. How many husband/wife argy-bargies do you know of that start over who is making too much noise with the a.m. Kelloggs? The Great Spaghetti fiasco occurs when Joan, Kim's mother, cooks up a great pot of pasta one time when she is in residence at Tara. Joan is not a bad chef at all and her spaghetti is renowned far and wide. What is more, the kitchen at Tara is perfect for cooking spaghetti—and anything else come to think of it—because it is huge and very well-equipped. Most of the operative devices are contained in a large island right in the middle of this very large room.

At the time that Joan produces the pot of spaghetti, Kim, Mandy and I don our bibs and tuckers, but Moonie, as usual, is nowhere to be seen.

So, just as the first forkful is pointed in the general direction of my stomach, who should walk in but Moonie. I can see immediately that he is not happy. Worse than that, I can see that he is extremely unhappy—and this is indicated by his almost comically sulky face. I never discover the reason for this face, but straight away he starts in on Kim.

"Where's my caftan?" he asks belligerently. "I thought you were going to get it cleaned."

So Kim tells him where it is.

"It's not there," he replies. "I've looked. It's not there."

This is one of those times when at least one out of the two people present is determined to have a ruck, and it is well known under these circumstances that there is nothing anyone can do to stop same ruck from occurring. It is like trying to halt a Sherman tank with a water pistol. There are roughly three more exchanges of words. Then Moonie seizes a milk bottle and slings it at Kim. It doesn't hit her, but it does shatter against the wall and a shard of glass flies out and cuts Mandy's face.

Naturally enough, Kim jumps up to attend to Mandy and while she is doing so she gives Moonie quite an earful to the effect that he is one of the world's most unpleasant people and that it is possible that his mother and father were not entirely married when he was born. For someone usually so quiet, she is very eloquent on this occasion and, at one stage, seems quite likely to support her eloquence with considerable physical violence. When it seems appropriate, I leap up and remonstrate with Moonie.

"Leave it out," I say—but that is as far as I get because Moonie rounds on me and makes like Genghis Khan after his team loses at home. BOFF! he goes on my earhole, which causes me a ringing in the head and persuades me to retaliate with a roundhouse left—not, unfortunately, before I fall against the handle of the spaghetti pot. It is quite extraordinary how large an area a small quantity of oily spaghetti can cover, and it is well known that the most effective method of spreading such pasta over a kitchen floor is for two full grown adults to roll around in it trying to strangle each other. Moreover, this activity is noted for its deleterious effect upon expensive clothes —though, needless to say, this particular phenomenon is irrelevant to Moonie on account of he dresses like a rubbish tip at home. I, on the other hand, am wearing a new pair of strides of which I am quite proud and which cost me a few bob. The spaghetti, and especially the Bolognaise sauce, do these strides no favours whatsoever.

Mandy is crying. Kim is crying. Joan is crying—or so it seems, though looking back, it may be that she is just aggravated that her meal is ruined. After some struggling, commonsense prevails and the fight ceases. Moonie stalks from the kitchen looking like an atomic bomb attack on an Italian restaurant— then, two hours later, walks back in right as rain and twice as noisy.

No, Kim is by no means a doormat—especially when it comes to protecting Mandy.

This Mandy is indeed a charming girl, and I know her from the time she is very small up until she is just about a teenager. She is bright, good at school and very quick on the uptake. She has no particular affinity for rock and rollers and their lifestyle and is far more interested in such subjects as are dear to the hearts of many female sprogs, by which I mean horse riding and ponies and so on.

She does not have very much time for Moonie, which is not surprising because he is not exactly the ideal father. Indeed he starts off his paternal career by forgetting that Mandy is about to be born, because just at that time he is tripping on acid and is not entirely sure who he is, let alone where he is or where he should be. It takes him two days to visit Kim after the baby is born, and even then he seems somewhat hazy about the purpose of his visit to the hospital.

Things do not improve much after this first encounter between father and daughter. For a kick off, Mandy sees very little of her father for, even when he is at home and not on tour, Moonie is constantly engaged in foolhardy schemes and the wholesale distribution of destruction. And when he is at home, Moonie is not especially enthusiastic about Mandy—or about any other child for that matter. This may be because children tend to be the centre of attraction and this militates against Keith's occupying that position.

Moreover, when Moonie is at home there is always plenty of rucking between him and Kim, and Kim usually comes off worst in this domestic sport. Mandy soon figures that it is Kim who does the looking after and provides the love and affection and attention which all children need to have.

So when she witnesses her mother receiving much GBH on the ears, not to mention actual GBH on various other areas of her person, it does not take Mandy long to develop a dislike of the perpetrator of same GBH. As a result, Kim attempts to keep Mandy away from Moonie as much as possible, and all the usual functions of having a child, such as taking her to school, attending school plays, and so on are carried out by Kim and, occasionally, by me.

By the time I am well established as Moonie's man, the rot is well set in his marriage and I find myself in a difficult position. Moonie often locks himself away in his room for days and nights on end and Kim sleeps on the living room sofa rather than go near him. Quite often she asks me to go out for a meal with her, or down to the pub for a few quiet bevvies, simply to get away from the house and enjoy a normal kind of evening. Of course, I am very sympathetic to Kim's position, but on the other hand I both like Moonie and am employed by him to be his man. This experience, hurtling between the pair of them like Mercury, the bleeding winged messenger, being as diplomatic as possible, equips me excellently for a stint in the Foreign Office, and one of these days I must apply to become the next ambassador to Iran or Ireland. These diplomatic missions, I am sure, are partly responsible for the marriage lasting as long as it does, though it is clearly doomed even when I first meet Kim.

Things come to a head one day after a real humdinger of a ruck, complete with doors slamming like machine gun fire. Kim turns to me and screams:

"That's it! I've had it. I'm off!"

Then her mother turns to me and screams:

"That's it! I've had enough. I'm off too!"

And I find myself screaming:

"That's it! Enough. I'm off too."

What happens is that I cart Kim off to her father's place in Bournemouth, where it turns out that I am welcome to stay, too, until I recover from a heavy overdose of Keith Moon. Now I know that Keith will immediately assume that I am at my parents' place and will phone them day and night until I return. So I phone them myself and tell them to tell him that I am in Brighton and cannot be contacted. Poor old Joan is *persona non grata* at her old man's place and she is undecided as to what to do. But we desert her and arrive in Bournemouth, where we get a very big hello from Kim's father. He looks much like a retired tea planter, which is quite appropriate for Bournemouth which, I dare say, has the largest proportion of tea planters (retired) per head of population anywhere in the world.

To cut a long story short, Kim and I commence to recuperate most effectively, what with the long walks along the beach and the generally relaxed air of this West Country resort. It is rather like recovering from shellshock after an over-long spell in the trenches. My parents contact me and tell me that they are deluged with messages from Keith, most of which read: come back soon—all is forgiven.

The days roll by and I soon begin to feel restless and in need of a little action. Plus I really do start to wonder if Moonie is

OK, because I know he is totally incompetent on his own. My mind is made up when Joan suddenly turns up and tells us that Keith is in a very bad way. It turns out that soon after we desert her, Joan realises she has nowhere else to go and returns to Tara and Keith and this is how she knows that he is falling apart.

By this time, Kim is feeling a little remorseful and, as I say, I am ready to resume my duties. Add this to the fact that Joan is not welcome in the (retired) tea planter's home, and it is enough to persuade us all to return to Chertsey and Tara House. Naturally, we arrange our transport so that we all arrive separately and however obvious this may seem to you, it fools Moonie. He is overjoyed at the coincidence that returns all his loved ones to him within a few hours of each other—and when his father turns up on a visit too, he practically bursts with joy and family sentiment. He is so happy that he becomes totally olivered and passes out for the best part of 24 hours.

Well, soon after this, Kim realises that it is time for her to quit and on this subject she gets much sound advice from the well-known DJ, Ann Nightingale, and her husband, who are both very hip to Moonie and the misery that he puts Kim through. I think it is also at about this time that she meets Ian McLagan, the keyboard player, and he too helps her to realise that there is no future whatsoever in her relationship with Moonie.

It is a massive break for Kim and it requires a great deal of determination, for there is no doubt that Moonie loves her and that she loves him. It is just impossible for them to live together. Nor is there any way that Moonie and Kim can sit down and talk things out. The only communicating Moonie ever does with Kim is via records, so that if they are in the middle of a ruck, Moonie will play: *Don't Be Cruel* by Elvis. If he wants to make up, then it's *Be My Baby* by the Chiffons. And if things reach a really tight pass, then it's Elvis again with *It's Now Or Never*. This may not be such a bad way of communicating at that, but it is somewhat limited unless you have a record library of about the size of the BBC and WNET put together.

So the day come when it is time for Kim to leave and, in truth, it is somewhat of an anticlimax. She simply waits until Moonie is asleep, then packs a case and takes it on her toes to a hotel near Heathrow Airport.

At first, Moonie does not believe he is alone. He thinks it is just a matter of finding her, and I even have to drive around the streets of Chertsey one night with Moonie, completely pissed, calling out to Kim. Of course, I know exactly where Kim is but I sympathise with her decision and know that it is the right one. So I stay schtum and make out that I have not got any more clue than Keith as to where she is.

In the following days and weeks it at last becomes clear to Moonie that Kim will not come back. For a while he becomes very maudlin and asks many questions such as:

"Why am I such a bastard?" and "How could I do this to the only woman I've ever loved?"

But to these questions there are no answers, or if there are then I do not know them.

Eventually Moonie gets used to the fact that Kim is no longer there, and what he does is to behave exactly as if the marriage is still on. In other words he fucks as many women as he can wherever and whenever he can. And when he is not doing that, he causes as much aggravation as possible. It is exactly as if Kim is still around, except that everything is a little more frenetic and obvious. Finally, it is as if Kim does not exist; as if Moonie never meets her and it is in this frame of mind that he meets Annette and she, I am sure, is the one who puts him right.

But this is for sure: for the rest of his life Moonie becomes quite emotional if Kim is mentioned or if anything happens to remind him of Kim. Years later, for example, when Annette, Moonie and I are in Malibu and feeling hungry, we decide to go out for an Indian meal. At the last moment, Annette changes her mind, and Keith and I go off to a little Indian gaff we know in Santa Monica. The waitress appears. She is an extraordinarily beautiful Indian girl with jet black hair and dark glistening skin. But she has very European features—even to the extent of a cute turned-up nose. In fact, she is a dead ringer for Kim. It is as if someone takes a photo of Kim and here is the negative. Moonie says nothing at the time, but he looks quite strange and shocked and it is no surprise to me when, in the car on the way home, he bursts into tears.

We never visit that Indian restaurant again.

When Keith first meets Annette, he is going with a chick who has the unlikely monicker of Joy Bang. Unhappily for Joy, she refuses one night to accompany Keith to Tramp, on account of having to return to the USA the following day and wishing to appear her best when she arrives there. Naturally, Moonie seizes the chance to go out alone. He is only in Tramp a few moments before he first sets eyes on Annette and decides that she is the one for him. There is a problem, however. She is accompanied. Moonie's solution is to slip one of the waiters a few quid to have Annette's unfortunate companion ejected from the club.

As is ever the case at Tramp, Moonie becomes totally blasted but nevertheless succeeds in taking Annette back to where he is staying, which is at Kit Lambert's flat. Whether he simply doesn't care that Joy Bang is in the flat when he turns up with Annette, or whether he is too pissed to remember that she is not due to leave for the airport until the morning, I cannot say. What I can tell you is that when I arrive at the flat to take Ms. Bang away, Moonie comes to the door looking absolutely shattered.

"Dougal, dear boy," he says. "What a night. I've had to keep both the girls happy—and I've had to keep them apart. I even locked Joy in the wardrobe for a while. But," he goes on, "wait until you meet Annette. Jesus Christ, Dougal, she is out of this world."

"Where is she?" I ask.

"She's just gone to get her things. She's moving in. So get hold of Joy and on your bike to the airport, dear boy."

I am just about to obey these instructions when Annette herself walks in, and I have to say that she is indeed a very beautiful piece of art. Moreover, it seems to be clear that she and Moonie are already falling in love, which is excellent news for me because all the looning about with Keith is beginning to grind my system into small pieces.

Shortly after this, Moonie and Annette leave for the States to visit Eric Clapton and it is on this trip that they decide to take up residence there, renting houses in Beverley Hills and Belair. Now when I say that Moonie and Annette fall in love, it is not the same sort of emotion as that which I witness between Moonie and Kim. It is quite different, but it is none the less very powerful. Not powerful enough, however, to prevent Moonie going back to his old ways, bevvying it up with the lads in LA and not bothering to phone home to say yes, no or how are you?

But Annette copes with this far better than Kim. She is surprisingly calm and relaxed and maybe this is because she is Swedish and Scandinavians are known for their phlegmatic approach to the problems posed by life and love. Mind you, if you or I had to live up there in the frozen north, eat the sort of rubbish they eat and put up with the Swedish male mentality, which has all the subtlety of a reindeer with a bumble bee up its arse, then maybe we would display this same fatalism too.

It is very hard to say exactly how Moonie's relationship with Annette differs from that with Kim. It is true that all the time they are together they very rarely actually go out together, which is very similar to what happens with Kim. It is also true that Moonie often looks at Annette as if she is an extension of Kim. Soon after they first get together, for example, Annette changes her hairstyle, which is brown bobbed, and dies her barnet blonde. When I first see it, Moonie says:

"Don't she look just like Kim, Dougal?" To which the answer is "only a bit"—and Annette is very dissimilar to Kim. She is entirely her own person.

Of course, during the early days especially, Annette has to face many of the problems that Kim faces. There is never any money around, despite the huge earnings that are taking place.

It only takes Moonie a couple of nights to blow several thousand dollars, after which he turns up at the house and gives Annette $48.50.

"Sorry, love," he says. "That's all there is. $40 for groceries and $8.50 for a few beers. OK?" And if there's no money for food, there's certainly no money for furniture. We have the sunbeds—but no mattresses, and instead of suntan oil, we're reduced to coating ourselves with Annette's salad dressing.

Yet at this time, it is doubtful whether there is another drummer in the world earning as much as Keith Moon.

Annette handles these mazuma shortages as well as she handles the emotional crises—though the time she actually witnesses Moonie screwing another bird, she is unable to maintain her cool. What happens is this: she opens the door to the study only to see Moonie flat on his back with an old toad astride him and hammering away. Moonie, who is highly juiced at the time, looks up, grins, then speaks to the toad as follows:

"Faster, love. Faster."

Annette burst into tears, rushes into my room and shrieks:

"Look, Dougal, he's fucking this chick in front of me! In our house!" There does not seem to be much that I can do about this state of affairs, although I do feel that it is somewhat out of order for Moonie to behave in this way. The matter is then taken out of our hands, for Moonie drags the toad into his and Annette's bedroom, locks the door and then continues the pork swordplay. It is only a few moments later that the sounds of *Ride, Ride The Wild Surf* come blasting out over the stereo and continue to blast out for over an hour.

Believe it or not, the next afternoon all is forgiven and love reigns supreme once more. Even after this episode, Annette visits Keith every day when he checks into the Cedar Sinai Hospital, hoping for a cure for his depression and alcoholism. She is certainly a remarkable chick.

The cure, incidentally, lasts as long as it takes us to get to the airport to check in for a flight back to London. When we arrive at the desk, we discover that of the three of us booked, only one is booked first class—and that is me.

"You must be fucking joking!" I say to the airline lackey, but even this display of English persuasiveness does no good. So while I am trying to rearrange the bookings, I tell the airline lackey to take Keith and Annette to the hospitality suite. With them out of the way, I proceed to lay greenbacks on every British Airways official in sight. Naturally, these greenbacks are well received, though I nearly lose my hand in the process and decide that it is probably safer to dangle an arm in a tankful of piranha fish than it is to dangle dollar notes in front of British Airways.

With the first class seats safely secured, I return to Keith and Annette in the hospitality suite—only to discover that Keith does not need an aircraft in which to fly. He is already higher than Saturn, fuelled by a handful of valium and three vodka and tonics. My heart sinks into my boots, for I know what is going to happen. Sure enough, once we are in the plane, Moonie heaves into the champagne and orange and after two hours he is uncontrollable. He throws his meal all over everyone. He tries to get into the cockpit to advise the pilots as to how they should control the engines. He falls asleep for a couple of hours, then wakes up screaming:

"YAHAAAAAAAA!!!!" so loud that the tailplane nearly drops off and I have a mild heart attack. When the captain announces that we will be landing in 30 minutes, Moonie drowns out the PA system with his portable cassette machine playing the Lone Ranger theme. And when we finally hit the deck, he switches tapes, stands to attention in the aisle with his trousers round his ankles and the machine blaring out *Land of Hope and Glory*. Stone me if this last effort doesn't receive thunderous applause from all our fellow passengers—though if you ask me this is not from any sense of patriotism, it is on account of the fact that everyone is so relieved that we land safe and sound despite having Moonie aboard.

Annette hardly bats an eyelid through all this. It just doesn't seem to faze her in the slightest and she sticks with Keith right up until the very end. I understand, in fact, that at the time Keith dies, he and Annette are discussing getting married and the whole thing. Much as I love Keith, I would not wish him on my worst enemy as a husband. Though if anyone could carry it off, it would be Annette Walter-Lax.

I Can't Help Myself

There is no question but that Keith Moon has a powerful effect on many women and that a very surprisingly large percentage of female persons find him most acceptable. Nor are all these female persons slags, groupies, hookers and scrubbers. Many of them are bints who are quite at ease in the upper echelons of society, who are not short of the odd bob and who are quite restful upon the eyes. Of these, of course, there must be a number who are out for a bit of rough adventure before they find their Lord Sir Right, and perhaps the heir to the throne of England, and Moonie is able to provide such adventure—more, perhaps, than these bints are able to handle. How many women genuinely like or love Moonie for himself is debatable, though I personally and emphatically place Kim and Annette in this category.

Now, when I express surprise at how many chicks rate Moonie I do not intend to do him down or knock him in any way because, at least when he has got his act together, he is by no means the ugliest turkey in the world and is the possessor of a most engaging personality. The main problem is that he very rarely does have his act together. Much of the time he lives like a creature created by the late H. G. Wells, emerging from his bed half shaven, eyes like piss-holes in the snow, and diving troglodyte-like into the nearest dimly lit bar where he takes on vast quantities of reviving medicines. At this stage his naturally engaging personality tends to become submerged beneath the manic Moon searching continuously for laughs, mayhem and, maybe, amnesia. But even in this state, Moonie will come up trumps and, if there are any birds to be pulled, it is Moonie who will be doing the pulling—regardless of the competition.

Early in his career as a movie star Moonie meets up with a young actor called Karl Howman, who is a nice enough bloke at that even if he is inclined to beat his breast about the strains and intricacies of the acting profession. As far as I am concerned Karl is good news because he is able to take the pressure off me in the matter of looking after Moonie, and I have many peaceful evenings and nights while Karl and Moonie are out on the town. Karl tells me that on one occasion he and a mate of his, a professional footballer of about the middle rank, meet Moonie in his suite at the Londonderry Hotel where they are joined by three young ladies. Like I say, the footballer is middle ranking, not bad-looking and is recognised here and there as a bit of a celebrity, though very junior to Moonie in this respect. Karl, though he is not Omar Sharif, is not Dr. Phibes either, which I only say by way of preamble to this story Karl tells me: Throughout the evening, Karl and the kicker are making concerted attacks upon the three birds, figuring that they must be in for a slice of beaver pie on account of Keith is completely ignoring the bints and is steadily becoming more and more inebriated. They do not seem to be doing too badly and are able to grasp various parts of the three bints' anatomies, though always being careful to keep a free hand available for chucking back the brandies. It is perhaps a shame that they concentrate so hard on the free brandy-chucking, because what happens is that they eventually pass out.

The next morning Karl awakes to find that the late General Heinz Guderian is conducting a blitzkreig in the region of his brains, but he is comforted by the knowledge that he is in a pleasantly comfortable bed and, as he can tell from sixth sense, that there is also present in this bed a body which may be able to offer him some shelter from the blitzkrieg. So he turns over, somewhat out of focus and sleepy, and feels about for the comfort that this body may provide. Unfortunately, what his groping hand finds is not so much the soft and pliant contours of the female form, but the huge, hairy and well-muscled arsehole of the pro footballer who, when he senses that his arsehole is being tampered with, sits bolt upright and says, very savage:

"Leave off, you stupid bastard, it's me."

Well this is a great shock to Karl because, unlike many followers of the Thespian arts, he is strictly addicted to tampering with bints and is personally not in favour of playing with gentlemen. This shock causes Heinz Guderian to make a momentary retreat and enables Karl to focus the minces. What he sees is this:

He and the pro kicker are warmly ensconced in the bed but Moonie and the three bints are tucked up together upon the floor, surrounded by cushions and covered with rugs, and it is quite evident from the movements taking place beneath these rugs that Moonie and the three chicks are playing most enthusiastically upon each others' pleasure domes and do not need or desire any assistance from Karl and the kicker. Naturally, it is extremely damaging to the actor's ego to see that he is rejected in this way, and Karl does not care to watch Moonie at work a moment longer. But, just as he is trying to creep away, Moonie's tousled and mischievous head bobs up from between an odd pair of legs:

"Morning, Karl, dear boy. How about a spot of something to eat . . ." then, realising the irony of this statement, he adds cheekily: "Or at least a cup of tea to go with this delicious breakfast." Then, with an evil wink, he resumes the kipper feast.

This Karl is the recipient of many Moon pranks. For example, shortly after his night with the pro kicker, he finds himself being chased around the Blue Boar motorway restaurant—with Moonie, stark naked, doing the chasing in a very fearsome and realistic way, shouting all the while:

"You're a fucking queer! You're bent! Just wait till I catch you, you fucking poove!" There is nothing too remarkable about this chasing and hollering, I suppose, except that it all takes place in broad daylight with a large audience of convent schoolgirls whose nuns are pausing at the Blue Boar for an innocent spot of lunch before resuming their journey northward.

Unlike many of Moonie's entourage, Karl at least tries to buy his round of medicine, though it is one of those strange contradictions that Moonie is rarely able to accept such offers and will rather stand the bill himself. One time, I find myself in company with Moonie and Karl in Manchester, which is a miserable sort of Northern city whose only saving grace is the fact that it is raining just about all the time. This means that there is no reason to stray very far from the comfort and warmth of the nearest bar or pub. But, in fairness to Manchester, it should be added that the city has many quite reasonable clubs and discos and one of these, Slack Alice's, belongs to George Best, who is once rated as a handy man with his feet. It is really quite surprising how many Irish folk arrive in this country and commence to earn a living playing some sort of sport, but maybe this stems from centuries of practice at skipping about the bogs while the great British army hurls musket balls and hand grenades at them. At this time, there is an incipient romantic connection between Best and Lulu the miniature Scottish rock and roller and also present in Slack Alice's is Dave Edmunds, who is highly skilled in the art of entertaining himself and his public. Moonie and Edmunds become mates while filming *Stardust* and because they are both dedicated to the perfection of medical science they cause the director of this movie no end of bother, what with being so pissed that they cannot remember where they are meant to be, or even who they are meant to be. Such amnesia is exacerbated by a game played between Moonie, Edmunds and Karl. One night, during an intensive course of Courvoisier, they decide that they are dissatisfied with their film names and wish to be called Alvin Avalanche, Jet Powers and Deep Rivers. On set the next day, Moonie and Karl forget about this agreement, though Dave Edmunds remembers. When Michael Apted, the director of the movie, says something to Dave he finds that he is completely ignored.

"Dave?" he says. "Dave! What's the matter with you?"

"My name," replies Dave, "is Jet Powers. If you wish to speak to me, kindly remember that that is my name. Jet Powers."

"Ah, come on, man. Don't piss about."

"Jet Powers," says Dave quite adamantly. "But you may call me Jet."

So Apted is forced to call Dave Jet whenever he needs to communicate with him. This episode only reminds Moonie and Karl that they are supposed to be Alvin Avalanche and Deep Rivers and the scene is repeated with them. By this time, Apted rightly assesses that the cause of his stars' attitude toward him is none other than the demon alcohol and he bans same substance from the set.

This causes the make-up girls no end of problems on account of the difficulty in matching the pre-ban facial colours to the post-ban colours and there are also many occasions when the camera operator is convinced that his apparatus is faulty and that there is a great deal of camera shakes going on when what is really going on is a great deal of Moonie and Dave Edmunds shake. This leads me to believe that what they need is a couple of crates of Lucozade, the well-known convalescence drink that comes wrapped and sealed in orange cellophane. When I appear on set with the Lucozade, Apted is delighted, believing that at last, when it comes to controlling Moonie and Edmunds, he has an ally.

"Very good, Dougal," he comments. "Thank you very much." I turn to Keith and hand him one of the sealed bottles and although he looks a touch surprised, he knows me well enough to unscrew the top and take a good swig. He too says:

"Very good, Dougal. Thank you very much." But of course

he does not let on that the Lucozade is in fact a strong mixture of brandy and ginger, which is exactly the same colour as Lucozade, and is much more efficacious in restoring life to such as Moonie. I overcome the problem of the cellophane seal by paying the geezer in the shop a few quid to empty out the refreshing convalescence drink and refill and reseal the bottles in a convincing manner. Edmunds grows especially fond of this Lucozade and it keeps him very quiet indeed.

However, this is an extremely large digression from Slack Alice's which is what I start out trying to tell you about. Well, Moonie, Edmunds, Karl and I are only in Slack Alice's on account of being thrown out of the Manchester Playboy Club, and the reason we are thrown out of the Playboy Club is that Moonie has so much medicine on board that he suddenly takes it into his head that the bunnies there are real bunnies. He commences to spear them with his eating fork and to throw knives at them. This is considered very out of order, especially as Keith's professional experience with drumsticks means that he is highly effective at short range with eating forks and knives, and these bunnies are suffering considerable damage to their bottoms.

As I say, Karl is the sort of geezer who wishes to pay his own way, and this week he has his entire week's wages on his person, which amounts to the grand total of £120. Now £120, though it is not exactly peanuts, is not a great deal of money when it comes to funding an evening out. But all through the evening, first at the Playboy and now at Slack Alice's, Karl is going on as how this time he wishes to pay the bill.

"Right, Dougal," says Moonie. "If he wants to pay the fucking bill, he can pay the fucking bill." He turns to one of the waiters.

"Champagne, dear boy. Over here. Dom Perignon. Four bottles to start with."

Up comes the champagne. Keith grabs hold of the first couple of bottles, fizzes them up and attacks everyone else at the table. Well, to cut a long story short, there's champagne all over the place and it's not long before Lulu disappears out of range, shouting:

"You're all bloody mad!"

By the end of the evening, Karl comes up to me, the bill for all the damage shaking in his hand.

"Here, Dougal," he says, looking round to see if Keith can hear. "You couldn't lend me a few quid, could you?"

The point of this diversion from the subject of Moonie and bints is that whereas we are all instructed from an early age that to pull a bird requires that she gets much attention and is generally made to feel wanted by the puller, this is not what Moonie does, because just about every time that Moonie is out and about there is so much chaos and mayhem going on that no bint will be able to think that she is the centre of attention or that she is wanted much. Indeed, unless she is fairly thick skinned she will feel completely surplus to requirements until, of course, it is time for the pork sword to be exercised. Usually when this time comes, there is someone around who is quite happy to accept the sword. But if there isn't, why then there are always the professionals who can be slipped a fatty.

One day, during the time we are filming *Stardust,* Moonie gets Charlie the driver to take him along to Trader Vic's in London to meet some mates. While everyone is there having a good jolly-up, Moonie feels the inclination to wave the magic wand—or at least to have something standing by in case he wishes to wave the wand later on in the evening. As it happens, there are no bints to hand so Moonie turns to Charlie and orders him to go out and find a couple of hookers. Now Charlie is not a connoisseur when it comes to chicks, and is not very practised at procuring hookers. So when he returns to Trader Vic's, looking quite pleased with himself for succeeding in following his master's orders, he has with him two girls who are by no means satisfactory substitutes for Jane Fonda—or even Henry Fonda, if it comes to that—in the matter of good looks. In fact, what Charlie produces is a matching pair of woofers and when Keith clocks them he says to Charlie:

"Tell you what, Charles, be a good chap and keep them down your end of the table. Have a few drinks."

"Yes, Mr. Moon. Very good, Mr. Moon."

Even Moonie's ardour is somewhat dampened by the presence of these two old dogs, but he does not seem to have the heart to actually give these boots the boot. Instead, he applies himself fervently to the medicine bottle and, for all I know, he is trying to cure his eyesight so that when he next looks at the hookers they will seem more attractive to men. But the cure is not entirely successful and the party decide to move on to Tramp. As everyone is about to leave, Charlie looks up and asks:

"What about these ladies, Mr. Moon?"

Moonie makes no comment on Charlie's generous description but merely answers:

"Bring them along, dear boy."

However, when the party arrives at Tramp, Moonie takes Charlie aside and instructs him to remain in the bar with the hookers while he and his mates have something to eat.

"But Mr. Moon, I can't do that," protests Charlie. "What happens if they want to eat too?"

"Give them some nuts, dear boy. Or possibly a bone." And while Charlie is trying to work this one out, Moonie retires to stuff his gob in the restaurant.

"Pacific prawns, dear boy," Moonie commands the waiter. "And a bottle of champagne." These Pacific prawns are very excellent indeed and Moonie proceeds to consume a considerable number of the exotic shellfish—though not enough to justify his bill which comes to exactly £16,000. Moonie calls the waiter over.

"Sir?" says the waiter, his voice cracking slightly.

"These prawns, dear boy . . ."

"Yes, sir?"

"Gone up a bit haven't they?"

"Oh, yes sir!"

"Appear to be about £400 each, dear boy."

Of course, it turns out that what Moonie is presented with is a bill for his previous visits during the past six months. But even this is not acceptable to Moonie, who demands to see a management figure. For once, however, the management figure proves to be unyielding and will not listen to Moonie's claims that he is a tax exile and is not even in the country during the past six months, let alone in Tramp. Now this is more or less the truth, and the reason for the massive bill is that whenever any member of the rock and roll fraternity visits Tramp at this time, he or she puts his or her bill down to Mr. Moon's account. These are the sort of friends that the rock and roll industry encourages, though I suppose it could be argued that this is only a fair response to the many pranks Moonie plays upon these people.

Well, the bill does not appear to be much of a problem because Moonie just produces a cheque book and draws a cheque on an account that is not in use and has no money whatsoever in it. He signs the cheque with a flourish, adds a huge tip and presents it somewhat airily to the management figure, who grovels appropriately and retires triumphantly to his management lair. Moonie then moves the party on to Harry Nilsson's flat, which is where he is staying, and on the way he picks up Charlie the driver and the two canine hookers. By now, fortunately, the brandies and the champagne achieve a small miracle and the two professionals do not seem to be such a bad prospect after all. At the very worst, they comprise an audience to which Moonie can perform, and so he decides to sing to them. Now Moonie does not possess much of a voice and in this respect he poses no threat to the established stars of rock and pop, but the song he chooses to sing is Harry Nilsson's *My Old Desk* and this requires an anyway halfway decent voice. Consequently, the hookers are not impressed—especially as, unbelievable though it may seem, they do not have the faintest clue who Moonie is, even when it is explained that he is the drummer of The Who. This is because these working girls are heavily into Diana Ross and Tamla Motown.

Eventually, despite the singing, Moonie hauls his tart off to bed and proceeds to take up the services for which she is procured in the first place. And as he avails himself of these services, he pauses every now and then to slip on a different funny mask, so that whereas the chick starts off being screwed by Laurel and Hardy (in quick succession), she ends up having congress with many famous faces of stage and screen. Next morning, when the times comes for Moonie to settle his account with her, she asks for £20, which seems perfectly reasonable but which Moonie claims to be excessive.

"After all, my dear, who else has been fucked by Laurel and Hardy, Buster Keaton, Harold Lloyd, Charlie Chaplin *and* Ben Turpin all in one night?"

But the working girl is insistent and says that despite these favours which Moonie arranges for her, she feels that £20 is a very reasonable price. So, overcoming her protests that she works strictly for cash, Moonie outs with the same cheque book he uses to square away the Tramp account and gives her a dud kite for twenty quid.

She goes away quite happy, though what she says about The Who when this kite bounces higher than the Eiffel Tower, I do not know.

The problem about being on tour is that we are often required to visit places which are only marginally more attractive to us than Belsen and, what is worse, that we arrive in such places knowing no one at all, knowing nothing about their entertainment value and usually at such a time as everything is closed anyway. These are exactly the circumstances under which Moonie and the boys hit Edmonton, Alberta, Canada, one Sunday afternoon.

It may be that Canada is a paradise for fishers, shooters, hikers, campers and other outdoor types, but it is certainly not the world's centre as far as the study of female anatomy or even curative tinctures go. In fact, in these respects Canada is very backward and there are many followers of fashion who will tell you it is no more than a toilet. This view gains much support when we find that, apart from registering us and allowing us to enter our rooms, the hotel is closed down. The bars are locked up tight. There is no room service. On further enquiry we discover, too, that the whole of Edmonton is locked up and that we have as much chance of finding any form of entertainment this Sunday as we do of opening oysters with a bus ticket. However, the one porter on duty in the hotel has a certain look about him and, with the leverage of a fistful of dollars, I pry out of him the information that he personally knows the madame who runs the local massage parlour and that it is just faintly possible, given the price of course, that a small quantity of wine and spirits may be forthcoming. The only problem is that this ferrety porter is a little doubtful about Moonie, and I can see that he is wondering if Moonie will blow away his contact with the massage parlour by abusing the masseuses and, of course, this will greatly lower the porter's future percentages. But it is quite remarkable how hotel porters the world over will trade long-term interests for short-term profits and another fistful of dollars procures the phone number we require.

"Do not fret, dear boy," Moonie says soothingly, "we will explain that we are IBM executives."

When I next see Moonie, he looks about as much like an IBM executive as he does like the Duke of Edinburgh. He is wearing his Noel Coward dressing gown, a pair of flamboyantly patterned shorts, orange flip-flops and an elegant lady's diamanté cigarette holder. Still, for all I know, this is how IBM executives —and maybe even the Duke of Edinburgh—dress when they are at home.

"Dougal, dear boy," Moonie commands, "fetch the champagne."

"What with?" I ask. "I haven't paid the bints yet."

"Then get some money, old chap. Run along to Regis and tell him I want 3,000 dollars."

This Regis is the tour accountant of the time and his second name is BOFF! Well that is what it sounds like and it is quite appropriate for any tour accountant since it is mazuma that provides the muscle needed to boff the many people who require boffing during any Who tour. However, this is only the sound of his name and it may well be it is spelt something like Bough.

"Regis," I say, when I track him down, "Moonie wants 3,000 bucks."

"Does he?" replies Regis, singularly unimpressed. "What does he want 3,000 dollars for? I mean, nothing in this toilet is open." He looks to Bill Curbishley for support, but Bill is an old hand at this game and stays very schtum. Of course I omit to explain to Regis that what we hope will soon be open is six pairs of masseuses' legs, for this is not the sort of argument that impresses tour accountants.

"No," continues Regis as he gains confidence, "tell him he cannot have 3,000 dollars." Even Curbishley agrees that this is a sensible decision. But when I point out that the even more sensible decision will be to let Moonie have the dough on account of it is due him anyway, and he will go raving mad and smash the hotel, and perhaps the town, to pieces, which will cost a lot more than 3,000 dollars, if he does not have his way, then Bill and Regis agree to hand over the necessary.

My next stop is the hotel porter and I swap 800 dollars for a few cases of champagne. Well, that is not entirely true. What I in fact swap 800 dollars for is exactly 400 dollars worth of champagne. But the consolation is that 400 dollars worth of champagne is a lot of champagne—especially as this is not very expensive or high quality champagne and, for all I know, it takes the additional 400 dollars to procure all this liquor in such a toilet as Edmonton, Alberta, Canada, on a Sunday afternoon. The ferrety porter scuttles away with his profit, leaving the champagne to be delivered by a lackey, and I return to Moonie's room. There I find that the six chicks from the massage parlour are arriving. That is the good news. The bad news is that five of them will be front runners at Cruft's the famous dog show, and even the one that stands no chance in the dog show is by no means Miss Alberta, or even Miss Edmonton. However, when Keith points this out, the chicks say:

"Well, what of it? You are not an IBM executive." There is no answer to this and so we settle down to make the best of a bad job and, in fact, it turns out that these masseuse bints, though they will not win any beauty contests, have a considerable sense of fun which becomes even further developed when they discover exactly who Moonie is.

It does not take too long for one entire case of champagne to be poured down the eight gullets present, but all that occurs in the way of action is a long discussion between Moonie and the birds as to the skills of various musicians. But the skills referred to are not the skills you would expect masseuses to be familiar with. No. They are talking about genuine musical skills and the conversation grows very tedious. Personally, I do not think it an economical proposition to invest 800 dollars in six dodgy bimbos just to get a lot of blag about rock music. What Regis Boff will make of this I do not know and, furthermore, I do not care to be in his vicinity if he ever finds out, for such a terrible waste of hard-earned dollars will surely cause him to live up to his name and commence hurling a few knuckle sandwiches and boot pies about.

With these thoughts in mind I retire to my room, faintly miffed that I find myself taking my trousers off to go to bed rather than to exercise the white-eared trouser elephant. But I do not get same trousers much beyond my ankles before the phone rings. It is Moonie.

"Come on, dear boy. Come and join the party. You're really missing something." So I return to what I hope will be an orgy of shocking depravity, but when I get there I find that, although the six birds are now partially undressed, nothing very exciting is showing and Moonie is giving them a right load of bollocks as to how he owns a gas well in Texas and will soon be one of the richest men in the world. Such conversations are not especially sexually arousing to me and I am about to leave once more when I am encouraged to remove my trousers by the fact that the girls are commencing to disrobe completely. *At last,* I think, *this is what I came for.*

It is really amazing how wrong you can be. Despite the fact that all eight of us are as near naked as makes no difference, no congress or union takes place whatsoever. Instead what comes off is a giant pillow fight with much giggling and shrieking and feathers flying about all over the place. It seems that all the chicks want is a few laughs. It is not clear whether this is because they take one look at Moonie's cricket set and do not wish to play with it, or whether it is because today is Sunday and Sunday is a day of rest even for Canadian masseuses. Whatever the reason, Moonie is perfectly happy with the situation, and if he is happy, why that is fine by everyone else because he is footing the bill. But now that the room is virtually destroyed and there are feathers all over the place and the pillows with which we are conducting the pillow fight are little more than empty pillow cases, there is very little to keep me here. So I retrieve my trousers from the debris, fix them about my person and retire to my room for some kip.

Once again the phone rings. *Sod it.*

"What is it now?"

"My dear boy, you cannot desert me in the middle of all this champagne. And, anyway, you're missing all the fun." This speech is punctuated by an extremely loud *crash* and I remember that at least part of my job is to try to keep Moonie out of trouble. So I heave on my trousers once more, all the while thinking that this up and down action must be wearing the material out and that I must request Regis to provide me additional allowance for replacement kecks. Back in Keith's room I find that the party is going on much as before; the feathers are still flying; everyone is still naked; the champagne is still pouring from the bottles and down everyone's throats; and Moonie is trying to fit the empty bottles up the masseuses' bottoms. But the masseuses do not wish to be fitted with empty champagne bottles, so it is time for another Moon diversion.

On this particular tour Moonie has a special bodyguard, a gigantic American front wheeler who is an ex-cop and built like a nuclear bomb-proof shithouse. It is not just that you can see the rivets that join him together, but that these rivets are reinforced by shipbuilding gauge welding. He makes the Incredible Hulk look like Pinocchio's hairdresser. His name is Isadore and this is his first rock and roll tour. He is originally requested to leave the Chicago police force on account of transporting a suspected mugger from the point of arrest to the police station inside the glove compartment of the patrol car.

You must remember that the background to what happens next is a hotel room that is one hundred per cent totalled and is knee deep in feathers to boot. There are empty, half-empty and broken champagne bottles littered around. The bed is collapsed. The curtains are in shreds. Every item of furniture in the room is either overturned or shattered. The girls are naked and coated in feathers. Moonie is naked, and the only reason that feathers do not cover his entire body is that they are rinsed off here and there by champagne. It is at this stage that I phone Isadore.

"Isadore? Isadore, is that you?" I demand, making as if I'm at panic stations.

"Yeah?" he replies. "Dougal?"

"Listen, man, you better get up here. I mean, right now! Moonie's gone raving. He's . . . Christ . . . for fuck's sake get up here. He's raped a chambermaid. I think she's dead, man. There's blood coming out of her mouth. Oh . . . He's done her in, man." And then I commence to sob and while this sobbing will not win any Oscars it is certainly effective enough to bring Isadore up to the room double geschvinn. He smashes through the door and there is the entire ghastly scene spread before him. The girl lying, legs spraddled, tomato ketchup all over her face. Moonie curled up in one corner banging his head against the wall and moaning to himself. Me and five other girls hysterical and sobbing.

"Jesus fucking Kerrist!!!" breathes this Isadore as he takes in the scene, and about three gallons of blood drains away from

his face, leaving it white and agonised. Just as he totters forward and seems about to faint, Moonie springs up from the
corner and addresses the girls, who miraculously cease to be
hysterical.

"Ah, girls, this is Isadore my bodyguard. I pay him 300 dollars a week and all he can eat. He's not a bad bodyguard. One
of the better ones, aren't you dear boy? He does anything I
ask him. Isadore!" Jaw trembling in amazement, Isadore faces
Moonie.

"Isadore," continues Keith, indicating his feather-encrusted
wanger. "I want you to do something for me. Pick these feathers
off me, there's a good chap."

"Ohhhhh, Gaaaaaaaad, Keith. I mean, you're having me on?
Like, this has got to be some kind of joke . . . ?"

With that he staggers out and we do not see him for a very,
very long time.

This little piece of theatre appears to bring things to a close
and, as I am finally convinced that there will be no third leg
exercises tonight, I heave up my trousers for the last time and
head for my own room and bed. I suppose that my years with
Keith must soften my brains and that if I am thinking straight
I must realise that the totalled hotel room, not to mention the
feathers, will cause aggravation with the hotel management
and that such aggravation will prevent a full night's kip. But,
blissfully unaware of what is to follow, I hit the hay and am
both surprised and hurt to be woken at seven a.m. the next
morning, only for the management to demand some explanations.

It transpires that the cleaners are most perplexed by a dense
trail of feathers that leads from Moonie's bedroom door, down
the corridor and on to the iced water machine. My explanation
is quick, but possibly not very convincing.

"Ah," I say. "Well, what happened was . . . Keith wanted
another pillow, otherwise he gets a stiff neck. When he's sleeping . . . know what I mean? Anyway, this pillow split as he
was getting it out of the cupboard and, obviously, someone must
have walked on the split feathers. He probably wanted a drink

of water during the night, you see . . ." Believable or not, at least this spiel gives me time to nip into Keith's room and hang a DO NOT DISTURB sign on the door. This gives me just a few moments to try and do something about the mess, but as I look around me I realise that this is a hopeless case. I might as well volunteer to clean out an elephant's cage with a teaspoon. The stink of dead champagne is overwhelming and, if anything, there are more feathers about than ever before, and feathers are very difficult items to clear up—especially if you open all the windows to try and clear the champagne stink from the room. Just as I am about to sink into despairing inactivity, there is a loud banging on the door. The cleaner wishes to know what the hell is going on and it is only with great difficulty that I prevent the Amazonian bint from forcing her way in.

I lean back against the door after winning this brief struggle, and then the phone rings. It is Bill Curbishley.

"Dougal? For Christ's sake get him out of there. The manager's going fucking mad and everyone along the corridor is complaining."

Well, there is absolutely no chance of getting Keith to help me—or even to help himself—in much of a hurry. He is completely wrecked. The average corpse will look very lively indeed in comparison, and it is a great piece of luck that no morticians see him in this state or they will cremate him immediately. His eyes are like pissholes in the snow and it is perfectly clear that he has no idea whether he is coming or going to Timbuctoo or is taking a Red Rover from Shepherds Bush.

Of course, there is no way that I can beat the manager's deadline, even though I manage to pack him up—and all his gear—and get him out of the room and into the corridor. The manager turns out to be one of those tough and very businesslike women who, when she sees the state Keith is in and his effect upon her rooms, exclaims:

"Jesus holy Christ!" and is ready to call the Mounties. Now I once see a movie in which these Mounties feature and it seems from this movie that Mounties are very no-nonsense guys such as always get their man—and even if it is not the right man, they are liable to boff you upon the crust as soon as look at you and shove you in the nearest nick for an indefinite period of time. What is more, they travel about on horses and it is well known that horses are savage and unpredictable creatures that will give you a quick nip and shit on your foot with no provocation whatsoever. It is clear, therefore that the time arrives for some very rapid talking and as Moonie is unable to say "one-two-three" this rapid diplomatic spiel is down to me. So I speak to the large and tough-looking bint as follows:

"Listen, I know what you're thinking, but it's a bit out of order to call in the Mounties isn't it? I mean by the time they're here and making enquiries all over the place, it's not going to do this hotel's reputation much good, is it? And anyway, think how much of your valuable time is going to be taken up—time which I'm sure you'd prefer to spend running the place, which, incidentally, is most definitely one of the best gaffs I've ever stayed in." But she does not seem to be too impressed until I add:

"Perhaps, taken all in all, and under the circumstances, it might be best if I remove Mr. Moon from the premises. Now. Immediately. Forthwith. If not sooner."

She gives off a look which will melt armour plating at one hundred yards and she says:

"Five minutes. That's how long you've got to get the little bastard out of here. Five minutes. And I want all the damage paid for. In cash. Now. And no one gets out of here until I've got the money." The long and the short of it is that I nip off and tell Regis what gives and, sighing in a really quite pitiful way, he dips into the coffers. I commence the Herculean task of dragging Moonie out of his room, down the corridor, into the lobby and, eventually, out the hotel. All the while he makes such helpful comments as:

"Ooooooooorrrrruuuuuuugggggghhhhh," and "Eeeeeeeeeaaaaaaaaa-iiiiihhhhhhh."

Several times he clings to various of the hotel's appendages and refuses to be budged an inch. But when this happens I simply point out that if we do not get the hell out of it we will all be arrested by the Mounties, placed in the pokey and the concert will be screwed up so that we will have no moolaw with which to spring ourselves.

Fnally we arrive at the airport, where we are forced to kip like a couple of winos. Moonie, of course, is spark out and it will make no difference whether he is lying upon a bed of nails or in a four-poster in Buckingham Palace. But this occurrence makes me reflect upon the human condition in general and, in particular, upon the condition of one Keith Moon and his sidekick P. "Dougal" Butler. He is supposed to be a rich and famous rock and roll star and I am supposed to be his faithful Sancho Panza. Nevertheless, here we are, stretched out on benches in an airport and attracting many suspicious glances from one and all. If we are not careful we will be turfed out of here too.

I keep recalling that the evening only starts out as a simple expedition, a search for reasonable quantities of medicine and a slice or two of fur pie. But, with Moonie, things often turn out this way. Getting laid is frequently an afterthought, simply a part of the general process of mayhem. As far as Moonie is concerned Germaine Greer and the feminist movement do not exist. Women are there for his entertainment—and then only when he demands such entertainment. Moreover, he makes little distinction between hookers and any other type of bint. Often, indeed, he prefers the uncomplicated hooker system as it does not intrude upon his private life or interfere with the vital business of having fun. Hookers do not often ask:

"Do you love me?" or "When are you going to fix the fridge?"

Of course, what with things the way they are in rock and roll, it is not often that one such as Moonie has to score with a hooker. There are many amateur talent shows to judge. Hookers are just more extreme.

Sometimes.

One of those sometimes involves six chicks from a massage parlour and the action takes place in an Indian restaurant. British rock musicians tend to develop a taste for Indian dishes early on in their careers because, in Britain, the local Indian restaurant is liable to be the only place still serving food after eleven o'clock. Moonie is partial to the occasional vindaloo and one night we make a thorough search hoping to discover a kosher, British-type Indian restaurant.

Sure enough, we discover a little gaff and there we spend a most pleasant few hours putting away the chicken vindaloo and striking up an acquaintance with the owner. It turns out that he is from Calcutta by way of Bradford, England, and when he discovers we are English he commences to yak on about the British, the English, the Empire and one thing and another. We all grow quite nostalgic and what with Moonie putting on a bravura Noel Coward and generally coming on like the last of the sahibs, the owner is eating out of our hands in no time at all. Moonie is a bit naughty with him, what with the sort of blag that reads like this:

"Of course, dear boy, I'm thinking of opening a place like this myself. In Malibu, Plenty of custom there, don't you know. English expatriates and such. Naturally, we'll need a partner. Someone who knows the ropes . . ."

"But . . . but . . . but . . ." gasps the owner in his caricature Peter Sellers accent that sounds halfway between a Welsh lunatic and a small motorboat. (Bradford, England, which has more Indians in it than Calcutta and Bombay put together, is reckoned to be the centre of the world's motor boat industry. This is on account of all you can hear in Bradford, England is: "But . . . but . . . but . . . but . . . but . . . but . . . but . . . but . . . but . . . but . . . but . . . but . . . but . . .")

"Then, of course," continues Moonie, "there are all the special functions one holds. I do think that Indian delicacies go down so well, don't you, Dougal, dear boy? Yessss . . . all we really need is the right partner . . ."

Later we take it on the toes with many salaams from the owner and the next night, bent on pleasures below the stomach, Moonie instructs me to call up a handful of hookers on the eau de cologne. So I phone the local massage parlour and order six of the best from the madame. I also tell her that we will be down to collect our order shortly. Unfortunately, when we arrive at the joint, we discover that our order seems to include more than a couple of woofers—but then this is so often the case and at least there is one good-looker amongst this lot. Moreover, they are a jolly bunch and they do at least recognise Moonie immediately, which puts him in a good mood. In fact, it puts him in such a good mood that instead of carting them all back to the hotel and revving up the beef torpedo, he decides to take them all out to dinner first. He also decides that as not many American bints ever savour the delights of Indian cuisine, it will be a pleasant change for them to try a tandoori or two.

It is closing time when we get there, but the owner is over-joyed to see us.

"But . . . but . . . but . . ." he says, and there are warm handshakes all round. We sit down around a large table and commence to nibble a bit of this and a bit of that. The birds are giggling away and trying out the various delights, while Moonie and I get stuck into some serious guzzling. Everything is hunky-dory and, by the time we are round to the mangoes and ice-cream, everyone else has taken it on the lammer and we are entirely alone. Moonie turns to me and says:

"Well, dear boy, I believe it is time for the cabaret. But first we must make sure that everyone is in the right mood for the entertainment to follow." With that he whips out a large bag of coke and tips the contents onto a clean plate.

"Brings us nine straws!" he calls to the owner.

"But . . . but . . . but . . . certainly, Mr. Moon!" He does not know what the hell is going on but there is electricity in the air. He susses that something will come off and that it will be something to remember. So he brings us the straws and I,

Moonie and the chicks commence to invigorate our hooters forthwith. The owner watches with great interest and, when Moonie offers him the ninth straw, he hedges somewhat. However, he soon sucks up a snootful and then nothing will stop him. He becomes so enthusiastic that we have to restrain him from hoovering up the entire plateful.

"But . . . but . . . but . . . Mr. Moon, you are certainly jolly good fellow! I am not meeting such a jolly good fellow as you in many a long time! I am thinking that whatever it is we are putting up our noses, it is a wonderful cure for many ailments—especially sadness of any kind. Is this not so?"

"And now," says Moonie," the very act you have been waiting for! The star turn! The climax of our show! Six volunteers from the audience, please! Six pretty girls! Well, six girls anyway. You six . . ." he indicates the six chicks who, of course, are further out of it than Mars. They giggle, wondering what it is they have to do. Moonie moves them over to the bar counter and he sits them up along the counter like half a dozen sparrows on a phone wire. Then he moves down the row instructing each bint to take her knickers off, to pull up her skirt and open up her legs. The owner's eyes are out like crabs' eyes, rolling about and rotating at lightning speed. His mouth is slightly parted and he is whispering to himself:

"But . . . but . . . but . . ." He is one hundred per cent dumbfounded.

Moonie now launches into a spiel such as magician and illusionists make before their acts:

"And now for your delectation and delight, the one and only, the great, the astonishing, the *astounding* Moonio will perform his world famous multi-clitoral stimulation—before your very eyes *and entirely without a safety net!*"

Next thing anyone knows, he dives into the first hooker's beaver pie and nibbles away. Then he passes on down the line, getting faster and faster all the while, just like one of those geezers who put up a whole row of spinning plates on stalks and then keeps them going for all he is worth. The bints, in fairness to them, cooperate in a most delightful manner—though it is true that they are more than somewhat glazed on account of the snorting that takes place beforehand.

The owner is practically a basket case by now. The *but* . . . *but* . . . *but's* have changed to:

"Oh blimey . . . oh blimey . . . oh blimey!" and they are issuing forth like machine gun fire. He is shaking his head . . . nodding his head . . . shaking his head . . . covering his eyes . . . peeping out from between his fingers . . . tugging at his ear . . . twitching his nose . . . blinking . . . stuttering . . . *twitching all over!* When Moonie suddenly looks up from between one set of thighs and offers the entire row to him, just like anyone else would offer a child a boiled sweet, he looks like he is going to explode all over the restaurant.

"Oh Mr. Moon! Oh Mr. Moon! Oh Mr. Moon . . . These are jolly fine girls! these are most *wonderful* ladies! You are jolly dashing fellow! But . . . but . . . Oh blimey!"

"What?" says Moonie. "Come on, dear boy, be my guest."

"But . . . but . . . but, Mr. Moon!" wails the owner. "*My wife! My wife!* Oh, my God, MY WIFE! She is coming back here soon and, oh, my God, Mr. Moon, she is undoubtedly not understanding. Oh blimey, no. She is not realising that this is the sport of the Raj. Oh, Mr. Moon, quite simply she will beat the living daylights out of my poor body if she sees me attempting this *wonderful* act of magic upon these *delightful* young ladies."

To make a long story short, we decide that he is such an obliging and nice geezer that the fairest thing we can do is to vacate his restaurant before his terrible Mrs. arrives on the scene and gives him a good seeing to. So we leave, waving a cheery goodbye. His last words to us are:

"Come back tomorrow, Mr. Moon! Oh please come back tomorrow! My wife will be away and we can have *wonderful* time with your ladies! Wonderful time. Oh, blimey, Mr. Moon, please, please come back tomorrow!"

But of course we never do.

What we do is to set the chicks free. This is a great surprise to me—not to mention a great blow—for I am all in favour of schlepping them back to the hotel to explore their naughty bits. But Moonie just hails a cab, piles the bints into it and when I protest, he laughs.

"Ah fuck it, Dougal. We've had a laugh. Let's call it a night."

The truth of it is that much of the time he just can't be bothered—just like the time he takes a chick back to Tara House to screw her. This is a chick who is crazy about Moonie and will do anything for him, including ski down Everest with a carnation in her earhole. Moonie never gives her even the time of day, so that when he suddenly rounds on her in The Speakeasy and tells her that if she comes home with him he will wield the bacon assegai, she virtually comes on the spot. As Kim is in the house, I have to surrender my room for the exercise, but when I nip back there later, for my cigarettes or something, I find the bint up and getting her kecks on. What happens is that Moonie climbs aboard, makes a feeble stab with the assegai, then falls asleep!

Maybe this indifference is on account of the fact that he scores with more women than anyone I ever meet. Among these girls are some shattering examples and, of course, there are also several who will make a fair showing at Crufts. He is not a Casanova. Not is he the sort of geezer who is so into himself that he must screw anything that moves just to prove what an all up guy he is. There are many pricks in the rock business like this, and Moonie is certainly not one of them. He does not take himself seriously enough to care whether he scores or what he scores with. His attitude may in many respects be callous and offensive, but it contrasts strangely with his basically very loving and generous nature.

My view is that in the long run any relationship that includes Moonie, casual or serious is inevitably one-sided. It must be on his terms. But, of course, whatever the feminists say, there are many bints who are happy to accept such terms. And probably many geezers too.

Possibly it is this take-it-or-leave-it attitude which makes Moonie attractive to women in the first place. For very many of them he appears to exert an irresistible attraction. And this attraction is not confined to those that wish to tamper with Moonie's cricket set. The best example that I can think of, of bints who have no interest in Moonies' chopper but wish to get to him, is the case of the Manson Girls. Now I do not know how many of you remember Charlie Manson and his Family of murderers but he is put away for a very long time. What happens is that plenty of dippy chicks—and not a few guys—continue to follow Manson like he is Jesus Christ and they are his apostles.

What's weird about this is that the chicks really are into Manson and the whole schmeer. Like they burn with the fire and they're all very, very serious and heavy. If they look at you like you're ready for conversion, then you better watch out because they mean Business with a very heavy B. It scares the Hell out of me, I can tell you, and in my time looking out for Moonie I see some pretty freaky things.

Now Moonie is like a candle to these Manson moths. I mean, they know all about his reputation—the booze, the women, the dope, the completely outrageous things he does—and they want him for a prophet to put on the mantelplace alongside Manson. And that's OK by me except that I have to spend so much time with Moonie, and if these chicks are traipsing after Moonie, they're also traipsing after me and that is a real piss-off.

Now you might expect that Moonie would like all this Black Magic and devilry being attached to him. But no, he hates it. It scares him shitless—and guess who has to keep it all away from him.

Yeah. Right in one. Me.

The first time these weirdos latch on to Moonie is on one of the later West Coast tours, and the place they do it is San Diego.

As long as I live, I can't forget the way these bints look. There's between three and six of them at any one time and they all dress in exactly the same cheap and bright red dresses. But the freaky thing is that they all look exactly the same. OK so one's taller than another. One's darker than another. One's got bigger tits than another. And one's fatter than another. But they all *look* exactly the same.

At San Diego, of course, we don't know that these chicks are Manson followers and we just figure them for another handful of freaks just like all the other freaks that lurk about rock bands. They even come backstage. But they don't want to screw or booze, or drop anything, or shoot up, or snort or . . . anything. They just stand and stare at Moonie and he really does hate all that. Which, again, is hardly surprising because Moonie is more wasted than Bikini atoll and is probably having a lot of trouble with working out exactly how many chicks in red are staring at him with exactly how many burning eyes.

Anyway, we all leave this gig and move on to the next one which is in San Francisco.

Now you must remember that there is some mileage between these two locations and, being the world famous and extremely rich Who rock band, we do not cover this mileage in any old charabanc. No, what we do is take a private jet from one to the other—and very nice it is too, what with plenty of champagne, not much less brandy and half a dozen pairs of legs wrapped around here and there. When we get to San Francisco, the first thing Moonie wants to do is get down to the massage parlour to see what local talent is available for immediate fornication. The lady that runs the parlour—at least I assume she is a lady despite a day or so's growth on her chin and forearms like George Chuvalo the Canadian heavyweight—lays on a choice. And pretty fair these ladies are. Pretty tasty, that is, in soft focus and not too many questions as to pedigree and track record and so on and so forth.

But they are certainly tasty enough for us not to be able to choose between them and to tell the massage parlour governor to send all of them up to the hotel.

So when they arrive at our suite we open a few bottles of California champagne and start on a bit of a jolly-up and I have to admit that all massagers appear quite hot to trot and well up to anything that seems to be well up to itself.

But, just as I'm about to loose off a few with two of these chicks in attendance, there's a knocking at the door and, like the born sucker I am, I go and open it.

Stone me but who should be standing there but the Manson girls in their red dresses, with all that heavy staring. What's more they've got a load of Tarot cards with them and copies of the Bible. Well, if that isn't too heavy for you, what is? Now under these circumstances the best thing to do is to call up the hotel security people and have these scary bints hurled out into the street and further if possible. Which is exactly what I do. But the whole episode does make me sit up and think a bit—which in turn makes the massage parlour girls ask me if I'm gay or something and do I want to get it up or not? And if not, is there anyone around who does? But even while I'm in there making like a good hetero lad and showing a bit of flag for the Old Country, I'm thinking to myself:

How the hell do these chicks get the bread to fly from San Diego to San Francisco and turn up at the hotel only an hour or so behind us?

After we play the gig at San Francisco, the next stop is Oakland and, as usual after the gig, we have a bit of a jolly-up, this one in the dressing room, which happens to be a fair size and relatively pleasant. Well, I'm standing close to the door when there's this terrible battering on it and no matter how hard I try I cannot kick this habit of opening doors. Now this is too much—there are the same Manson girls, standing and staring, and before I can recover my equilibrium, or even my balance, they start rapping on as how Keith and the band should join the Manson sect and follow the devil and all that caper. Of course I have them thrown out, but answer me this: how do they keep getting through the lines of heavy security muscle that surrounds the famous Who rock band at all times of day or night?

Moonie is well freaked by these spooky ladies. I mean, he really hates it but, fortunately, I can tell him to relax because the next gig is in Portland, Oregon, and there's no way these bints can turn up there.

Right?

Wrong!

I'm first off the airplane and down the gangway and into the service area and who do you think is waiting there?

Six look-alike chicks in cheap red dresses.

Now, of course, it is just possible that after we see them in Oakland and chuck them out they make for the airport and catch the first plane to Portland. I concede that this is entirely possible. Also it may be that they have the dough to do this. Nevertheless it is pretty freaky to find these birds actually at the airport and waiting for us to get off the plane.

Moonie? Well Moonie completely shits himself.

I mean, I can't do anything about getting rid of these bints at the airport. They're not doing anything out of order. Staring fixedly at rock stars is all part of the airport scene. I hustle Moonie out of there double quick, into the limo and straight to the hotel.

There's no sign of the bints at the hotel and after a few brandies Moonie and me begin to relax and enjoy ourselves. After all, when I say that Moonie shits himself on seeing these freaks, I have to point out that there is a very strong possibility that my own underwear may also become besmirched. What is this world coming to, I ask myself, when half a dozen daft looking birds can transport themselves around the country as quick as Superman on bennies?

Later, we do the gig—a good one, as it happens—and after a few bevvies we decide on an early night for once, because we are both well knackered. So we get back to the hotel in the limo, zip into the reception area and call up a lift to take us to the suite, where we have a well-stocked bar. What's more, just in case you feel we may be taking this early night game a little too far, we have with us a couple of birds we dragged off from the gig. I mean, let's face it, there's early nights and early nights.

While we're standing around at the elevator doors, giggling and doing a little of that off-hand groping, the lift arrives, the doors slide open and I can't believe my eyes. It's the Manson girls and they immediately start up with all this caterwauling and waving Bibles and Tarot cards around, imploring Moonie to join the act, making such suggestions as:

"Charlie is the sun and you will be the Moon." Very good, I think to myself.

Moonie leaps back like a kangaroo with a hot stone in its pouch, grabs the chicks from the gig, which proves that he sometimes gets his priorities right, jumps into another elevator that just arrives, and screams at me:

"Get rid of them! Get rid of them!"

So what I do is get round to hotel security. Three huge geezers appear and ask me what's the matter and I tell them that Moonie is being pestered by some freaky Manson followers and the best thing to do is track same followers down and evict them into the street before something nasty comes off in this expensive and luxurious hotel.

It seems that these huge geezers must hear my voice above the knocking of my knees and I must say that one advantage of being on the road with a giant band like The Who is that money talks. I mean, these same security guys must hate everything that we stand for, what with having to sort out seven types of mayhem wherever they come across a band like this, but what they do know for sure is that we do have dough and plenty of it. And what this dough means is that we've got muscle. So when I tell them that they should find these chicks and deport them from the hotel, they're off like a couple of rats up a drainpipe.

Once I organise this violence, I go off up to the suite hoping to catch up on the groping and poking that I know must be occurring. But when I get there all I find is the chicks we bring over from the concert and, although they seem to be quite happy guzzling the champagne and stuffing coke up their hooters, they also seem to be somewhat surprised that they are getting all this luxury behaviour without the world famous rock star and his personal getting into their bodies as much as possible. And I realise that if we do not get into these bodies in the near future, these bodies are liable to do a legger and take off on account of no one is taking any notice of them.

And just while I'm thinking this, the phone rings. So, of course, I answer it and who is it but hotel security again.

"Mr. Butler," the man says, "we got rid of the chicks from upstairs, but there's one down here who seems really weird. I means she's just sitting here and moaning and groaning. You'd better get down here, sir." And when I arrive downstairs the security man takes me by the arm and walks me over to the lounge area where this Manson chick is sitting, back to us, in a kind of red coat with a hood over it, and this chick is making a noise as follows, very low and sinister:

"Ooooooooooommmmmm. AAAaaaaaaahhhnnnn."

And although I have to say that momentarily I find this apparition very scary, I recall something in the back of my mind that makes me go up to the figure and prod it quite severely in the back. I have to admit, however, that I stand well back while doing the prodding.

The figure turns round, the hood falls down from its head and there it is—Moonie.

"Ah, dear boy," he exclaims, "got rid of them, have you? We'd better get up there and wield the pork sword, what?"

The security man is looking pretty well bemused and I expect I'm looking well relieved myself. Certainly I feel quite proud that I remember from way back that one time in London Moonie buys himself a very tasty red velvet dressing gown complete with hood.

Well, that is all there is to the Manson girls story—except for one more appearance. It happens when we're on a gig in Edmonton, Alberta, and Moonie gets a call from Annette, who's shacked up in their house on Malibu beach, right next to Steve McQueen's gaff.

What this call says is that there are two birds, all dressed in red and giving her plenty of wounding on the ears about Manson and Moon, kipping under the house. Moonie goes berserk when he hears this, and I have to call the police to have the chicks taken out and shot or whatever else can be done. But apparently even Moonie is not as crazy about this incident as McQueen himself, because McQueen is on the Manson short-list and when he hears as how there are two Manson girls in the house next to his, what does he do?

He shits himself too.

What with one thing and another, these chicks in their cheap red dresses are causing a boom in local Chinese laundries.

Only a few days after this scene we're back in Malibu and staying in the house. The bedrooms in this all-American dream drum are on the ground floor and the living quarters are up above, with a view out over the Pacific like you are in Paradise. This particular night I am well akip in my room, the body only too grateful for a few hours free from abuse, and building up the energy to take care of Moonie over the next few weeks when, all of a sudden, Moonie's in my room and shaking me.

"Hey listen, man," he whispers very violently in my ear, "there's someone up there. You've got to go and see who it is, man."

It just shows how fast akip I am that I next find myself out of bed and picking up a giant size flashlight, with a handle a yard and a half long and full of very heavy dry cells indeed. Certainly, I do not react this enthusiastically to the possibility of danger when I am properly awake.

I turn to Keith and ask him if he calls the police and he

replies that as soon as he hears the noise Annette rings the local cop shop. So we creep toward the stairs and I turn to Moonie and say:

"You go first, man."

"Fuck that," he answers. "*I'm* paying *you. You* go first." There really is no answer to that, so I go first and as I go up the stairs I can see out through one of the big all-American dream aluminium double glazed windows and out there, in the moonlight, is the complete all-American cop scene, with more bogies, cars and Christ knows what all else that you can imagine. I mean it's like someone threatens to hijack the Queen of England and she is in our house. And then from out of nowhere appears this helicopter complete with searchlights.

At this stage I realise that the odds in this encounter are marginally in my favour, so I go on up the stairs, open the door and walk straight into another Manson girl.

I'm so keyed up that all I can do is give her the most violent smack round the head with this combat-duty flashlight and she falls to the deck, spark out, like she's dead.

Of course, I am quite pleased with myself and I go downstairs, throw open the door and—wallop!—before I can say yes, no or thank you there's a huge cop with an even huger shooter, a Magnum automatic, stuck up my hooter—into my left nostril in fact.

"Sheeeeeyitt, man! You're lucky. You nearly got your fuckin' head blown clear off!"

"Oh, man," I whimper, "I was only going to invite you in for a cup of tea."

Act Naturally

If you leave school at sixteen, become a massive rock superstar at seventeen, an international celebrity by the time you're twenty-one and a potential millionaire by the time you're twenty-three, where do you go from there? This decision is made even harder to reach if you are often surrounded by a bunch of grovellers who never disagree with you, especially if they think it might cost them either a quid or two or their place in your entourage, and if every woman—slag or lady, bint or bird—aims herself open-legged at your cricket set before you even have time to shake hands.

In Moonie's case, the answer is to become a movie star and this, of course, is the direction in which he is headed when that great casting director in the sky decides that he has a bit part for him in the greatest epic of all and so pulls his earthly union card. Most people in the movie business agree that Moonie will make a superb character actor in the English Robert Newton/ Oliver Reed style. Moonie's only problem is that he is liable to over-rehearse with the brandy bottle between takes.

There is no question but that the few times that Moonie features amidst the poodle fakers and ponces he turns in very promising performances, but also shows that he does not have the necessary discipline to become a full-time, big-time movie star which is, of course, where such as Oliver Reed score whatever their off-screen records show. The rock business, in its own strange way, is well able to cope with such ill discipline, not least because The Who and most bands of this stature own their own studios and facilities and are more or less in control of the finances. Whenever Keith is due to record, the other members of the band tell him that the session is booked at least four hours earlier than is in fact the case.

"Listen, Keith," they say, "we want to kick off at twelve and we don't want to hang about all fucking afternoon waiting for you." They know that Moonie anyway will be three hours late, and maybe four, so they turn up, along with the engineers and crew, around three and Moonie himself appears between three and four, looking sly and dead chuffed because he thinks he causes the other members of the Who to lurk about waiting for him. Of course, the other three encourage him in this illusion by slagging him off good and proper for turning up late and delaying the proceedings.

This kind of behaviour cannot be tolerated in the movies because every minute lost is another few grand down the pan and the people who finance movies will not put up with this even if the star is the legendary Keith Moon.

"What about Marilyn Monroe and others like her?" you ask. "It is well-known that she is never on time in her professional life and that even when she does manage to reach the right studio she never knows her lines." The answer to this is that Marilyn Monroe and others of this type have their days, by and large, many years ago when the world is a more tolerant place in the matter of throwing ackers about and nowadays, especially in the great British film industry, such profligacy is frowned upon. Even the so-called hell-raisers are usually referred to in terms such as these:

"Oh yes, he/she snorts (or screws/buggers/pops/drinks) but he is very *professional*." By which they mean he/she turns up on time, more or less upright, and more or less familiar with the writer's original lines. Such behaviour seems to cast some doubt as to the degree of degeneracy in question because, to get back to Keith, there is no way that anyone abusing their brains and bodies like Moonie does can actually turn in a regular and professional acting performance on demand. It has to happen on his terms, and there are not many film directors who can handle that as they feel it is a personal affront and very damaging to the ego.

There is another reason why Moonie may never be a highly successful actor. He is not the sort of person who can manage large chunks of Shakespearian verse, or even tracts of Tennessee Williams, no matter how many prompts, idiot boards and cue cards are provided. *Once more unto the breach, dear friends . . .* is liable to become *Once more to Beachy Head, lads, or stop up the brandy bottle.* Furthermore, Keith's personality is such that he will never be able to accept that he is not the star of every movie. As it is, in his brief movie career his presence on screen reduces most of those around him to the role of extras. If, by any chance, he is not recognised as the star on-screen, then Moonie will go to any lengths to ensure that he is the most noticeable person on the set, taking the piss out of his fellow actors, the director, the technicians and anyone else within range.

That'll Be the Day is the first movie to feature Keith Moon. As I previously mention it is all about growing up in England during the nineteen fifties and is quite highly regarded, though it certainly will never feature in any lists of the top ten films of all time. Moonie's role is very small, not much more than a cameo, and he plays the drummer of a struggling rock and roll band. Whenever he is on screen he dominates the proceedings with very little effort, which is not entirely surprising as he does little more than play himself. But it is off the screen and on the set that he really comes into his own because film sets are cluttered up with exactly the right sort of equipment for playing pranks and merry japes.

He arrives in typical style, turning up on location in the Isle of Wight in a helicopter, which in the normal course of events will cause little comment. But Moonie is not content to land at the nearest heliport, or even upon the lawn of the location hotel. He wishes to land on the roof of the hotel, which the architect who designs the hotel never envisages, being as he initiates his drawings around about the time that the Wright Brothers are gawping at our feathered friends and wondering how to emulate same—at least that is the impression this hotel's plumbing gives. Moonie therefore requires me to provide a helipad.

"Dougal, dear boy. Arrange a landing for me. I will be piloting my helicopter and I intend to land on the hotel." Well, Moonie can no more pilot his own helicopter than he can perform brain surgery. But I understand that he wishes to cause an impression by pretending to do his own Red Baron act and who am I to deny him this pleasure? So I do not demur when he commands me thus:

"Make a large cross on the roof of the hotel so that I know which hotel to land on." It occurs to me that the hotel management will object to the entire manoeuvre if it sees me painting whitewashed crosses all over the building, but Moonie has this problem sussed too.

"What you do, dear boy, is collect up a few waiters and get them to make the cross out of tablecloths. Slip them a few quid if you have to." I am in the middle of pointing out that I have roughly five bob on me, and that these waiters are unlikely to accept American Express plastic, when I find that I am speaking to a dialing tone. So I borrow a tenner and slip it to the head Italian, who in turn orders various minion Italians up onto the roof with plenty of second best tablecloths.

It is a most impressive sight when Moonie swoops out of the sky, dead on time—which is a sure sign that it is not Keith doing the piloting. He makes a beeline for the roof, which is quite crowded what with the various Italians standing by to watch and maybe pick up the pieces. I ask myself who is doing all the waiting at the tables below. All proceeds in the approved fashion of the manual of British helicoptering until the chopper is just a few feet above the table linen. Then the wind from the rotor blades causes all this linen to flutter off to the edge of the roof and one of the Italian waiters nearly flutters off with it in his efforts at recovery.

Moonie is delighted with his reception. He is in full Red Baron drag, with furry flying jacket, leather helmet and so on, and does not seem in the slightest fazed by the obvious fact that there is a highly professional chauffeur in the driver's seat and that it is this chauffeur and not Moonie who achieves the perfect landing. Very soon we are all ensconced in the hotel bar and Moonie is already planning ways to enliven the proceedings in this staid Isle of Wight holiday hotel, that is more accustomed to receiving coachloads of distressed gentlefolk than it is to entertaining film crews, actors and their ilk. What he is not doing is learning his lines and when I mention these lines to him, believing that they are essential to the filming, he just waves his hand about and says:

"When you're a natural, dear boy, you don't have to worry about incidentals like learning lines." He has so few lines, anyway, that I figure he will manage OK. Moonie's arrival gives me great pleasure because I am finding that this filming malarky is not all that it is cracked up to be and consists largely of hanging around for hours on end, playing cards and listening to actors cracking on about the time they play Abanazar in panto in Barrow-in-Furness.

Though this hotel is not what you or I would choose, it fancies itself as an "in" place and prides itself on staging such exciting events as dinner dances that feature The Roy Gristle Trio, and exhibitions of art and sculpture by persons who are registered as blind. This particular evening there is a fashion show and while this show will not rival the Spring Collection of Yves St. Laurent, or even the stamp collection of my Uncle

Eric, it does have the advantage of attracting various examples of the local crumpet who are supposed to parade about in naff evening dresses and awful trouser suits for the delectation of the local followers of fashion. The only question that remains to be answered is how do we get amongst this talent?

The etiquette handbooks suggest that the correct method is to stand suavely by the bar, wait until one of the lovelies pops in to wet her whistle, then order up a bottle of champagne and introduce oneself. Moonie, however, has other ideas though he at least starts off by standing by the bar. His attitude, however, is not suave, because he is rapidly very pissed indeed by drinking large quantities of brandy and ginger. From this bar, the fashion caper is just about visible and Moonie is increasingly interested in the bints that parade there. He is a sucker for model bints anyway.

"Dougal," he remarks innocently. "This show needs livening up. What it needs is a guest appearance by someone whose sense of fashion is renowned throughout the civilised world. That is to say, me."

"Listen, man," I reply, indicating his flying outfit, "that may be OK for landing on hotel roofs but it sure as hell isn't the latest thing."

"True. You are quite right, Dougal. What this needs, dear boy, is something a little more risqué. Something with a degree of *je ne sais quoi*."

"Do what?" I exclaim as Moonie struggles out of his flying suit and stands there in a decidedly grubby pair of Y-fronts. Strange. The one thing he seems to prefer to dressing up is jumping about with absolutely no gear on whatsoever.

These Y-fronts look like they are getting on in years even at the retreat from Dunkirk and, indeed, from their appearance they probably witness same retreat. Anyway, they are by no means haute couture even for a toilet like the Isle of Wight. Though I am very entertained by this turn of events, I don't know quite where to look because I can see that many punters present are beginning to give us the peculiar eye.

But the peculiar eye we receive in the bar is nothing to the looks Moonie gets from the local followers of fashion while he is capering about upon the model's catwalk. This capering is performed in conjunction with a pretty little bint who is wearing a nice off-the-shoulder number in pink tulle. Moonie starts to jive with the bird as she is parading up and down the catwalk and she is no little annoyed at the intrusion, especially as Moonie is giving a loud and discordant rendition of *Little Old Lady from Pasadena* all the while.

The point is that when Moonie arrives anywhere—let alone a film set—he is not inclined to behave like Laurence Olivier or, indeed, like any other geezer who is a fair hand at the performance of thespian arts. No, he regards the making of films as one big joke from beginning to end. He is not impressed—even if he knows—that every delay in the schedule, every minute lost, costs the producers many hundreds, and maybe thousands, of pounds. One time, during *That'll Be the Day*, Moonie delays the proceedings by a couple of hours just for the sake of a few more laughs. The director of this film, Claude Whatham, is just about to launch into a take and his assistants are calling for quiet on the set and standby, please, and all the other things that assistants are supposed to call for. The scene he is about to film is set in a dance hall and is complete with a couple of groups and a load of extras who are playing the punters so, one way or another, there are several hundred people and half a billion quids worth of equipment strewn around. In fact, the entire scene is typical of all movie sets where, despite the fact that the great British film industry is about as healthy as the economy of Haiti, it seems to be necessary to have half the population of the world present and unionised before a camera can be switched on. We are told, however, that things are now improving in the great British film industry and that it is no longer compulsory to employ two hairdressers, one of the straight hairs and one for the curly bits.

"Quiet everybody, please. Quiet on the set!"

"Standby."

"First positions, please."

"Quiet . . . *quiet, please!*"

"Turn sound . . . camera . . ."

"THE GERMANS ARE BOMBING NEASDEN . . . AN H-BOMB IS ABOUT TO FALL ON NEASDEN! THIS IS AN OFFICIAL ANNOUNCEMENT: YOU ARE DIRECTED TO GO IMMEDIATELY TO THE NEAREST BOMB SHELTER WITH YOUR GAS MASK: I REPEAT . . ."

"What the fuck?"

". . . YOU MUST WEAR YOUR GAS MASKS AT ALL TIMES . . ."

"Cut! *Cut!* CUT!!!"

Now, of course, this dialogue about the Germans raiding Neasden by air is by no means included in the script of *That'll Be the Day,* and it is especially not intended that these lines should boom out from the speakers on the set. Claude Whatham, who is no thickie, immediately realises what gives here and screams:

"Find the loony! Find that bastard!"

All the minions start running around like chickens without any heads, searching here, there and everywhere for Keith and, although it is quite clear that he is somewhere on the set and is speaking out over the PA equipment, it is not quite so clear exactly where he is located.

"Find him!" screams Claude and the minions scurry even more fervently because Claude's word is God's word on this set and the lucky minion who finds Moonie may also find himself suddenly elevated to Assistant Director's Third Assistant— at least for the rest of the day. Moonie's voice, meanwhile, rants on:

"DO NOT TRY TO FIND ME. I REPEAT: DO NOT TRY TO FIND ME. I HAVE A GATLING GUN AND I WILL NOT HESITATE TO USE IT. I AM ARMED AND EXTREMELY DANGEROUS."

"Find him!" screams Claude.

Scurry, scurry! Rush, rush! Peer, peer! go all the minions, but what with all the equipment and cables lying about the place and all jumbled up like a gigantic spaghetti, looking for a lead that has Moonie on the end of it is like looking for a tadpole in a pot of black paint. Moonie continues over the PA in a very pompous BBC-type announcer's voice:

"YOU WON'T FIND ME. I AM IMPOSSIBLE TO FIND."

"Jesus Christ get that bastard out of here!" rages Claude.

"Yes, Claude. Of course, Claude. Certainly, Claude!"

"IF THERE ARE ANY POLICEMEN HERE, I AM SMOKING A JOINT AND INJECTING HEROIN INTO MY MAIN ARTERY AT THE SAME TIME. EVERYONE ON THIS FILM HAS THE CLAP. AND CRABS. EVERYONE PRESENT IS INSTRUCTED TO REPORT TO THE NEAREST SPECIAL CLINIC. ALL THE GIRLS IN THE ISLE OF WIGHT ARE SLUTS AND HOOKERS AND EVERY ONE OF THEM WILL DROP HER KNICKERS AT THE SLIGHTEST PROVOCATION."

Not only is Claude Whatham going berserk, the female extras are beginning to generate a degree of resentment at Moonie's casting such slurs upon their characters. Moreover, the search and destroy operation that is being mounted to find Moonie is doing plenty of searching and even more destroying of the very expensive sets. Plugs are being unplugged and leads are being unravelled—but still the voice booms on:

"TAKE NO NOTICE OF CLAUDE WHATHAM. HE IS BEING REPLACED BY ANOTHER DIRECTOR. A NEW DIRECTOR IS ON HIS WAY FROM THE LABOUR EXCHANGE AT THIS VERY MOMENT. CLAUDE WHATHAM IS NO LONGER WANTED ON THIS MOVIE BECAUSE HE IS STUFFING THE CASTING DIRECTOR. DON'T DENY THIS, CLAUDE, BECAUSE WE HAVE SEEN YOU . . . WE'VE ACTUALLY WATCHED YOU SCREWING THE CASTING DIRECTOR."

At this stage I am not a little concerned that Claude seems to be tearing his hair out by the handful. Moonie is nowhere in sight and I wonder if, somehow, there is a tape recorder rigged into the system. Eventually, however, someone remembers that some of the speaker cabinets on stage are not real speaker cabinets stuffed with electronics, but are mock-ups which are hollow inside and from one of these dummy cabinets someone traces a tiny and inconspicuous lead. When the back is ripped off this cabinet, there is Moonie, crouching, microphone in hand.

"Tee, hee, hee," he says. "That livened things up a bit, didn't it dear boy?"

Moonie is certainly capable of taking his reach for attention to quite staggering lengths. He is very conscious of his star status and will become very neurotic if he is around anyone he thinks—rightly or wrongly—is getting more public acclaim than him. This tendency is made worse by the fact that even the biggest rock stars, by which I mean musicians playing in rock and roll bands as against pop stars like Cliff Richard or Donna Summer, despite the fact that they may sell millions of records all around the world, are often completely unrecognised by Mrs. Spriggs of 43 Acacia Avenue. She will instantly recognise Cliff Richard because she constantly sees him on telly singing dozey love songs. She also sees him doing guest spots on variety shows and chat shows. But rock and roll musicians do not often take part in these events and, anyway, bands like The Who concentrate more on albums than they do on singles. Led Zeppelin are in a very similar position. They are right up there in the top league of sellers and rock fans everywhere recognise them. Nevertheless, they remain a totally unrecognisable entity as far as the Mrs. Spriggs of this world are concerned. Assuming he is not wearing his attention-getting gear, I dare say that Jimmy Page will be able to wander round London or Los Angeles unmolested by the general public.

The star of *That'll Be the Day* is a young geezer by the name of David Essex and he is, perhaps, a medium star, what with the odd hit record, boyish good looks, a spot of acting here and there, telly appearances and, of course, plenty of do re mi. At the time of the filming he is very hot indeed. His hit record *Rock On* is recently Number One in the UK and the USA. What is more, he has great Mrs. Spriggs-appeal and is on *Top of the Pops* and similar telly shows all the time. Many bints ask him for his autograph, amongst other things, and, indeed, if he is connected to the national grid, this country will have no energy crises. Essex is a fairly straight geezer with all this heat and fame but, inevitably, it does not please Moonie at all. He is very jealous. The way he sees it is that it is bad enough that Essex, and not Moonie, is the star of the movie.

The *Rock On* Number One hit malarkey is the straw that breaks the camel's back.

One day Moonie suddenly bursts in the hotel where the film crew is staying waving a newspaper about and shouting and generally carrying on.

"Hold everything," shouts. "Hold everything, dear boys. I have an announcement to make. I have just become the third richest man in the world." Naturally there are a few comments made along the lines of:

"Oh yeah?" and "Bullshit!" But Moonie is not in the slightest surprised or fazed.

"Yes," he continues. "It's true. Years ago I bought shares in a silver mine in Australia and this mine has just become the hottest thing in the world. As you know, silver is very buoyant at the moment, and this mine has discovered two massive new seams. I am now worth roughly £186 million and I invite you all to celebrate my good fortune. We'll have a party tonight in the hotel and everything's on me. Right?" Well it all goes to show how full of bullshit this entire business is because, despite a few sceptical looks here and there, most everyone raises a cheer and even the sceptical few are convinced when Moonie shows them the newspaper he is waving about. It reads:

ROCK STAR MOON BECOMES BILLIONAIRE OVER-NIGHT.

There is much glad-handing and congratulations all round and, of course, everyone is well into the idea of free booze and a jolly-up even if Moonie has to pay for same out of his granny's Post Office savings.

Come the evening, everyone gathers in the hotel bar and Moonie starts to order up the medicine. At this activity he is one of the all-time greats, the Juan Fangio of drink orderers. Consequently, in no time at all the hotel bar is jammed up with raucous drunkards who very quickly drive the respectable residents out of the hotel. Whoever else is present, there is no question but that Moonie is the star of the show and is in absolutely top form.

Just when things are at their most spectacularly noisy and it seems highly unlikely that the party could become more explosive without detonation actually taking place, the Dubliners enter.

Strictly rock fans may not suss that the Dubliners are an Irish band that sings such songs as *Seven Drunken Nights* and, by all accounts, believe that such songs cannot be sung without personally experiencing these seven drunken nights—preferably at least once a week. The Dubliners are quite surprisingly Irish-looking, what with having large, florid faces and plenty of beard here and there. Most of their music tends to go:

Yiddly-tiddly-diddly-diddly—ah—yiddly-tiddly-diddly ad infinitum (or even ad nauseam if you do not care for this sort of music) and they are a most entertaining act indeed. In fact, the quantity of *yiddly-tiddly* in the Dubliners' act is only exceeded by the amount of medicine that is required to produce any *yiddly-tiddly* whatsoever. In fact, the Dubliners, it is said, are able to consume medicines faster than a coachload of Australians on their way to a test match.

The reason that the Dubliners are at hand is that they are staying in this hotel while they are on tour in the area, and Moonie quickly encourages them to join in with the jolly-up by thrusting large measures into their hands. In very quick time, the Irish geezers out with their instruments and what we have going is a kind of Anglo-Irish jam session. Moonie is playing upon anything that comes to hand and there are accordions, flutes and all sorts of Gaelic-style instruments sounding off. The end result is a bit like something out of the *Muppet Show* but a good time is had by all, except, possibly, by the hotel management and anyone with a built-in aversion to *yiddly-tiddly-diddly-diddly*.

This jollification cheers Moonie up no end but, unhappily, the price for this boost to the ego must eventually be paid and the time to pay is at the crack of lunchtime the next morning. I go to Moonie's room and discover him in tears. And the cause of these tears, which are real and copious, is not so much the pain that is left behind by the medicines of the night before, as by a bill, the size of which will bring tears to the eyes of anyone who is not either J. Paul Getty or A. Khashoggi. Although the first couple of figures on this bill are not very large in themselves, they are followed by an infinite number of zeros and it is these zeros that cause Keith to break down. As bills go, this is interesting, informative and even quite imaginative, as it lists and itemises every single expenditure including things which get damaged, such as occasional tables and fruit bowls, and it stretches four or five yards when laid out.

You may be thinking that a man the newspapers claim to be worth £186 million will not worry too much about his entertainment bills. On the other hand you may be thinking that Moonie is by no means worth the said amount and the newspaper story and his claims are nothing more than a pack of lies. The latter is, of course, the correct interpretation, as I very well know throughout because it is I who has to visit the nearest joke shop in order to get Moonie's story printed up on a dummy newspage.

Moonie is really quite desperate.

"I haven't got any money," he keeps saying. "I can't even pay this fucking bar bill. Why do I do these things, Dougal? Why? I can't understand it." He is really quite broken up and it is one of those occasions when there is not much I can either say or do. Of course the bill will be paid, even if it is me who has to fork out the American Express to do so. Of course he has plenty of dough, even if most of it is notional at this point in time. What he is really peeved about is that he has to resort to deception and lies to come across as a bigshot. He firmly believes that his place in life is right up there at the top of the tree—both in terms of finance and celebrity. If anyone eclipses him, however temporarily, then he becomes very depressed and this is when he gets himself into trouble.

After a long while he comes round, but this feeling that he should be the star of the show is never far away all the while we are filming. By the time *Stardust*, the sequel to *That'll Be the Day*, is in production, this feeling is with Moonie constantly and this probably explains the outbursts of childish temperament which follow.

We are filming in Manchester. *Stardust* is the story of a band that makes it from scuffling club gigs to international superstardom. It is a sort of fictionalised version of the Beatles story and the band in the movie is called The Stray Cats. The members of the band are played by Dave Edmunds, who, of course, does very nicely thank you in the music biz in real life; Karl Howman, an actor I mention elsewhere; Moonie and David Essex as the lead singer. We are on location in the Belle Vue, a large venue in Manchester, and the idea is that The Stray Cats are just beginning to get plenty of hysteria. The hall is chock full of extras, all decked out in sixties gear, and they must perform plenty of screaming and hysteria at the Cats. As Essex is the lead singer he, of course, must command more of the hysteria than anyone else, especially female hysteria. (The storyline goes on to tell how this character becomes a superstar solo act and eventually goes somewhat bonkers with the strain of it all.)

The bints that are dragged in as extras perform a fine job and if I already do not know what is going on I will think that here is a genuine case of fan-hysteria. These birds are waving a picture of Essex around, screaming their heads off, and are pushing and shoving in the approved manner. During these scenes I can tell that Moonie is becoming more and more unhinged by the fact that he is not the centre of attention and things get so bad that, on one occasion, I go backstage and find him in tears again, breaking up.

Bloody hell, I think, *here we go again.*

I ask him what the problem is and he says:

"I've been here before. I've done all this before. I've smashed up this fucking dressing room. I've had birds screaming and carrying on right in this hall—and I'm still not the leader of the band. Why? Why am I just the drummer? Why is everyone holding up David Essex's picture? Why are they all shouting for him? Why don't they want me?"

"Come on, cock," I say. "What are you on about? It's only a film. A movie. Make believe. You're a fucking actor. You're acting the part of a drummer in the group."

But even as I talk to him I realise that he completely forgets that he is in a film and that he believes that this is real life. Sad though this may seem, it is certainly not the only occasion on which reality and fantasy become inextricably intermixed for Keith Moon. It is almost as though he enters another dimension in which only imagination exists. Once, I have to pretend to be the manager of a large hotel, because that is where he thinks he is and it will just be too complicated to go through the whole process of convincing him that this is not the case. I have to pretend to be room service, too, and take plenty of verbal battery on the pearly listeners when he finds that the breakfast that I lovingly fry is not up to West Coast standards —especially in the orange juice department.

So here he is weeping and wailing and quite obviously believing that he is at the Bell Vue with The Who, that The Who are never going to make it and that he will spend the rest of his life schlepping around such toilets. All this stuff about not being the leader of the band is quite significant, too. Is this what he thinks all the time he plays with The Who? If so it is really very much a shame because it is a fact that however pissed off they get with him, the boys in the band love Moonie and by no means do they think of him as anything other than an equal in a great and exciting enterprise. Maybe this is the time that I finally realise that Moonie has such a giant ego that one day it will inevitably land him right in the excremental matter for good.

What eventually cures him, of course, is a couple of large brandies, a few words of commiseration and a spot of generalised jollying-up. Maybe you are thinking *no wonder the poor sod gets to have medicinal problems what with his personal filling him up with liquor at every conceivable opportunity.*

Maybe you are right at that. It is strange how there never seems to be a doctor or a strait-jacket handy when you need it.

One aspect of Moonie's character that is truly surprising is the lengths to which he will go to be admired by people who rate him anyway. There is no doubt that despite, or because of, his lunacy he is one of the best-liked music business figures. Though he is probably the worst money-manager in the world (apart from the succession of Government treasury officials) Moonie is also genuinely rich and famous. Virtually all his peers reckon he is one of the all-time greats when it comes to playing upon the drumskins. So what else should he need? Why take so much trouble to seem either childish or megalomanic? Maybe the truth is that when he is with anyone outside the rock business, whether they are lawyers or actors, doctors or architects, he is both jealous and insecure. He cannot relate his achievements to theirs and does not see that they all recognise his success, that even the ones who disapprove of him most also probably have a sneaking envy of his way of life. This whole feeling is made worse by his realisation that some actors achieve the same degree of adulation, recognition and cash success, and that these actors can go on far longer than any rock star. Whereas an actor can grow old gracefully and lose little of his or her appeal (though this argument tends to collapse when it comes to the bints who rely on a certain amount of déshabille in the Bristol area) there is nothing more pathetic than a geriatric rock and roller—as anyone who sees Presley in his last years will testify. Of course, there are exceptions such as Bo Diddley and Chuck Berry, but these are really museum pieces who are still alive and I am sure that none of the boys wish to be playing *Pinball Wizard* just prior to clocking into the local Post Office for their pension.

Not to put too fine a point on it, Moonie, deep down, seems to feel at a great disadvantage when he is with movie people, and therefore feels that he must build himself up. He cannot see how transparent his act seems when he puts it on—though, to be fair, not many movie people have the nous to see it either. But then they are usually so engrossed in how they appear that they are oblivious to everyone else. You can see a similar phenomenon if you put a small mirror in a birdcage. Still, however transparent Moonie's acts, they often give off several guffaws here and there.

On one occasion, when we are forced for no good reason that comes to mind, to stay in one of a grotesque chain of hotels, none of us can obtain any medicines. There is absolutely no chance whatsoever of any staff member of this hotel obtaining same. It is difficult enough to obtain a cold bottle of wine after nine o'clock in the evening in the dining room. We are debating what to do when Moonie suddenly outs with:

"No problem, dear boys. No problem at all. We will simply go to my hotel."

Obviously, someone pipes up:

"But, Moonie, this *is* your hotel."

"No, no, dear boy," replies Moonie. "I mean *my* hotel. The hotel I own."

"Oh," says the cynic. "And where is that?"

"Just down the road. We'll go over there now. I've got a private suite there and it's well stocked with this and that. Come on."

This may not seem like the most convincing story in the world, but Moonie is definitely one of the all time great liars, and whereas I know him very well, the others present are not especially familiar with his ways. So, by the time Moonie completes the blag as to how long he is a hotelier and how he does not like to talk of it, or even stay in it, in case people think he is being flash, it is clear that the actors present swallow the story hook, line and fishing rod.

When we pull up at Moonie's hotel, it is one of those monstrosities about two hundred stories high and covering an area the size of Manhattan. It is so large that even the actors, who are very gullible indeed, are having their doubts as to the ownership of the gaff. But Moonie gathers everyone up and marches directly to the reception desk. He open with:

"Ah, good evening, dear boy. My usual suite, if you'd be so kind." The bloke looks a bit blank, then says:

"I'm sorry, sir. I don't understand. Exactly who are you?"

"Come along, come along," says Moonie. "I don't have all night you know. I want my suite and I want you to send up some cold meats and salads and half a dozen bottles of champagne." This geezer on the reception remains extremely blank.

"But who are you, sir?"

"Who am I?" responds Keith, leaning nonchalantly on the desk and looking round at the actors with a knowing smirk. "That's rich, that is. I, dear boy . . ." and here, with impeccable timing, he turns back to the unfortunate, "just happen to be the owner of this hotel and if you don't sort out this matter instantly, I will have you dismissed. In fact, I will make sure that you never work in the hotel and catering trade again. Anywhere."

"I'm sorry, sir, I can't authorise . . ." The geezer is certainly game, but he is no match for Keith Moon.

"RIGHT. THAT'S IT. CALL THE MANAGER. AND YOU MAY REGARD YOURSELF AS ON THE DOLE. FROM NOW! OUT!"

One of the actors with us who specialises in sensitive roles is a little upset at this high handed behaviour.

"Here, Dougal, this is a bit out of order isn't it? I mean, perhaps the bloke's new on the job or something."

"Ah, well," I reply, "Moonie's a hard man when it comes to business. He won't tolerate slackness, you know." While this dialogue is taking place, Moonie has got hold of the manager and is speaking to him in a most animated fashion. Words such as "sack," "dismiss," and "stupid bastard" can be heard. Next thing, the manager marches over to the receptionist and gives him audio GBH:

"What do you mean by this? Don't you know this is Mr Moon? He owns the bloody place—not to mention half of Manchester. How dare you insult him? I can't tolerate this. You're fired. Now. Instantly. Get out. I'll send you your cards."

Of course, the receptionist is most downcast and commences to mumble about his wife and three children who, it seems, are unable to subsist without his meagre paycheck, and what about his crippled grandmother who requires expensive medical treatment in America? But the manager is relentless, insists that the receptionist leave this very night and then stalks off to fix up Moonie's suite.

Next thing we know the receptionist disappears, then almost immediately reappears with his hat, coat and a small suitcase. He takes it on his toes out of the hotel.

The actors, and especially the one that specialises in sensitive roles, are flabbergasted. They plead with Moonie and ask if he does not think it a bit strong to give the poor man the heave ho, especially as he is encumbered with the wife, three children and crippled granny who must be expensively treated in the USA.

"The thing is, dear boys," retorts Moonie with glacial disdain, "when you are in the catering business, which is of course just one of my many interests, you have to be absolutely ruthless with the staff. Give them an inch and they'll take a mile. Inefficiency starts to creep in—and then where are you? Before you know what's what, Egon Ronay docks you a star or two and the whole thing goes to the dogs. No, believe me, these people only understand the mailed fist. You've got to be cruel to be kind." He continues in this vein, sounding for all the world like something by Keith Joseph out of Mrs. Thatcher. It is, indeed, fortunate that I realise that what really happens is that Moonie slips everyone concerned a few quid to play along with his little jape, otherwise I will begin to wonder what I am doing working for someone who makes Albert Speer seem like Ralph Nader when it comes to labour relations.

There is no question that, all in all, working in the movies with Moonie is a great laugh for, although they take making pictures more seriously than rock and rollers take making rock and roll, movie people are, by and large, a fair bunch of jokers, even if some of them do come the old madam here and there. As long as the epic masterpiece is not too badly interfered with, they are quite prepared to experiment with the medicines, tamper with the bints and generally misbehave in a quite disgraceful fashion. And, of course, the great thing about making movies is that there are so many people interacting in an ever changing string of locations that there is continual ferment—and this is well-known to be conducive to laughter and pranks.

In *Stardust*, it is necessary to recreate the old Cavern Club in Liverpool, which is where the Beatles first spring to fame. These scenes are, in fact, filmed in Wapping which is well-known as a bit of a toilet in the East End of London. No offence to those from Wapping, of course, but even they will admit that there is a slight shortage of elegant boulevards and soigné cafes and a general air of gracious living. It is by no means in the real estate agents' top ten. In fact, it is in their bottom five . . . a right khazi and the reason why we are filming there is that a right khazi is what is required. The location people excel themselves by finding this spot and before anyone knows what's what we are filming a scene where The Stray Cats pull their van up outside what is supposed to be the Cavern Club but is, in fact, slap up against a famous pub which is a great tourist trap and goes by the name of The Prospect of Whitby.

It is the end of the day and everybody concerned is pretty well knackered. The shot is repeated many, many times, as is the wont of film directors. David Essex and Adam Faith are sitting in the front of the van, as befits the star of his band and his manager, and in the back are Moonie, Paul Nicholas and Karl Howman. They are partitioned off from Essex and Faith so that it is really quite private in the back. In the lull before the next shot, four

Japanesers, all festooned with cameras, spectacles and teeth, issue forth from the Prospect of Whitby, see the geezers in the back of the van, which has its doors open, and ask them what gives. It just happens that the situation is such that the Japanesers cannot see the lights, cameras and other such things that are necessary to turn life into art. But before Moonie or anyone else can dream up an answer as to what gives, one of the Japanesers, a most cordial fellow, sticks his bonce into the van and asks:

"Ah, so you gentremen are musicians?"

"That's it."

"You pray lock rorr?"

"Yeah. Matter of fact we're just on our way to play in a night-club round the corner."

"Ahhh. Excrerrent. You dilect us to night crub? We enjoy trypicar Engrish nightcrub. In Japan, evlyone rove lock rorr!"

The upshot is that the Japanesers are invited to jump in the back of the van and offered the inducement of a free pass into the night club if they will help the lads with the gear. Naturally they are well chuffed to fall in with an Engrish lock rorr band, so they pile in. It turns out that this is a works outing for a Japanese fountain pen company, and the first thing they do is to hand around freebies.

A few seconds later comes the call for *Action* and Faithie drives the van round the corner, totally unaware that it is full to the brim with Japanesers. He pulls up outside the "club." The cameras are rolling quite merrily and everyone is busy being an "actor." The van doors open so that Messrs. Howman, Edmunds, Nicholas and Moon, alias The Stray Cats, can exit. But instead, what happens? Out fall four confused looking Japaneser tourists, blinking in the glare of the lights.

"Ah, soo," says the head Japaneser. "What the fucking herr going on?"

"Tee hee hee," reply Moonie and the lads.

Considering that they are not treated at all well by the powers that be, the orientals do take this little prank in good spirits. By the time Moonie and the others fill them in as to what comes off and hand around a few autographs, the Japanesers are most enthusiastic about the movie and wish to become Toshiro Mifune. In the end they have to make do with dishing out a few more fountain pens before making off into the night. Considering they cause the demise of the great British motorcycle industry and are in the process of completing same toward the great British car industry too, they seem to be good blokes.

When it comes to situations that can be turned into comedy, you might think that a motorway cafe offers less potential than most. After all, what is funny about a depressing joint whose interior decoration is confined to dirty coffee cups, half-masticated doughnuts and a few soggy chips?

What could produce fewer laughs than plastic tables and floors that are slowly being eaten away by the regular spillage of acid-based gravies? Anyone that spends any time on the road with rock and roll bands must come across his fair share of motorway cafes, and no one in the entire history of rock and roll touring ever comes across one that does not rival Wigan on a wet Monday morning, as a source of gloom, despondency and general depression.

All this leads into another *Stardust* incident which involves The Stray Cats in a motorway cafe scene—the idea being that the band is touring the UK and is stopping off in this cafe for a bite to eat. The cafe chosen for the film is highly representative of its type having slightly less grace and charm than a third rate knacker's yard. On the other hand, it does possess a manager whose boundless enthusiasm is only matched by his complete inability to grasp the fact that he is the overlord of a squalid greaserama and not a five star hotel.

This manager clearly believes that to star his rip-off joint in a movie will do wonders for business and cause it to become the frequent haunt of stars of the silver screen and other famous personalities. He seems to have some crazy, lunatic dream in his bonce whereby HRH the Princess Margaret turns to her companion and speaks:

"I say, why don't we all pop up the M1 tonight to that delightful little motorway cafe that was mentioned in Country Life last week. I hear their double sausage, egg and chips is simply out of this world—and Foggy says the steak pie and beans is too too divine."

From this you may gather that this manager is a certifiable lunatic and despite the fact that all we are after is a couple of scenes in a typical motorway cafe, he insists that all the tables and chairs are neatly arranged, that everything in sight is polished (though here he has a problem because none of his staff ever see polish in their lives, and one of them faints at the sight of a dustpan and brush). All in all, he carries on like the maitre d' of The Dorchester, which is really quite pathetic and only succeeds in making the flies on the Danish pastries feel uncomfortable.

The first shot entails the lads in the band all queueing up for their rations of grease, and on the counter by which they are standing there are many plastic panels to promote the day's special, such as prunes and custard and fried plaice and chips. The manager is most keen that they should be included in picture and he takes special care to ensure that they are relatively clean and legible.

Filming continues and a few takes are attempted. Then, as usual, there is some sort of cock-up and there is a break while the head cameraman tries to clear his equipment of the grease that clogs up the works on account of him filming within twenty-five feet of the kitchens. Naturally, I keep an eye on Moonie to try and keep him in order. But he seems to be remarkably quiet and is in a corner with Karl Howman. They are rapping away, huddled over something, so I ignore them and continue trying to drink a cup of coffee which the manager thoughtfully gives me. Though what he has against me at this stage, I do not know.

This scene is set up once more and the camera, now free of frying grease, seems to be working in the approved and kosher manner. The Stray Cats poke around at the dubious comestibles on view and shuffle forward in the queue.

Suddenly, there is a colossal commotion and a great deal of shouting and arm waving. I move across to take a gander and what I see is this lunatic manager prancing about in front of the camera gesticulating insanely. Well, as far as I know, the script does not call for a cafe manager to impersonate a Matabele dancer, so I gather that all is not well.

"Stop! Stop it! Stop the cameras! I won't have it! You've got to stop! I'll sue you all! You'll never come here again!" This last is not a threat to take too seriously—in fact, if it is a promise, most of the great British people will heave a collective sigh of relief. Just as I am thinking this, I catch sight of the cause of all the aggravation. Along the top of the counter, the "Today's Specials" cards are most tastefully arranged and their white plastic letters show up most effectively against the black plastic backgrounds. But instead of promising the culinary delights previously mentioned, they now proclaim the immediate availability of:

Fried Shit and Chips

Prunes and Piss

Bollocks on Toast

Inevitably, Moonie is absolutely convulsed with laughter and he can hardly stand up.

These and many other incidents will lead you to believe that Keith Moon does not have the correct degree of deference and/or respect when it comes to those who are in charge of movie-making—be they directors, producers, stars or writers. To Moonie there is only one act of creation and that is to sit behind the biggest set of drums in the world, behind the best rock and roll band in the world, and then to beat the shit out of those drums to drive the band into producing some of the best sounds ever to come from musical instruments. This is what he is very good at. Moonie relishes the freedom of rock drumming and this freedom enables him to create on the spot, with little or no forethought—for, no matter how full of ideas Moonie is, and ideas come to him thick and fast, he is hopeless at organising himself to carry those ideas through. Meetings, conferences, plans of action, *let's try it another way*—these are not the things Moonie understands and movies are very dependent on these things.

Moreover, although members of the movie business do not usually qualify for founder membership of the Festival of Light and are apt to overindulge and point their mutton javelins at each other's wives and girlfriends, most of them realise that there is a time and a place for everything. By and large, they do not cock up their professional appearances. Moonie, on the other hand, has no such inhibitions and will cock himself up, and anyone else who is within range, at the drop of a bottle. For example, he visits Karl Howman one time when Karl is in a play which goes by the name of *Teeth and Smiles*. It is written by a geezer called David Hare, who is generally regarded as being quite up-and-coming in the writing game, and it has more than one long word in it, as befits a play that is on at the Royal Court. What's more there are several very kosher actors in it, such as Helen Mirren. After the play, Moonie wishes to pay a call on his mate Karl, so what he does is blag his way to the stage door and into the dressing room. There, the first thing he does is to leap upon Karl and wrestle him to the ground, which is most embarrassing to Karl as it is witnessed by several theatrical types present.

This is quite bearable, though, and everything remains OK until the end of the play comes up and it is time for the Thespians to take their curtain call. Now, to many such players, this is the most important part of the evening and it is the reason many of them go upon the stage in the first place. So they are not too delighted when Moonie insists on taking a bow with them. He is virtually on stage before anyone can restrain him.

"Here," he says, protesting at the hands laid on him. "I only want to take a bow." Helen Mirren very reasonably points out that he is not in the play and is therefore not entitled to take a bow.

"What are you talking about?" replies Moonie. "I always go

on stage with Led Zeppelin when I am at their concerts. And Eric Clapton. What's so special about this?" One way and another, however, he is prevented from startling the patrons of the Royal Court theatre with an unscheduled appearance, much to the relief of all—especially Karl. But Karl's tribulations are not yet over because he foolishly invites Moonie over to the pub next door to have a few bevvies. For all I know, Karl feels that it is the least he can do to try and make up for Moonie's disappointment at not being able to take a curtain call. Everyone in the play, including its scribe, David Hare, is in the bar and they are all talking quite amiably. Moon changes all this by button-holing David Hare.

"Listen, dear boy," he says, "I have an interest in the career of young Karl here and I want you to make sure you always see him right. Young Karl will be a star and I want you to remember that. If I ever hear that you have given him a bad part, or any other sort of bum steer, I shall want to know why. Do you know what I mean?"

Naturally, Karl is somewhat embarrassed by all this and has to bicycle very hard indeed to cancel out this uncalled for testimony as to his acting prowess. But Moonie cannot see that he in any way is committing a gaffe. He has no idea that he does not carry the weight with these people that he does in the rock business.

So, despite the fact that Moonie is undoubtedly a natural actor and despite the fact that acting offers him perhaps the only way out of the trap he creates for himself with his manic rock and roll life, he never does give it his best shots. He has several other parts than the ones I mention here, including that of a nun in Frank Zappa's *200 Motels*, Uncle Ernie in Ken Russell's *Tommy* and a poovy dress designer in Mae West's *Sextet*. To all outward appearances, incidentally, Moonie and Mae West get on like a house on fire in the very brief hours they work together. Maybe it is a case of each recognising the outrageous in the other. It is interesting that despite the fact that these masterpieces are given a right good slagging by the people who are meant to know what's what in movies, and singularly fail to place bottoms in cinema seats, almost without exception Moonie gets a small rave notice.

Of course, this is no great shock to me, for Moonie's whole life is a movie which he produces, directs and stars in himself. He even finances it and expects very little return. He often says:

"I am the best Keith Moon-type drummer in the world." It is a great shame and a pity that he will never say:

"I am the best Keith Moon-type actor in the world."

Who's
Sorry Now?

Malibu Beach, California, USA is a long, long way from Shepherds Bush, London, England. In fact, Malibu Beach, is not the sort of place an ordinary young bloke from London is likely to wind up in. Or can normally expect to end up in, come to think of it. But there again, once the old foot is on the bottom rung of the rock and roll ladder, there's no telling what might happen. And, in fact, this is what happens to me—just a couple of years after entering the rock and roll biz—BOFF!—there I am in Malibu.

Not so very long ago, of course, the only way that a miracle like this can occur is by winning the football pools, or maybe becoming a film star or maybe spending twenty odd years working like hell at your own business. Now all you have to do to see the world is join the rock and roll army.

There is no place like California. I mean Moonie and me see a lot of places in a lot of countries but there's no place like California—which is why, of course, Moonie eventually buys a place on Malibu Beach.

Like everyone says, best or worst, it happens in California first. It is all the good things and all the bad things about living in the late twentieth century all rolled up into one. There are geezers there with more money than any working person—and especially any English working person—can imagine. And I don't just mean film stars and rock stars and oil tycoons. Secretaries, plumbers, bank clerks and such types with very ordinary jobs live like no one in England can dream of. I mean, there's this chick in LA works for a PR guy as his personal assistant. No big deal. No funny business in the sack. Just an ordinary job that might pay the rent in London, and perhaps a bit more to run a Mini and leave a few bob spare for a couple of drinks at the weekend and a late night Chinese meal to soak up same. But this chick in LA has the big Pontiac sitting in the garage, the beautiful apartment right on the waterside at Marina del Rey and she thinks nothing of taking a quick flight to Lake Tahoe or SF for the weekend just to see friends.

Then, of course, there's all this technology stuff. Everyone has access to the most amazing gadgets. There are cars with computers in them that tell you how many miles you do, how many gallons the car's using, how much those gallons cost and if that doesn't make you shit yourself, the computer can probably tell you when you're due to visit the can next.

There's air conditioning everywhere and most homes have just about every conceivable appliance too. Even electric cocktail sticks. Not to mention swimming pools, saunas, jacuzzis and the like. I should think the average California home uses up more electricity in a day than it takes to run the entire British Railways for a year.

There's always a catch, of course. Amongst all this affluence you've got some of the rottenest slums I ever see—like Watts. Plus someone gets knocked off or mugged every couple of nano-seconds. Plus—and this is really hard for Europeans to handle—LA has got virtually no transport system. There are one or two buses, but they're few and far between and they only run along the main streets. In LA it is simply assumed that everyone has a car. I mean if you haven't got a car you are really at the bottom of the dung heap. And if you start walking about the chances are you will be arrested on suspicion of being suspicious.

All I'm trying to say, really, is that when Moonie and I are living in Malibu it is like an alien world and very different indeed from the places we grow up in. Don't get me wrong—we have a great time and while we often talk about the sort of place California is, we do not have any hang ups about it. We've got a fabulous house right on the beach and next door is Steve Mc-Queen. We've got more birds than you can shake a dick at. We've got a lot of good mates with whom we can raise mayhem when required. And, except for the times Moonie pisses it all away, we've got a lot of dough to spend.

But Keith and I are both very English. I mean, Moonie is a lunatic but he's right in the tradition of great British eccentrics. And I'm the sort of geezer who likes a game of darts and a few pints down the pub when all is said and done—though it is true that in Malibu I have quite a reputation as a professional organiser of jolly-ups.

So it is really quite ironic that when Moonie and I finally split, when the last great bust-up comes, it all happens in Malibu among the palm trees, the health freaks, the surfers and the whole American dream. Maybe if we are both at home in the good old UK this final scene will not be quite so traumatic.

And that is what it is. A trauma. By now you understand the background to it all. Moonie is a very freaky geezer and he does not have many friends—not proper friends that he can sit and talk to; that he can rely on and do not expect him to put on a funny costume at all times and caper about to make them laugh. When it comes right down to it, I am just about all he has.

This is not an exaggeration. Of course, I start my time with The Who and Moonie as just another arsehole who heaves equipment about and is generally of no account. But later I become the man who keeps Moonie together—not just making sure that he arrives on time at the various gigs, but really helping him to keep a grip on what little reality there is for a geezer like him.

Consider this guy. He is a personal, mobile catastrophe. He's got a colossal ego, too huge to relate to normal people on any normal level. But on top of it all he is really a loving and generous man who needs an outlet, and perhaps because he does not have that outlet in the conventional sense, he explodes all over the place into outrageous behaviour. And, in most cases, it is me who has to carry the can for these explosions.

Now you must not get this wrong. Moonie is by no means a poove. Far from it, although I will not be in the slightest surprised if he gives some geezer one up the bum just to shock and horrify some old biddy. I mean, it is the sort of thing he might do on the front lawn of the most exclusive country club in Massachusetts. Moonie will do anything if he thinks there are enough people around who do not want him to do it. No, Moonie is not bent. And I am not an iron either. But the relationship between us is very close indeed and during my time with Moonie I do take on a lot of emotional, practical and organisational problems so that when the split comes it hits us both pretty hard— and when Moonie realises just how much weight I remove from his shoulders he takes my leaving very badly indeed.

Of course, I am very well rewarded for what I do and I do not want you to think that I am moaning and groaning about what I have to do for my money. Far from it. The only reason I experience so many things, see so many places, meet so many people, practice up on my sexual intercourse and generally have so many laughs is that I am attached to a great superstar. No, I am not complaining—I am merely trying to set the scene.

Now, the great rock and roll business knows no loyalties. It picks you up and puts you down with equal ease—it's all a matter of luck and money, and I am well aware that my time in this business is limited and, while I am in it, I develop a great interest in movies and how they are made. Gradually I come to think that when the rock and roll adventure is over I will try to squeeze my way into the movies in some or other manner. Funnily enough, hanging around rock and roll bands is quite a good way to break into movies because, especially in LA, the two things go hand in hand and everyone hangs out together. It is probably true to remark that rock and roll now appears to occupy about the same position as the film business in its heyday when there are many stars on contract to such legendary figures as Louis B. Mayer and Sam Goldwyn. Now, if you ask the geezers who drive the hired limos who their customers are, they are liable to tell you that they spend most of their time contracted to record companies, driving rock and roll stars around and about the place.

Moonie always says to me that if I get a good offer, wherever it comes from, I should take it, and furthermore, that he will help me make best use of same offer and generally encourage me to make a success of myself. It seems that in his saner moments Moonie realises that I cannot be running around after inebriated, drugged and halfway insane rock stars when I am forty years old—no matter how entertaining that may be for a while.

What with The Who being so famous and Moonie being such a personable and much sought-after geezer, it is not surprising that he appears in several movies and, because I am ever present, I feature in these activities too. We have a load of laughs but all the while I am beavering away and trying to get as much experience on movies as possible, and generally making my number with the chaps in charge of all the filming caper.

It seems that I am quite successful in this because David Putnam, who is the guy that produces one of these films, is impressed by the manner in which I manage to keep Moonie together and the fact that I make myself useful around the place, helping to arrange locations and so on. Well, of course, when you are used to covering Moonie's tracks helping to or-

ganise locations is like falling off a log. Anyway, this Putnam
says to me that I should join the ACTT by which he means to
say that I should get myself into the film technicians' union.
Well, I apply for same union card but for one reason or another
the application is thrown out, so I forget about my film career
for a while and continue to excite myself by means of various
medicines and the sort of activities that go on around Moonie.

But, eventually we get involved in the movies again because
The Who buy Shepperton Studios and begin to film *The Kids
Are Alright* which is all about the rise of the band and features
the band on tour and in concert. Naturally, Moonie stars in a
pretty big way and many people agree that he turns out to be
the main turn in the movie. Naturally, in the course of my job
I spend much time schlepping Moonie around the film sets
and making myself useful. In fact I make myself so useful that
Jeff Stein, who directs the movie, makes me his assistant.

While we are filming we fly to LA to do some sequences in
Moonie's house at Malibu and I find myself doing a great deal
of organising and hustling about. I recall for example, that one
time I have to go and interrupt a Bob Dylan recording session
to borrow some lighting equipment. And let me tell you that
the Big Zim does not take kindly to having his recording sessions
interrupted.

Well the upshot of all this is that I get on so well with Jeff
Stein that he asks me to work with him on a permanent basis.
Now, of course, this is the sort of break that I am looking for,
so when Jeff asks me to discuss the deal over dinner, I go like a
shot. It seems the first thing I must do is fly back to London
with him when we finish shooting in Malibu, to help with the
remainder of the filming of *The Kids Are Alright*. This means
that I must leave Moonie behind because by now he finishes
his part in the movie.

It is true that during these talks with Jeff, which stretch over
several days, I notice that Moonie is giving me the occasional
strange look and that he does not seem too cheerful about my

good fortune. But then I remember that he also says that I should grab my chances as they arise, so I do not worry about the black looks too much.

Until, that is, I return to the house at Malibu one night and find a big notice pinned to my bed. And what this notice reads is:

YOU'RE LICKING PRODUCERS ARSES. GOOD LUCK. MOONIE.

Now I am well choked by this. I mean, I consider that in the time I am with him I look after Moonie pretty well and, while it is true that he pays me for this service, I cannot do this for ever. He also knows how much this break means to me because we discuss the matter on many occasions. It is not as if the whole thing comes as any surprise or as if I am in any way underhand about what is happening.

The next day is pretty weird. Moonie is a bit sheepish about the notice on the bed and, to begin with, makes out that he is sorry about it and that he will release me when I am ready to go. Of course, I am very fond of Moonie and there is no way I wish to end up on bad terms with him, so I am very pleased that he seems to be over his downer on me. The whole thing is made easier by the fact that Moonie already finds a replacement for me, a bloke who goes by the name of Keith Allison. And just to show you how things go up and down in the great rock and roll business, this Keith Allison once has a big hit single. A number one as I remember it. And here is Keith Allison prepared to work as Moonie's runaround for what is, relatively, not too much mazuma. Mind you, there are many musicians who prefer to be roadies or other similar hangers-on, rather than leave the business altogether. I suppose it is quite similar to being addicted—and, of course, many of them believe that if they hang around long enough their chance must come again.

So everything in the garden is hunky-dory—until we start the day's filming and the filming involves drinking. But, whereas brandy and ginger usually gets Moonie well jollied-up, this time he gets very depressed and moody and nasty. Then he starts to take it out on me, doing everything he can to put me down in front of the film crew and everyone else. Now I am not the sort of bloke who can take much of this type of opposition without throwing a few knuckles here and there. But, because it is coming from Moonie and I know that he is having a bit of bother with his head, I simply take him on one side and ask him what it is all about. He is very truculent and says to me like this:

"Right, Dougal, you cunt. Are you going through with all this fucking film business?" His eyes are hot and angry-looking and I must confess that at this stage I am resigned to our discussion ending in bloodshed. Nevertheless, it is too late for me to back down—which I have no intention of doing anyway. So I reply:

"Yes, I am."

"Is that what you really want to do?" he sneers.

"Yes it is."

"You're a cunt," he says. "If you leave me, you don't come back."

"Right," I say.

"No, you're a cunt." And now his words are really running into each other, like he's very pissed. "You're a cunt. I mean it. Leave me and that's it. You don't come back."

"Listen, man," I say, making one last effort to reason with him. "Listen, man, you know this is something I really want to do. And what's more, you're always saying that you'll help me. So what's all this about?"

But all Moonie does is to start on about how The Who now own Shepperton Studios and how he is in charge of all publicity. Then he tells me I can be his assistant on this side of the business, at double the wages I'm on at the moment.

"No, man," I reply to this spiel. "I really want to do the gig with Jeff. It's a big break for me. I could really go places."

"Ah fuck off, Dougal, the only place you'll go with him is straight up the fucking pictures."

"Yeah, maybe. But I want to give it a go."

Moonie walks away without saying anything more. He's like a small kid sulking.

When we finish the day's shooting, Moonie is still acting a bit funny but we climb into the Lincoln Continental to go for something to eat. We get through the meal OK and Moonie even seems to be getting used to the idea of me slipping off to London. But I start to relax too soon, because as we're crusing back home down Pacific Highway, Moonie suddenly turns to me and shouts:

"Right. This is it! It's either me or the film business." Then he really turns the venom on and what it turns out he's saying is that it is either him or *no* film business because if I do not work for him I will not work for anyone ever again. And I especially will not work in films because he, Moonie, knows everyone in the business and he'll make sure that no one in movies anywhere in the world will want to know about Peter Butler.

Charming! I think to myself, but I do not say anything else other than my mind is made up and I intend to work with Jeff Stein. Moonie relapses into silence and the drive back to the house seems to take ten times as long as it normally does.

We park the car and walk round to the patio. Keith suddenly rounds on me and snarls:

"So that's it, is it?"

"Yeah. That's it."

Then with no warning Moonie goes mad and swings a punch at me. Well, this catches me unaware and I am rocked back on my heels. Now Moonie has plenty of balls, but he is not a very scientific fighter at the best of times. Also, he is extremely pissed. So, although I am surprised and have to step back, I come forward immediately and, unlike Moonie, I have experience of rough-housing. What is more I do not take very kindly to being swung at. So I let go with a short left and—BOFF!—there's Moonie flat on his back.

Well, after a count of five, Moonie's back on his feet and he's fighting mad. Now, I do not want to hurt Moonie any more than

I wish to be hurt myself so what I try to do is sort of hold him off
at arm's length until he is calm enough to realise that we are not
behaving entirely in a civilised manner. But he comes on at me
like a warthog on amyl nitrate and despite my efforts he manages to get hold of my shirt front. Then with a great heave he
rips the shirt open and catches hold of all my gold chains, such
as are very fashionable on the West Coast at this time. He
wrenches them off and hurls them out onto the beach. And, to
tell you the truth, it is this that infuriates me more than anything
else—perhaps because I do not as yet realise exactly what a pass
Moonie and I arrive at, but more likely because these gold
chains cost me a lot of sweat. So I push Moonie away and I
storm off up the beach to look for all this gold. Moonie meanwhile stomps off into the house. Of course, I never find the
chains and I expect they are now the property of some California
beach bum. If they are and he is reading this, he can have them
inscribed "As hurled by Keith Moon."

Of course, all this activity is accompanied by much shouting
and screaming and cursing, and this noise brings out our next
door neighbor, who is none other than Steve McQueen. He sees
me grovelling about in the sand and strolls over to ask what
comes off. When I tell him, he simply remarks:

"I tell you this, Dougal, that's the best day's work you've ever
done. No question about it. I mean, you stick with Moonie and
you'll end up dead one way or another. The guy is a nutcase."

I have to admit that at this stage I am in the right mood to
agree with Steve McQueen, but all I do is go into the house,
quietly pack my bags and then shove off out of it.

Well, there is still a bit of time before I am due to return to
England with Jeff Stein, so the first thing to do is find accommodation. Fortunately this is not too difficult, as I am quite
friendly with a young geezer whose mother and father are both
zillionaires and who own more property than the Roman Catholic Church. This young geezer lives just down the road from
Moonie's place, so I roll up there, get a very large and cheerful
"Hello" from him and immediately install myself. As it happens,

I do have a few dibs stashed away in the bank, so I am not in any immediate difficulties and can maintain my lifestyle for anyway a few weeks. I very soon grow to enjoy this break. I lie back in the California sunshine, tequila sunrise in hand, and watch the various shapely golden-haired bints that pass by with great frequency. It is a relief not to have to worry about whether Keith is planning to steal the Queen Mary, is throwing bricks through the windows of the local branch of the Bank of America, or is in jail, or what.

The days pass pleasantly because California is the best place in the world that I know in which to do nothing. The whole place is designed for laid-back living. I get up in the morning round about eleven o'clock, take a leisurely dip in the pool and partake of an avocado salad, or something similar, for lunch. Then there's just enough time for a little more lazing around the pool before it is time for the cocktail ritual. California is heavily into cocktails and during my time there I learn to make many, such as Margaritas and Harvey Wallbangers, and I teach the local denizens a few of my own. One that goes down particularly well is the Sherry Whossname, a concoction of very dry sherry, brandy and lemonade which makes you look upon sherry with a newfound respect.

So I pass my days in this fashion and in the evening I generally go to a little bar a few miles along the Pacific Coast highway. At this time they have a great band playing there called Trancus, and I am soon very friendly with the guys in this band and am able to give them the benefit, such as it is, of my years in the business.

I am sitting there one night, quietly digging the band, when in comes this geezer who works for Moonie, driving his motors and so on. He comes up to me and says:

"Moonie wants to see you, man. He's in the motor outside."

Well, I think to myself, *if he wants to see me, he can fucking well come in here, and see me.* And I make this dude know that that is what I feel, but he just replies:

"No, man, come on. Moonie really does want to see you. To

go off and have a few drinks." So I think to myself *What the hell?* and I wander out into the night. Sure enough, there is Moonie, sitting in the back of the Continental. Even though it is hot enough to make a camel think twice about taking any form of exercise, Moonie has got his fur coat on.

"Hello, dear boy!" he says as if nothing unpleasant ever passes between us.

"Hello, Moonie," I reply.

Then I jump into the motor and we glide off. I will say this for Yanks, when they make a car they make a car, and the Lincoln Continental is such. It may not be too hot on the cornering. It may be like a truck to park. It may cost you the Bank of England to keep running. But, when it comes to giving the effect of a large, silent and somewhat sinful bedroom in motion, the Lincoln Continental is simply tops. But the lack of any noise whatsover in the back of this motor is only emphasized by the complete lack of noise from Keith Moon.

Once he is over giving me the sheepish "Hello," he clams up tighter than a Scottish bookmaker's wallet, and, naturally, I do not say anything either because I am waiting to see exactly what the score is before I start in on the quips and the light conversation.

Moonie and I are completely alone in this car because Moonie operates the thick glass partition that separates the chauffeur from the general proceedings in the back seat. And this is another count on which I must compliment the Lincoln, because with this partition the chauffeur can be practising his Robert Plant impressions and you hear nothing at all in the back seat.

Then, without looking at me, Moonie suddenly speaks.

"You can't leave me, Dougal," he says.

Oh Christ, I think. *I might have known it.*

"Look, Moonie," I reply, "the decision is made. What you did to me out on the beach is unforgivable. And all that act with the film crew . . . I mean, how can I work for a bloke who tries to make me look a complete cunt?" Then he turns to me and I can see that his eyes are full of tears—and that really does choke me up—and he says:

"Whatever I earn, you can have half. Fifty per cent of what I make. Right?" This may seem a pretty fantastic offer, but by now I am so determined to get on, get out and get moving that I do not hestiate. Do not give it a second thought.

"You're crackers," I say. "But I stand by what I'm telling you. I'm going back to England when Jeff leaves. I appreciate the offer, man, I really do. But my mind is made up. I'm going."

Well, what happens next I cannot believe and, to tell you the truth, I do not care very much to write about it. It really fazes me, because what happens next is that Moonie, king of the rock and roll ravers, breaks down and cries like a baby. It is a really hyterical outburst, and all I can think of is to get him into a quiet bar somewhere where I can hurl a few stiff ones down him. So I press the electrics that operate the window partition and tell Moonie's driver to take us on down to Alice's Restaurant, which is just a bit further along the Pacific Highway. When we arrive there I drag Moonie in and order up a quick succession of brandies accompanied by ginger ale.

This Florence Nightingale act has a fairly rapid effect, which is further accelerated by the fact that Moonie is pretty peeved with himself for cracking up in the first place. So, after a few more bevvies, he begins to perk up and soon he is carrying on in the old manner, spieling to the waitresses, slagging the other punters in the place, downing liquor like Prohibition is about to commence tomorrow, and generally making plenty of speed— not to mention noise.

Later, when I get him home, he acts quite normally and even shakes my hand, wishing me luck.

I wish the story could end here with Moonie and I good mates, him going his way and me going mine. But it is not that simple. I am round at a friend's place only a couple of days later where I here someone says:

"Hear about Keith, man? He's in Malibu jail." This does not

surprise me, of course, because Keith is no stranger to the inside of various jails all round the country—and plenty in other countries too. What happens, apparently, is that Moonie is found driving up and down the Pacific Highway in Annette's Mustang and wearing nothing but a pair of red Y-front pants and a thick fur coat. That in itself is probably not an offence, especially in the state of California, but, of course, when Moonie is arrested, which occurs because he runs out of petrol, stops at a filling station and has no cash to pay for the gas, he is well out of his tree and waving a bottle of brandy to boot.

The next day I hear that he is pissed again, this time at a place called the Crazy Horse, which is just opposite Alice's Restaurant. But this time he is slagging me off well and proper, telling the world in general what a cunt I am and how I betray him, how no one in the entire universe must ever trust me or give me a job of any description, and I do not know what all else. He then has another series of near misses in the Mustang and winds up under arrest once more.

Because I feel somewhat guilty, I also feel genuinely sorry for Keith. He is not capable of coping on his own, but at the same time I just do not feel able, any longer, to handle him. It is true that in the ten years I have some wonderful, some amazing, times with the guy; more amazing than I can ever expect when I am a saucepan in West London. But what Moonie never seems to understand is that I do not owe him the rest of my life on account of those ten years. Every party ends sometime and Moonie's and my party comes to an end when Jeff Stein offers me the gig on *The Kids Are Alright*. And, if Jeff never offers me that gig, the end will still come—and soon. Because, I am beginning to feel the strain. Smashing up hotel rooms, driving about pissed, screwing in every conceivable place, with every conceivable type and using every conceivable variation, generally causing riots and behaving unlike a responsible and tax-paying citizen is a lot of fun. But in the end it begins to pall. It is clear to me when I decide to split that I have a choice in these matters—I can call it a day. But, sadly, Moonie does not have such a choice. He is a prisoner of his own nature. He is locked into a certain pattern of behaviour—just as surely as swallows migrate, salmon spawn and squirrels hibernate.

It is just about a year after I leave Moonie that he dies, but before he dies, I do see him a few times. There is one occasion when I am working full time for Jeff Stein, and we are filming a Who gig at Kilburn State Theatre in London. At this time I am the official Assistant Director on the movie—or at least one of the official Assistant Directors—and I have to do a great deal of hustling about. Now, this hustling delays my meeting up with Moonie, and, to tell you the truth, as the time to meet him approaches, I find that I am dreading it—but looking forward to it at the same time. I mean, I really hope that he is getting on all right.

Anyway, it is inevitable that I meet up with the band, including Moonie, on the shoot. This meeting takes place in the dressing room at the gig. As it happens, I have no need to be concerned beforehand, because everyone gives me a very large *Hello*! indeed, none more so than Keith, and fairly soon we're hitting the brandies and ginger, and later we do without the ginger as it seems to be getting in the way of the brandy. Well, eventually, I have to perform one of my functions as official Assistant Director, this function being to get the performers in front of the camera. So when the time comes I stand up on my feet, a little uncertain in the balancing act, it's true, and speak as follows:

"On set, please, gentlemen!"

When this command is greeted with universal shouts of:

"FUCK OFF, DOUGAL!" I know that it's business as usual and I must say that I am very happy about it. After this episode, Moonie says to me:

"You fucking idiot, Dougal. Why don't you come back?" But I know I can't go back to Moonie. He knows it too. On the other hand, we both know we're mates again.

And that's what it's all about, really, isn't it?

After this, I see Moonie a few times, and most of those times he asks me to come back. We meet up at Shepperton Studios, at his flat, and have numerous phone conversations. But I stick to my chosen path, and I assume the role, I think, of Moonie's mate and confidant. Then he ups and dies, and a very strange thing happens.

Just before the funeral, I get a phone call from one of the roadies. He sounds quite nervous and what he tells me is that I am barred from attending the funeral and that this is on Annette's instructions. Naturally, this upsets me quite considerably and anyway I do not believe that Annette issues such instructions. It is true that we are never very great friends, but there is certainly no bad feeling between us and we share many good times. However, the call throws me slightly and I ask Keith's mother, with whom I am always on excellent terms, what she thinks about it. She is most indignant and insists that I go with her. In the event, it is Roger Daltrey who takes me to the funeral, where I also see Annette and, from her reaction to me, I am more sure than ever that she never tells anyone I am not wanted around on this day.

The mystery is never solved.

Reading through this account of my time with Keith Moon, it occurs to me that nothing really *happens*. Sure, plenty of hotels are wrecked. Bints are rumped. Medicines are taken. People are shocked. But in most of the books I read wars are declared, people are stabbed, shot and beaten up. Spies spy. Murderers murder. Lovers love.

For a while this worries me, because I figure that this is a book too. Things should happen like in other books. But then I remember that this is about just one person. It is, by and large, the true story of ten years of that person's life and of course these ten years are not to do with wars, murders and spies. They are to do with someone who in his time is perhaps the most talented and innovative rock drummer in the world. And the saddest thing that this geezer does, the thing that makes it all such a waste—the one thing that really *happens*—is that Keith Moon ups and fucking well dies.

Glossary

Ackers: money, cash
Argy bargy: argument, conflict
Aris: arse, ass, bottom, buttocks (rhyming slang—Aristotle/
 bottle, bottle and glass/arse)
Arseholed: extremely drunk
Ava Gardner: avant garde

Bacon assegai: male organ
Barnet: hair (rhyming—Barnet Fair)
Barney: argument, altercation
Beaver pie: female sexual organ
Beef torpedo: male organ
Beezer: nose
Berk: cunt, denoting stupid or worthless person rather than
 sexual organ (rhyming—Berkeley Hunt or, according to some
 sources, Berkshire Hunt)
Bevvy, bevvies: drink, drinks
Biddy: old woman

Bint: female person (slightly derogatory)

Bird: female person

Blag, to: to bullshit

Boatrace: face (rhyming)

Bollocks: testicles, but often used figuratively to denote non-sense, rubbish

Bonce: head

boodle: money, assets, fortune

Boot: female person (derogatory)

Boot, to be given the: to be fired, dismissed

Boot pie: kick while fighting (cf. *knuckle sandwich*)

Boracic: skint, without funds (rhyming—boracic lint)

Box, to be out of one's: to be out of one's senses, drugged, drunk

Brahms and Lizst: drunk (rhyming—Brahms and Lizst/pissed; also sometimes Mozart and Lizst)

Brass: extremely cold (from "cold enough to freeze the balls off a brass monkey")

Bristol(s): breast, breasts (rhyming—Bristol City/titty)

Brown bread: dead (rhyming)

Buffalo Bill: pill (rhyming)

Buggered: bothered, as in "I can't be bothered"; also some-times stymied, baffled or finished (cf. fucked as in "completely fucked")

Bugle: nose

Bullet, to be given the: to be fired, dismissed

Bunny: talk (shortened form of bunny rabbit, which in turn derives from rhyming—rabbit and pork)

Cabbage: money

Chopper: male organ

Chuffed: pleased, proud, gratified

Clap: venereal disease (hence "round of applause")

Clappers, to go like the: to go very rapidly

Clock into: to check in for work via clock that marks working hours completed

clock to: to notice, look at

Clogs, to check in: to die

Cobblers: balls, testicles (rhyming—cobbler's awls)

Cock, cocksparrow, cocksparrer: conversational vocative meaning "old chap" (not to be confused with "old chap" meaning male organ, also known as "cock"; cf. American "man" as in "hey man")

Crackers: insane

Cricket set: male genitalia

Crumpet: attractive, desirable female person(s); usually available

Crust: head, especially top of (rhyming—crust of bread)

Cyril Lord, to do a: hit the carpet, collapse (from British carpet magnate whose company collapsed)

Derby: belly (rhyming—Derby Kelly)

Dibs: money

Dick: male organ

Dog and bone: telephone (rhyming)

Dong: male organ

Do-re-mi: money

Duff up, to: to beat up, assault violently

Earwig, to: to listen, eavesdrop

Eau de Cologne: telephone (rhyming)

Eric Delaney Drum Tutor: standard beginners' instruction manual by well-known British band-leader

Fag: cigarette

Fatty, to slip a: to insert the male organ, have sexual intercourse

Festival of Light: British puritan movement

Front wheeler: Jew (rhyming—front wheel skid/yid)

Fruity: desirous of sexual intercourse

Fur pie: female sexual organ.

Gaff: home

Gander: look

Gash: derogatory term for female genitalia and, by extension, available female persons; can also mean rubbish, unwanted material

GBH: Grievous Bodily Harm

Geed up: excited or enthused; but to gee someone up can mean to tease them

Geezer: male person

Geschvinn: very quickly

Ginger beer: queer, homosexual (rhyming)

Glom: look at, scrutinise

Gob: mouth

Handle: name

Heave ho: sack, termination of employment

Hepworth's three-piece: suit by well-known English multiple tailor

Herbert: stupid or worthless male person

Hoity toity: snobbish, with pretensions to social position

Hooter: nose

Hrrrrrrnnnnn Jimmeh: guttural sound frequently uttered by Glaswegians; believed by some researchers to mean "hello James"

Iron: homosexual (rhyming—iron hoof/poof)

Jack in, to: to give up, break down, finish, end it all

Jam jar: car (rhyming)

Jimmy Logan: Scottish entertainer not usually appreciated by rock audiences

Kecks: trousers

Kenneth McKellar: see *Jimmy Logan*

Khazi: lavatory; sometimes spelt "carsi"

Kip: sleep

Kipper feast: cunnilingus

Kite: cheque

Knackered: very tired
Knuckle sandwich: fist, punch

Limo: limousine
Lungs: breasts
Lurker: worthless person, hanger-on

Malarkey: nonsense
Marbles, to lose: to go insane
Mastermind: English TV quiz show designed to assess intelligence and/or knowledgeability
Mazuma: money
Minces: eyes (rhyming—mince pies)
Minicabber: unlicensed hire car driver
Mod: member of youth sub-group which developed in England in the early 1960's; characterised by enthusiasm for pill-popping, neat mohair suits and short hair; usual method of transport much-modified Lambretta and Vespa scooters; musical tastes ska, Motown, the Who and other English Mod groups of the era; at the time of writing (Autumn 1980), Mods are flourishing again
Monkey's, to give a: damn (as in "I don't give a monkey's")
Moolaw: money
Mutton javelin: male organ
Naff: tasteless, worthless, without style
Napper: head
Nick, to: to arrest, charge with an offence; also to steal
Nous: common sense

Old Bill: police
Olivered: drunk (rhyming—Oliver Twist/pissed)

Pen and ink: stink (rhyming)
Pictures, up the: defunct, inoperative, ruined, down and out
Pissed: drunk
Pissed off: angry, unhappy

Plonker: male organ
Poodle faker: pretentious person, often of ambiguous sexuality
Poofter: homosexual (from poof)
Pork sword: male organ
Potatoes: money
Potty: insane

Raspberry: heart (from rhyming—raspberry tart)
Red Rover: bus excursion ticket available from London Transport
Ring piece: rectum
Roller: Rolls-Royce
Round of applause: veneral disease (from clap)
Ruck: argument, conflict
Rump, to: to have sexual intercourse with
Rumpole of The Bailey: fictional English barrister created by John Mortimer and made popular by TV series starring Leo McKern

Saucepan: child (rhyming—saucepan lid/kid)
Sausage: male organ
Schmutter: clothing
Schtum: totally silent
Scratch: money
Scrubber: unattractive female person of low status but accommodating nature
Sherbert: beer or other alcoholic drink
Slag: see scrubber
Slag off: denigrate
Snotty: bad tempered and/or snobbish and/or bumptious
Sprog: small child
Strides: trousers
Stroppy: belligerent, argumentative, angry
Suss, to: to discover, deduce

Tanner: sixpence coin

Teddy Boy: youth sub-group coming to prominence in Britain in the fifties; dress and appearance a stylised version of Edwardian fashions, e.g., long drape jackets, double-breasted waistcoats, slim neckties, drain-pipe trousers, elaborate, heavily greased and curled hairstyles often incorporating exaggerated kiss curls, long sideburns and duck-tails: prone to wear thick crepe-soled or winklepicker shoes; partial to authentic rock and roll, gang violence and general outrage (though the latter aspects have been greatly exaggerated); the style is currently enjoying a revival in even more extreme form

Tesco: British supermarket chain

Third leg exercise: sexual intercourse

Tin tack: sack, termination of employment (rhyming)

Toes, to take it on the: to run away, depart, exit

Twat: literally, female sexual organ; but normally only used figuratively, to denote stupidity or worthlessness

Wanger: male organ

Wank, wanker: masturbate, masturbator

White-eared trouser elephant: male organ; for orgin, stand in front of full-length mirror, unzip trousers and completely expose member, turn pockets inside out to form elephant's ears, complementing trunk if member of sufficient size; if not in possession of male member, call nearest musicians for volunteers

Wobble, to throw a: to become frenzied, freak out

Woofer: dog, unattractive female person